Aiding Democracy Abroad

The Learning Curve

Thomas Carothers

Carnegie Endowment for International Peace
Washington, D.C.

D1446109

© 1999 by the
Carnegie Endowment for International Peace
1779 Massachusetts Avenue, N.W.
Washington, D.C. 20036
202-483-7600
www.CarnegieEndowment.org

To order, contact:
Hopkins Fulfillment Service
P.O. Box 50370
Baltimore, MD 21211-4370
Tel: 1-800-537-5487 or 1-410-516-6956
Fax: 1-410-516-6998

Cover: Sese/Paul Design

Library of Congress Cataloging-in-Publication Data
Carothers, Thomas, 1956–
    Aiding democracy abroad : the learning curve/Thomas Carothers.
        p. cm.
    Includes bibliographical references and index.
    ISBN 0-87003-168-6 (cloth)—ISBN 0-87003-169-4 (paper)
    1. Democracy. 2. Democratization. 3. Technical assistance. I. Title.
JC421.C246   1999
321.8'071—dc21   99-045358

Sixth printing, September 2009

CONTENTS

Foreword

Democracy promotion surged to the top of the international policy agenda at the end of the 1980s with the fall of the Berlin Wall and the outbreak of democracy movements around the world. Ten years later, making democracy work and finding a means through which outsiders can help remain a high priority in countries as diverse and demanding as Russia, Indonesia, Nigeria, Serbia, Kenya, and Peru. Policy makers use various methods to spur countries toward democracy, from economic sanctions and diplomatic persuasion to the force of arms. Their most common tool, however, is democracy assistance—aid programs explicitly designed to bolster democratic institutions, processes, and principles. Such efforts have expanded rapidly in recent years. The United States now spends over $500 million a year on democracy aid and is by no means the only actor in this field. Nearly every major donor country, as well as a growing number of international institutions and private foundations, are involved. Taken together, these many initiatives constitute a major new area of international cooperation. Moreover, by fostering a multitude of cross-border exchanges of knowledge, people, and resources, they are a significant element of globalization.

Though vast and relatively open to public view, the burgeoning domain of democracy assistance is not well understood. Many people have an instinctive sense that such programs are a good thing. Others react with skepticism or suspicion about the very notion of one country trying to influence another's political affairs. Yet few on either side build their case on detailed knowledge. Despite thousands of programs carried out in over a hundred countries in recent years, the most basic questions about democracy aid—what it accomplishes, where and why it fails, and how it can be improved—have remained unanswered, at least until now.

In this book Thomas Carothers provides much-needed answers to the fundamental questions about democracy assistance. He has given the field what it has lacked for so long—a defining text, one that includes a history of the field, comprehensive treatment of all the principal forms of democracy aid, and systematic studies of the key issues of strategy, implementation, and evaluation. He weaves in case studies from four corners of the world—Guatemala, Nepal, Zambia, and Romania—and enlivens the book with frequent real-life examples. Throughout, he takes a consistent line that one might call "tough love." While sympathetic to the idea of helping other countries become democratic, he is clear-eyed about and often critical of what actually happens on the ground. He finds that while democracy promoters often fall short of their goals, they are moving, albeit slowly and unevenly, along a positive learning curve. And he suggests ways to accelerate that movement.

Thomas Carothers is exceptionally well qualified to give this grand tour. A lawyer by training, he has built a reputation as a leading expert on democracy promotion, one of the few who combines extensive practical experience working on aid programs with a capacity for insightful analysis and cogent writing. The book builds on his earlier works on democracy promotion in Latin America and Eastern Europe, representing the culmination of many years of work in and outside of government and a tremendous amount of field research.

With its topical subject matter, analytic rigor, accessible prose, and constructive critiques, this book is an admirable example of what the Carnegie Endowment aims to offer on many fronts. I believe it stands as a major contribution to this field.

Jessica T. Mathews
President
Carnegie Endowment for
International Peace

Acknowledgments

I owe an enormous debt of gratitude to the hundreds of people in Guatemala, Nepal, Zambia, Romania, the United States, and elsewhere who generously gave their time in interviews with me and my research partners to talk about their experiences with democracy assistance. If I were to name some I should name them all and so I must thank them anonymously; in any event more than a few will prefer that status. Marina Ottaway, Stephen Golub, and Michael Shifter were ideal research partners. They accompanied me on research trips abroad, enriched my understanding of other countries, and consistently challenged and improved my analysis. Larry Garber, Chris Sabatini, and David Yang read substantial portions of the manuscript in draft and gave me extremely helpful suggestions to improve it. Their colleagues at the organizations for which they work (the U.S. Agency for International Development [USAID], the National Endowment for Democracy, and the U.S. Department of State, respectively) should be assured that what critical comments remain in the text about those organizations are very much my own views. Matthew Frumin provided moral support and a sounding board for ideas. Lisa Peterson of USAID graciously helped me obtain figures on USAID's democracy-related expenditures.

The Carnegie Endowment has been the perfect home for this project and for all my work in the past six years. I thank Carnegie President Jessica Mathews, Vice President Paul Balaran, and former president Morton Abramowitz for their unflagging support. Four Carnegie junior fellows, Sabrineh Ardalan, William Barndt, Theresa Chung, and Nicole Dannenberg, were invaluable research assistants. Dianna Christenson and Maria Sherzad prepared the manuscript and helped me in countless other ways. Sherry Pettie, Carmen MacDougall, Tom Skladony, and Mary Downs ably turned the manuscript into a book. The outstanding Carnegie librarians, Jennifer Little, Kathleen

Daly, and Chris Henley, promptly fulfilled my requests for books and articles.

I am also deeply grateful to the Ford Foundation, especially Mahnaz Ispahani, for the generous financial support that made the field research possible and sustained the project generally. With her linguistic talents and consistent good humor Alice Phillips made the editing process a pleasure.

I also need to make several disavowals. Over the years I have worked on democracy programs with various organizations, either as an employee or a consultant, including the U.S. Department of State, the U.S. Agency for International Development, the National Democratic Institute, the International Foundation for Election Systems, and the International Institute for Democracy and Electoral Assistance. The views in this book do not represent the views of those organizations. In addition, given that I discuss briefly in this book the work of the Soros foundations network, I should note here that in 1999 I became a member of the board of directors of the Open Society Institute–Budapest, which has oversight responsibility for many of the activities of the Soros foundations network. Again, the opinions expressed herein are entirely my own.

I thank my children, Christopher and Vera, for pretending convincingly that the various chocolates and other presents I brought back from the research trips abroad were a reasonable exchange for my absence. Above all, I owe much to Laura Bocalandro, my wife. With her own demanding work as an international finance lawyer, she did not perform the sorts of tasks other authors always seem to thank their spouses for—she did not discuss every idea with me, edit every page I wrote, and urge me on to completion. I am most grateful for that and for the fact that whenever I reappeared after another foreign trip she always met me at the airport, with a smile.

PART ONE

Setting the Stage

1
A New Field

For generations, American leaders have emphasized the promotion of democracy abroad as a key element of America's international role. President Woodrow Wilson proclaimed that America was fighting World War I "to make the world safe for democracy." In the 1920s and 1930s, U.S. politicians cast the various military interventions in the Caribbean and Central America as missions to establish democracy. In World War II, America fought against fascist tyrannies in the name of freedom. U.S. officials of the postwar period emphasized democracy promotion as they formulated a policy toward a vanquished Japan and Germany and then framed the emerging cold war as a struggle to preserve "the Free World." In the early 1960s, President John Kennedy embraced the idea of a noble campaign to foster democracy in the developing world. Two decades later, President Ronald Reagan renewed the democracy theme by casting his ardent anti-Soviet policy as a democracy crusade. In the 1990s, Presidents George Bush and Bill Clinton asserted that democracy promotion was a key organizing principle of U.S. foreign policy after the cold war.

Looking behind this long chain of impressive policy rhetoric, one sees a less consistent policy reality. Countervailing interests, both security-related and economic, have often outweighed or undermined a U.S. interest in democracy. Throughout the twentieth century, the United States has maintained friendly relations with dictatorships and intervened in other countries' internal affairs for purposes far removed from the promotion of democracy. Prodemocracy rhetoric has regularly exceeded reality and has sometimes been used deliberately to obscure a contrary reality. Nevertheless, democracy promotion is an important part of America's international tradition, even if its application has often been inconsistent. American foreign policy of the past 100 years cannot be understood without serious attention to the democracy ideal. And the history of democracy around the globe during the same period is incomplete without sustained attention to the role of the United States on the world stage.

In the past twenty years, democracy promotion has been a particularly significant part of U.S. foreign policy. One reason has been the unfolding of "the third wave" of democratization in the world, the expansion of democracy that began in Southern Europe in the mid-1970s, spread to Latin America and parts of Asia in the 1980s, then accelerated dramatically from 1989 on with the fall of the Berlin Wall, the breakup of the Soviet Union, the unexpected surge of democratic openings in sub-Saharan Africa, and further democratization in Asia. As dictatorships around the world have fallen and societies as diverse as Bolivia, Bulgaria, Mongolia, and Malawi have attempted transitions to democracy, the U.S. government has frequently responded with support. Its democracy-related policies and programs have been prompted by the global movement toward democracy more than the reverse, despite what Americans involved in democracy promotion like to claim.

Another cause of the greater attention to democracy has been the ideological evolution of U.S. foreign policy since the late 1970s. Through its human rights policies, the Carter administration put the government in the habit of paying attention to the domestic behavior of other governments, beyond the limited cold war concern about leftist insurgencies and takeovers. The Carter team did not, however, highlight democracy per se, both because few countries in those years were engaged in democratic transitions and because Carter officials generally believed in political noninterventionism (distinguishing their human rights advocacy from efforts to produce particular political outcomes in other countries). President Reagan raised high the democracy banner, seeking a moral dimension for his heightened anti-Soviet approach. The actual role of democracy promotion in Reagan's foreign policy was uneven; it evolved substantially, from the early line of accepting anticommunist dictators as necessary allies to a limited but growing willingness to support democracy against tyrants of either the left or the right.

The end of the cold war gave rise to the appealing notion that the traditional tension in U.S. foreign policy between *realpolitik* security interests and Wilsonian moral interests was over. Both President Bush and President Clinton, along with their top foreign policy advisers, repeatedly declared that in the reconfigured world, promoting democracy serves not only moral interests but also practical ones, thereby bridging the longstanding realist-idealist divide. Democratic governments, they asserted, do not go to war with one another, produce refugees, or engage in terrorism. They make better trade partners, and further pragmatic U.S. interests in other ways as well. As Clinton declared in his second State of the Union address in 1995, "Ultimately, the best strategy to ensure our security and to build a durable peace is to support the advance of democracy elsewhere." The democracy rhetoric escalated across the decade, leading to sweeping, utopian declarations such as Clinton's prediction in his second inaugural address that, "The world's greatest democracy will lead a whole world of democracies."

High-flying rhetoric and the end of the U.S.-Soviet rivalry notwithstanding, security and economic interests still often point U.S. policy in a contrary direction. In more than a few countries, including Kazakhstan, Saudi Arabia, Egypt, China, Indonesia (before the fall of President Suharto in May 1998), Armenia, and Azerbaijan, the Bush and Clinton administrations downplayed democracy and pursued friendly relations with governments for the sake of interests ranging from oil and trade relations to regional security and stability. Democracy promotion remains at most one of several major U.S. foreign policy interests, sometimes complementary to but sometimes in competition with other, stronger interests.

Nevertheless, the promotion of democracy is playing an important role in U.S. foreign policy. In many countries, especially in Latin America, Eastern Europe, and sub-Saharan Africa but also in parts of Asia, the former Soviet Union, and the Middle East, the United States has attempted to support transitions away from authoritarianism. The foreign policy bureaucracy is gradually habituating itself to the concept. U.S. officials no longer automatically view democracy promotion as a marginal idea pushed only by a fervently pro-American right or a touchy-feely, do-gooder left. U.S. missions abroad now at least formally incorporate democracy promotion into their strategic plans and it is a major line item in the foreign affairs budget of the United States.

TOOLS OF THE TRADE

When policy makers decide they are going to try to promote democracy in another country, they typically reach for various tools. The officials may use diplomatic measures, as either carrots or sticks: criticizing a government that is backtracking from democracy, praising a prodemocracy leader, granting or withdrawing high-level diplomatic contacts in response to positive or negative developments, and so on. Or they may apply economic tools, again as carrots or sticks: economic pressure, such as sanctions, on governments that crush democracy movements; or economic rewards, such as trade benefits or balance-of-payments support for governments taking steps toward democracy. In extreme circumstances, the United States may even employ military means to promote democracy, intervening to overthrow a dictatorship and install or re-install an elected government—although U.S. military interventions that politicians justify on democratic grounds are usually motivated by other interests as well.

The most common and often most significant tool for promoting democracy is democracy aid: aid specifically designed to foster a democratic opening in a nondemocratic country or to further a democratic transition in a country that has experienced a democratic opening. Donors typically direct such aid at one or more institutions or political processes from what has become a relatively set list: elections, political parties, constitutions, judiciaries, police, legislatures, local government, militaries, nongovernmental civic advocacy groups, civic education organizations, trade unions, media organizations. Unlike the other tools of the trade, democracy assistance is neither a carrot nor a stick. It is not awarded for particular political behavior, nor is it meted out as punishment for democratic slippage (though people in recipient countries may sometimes view it as such).

Prior to the 1980s, the United States did not pursue democracy aid on a wide basis. In the past two decades, such aid has mushroomed, as part of the increased role of democracy promotion in American foreign policy. It started slowly in the 1980s then expanded sharply after 1989 with the quickening of the global democratic trend. By the mid-1990s, U.S. annual spending on such programs reached approximately $600 million and now exceeds $700 million.

A host of U.S. government agencies are involved in this work—primarily the U.S. Agency for International Development (USAID) and the U.S. Information Agency (USIA—now being merged into the Department of State), but also the Departments of State, Defense, and Justice, as well as several quasi-governmental organizations (government-funded, privately run), including the National Endowment for Democracy (NED), the Asia Foundation, and the Eurasia Foundation.

These organizations in turn support several dozen American groups that implement most of the U.S. democracy programs in other countries. These groups fall into several categories: nonprofit organizations largely or wholly devoted to one or more areas of democracy promotion—such as the International Foundation for Election Systems, the International Republican Institute, the National Democratic Institute for International Affairs, the Carter Center, the American Bar Association's Central and East European Law Initiative, and the American Center for International Labor Solidarity; universities, research institutes, and policy institutes that sometimes take on democracy projects; and for-profit development consulting groups, usually Washington-based, that have added democracy work to their portfolio of development specialties, including Management Systems International, Checchi and Company Consulting, Development Associates, Chemonics International, Creative Associates International, and ARD. Some American private foundations also sponsor activities that bear directly on democratization abroad, especially relating to civil society development, though they operate separately from the world of official U.S. democracy aid.

Within this array of government, quasi-government, and nongovernment organizations underwriting or implementing democracy programs are thus many people who work substantially on democracy promotion. A core of several hundred people in key positions in those organizations drive the field, but several thousand take part on a regular basis and constitute the newly emerged and still growing community of American democracy promoters.

The reach of such assistance is broad. In 1998 the United States carried out democracy programs in more than 100 countries, including most countries in Eastern Europe, the former Soviet Union, sub-Saharan Africa, and Latin America, as well as many in Asia and the Middle East. The current wave of democracy aid is by no means the first for the United States, as readers will see in the next chapter. The democracy programs of the 1980s and 1990s, however, are by far the most systematic, sustained, and wide-reaching that America has undertaken.

The recent surge of democracy assistance is by no means exclusively or even principally a U.S. story. The relaxation of ideological tensions after the cold war, combined with the movement toward democracy in many regions, have put democracy on the global agenda in a much more far-reaching way than ever before. In the past ten years, aiding democracy has become an international cottage industry, with a remarkable range of actors entering the field. Almost every major country that gives foreign assistance now includes democracy programs in its aid portfolio. Numerous international or multilateral institutions, including the United Nations, the Organization of American States, the Organization for Security and Cooperation in Europe, the European Union, the Inter-Parliamentary Union, and the Council of Europe, sponsor democracy programs. Many Western political parties, labor unions, foundations, and other nongovernmental organizations are active. The international financial institutions have begun committing resources to promoting good governance, which, although theoretically distinct from democracy promotion, often substantially overlaps with it in practice.

LACK OF LEARNING

Although democracy aid has become a remarkably extensive field of activity, it remains understudied and poorly understood. Some of the more experienced people and organizations in the community of democracy promoters are gaining considerable expertise. They rarely distill their knowledge into written form, however, and when they do it is usually in informal internal memos. Some of the organizations involved carry out evaluations of their own work, but those reports rarely circulate outside the sponsoring organizations and, for reasons discussed at length later, rarely cut deep. Those in the business of dispensing democratic aid are much more inclined toward action than retrospective reflection. Bureaucratic imperatives reinforce this tendency, above all the pressure to keep moving from one project to the next. It should be said as well that many democracy promoters are temperamentally resistant to critical reflection. Missionary zeal pervades the field, bringing with it a disinclination for self-doubt and a reflexive belief in the value of the enterprise. On top of all this, democracy assistance, as with all types of foreign aid, is a competitive business. Democracy groups are not motivated to share their knowledge and best ideas with one another or to make public (or even to engage in) tough-minded reviews of their own performance. To the extent that they produce reports for external consumption, such publications are by necessity usually more public relations efforts than anything else.

Little systematic learning has been added to the field from outside the circle of practitioners. Academic specialists—whether in international relations, comparative politics, or development studies—have not devoted much attention to the subject. Political scientists have shown considerable interest in democratization, producing a large literature on democratic transitions, particularly relating to Southern and Eastern Europe and Latin America. They have shown relatively little interest, however, in democracy assistance. Often unaware how extensive democracy aid has become, scholars assume it is of minimal importance in the overall picture of any given democratic transition. To the extent they are aware of it, they tend to see it as a practical domain that poses few theoretical questions of the sort that motivate scholarly inquiry. Moreover, some American academics still automatically assume, as they learned to do during the cold war, that U.S. aid to promote democracy abroad is little more than a way of forcing the American system on other countries or sugar-coating self-interested interventions in the internal politics of weaker nations.

The media dip into the subject only occasionally, during high-profile elections in politically transitional countries, when they work alongside international election observers and focus on the role of the United States or the international community in the vote. The media are far less likely to examine other types of democracy assistance: it is hard to make much of a story out of a training program for parliamentary staff, technical assistance to municipal governments, or an exchange program for civic educators. The result is a distorted picture of democracy aid, one fostering the oft-repeated view that democracy promoters push elections at the expense of other elements of democratization. Every so often a journalist will suddenly discover that there *is* democracy aid beyond elections, and make a brief investigative foray, usually with the bold aim of ridiculing the whole endeavor as the work of naïve fools. After an enthusiastic, superficial bout of bubble-bursting, the journalist moves on, leaving behind an angry, sputtering set of democracy promoters. Such episodes produce little insight and tend to make an already defensive and sometimes self-righteous community of assistance practitioners even warier of sharing information with the outside world or engaging in open debates about what they do.

The lack of much formal accumulation of knowledge about democracy aid has negative consequences in the practitioner community. One is insufficient cross-learning about promoting democracy among different regions or among different sectors in recipient countries. Another is the dispiriting tendency toward constant reinventing of the wheel in aid organizations as personnel shift into and out of positions, particularly in groups working in the field for the first time. People often seem to believe that merely being a citizen of a democratic country qualifies them splendidly to promote democracy anywhere else. Utilizing their own limited instincts and ideas about how democracy is supposed to work, they generate programs with little help from any body of learning other than occasional reports containing lists of anodyne lessons learned ranging from "Be sensitive to the local environment" to "Democracy is not achieved overnight."

The scarcity of systematic study also has detrimental effects on the position of democracy aid within the world of foreign policy and international affairs. It increases the tendency to judge democracy aid according to preformed assumptions and prejudices rather than on the basis of reality. The most basic questions about the field, such as, "Does it work?" and "Do we know what we're doing?" are left unanswered for most observers. Public discussions about democracy aid remain stuck in unhelpful extremes, with the aid programs portrayed either as heroic endeavors critical to the future of democracy or as a cascade of boondoggles that primarily benefit self-interested aid givers and consultants. Neither side in such debates learns much from the other, and the more useful, accurate middle ground is left underdeveloped.

TAKING STOCK

This book is a response to the lack of systematic study of democracy assistance. Ten years after 1989—the starting point for much recent democracy work—it is a natural time for taking stock. I attempt in this book to draw together the essential elements of and questions about democracy aid to help define this emergent field as a field.

There are obvious limitations in any attempted overview of such diverse activities. Tracing the evolution and analyzing the effects of the thousands of U.S.-sponsored democracy aid projects in dozens of countries around the world during the past two decades is impossible. No one category of democracy aid can be fully discussed here. No one recipient country can receive definitive treatment. I do aim to establish an analytic framework for understanding the field and to set out at least basic lines of analysis for all the major elements of the framework.

As I make clear throughout the book, I believe that the shortcomings of democracy aid are many and serious. Nonetheless, I also believe if one takes the broader view, many democracy promoters are learning as they go along. The positive trend is not dramatic, steady, or rapid, yet it is real. One of my main purposes in writing this book is to capture the main elements of this learning curve to further its consolidation and advance.

The chapters of the book track my analytic framework for the field. Chapter 2 traces the history of U.S. democracy assistance from the 1960s through the 1990s, focusing on the evolution of such aid, its place within overall U.S. foreign policy, and the question of whether the efforts of the 1990s are a repeat of those of the 1960s. Chapter 3, an interlude for skeptics, directly addresses the core doubts that such persons usually have about democracy aid. Chapter 4 introduces the four country case studies, on Guatemala, Nepal, Zambia, and Romania, that are developed throughout the book.

Chapter 5 examines the all-important question of strategy, identifying the models of democracy and democratization that structure U.S. democracy aid programs as well as recent attempts to develop more nuanced approaches. Chapters 6, 7, and 8 analyze the main types of democracy assistance, for each looking at its specific forms, the principal challenges in making it effective, and how it is evolving over time. Chapter 6 covers elections aid and political party work. Chapter 7 takes up programs directed at state institutions, including constitutions, judiciaries, legislatures, local government, and militaries. Chapter 8 explores aid to civil society, with particular attention to advocacy-oriented nongovernmental organizations, civic education, independent media, and trade unions.

Chapter 9 reviews how democracy aid is implemented on the ground; it includes a critique of the standard project method and a look at the trend toward more locally sensitive methods. Chapter 10 considers the question of evaluation, offering a critique of existing methods and suggesting some better ways of proceeding. Chapter 11 assesses the effects of democracy aid. Chapter 12 sums up the learning curve to date, points out how it should be broadened, and presents its implications for U.S. policy.

My focus throughout is democracy aid funded by the U.S. government, with only occasional commentary on the work of other donor countries, international organizations, and private foundations. I give particular though not exclusive attention to the programs sponsored by USAID, because it is by far the largest source of such aid. My emphasis on U.S. efforts reflects the fact that the bulk of my experience lies in this realm. Although this is a limitation, I do not believe it is a fatal impediment to an overview of the whole field, given that the United States moved into democracy assistance earlier than most other actors and has been the largest single democracy donor. Moreover, I believe that much of my analysis is applicable or at least directly relevant to democracy assistance generally, whatever its source. Certain distinctive features do mark U.S. aid—notably the projection of certain America-specific ideas about democracy and the political baggage that inevitably accompanies Americans doing political work abroad. At root, however, most forms of Western democracy assistance, whether from Sweden, Spain, Australia, the Organization of American States, Canada, the United Nations, the European Union, or the United States, are not all that different from each other, despite what non-U.S. actors often like to think. In fact, comparing democracy programs sponsored by varied governments and international institutions, what is most striking is not their differences but their similarities.

CASE STUDIES AND OTHER SOURCES

In writing this book I have drawn heavily from two sources. The first is my personal experience as a practitioner and analyst of democracy assistance since the mid-1980s. My first exposure to the field came in 1986–1987 when I was detailed from the legal adviser's office of the State Department to a newly created office for democracy programs in the Latin American bureau of USAID. Late in the decade, after leaving the government, I carried out extensive research on the policy process surrounding democracy aid and wrote a book on U.S. democracy promotion in Latin America during the Reagan years. I broadened my involvement in democracy programs through diverse consulting assignments in the first half of the 1990s for the National Democratic Institute for International Affairs and the International Foundation for Election Systems, in Eastern Europe, the former Soviet Union, Africa, Asia, and Latin America. In 1993 I established the Democracy Project at the Carnegie Endowment for International Peace in Washington, D.C., for the purpose of studying democracy assistance. Through the Democracy Project I have carried out field research on numerous aid efforts, organized many study groups and seminars with practitioners and scholars on different aspects of the subject, worked as a consultant on democracy aid projects in different regions for several U.S. and international institutions, and written numerous articles on the subject. I draw on all these experiences here, especially my observation of projects in the field and countless formal and informal conversations with both aid practitioners and aid recipients over the years.

A second, more specific source is a set of four studies of U.S. democracy assistance that I designed and carried out from 1996 to 1998. For each of the four case studies—on Guatemala, Nepal, Zambia, and Romania—I first gathered extensive information in Washington through documents and interviews on all publicly funded U.S. democracy aid programs in the country from the late 1980s on. I then traveled at least twice to each country to interview people who had participated in, observed, or were otherwise knowledgeable about the U.S. democracy aid efforts. For the case studies in Latin America, Africa, and Asia, I was assisted by three American researchers, each of whom is a specialist in democratization in his or her region of specialization and is knowledgeable about democracy aid. These research partners—Michael Shifter for Latin America, Marina Ottaway for Africa, and Stephen Golub for Asia—traveled with me on the field visits and carried out further field research on their own. In the case of Romania, I incorporate some of the findings from extensive research on U.S. democracy assistance that I did in 1994 and 1995 for a book of mine published in 1996 on U.S. democracy aid to Eastern Europe, focused on Romania. I updated that research with additional visits to Romania in 1997 and 1998.

In carrying out the field research, my research partners and I strove to understand not only the substance and effects of the U.S. and other democracy aid programs in each of the four countries but also how democracy aid looks from the recipient end. We followed the evaluation guidelines that I set out in chapter 10. We made a point of talking not just to people who received the assistance, for example, but to others who were not included in the aid programs but were knowledgeable about the sectors in question. We took a highly qualitative approach, asking in an open-ended fashion about the effects of programs rather than quizzing interviewees on whether the programs reached particular preset goals. We tried to make clear that we were interested in what was being learned on all sides, whether or not the story involved mistakes or misadventures.

Given the large number of countries in which U.S. democracy promoters operate, no small group of cases can be perfectly representative of the field. Nevertheless, Guatemala, Nepal, Zambia, and Romania provide some useful representativity. They are on four different continents. Each has been host to a set of U.S. democracy aid programs that are fairly typical of the programs that the United States has recently sponsored in that region. Their democratic transitions (or attempted transitions) were part of the democratic wave of the 1980s and 1990s. Each has ended up in the large, gray middle zone of so many transitions of that period, having neither moved rapidly and painlessly to democracy nor fallen back into outright authoritarianism. They are not the exceptional cases that have attracted the lion's share of international attention—such as South Africa, Poland, Russia, Chile, El Salvador, or the Philippines. They are instead part of the less visible but much larger group of transitional countries that had their moment in the news briefly during their initial democratic opening but have since grappled with democratization out of the limelight, aided by low-profile but nonetheless often substantial U.S. and other Western democracy programs.

I have not written up each case study as a separate chapter. I introduce the cases in chapter 4, and present some concluding thoughts about each in chapter 11. In between I have woven material from the cases into the other chapters, both directly, as examples intended to illuminate specific points, and indirectly, as learning that helped shape my overall analysis. This method makes it difficult to go into great detail or tell a complete story with the cases, but it spares readers a book dominated by long, detailed studies of countries in which few people have an all-consuming interest.

AVOIDING ROSY ASSUMPTIONS

I have discovered over the years that if you take democracy assistance seriously as a subject for analysis and writing, some people automatically suspect you of harboring rosy assumptions, in particular two: first, that democracy is advancing steadily around the world and clearly works well for all countries, regardless of their political background or economic condition; and second, that the grandiose official rhetoric about the central place of democracy promotion in U.S. foreign policy is really true. In fact, however, neither of these assumptions informs my outlook or this book.

With regard to the state of democracy in the world, it is true that significant advances have been achieved in some parts of the world in the past twenty years. Most East European countries have made substantial democratic progress since 1989 and appear headed toward political and economic integration with Western Europe. In Latin America, the institutional performance of many democratic governments remains weak, but democracy has shown greater staying power than many analysts predicted when the region returned to elected, constitutional governments in the 1980s. Several East Asian countries, notably South Korea, Taiwan, Mongolia, and Thailand, are making serious efforts at democratizing, and in much of the region the notion that democracy is an unnatural Western implant has faded. At least a handful of sub-Saharan African states have managed to keep basically on track with democratic transitions begun in the early 1990s. More broadly, all around the developing world and former communist countries, the concepts of political pluralism, governmental accountability, and the right of people to choose their own leaders are discussed and considered much more widely than in the past.

At the same time, the much-heralded global democratic trend has fallen short of expectations. In the mid-1990s, significant retrenchment and backsliding from initially promising democratic transitions began to occur. Many of the former Soviet republics are now dominated by semiauthoritarian or outright authoritarian leaders. Russia remains a democracy in form but threatens to go badly astray politically if the socioeconomic situation fails to improve. In Africa, a distressingly large number of countries attempting transition have lapsed into civil war, coups d'etat, or resurgent strongman rule. The liberalizing trend that made itself felt in the Arab world in the second half of the 1980s has come to little. South Asia has stopped moving forward on democratization. In many parts of the world, disillusionment about democracy has replaced the infectious enthusiasm of ten years back as citizens watch fledgling elected governments wallow in corruption, incompetence, and instability. Democracy continues its post-cold war reign as the only political ideology with broad international legitimacy. Nonetheless, it has become painfully clear that many countries face a tremendous struggle to make democracy work. It is all too common for countries attempting political transitions to achieve the forms but not the substance of democracy.

The analysis here rests on this mixed review of the state of democracy in the world. Democracy aid was relatively easy to sell and often easy to implement when the political winds were at its back in the first half of the 1990s. Today, with democratic setbacks and failures more frequent, democracy aid faces a harder road, forcing democracy's promoters to try to sharpen their skills. I chart their learning curve.

As for the place of democracy promotion in American foreign policy, I take as a starting point a similarly mixed picture: although its role has expanded since the mid-1980s, it remains at most one of several main U.S. interests, sometimes compatible with and sometime contrary to economic or security interests. When contrary, it is usually overridden. This semi-realist approach to democracy promotion has been adopted by both the Republicans and Democrats and is unlikely to change anytime soon.

My aim here is not to lament this state of affairs or to issue a clarion call for a vigorous new embrace of the Wilsonian ideal as the twenty-first century dawns. I do believe that American policy makers should give greater emphasis to democracy promotion and that it should play a major though not necessarily dominant role in U.S. foreign policy. I have learned from living in Washington, however, that even the most eloquent calls for bold new directions in U.S. policy, foreign or domestic, often go unheeded. My approach instead is to try to help foster understanding and more effective use of one of the central tools of democracy promotion. As knowledge and use of new policy tools improve, new policy directions become possible. Working upward from method to principle is not how Americans usually approach foreign policy, especially when it comes to democracy promotion or other issues suffused with high principle. It is necessary in this domain, however, given the continuing gap between expectations and accomplishments and the substantial body of experience that now exists.

2
The Rise of Democracy Assistance

Democracy assistance tends to live in an eternal present. Democracy promoters talk at times, vaingloriously, of participating in "history in the making." Yet they rarely have much sense of history about what they do, either with regard to the countries in which they are working or to the enterprise of using aid to promote democracy. U.S. democracy assistance does have a history, one that has consequences for the shape and success of aid efforts today. After the Spanish-American War, the U.S. government attempted to set up electoral systems in Cuba and the Philippines. Similarly, as part of the many U.S. military interventions in the Dominican Republic, Honduras, Panama, Nicaragua, Haiti, and elsewhere in the Caribbean and Central America in the first few decades of the twentieth century, the United States sponsored elections to produce governments to replace those it had just ousted. Political aid programs ranging from constitution writing to civic education were part of the successful efforts to help reconstruct and democratize Germany and Japan after World War II.[1]

The bulk of the story, however, takes place beginning in the 1960s. When foreign aid became a major component of U.S. policy toward the developing world in the 1950s, democracy promotion was not a priority. Aid rested on a straightforward security rationale: economic and security assistance would bolster friendly governments, whether dictatorial or democratic, against the spread of Soviet influence. It was only with the arrival of the Kennedy administration and some new thinking about the relationship of development and democracy that the idea of giving aid specifically to promote democracy caught on among policy makers. This chapter traces the history of U.S. democracy assistance from the 1960s on, covering the rise of interest in using aid to promote democracy in the 1960s, the decline of that interest in the 1970s, the refound initiative in the 1980s, and the tremendous increase in assistance for democracy in the 1990s. The focus throughout is not only on the types of democracy aid undertaken in the different periods but the changing policies behind them and the reasons for the cycle of interest and lack of interest within the U.S. government.

THE FIRST WAVE: THE 1960s AND 1970s

In the 1960s, anticommunism dominated U.S. policy toward the developing world. The United States was competing with the Soviet Union for influence over and the loyalty of third world governments, and fighting on many fronts to combat the spread of leftist movements and regimes. At the same time, the U.S. government, particularly the incoming Kennedy administration at the start of the decade, also had idealistic—one could even say hubristic—goals.

The Kennedy Push

President Kennedy and his team believed that the United States had a unique capacity, as well as the duty or even the destiny, to do good in the world. They were certain that with the proper application of energy and resources America could help third world nations rise out of poverty and move from dictatorship to democracy.[2] The pragmatic anticommunist objective was by far the stronger of the two interests, and often ended up conflicting with or overshadowing the idealistic goals. Initially at least, however, U.S. officials of the 1960s had a framework for thinking about economic and political development—modernization theory—that seemed to reconcile their interests. Reduced to bare essentials, modernization theory conceived of development as a linear process ending up in an American-style social, economic, and political system—and held that the various elements of the development process would be mutually reinforcing. In particular, economic development would generate democracy by helping countries achieve a middle class, a high literacy rate, and other socioeconomic features then considered preconditions for democracy.[3]

Translated into policy terms, modernization theory promised that promoting economic development in the third world would simultaneously do good (reduce poverty) and serve the goal of fighting communism: helping countries grow economically would prevent empty stomachs from making revolutions and would foster democratic, therefore pro-Western, systems. A crucial tool for this policy was economic aid. Influenced by Eugene Rostow's optimistic work on development economics, Kennedy administration officials believed that timely injections of aid would launch underdeveloped countries into economic takeoff. Building on groundwork Kennedy had laid in the late 1950s as a congressman, particularly the Kennedy-Cooper Resolution of 1959 that called for greater attention to the development needs of South Asia, the Kennedy administration increased U.S. foreign aid by 33 percent and strengthened the institutionalization of foreign aid through the creation of the United States Agency for International Development (USAID) and the Peace Corps.[4]

Although U.S. officials began to view foreign aid as a tool to promote democracy abroad, the assumed aid-democracy link was largely indirect: aid was expected to produce economic development, which in turn was expected to foster democracy. Aid was not directly targeted at political institutions and processes and thus was not democracy assistance in the sense the term has come to be used in recent years. To the extent that U.S. aid programs of the 1960s tried to shape government institutions in developing countries, they focused on strengthening public administration. In the many new states emerging with the decolonization of Africa, Asia, and the Middle East, U.S. aid officials sought to build up the administrative capabilities of what were typically fragile, inexperienced state institutions. These programs, which focused on budgeting, project development, and personnel management, and other bread-and-butter organizational issues, had no specific democratic focus. They aimed to increase governments' technical capacities and were often carried out with nondemocratic regimes.[5] A generation later, pushing free-market reform policies, Washington would urge countries to dismantle many of the top-heavy administrative structures set up by these earlier programs, and U.S. democracy programs would strive to reduce the dominance of the executive branches that the earlier programs had helped strengthen in many countries.

The most sweeping and intensive application of the United States' new approach to the developing world in the 1960s was in Latin America. Fidel Castro's takeover in Cuba in 1959 had been a rude shock for Washington, and heightened the fear that Latin America was fertile ground for Soviet influence. In 1961 President Kennedy launched the Alliance for Progress, a bold, far-reaching U.S. aid initiative that sought to transform Latin America into a region of prosperous, democratic countries, thereby inoculating it against Soviet influence. Although consisting primarily of economic aid, the program was also intended to advance democracy—U.S. officials believed that economic progress in Latin America would build the societal base for democracy, particularly a large middle class. In addition, the Kennedy administration planned to give vigorous diplomatic support to moderate civilian reformers against reactionary military elements, further bolstering democracy in the region.[6]

The experience of the Alliance for Progress was mixed at best. The U.S. aid contributed to substantial growth in many Latin American economies, but the takeoff to modernization never happened. Poverty, inequality, poor education, erratic public health systems, and other socioeconomic failings remained widespread in the region. Moreover, what growth did occur did not generate democracy. Quite the opposite—many Latin American countries slid into military dictatorship in the 1960s. The Kennedy administration ended up retreating from its intention to support democratic governments. Faced with rising populist movements and left-leaning leaders in a number of Latin American countries, the administration began backing new military dictatorships on anticommunist grounds, an initial tendency that hardened into consistent policy in the Johnson years. The disappointments of the Alliance for Progress epitomized the United States' broader frustration with attempting to promote economic and political "modernization" around the third world during the 1960s.

Title IX

As the 1960s unfolded, some in the U.S. policy community, including several congressmen, some scholars, and some aid officials, began to question the indirect approach to promoting democracy through economic aid. They feared that if the benefits of economic growth in developing countries remained concentrated in elite circles, the positive political development would not occur. Instead, the growth would reinforce existing structures of political domination and repression. They began to urge that U.S. assistance specifically attempt to foster increased popular participation in economic development as a first step toward focusing more directly on political participation and development. Two U.S. congressmen, Donald Fraser and Bradford Morse, both members of the House Foreign Affairs Committee, became the leading advocates of "a basic reorientation in our thinking . . . to put social and political evolution as the first concern of our foreign assistance program with economic aid playing the supporting role rather than the other way around."[7] In 1966 they sponsored Title IX of the Foreign Assistance Act of 1961, a legislative directive to USAID: "In carrying out programs authorized by this chapter, emphasis shall be placed on assuring maximum participation in the task of economic development on the part of the people of the developing countries, through the encouragement of democratic private and local government institutions."[8]

This language suggested a major redirection of U.S. foreign aid toward an explicit fostering of democratic institutions. In practice, however, Title IX did not produce such a shift. Two interpretations of it co-existed in Washington in the years immediately after its passage. One, emphasizing the latter clause of Title IX, viewed it as a mandate for a focus on assisting democratic institutions; the other stressed the first words of the provision and held that Title IX was only about ensuring greater participation in economic development, not democracy building per se. USAID, which for reasons discussed below was hesitant to get involved in political work, hewed to the latter interpretation.[9]

USAID sponsored many studies of participation in the development process. The agency established criteria for assessing the extent to which specific projects fostered increased participation in economic development and rated all its projects on their degree of "Title IX emphasis."[10] Title IX may have led to some increased attention to the participation of people in aid-receiving countries in economic and social development projects, especially in health, agriculture, education, and housing. It certainly resulted in a slew of conferences, research projects, and papers, the creation of a Title IX division within USAID, and a great deal of talk in the aid community about participation and development. It did not, however, result in a set of aid programs explicitly designed to promote democracy.

Beginning in the latter half of the 1960s, USAID did initiate programs directed at sectors or institutions that today are considered the domain of democracy assistance, including legislatures, legal institutions, civic education, labor unions, and local government. These programs' activities were often similar to those of democracy programs of the 1980s and 1990s. They were not, however, conceived of as democracy promotion. They concentrated on economic and social goals and were viewed as new forms of development aid. And they were often carried out in nondemocratic countries. A major USAID-funded program to strengthen the institutional capacity of national legislatures in developing countries including South Korea, Brazil, Ethiopia, Lebanon, and Costa Rica, for example, was developed in the late 1960s and carried out in the 1970s. The underlying assumption was that more competent, efficient legislatures— whether part of democratic systems or not—would further the economic and social development of third world countries.[11]

The law and development movement entailed a broad range of legal development initiatives throughout the 1960s and the early 1970s, mostly in Latin America, Asia, and Africa, sponsored by both USAID and private sources in the United States, especially the Ford Foundation. The passage of Title IX spurred increased USAID involvement in this domain. Programs emphasized legal education, particularly the goal of trying to recast methods of teaching law in developing countries in the image of the American Socratic, case-oriented method. Based on a jumble of vague but ambitious ideas about development, the thinking was to encourage lawyers and legal educators in developing countries to treat the law as an activist instrument of progressive social change.[12]

"Civic education" became a buzzphrase at USAID in the late 1960s, after Congress modified Title IX in 1967 to include a specific clause referring to it. Large-scale civic education programs were set up, especially in Latin America. Such programs included some explicit teaching of democratic values in the classroom. But they emphasized the fostering of voluntary participation by citizens in diverse social, cultural, and economic spheres, the notion being that increased participation was generally beneficial to development.[13]

Strengthening labor unions abroad was also a component of U.S. assistance in the 1960s that USAID highlighted as involving a high degree of Title IX emphasis. U.S. government support for the international work of the American Federation of Labor–Congress of Industrial Organizations (AFL-CIO) predated Title IX by decades. The overriding motive of the AFL-CIO's work throughout the cold war was neither democracy promotion nor economic development, but a strenuous anticommunism. The AFL-CIO was committed in all the countries it worked in—dictatorships and democracies alike— to undermining left-leaning labor unions. It received extensive CIA funding in the 1950s and 1960s and contributed actively to U.S. undertakings to topple or discredit leftist politicians abroad.[14]

U.S. aid officials added local government strengthening to their portfolio in the 1960s. "Municipal development" in poorer parts of the world was suddenly a fashionable aid concept and was viewed by USAID as a participatory, Title IX approach to economic development. USAID funded projects that trained local government officials, supported local government associations, and provided technical assistance in project design, finance, and implementation for local government entities. Although similar to many U.S.-funded local government assistance projects of the 1990s that are characterized as democracy-building efforts, the municipal development projects of the 1960s and 1970s were not cast as such. Their stated goal was to enable local governments to play a more active role in development, and they did not focus on the representative aspects of local government. Indeed, many were carried out in countries run by dictators and those regimes accepted the projects as compatible with their rule.[15]

Although political aid was only a small part of U.S. foreign aid, other U.S. funds were being spent to influence the political life of foreign countries. Both in the developing world and in Europe, the Central Intelligence Agency engaged in numerous covert efforts to bolster selected political parties, to tilt elections, and otherwise to influence political outcomes, to thwart leftist movements and to ensure that governments friendly to the United States stayed in power.[16] Although sometimes described by its practitioners as support for the cause of democracy, such political work was anticommunist above all, and dictatorial regimes were often the beneficiaries. Moreover, the CIA's methods, particularly the covert schemes to manipulate elections, were patently antidemocratic. Although some of this activity stopped in response to public revelations in the late 1960s and early 1970s, it created a powerful legacy of domestic and international suspicion about any involvement of the U.S. government in elections or political parties abroad—a legacy with which democracy programs of the 1980s and 1990s have had to contend.

Why Title IX Fell Short

It is worth considering why, despite the intentions of Title IX's sponsors, democracy promotion did not become a significant element of U.S. aid in the late 1960s and early 1970s.

In the first place, Title IX was a congressional initiative, a mandate externally imposed on USAID. It did not establish or set aside special funds for a new set of assistance programs, was broadly worded, and was passed after little consultation with the agency. Moreover, Title IX went against the grain of deeply held beliefs and well-established practices in the U.S. foreign aid bureaucracy. The great majority of USAID officers were wary of direct involvement by the agency in political development assistance. They thought USAID—being an economic development organization—was ill prepared to influence the political life of other countries through aid programs. Attempting to do so, they feared, could jeopardize its other programs and involve it in foreign policy controversies and undertakings better left to the State Department and the intelligence agencies. Direct assistance for political parties, elections, and political education sounded to many USAID officers like out-and-out meddling in politics, something they were disinclined to do.

Title IX's effect was also limited because it was out of phase with the political tide in the developing world. Democracy was in retreat in the 1960s. Throughout Latin America, elected civilian governments were being ousted by military leaders. In much of Africa and parts of Asia and the Middle East, new constitutional governments that had emerged from decolonization were turning into or being replaced by one-party regimes. Title IX was enacted in part because of this retrogression of democracy, but the backward movement made Title IX difficult to implement. As countries slid into authoritarianism, U.S. aid officials had few opportunities to work cooperatively with pluralistic institutions or politicians and few reasons to be optimistic about work to promote democracy.

Furthermore, in those years the gap between democratic goals and the realities of U.S. policy in the third world grew enormous. Essentially, U.S. policy in the developing world was to fight actual and perceived communist movements, leaders, and governments. This was ostensibly to preserve the borders of the "free world," but the United States often ended up backing undemocratic governments and repressive militaries, as well as employing blatantly antidemocratic means, ranging from covert funding of political favorites to political subversion campaigns. Under these circumstances, for USAID to have launched a campaign of democracy building would have been irrelevant at best.

The few assistance programs that had some democratic content were often contradicted and rendered pointless, even dangerous, by Washington's overriding anticommunism. In Guatemala, for example, USAID funded a large program in the late 1960s and early 1970s to train rural leaders, so as to give rural communities more say in their own development. At the same time, the Defense Department and the CIA were actively supporting the Guatemalan military's counterinsurgency campaign against the small but growing guerrilla forces and all organized political opposition. A USAID study sponsored in the 1980s reported that more than 750 of the rural leaders who took part in the agency's earlier program were murdered in the war between the U.S.-backed Guatemalan military and the leftist rebels.[17]

Back to Basics

By the close of the 1960s, disillusionment in the United States with foreign aid, and with the whole idea of trying to produce economic and political modernization in the third world, ran deep. The shining hopes of the early 1960s had not been realized. Despite unprecedented amounts of aid, poverty and misery were still rife in the developing world. Moreover, what economic growth had occurred had not produced the expected payoff in politics. If anything, democracy had retreated in Africa, Latin America, and elsewhere. Repressive dictatorships were multiplying, and leftist ferment and active insurgency were on the rise. Professor Samuel Huntington of Harvard University had done serious damage to the intellectual framework of modernization theory with his seminal *Political Order in Changing Societies* (1968), in which he argued that economic progress in underdeveloped countries did not lead inevitably to democratization but in fact was often destabilizing and conducive to the rise of authoritarianism. The unpleasant realities of third world politics and economics were taking care of what remained of the theory.

In the late 1960s, the Nixon administration shifted policy into a realist mode, one evincing a palpable disregard for the sovereignty or fortunes of most third world countries (beyond an anticommunist interest) and a deliberate lack of interest in any moral mission for the United States. In the foreign aid realm, the United States and other Western donors de-emphasized economic growth and stressed basic human needs. They allocated assistance primarily to help third world governments provide their citizens basic goods and services such as food, shelter, and medicine, eschewing the idea of a natural connection between economic development and political development. This approach was ecumenical about the relative desirability of different political systems, reflecting a strong reaction to the idealism of modernization theory and the political relativism common among liberals during that period who dominated the U.S. development community. Although over time the basic human needs approach generated an interest in grassroots-oriented, participatory programs, there was little emphasis on democracy per se. Title IX faded from sight by the mid-1970s.[18]

The latter 1970s saw the rise of human rights in U.S. foreign policy. In tune with Americans' questioning of their country's role in the world after the Vietnam War, President Jimmy Carter made human rights a major theme of his foreign policy. Little new democratization was taking place in those years, outside of Southern Europe. A human rights focus thus meant attention to basic violations of rights—torture, political murder, and other serious forms of repression—rather than to higher-order political norms such as free expression, freedom of association, and the right to genuine, periodic elections (a right enshrined in the Universal Declaration of Human Rights). Furthermore, although Carter's human rights policy implied intervention in other countries' internal affairs, Carter and most of his top advisers prided themselves on their commitment to noninterventionism in others' affairs—their reaction to the U.S. anticommunist interventions in Chile, Guatemala, Vietnam, and elsewhere. They stressed the universalistic grounding of human rights advocacy in international law, and saw it as separate from any sort of political crusade. Carter did support free and fair elections when the electoral process in the Dominican Republic threatened to fall apart in 1978, but this venture into the democracy arena was exceptional and reflected the unusually long history of U.S. involvement in that country's political life.

Carter's push on human rights, partial and sometimes ineffective as it was, contributed to some later democratic transitions, especially in Latin America, by directing attention to the core issues of political freedom and governments' behavior toward citizens. And as former CIA director Robert Gates acknowledges in his memoirs, the human rights scrutiny of the Soviet Union through the Helsinki process begun in the mid-1970s turned out to be important in the eventual demise of Soviet communism.[19] The Carter human rights policy did not at the time, however, constitute a shift to a democracy focus. Nor did it generate much in the way of democracy aid. It relied mainly on diplomatic measures, aid cutoffs, and some forms of economic pressure; it did not rest on the use of new types of aid. Congress did enact Section 116(e) of the Foreign Assistance Act in 1978, authorizing the use of assistance funds for projects to promote human rights. Some projects were initiated in the late 1970s pursuant to this section, such as ones funding legal aid centers in Latin America, but they were small-scale.

A NEW WAVE: THE 1980s

At the beginning of the 1980s, programs to promote democracy abroad were an insignificant part of U.S. foreign aid. By the end of the decade, such programs were under way in many countries and democracy promotion was close to becoming one of the four core priorities of U.S. foreign aid. This evolution was striking but it was neither steady nor simple. The rise of democracy assistance was clearly related to the heightened anticommunism of Ronald Reagan's foreign policy. Yet the relationship was complex and controversial. The democracy theme arose in the early 1980s as part of the Reagan administration's combative anti-Soviet posture. Yet democracy promotion became an assistance priority during the 1980s mainly as a result of the moderation of Reagan's anticommunist focus, particularly in Latin America and Asia. A moderating trend from the first to the second Reagan administration led officials to take more seriously the idea of developing the political component of the military-oriented policy toward Central America and to shift away from support for friendly tyrants in decline, as in Chile, Paraguay, Haiti, the Philippines, and South Korea. That evolution in policy prepared the way for the creation of programs assisting elections, the administration of justice, and other key areas in the new wave of democracy aid that unfolded in the 1980s.

The War of Ideas

President Reagan took office determined to challenge the Soviet Union and reverse what he perceived as the United States' weakening geostrategic position. Military force—both the building up of the U.S. arsenal and renewed military assistance for friendly anticommunist governments, especially those facing leftist insurgencies—was the core of the new policy line. Yet ideological tactics also had a role. Members of the Reagan team were disturbed by what they saw as a defeatist attitude among American and other Western intellectuals about the future of democracy as a political ideology, and by the Soviet Union's considerable investment in scholarship programs, media projects, and propaganda campaigns to spread the gospel of Marxism-Leninism. President Reagan's initial foreign policy team believed that the U.S. government should fight back in the war of ideas with a substantial program of international activities to promote democracy as an ideology.

In 1981 White House officials began planning a set of such activities—international conferences on democracy, exchanges to expose foreigners to American democracy, book translation programs, increased radio broadcasting into communist countries—under the rubric "Project Democracy." They did not envision Project Democracy as part of U.S. foreign aid, but rather a form of public diplomacy that would be run out of the cultural outreach arm of the foreign policy bureaucracy, the U.S. Information Agency.[20]

In the same period, a separate initiative to set up a publicly funded, privately run foundation to promote democracy abroad—what would become the National Endowment for Democracy—was taking shape. This idea did not originate with the Reagan administration. The late congressman Dante Fascell (D-Fla.) had introduced a bill in Congress as far back as 1969 to create such an institute. From the mid-1970s, a diverse collection of political activists began talking together to move the idea along; the group included Fascell, Lane Kirkland (AFL-CIO), William Brock (Republican National Committee), Charles Manatt (Democratic National Committee), Michael Samuels (U.S. Chamber of Commerce), George Agree (a political scientist), and Allen Weinstein (a historian). Their early plans were based substantially on the *Stiftungen*, German political party foundations, particularly the valuable role the *Stiftungen* played in the democratic transitions in Spain and Portugal in the mid-1970s. The AFL-CIO was especially interested in a U.S. democracy foundation as a new source of public funds for its international activities, to replace the CIA support it had lost in the late 1960s.[21]

The Reagan administration was sympathetic to the notion of such an organization, seeing it as consistent with, though organizationally different from, Project Democracy. President Reagan gave both efforts a major boost in June 1982 with his much-quoted speech before the British Parliament in which he announced his intention to develop a global program of democracy assistance:

> The objective I propose is quite simple to state: to foster the infrastructure of democracy, the system of a free press, unions, political parties, universities, which allows a people to choose their own way to develop their own culture, to reconcile their own differences through peaceful means.[22]

The next year, Congress considered proposals for both Project Democracy and the National Endowment for Democracy. Although intended as complementary projects, emphasizing direct and indirect roles, respectively, for the U.S. government, the two ended up as rivals for congressional support. Some House Democrats were skeptical about Project Democracy, seeing it as a disorganized, hastily assembled set of initiatives that risked becoming heavy-handed efforts to push American ideas about politics at unreceptive foreigners. Although uncomfortable with the "America Knows Best" hubris that surrounded both proposals, they preferred the NED for its bipartisan structure and its partial separation from executive branch control. Congress eventually rejected Project Democracy, appropriating funds for only a few of the proposed activities.[23] It gave the NED $18 million, in contrast, less than requested, but enough to get it going. Project Democracy, in its proposed form, largely faded away. Some of the administration officials most interested in the public diplomacy concept pushed a narrow, domestically oriented campaign to try to generate American public support for the administration's anti-Sandinista, procontra policy toward Nicaragua.[24]

President Reagan inaugurated the National Endowment for Democracy in December 1983, and it has operated continuously ever since. It is financed by the U.S. government, but is a private nonprofit organization with an independent board of directors, management, and staff. The Endowment, whose annual budget is now approximately $30 million, has four main grantees, which in NED's first ten years received most of its money, but which now get approximately 55 percent (the rest going to discretionary grants and for administrative costs): the Center for International Private Enterprise, the American Center for International Labor Solidarity, the International Republican Institute, and the National Democratic Institute for International Affairs, affiliated, respectively, with the U.S. Chamber of Commerce, the AFL-CIO, the Republican Party, and the Democratic Party. Each of these organizations is independently run and has its own areas of activity. The Center for International Private Enterprise promotes free-market economic policies in other countries, with the rationale that such policies reinforce democratization and are necessary to democracy. The American Center for International Labor Solidarity supports the development or strengthening of independent trade unions abroad, believing that independent unions are critical to democracy. The two political party institutes concentrate on fostering democratic processes in other countries, through programs for promoting free and fair elections, bolstering political parties, developing civic education, and strengthening parliaments.

During its early years, NED exemplified the keenly anticommunist tenor of the democracy promotion movement of the time. By far the largest recipient of NED's funds was the AFL-CIO, whose international outreach work was stridently anticommunist.[25] The AFL-CIO carried out some programs of dubious value in spreading democracy, several of them aimed at battling leftist intellectuals or political activists in Western Europe—through, for example, a labor organization for professors and students in France intended as "a counterweight to the propaganda efforts of left-wing organizations of professors active within the university system."[26] Similarly, the newly founded Republican Party Institute launched anticommunist projects in Europe and Latin America such as support for an effort to find "private enterprise solutions for economic problems in those regions of Portugal that are communist-dominated."[27] NED's early anticommunist focus lessened, however, as the cold war wound down and the relationship in U.S. policy between anticommunism and democracy promotion evolved.

The Crucible of Central America

Congress's rejection of Project Democracy in 1983 put a halt to the early Reagan administration's idea of creating a large-scale, centralized set of democracy assistance programs within the U.S. government. The NED had been created but was relatively small and operated outside the government. In the mid-1980s, however, democracy assistance began to become part of U.S. policy toward one particular region—Latin America, or more specifically, Central America. Understanding this requires a brief review of the evolution of the Reagan administration's hotly debated Latin America policy.

The initial Reagan approach to Latin America followed the unrepentant anticommunist line set out in Jeane Kirkpatrick's much-cited 1979 article in *Commentary*, "Dictatorships and Double Standards," which held that the United States must support friendly anticommunist authoritarian regimes in developing countries rather than risk their falling to potential totalitarians of the left. The early Reagan team (which included Kirkpatrick as UN ambassador) moved quickly to rekindle relations with the dictatorial, anticommunist regimes of South America that President Carter had criticized on human rights grounds. In Central America, the Reagan administration saw the leftist insurgencies in El Salvador and Guatemala, as well as the new Sandinista government in Nicaragua, as Soviet-sponsored arrows aimed at the United States' strategic underbelly. Reagan's advisers decided to draw the line in El Salvador. That meant a military-oriented policy—above all, opening the aid spigot to the beleaguered, brutal Salvadoran military. In its early form, the Reagan policy toward Central America paid little heed to whether the governments the United States sought to shore up were democratic or not, so long as they were anticommunist.

This hard-line approach soon encountered new realities in Latin America and underwent a moderating trend. The renewal of ties with the ruling generals in Argentina, Brazil, Chile, and other South American countries went nowhere, derailed by the 1982 Falklands War and the unexpected spread of democratic transitions in that region. By 1983 the Reagan administration was bypassing the Argentine generals to congratulate Raúl Alfonsín on his election to the Argentine presidency and hailing a democratic trend in South America.

As for Central America, obtaining approval from the Democrat-controlled House of Representatives for increased military aid to El Salvador, Guatemala, and Honduras proved contentious, due to those countries' poor human rights records. In addition, career U.S. diplomats working alongside the Reagan appointees pushed for a more moderate policy line, insisting that to defeat leftist insurgencies the governments of Central America would have to win the loyalty of their citizens by becoming less oppressive and more democratic. The early Reagan team began developing a political component to its overall policy, aimed at encouraging transitions to elected, civilian rule in El Salvador, Guatemala, and Honduras. It started pitching this Central America policy as a democracy campaign, that label provoking much controversy and some fury in the American policy community. Critics countered that the policy's political component was window dressing, subordinate to the military thrust. They also asserted that what Reagan officials called democratization was superficial change—elections that put civilian leaders formally into power but left the underlying structures of repression intact. These critiques had considerable validity, especially in the early 1980s. Over the decade, however, U.S. policy toward most of the region did evolve. The political component gained in importance against the military component and U.S. officials gradually moved from the simplistic equation of elections with democracy to more substantial exertions on democracy's behalf.

As part of this evolution, the U.S. government developed assistance efforts specifically directed at democracy promotion, along two principal lines: assisting elections and strengthening the administration of justice. Both got their start in El Salvador, the crucible for much of the Reagan administration's Latin America policy. When El Salvador held Constituent Assembly elections in 1982 as part of its wrenching transition to civilian rule, the State Department (with USAID funding) arranged for a group of prominent Americans to observe the balloting and report on it to Washington. This superficial, highly politicized observation mission (which USAID resisted supporting until Secretary of State Alexander Haig insisted) was the first step toward dozens of electoral aid programs in Latin America and elsewhere in the 1980s.[28] For the presidential election in El Salvador in 1984, USAID paid for computers and a voter registration system to help ensure that the elections were credible (while the

CIA provided covert funds to José Napoleón Duarte, the Christian Democrat with genuine democratic credentials, to help ensure the election came out the way the Reagan administration wanted).[29]

U.S. assistance to improve the administration of justice, which became the largest area of democracy aid in the 1980s, also started in this period. Early in the decade, the State Department was under great pressure from Congress, the media, and the human rights community in the United States to do something to reduce the horrendous number of human rights abuses by the Salvadoran armed forces. Neither the White House nor the Pentagon was especially interested, seeing the issue as a distraction from the central task of defeating the Salvadoran guerrillas. In the State Department, officials trying to work with the Salvadoran government to resolve some of the more high-profile political murders (such as the 1980 assassination of Archbishop Oscar Romero and the 1981 killing by Salvadoran security personnel of four U.S. churchwomen) were struck by the incompetence of the Salvadoran judicial and police systems. Led by James Michel, then the number two official in the Latin America bureau of the State Department, an interagency working group oversaw the design in 1983 of a $9.2 million assistance program for the Salvadoran judiciary. The project, which included judicial training and the setting up of both a law reform commission and a special investigative unit to investigate human rights cases, operated from the rationale that improving the human rights situation in El Salvador, and developing democracy in general, required improved administration of justice.[30]

From these beginnings in El Salvador, both major strands of the new democracy-related U.S. assistance in Latin America—elections and the administration of justice—grew rapidly. USAID and the National Endowment for Democracy sponsored election assistance projects in Guatemala and Honduras in 1985, Haiti in 1987, Chile in 1988, Paraguay in 1989, and Nicaragua in 1990, and underwrote the establishment of the Inter-American Center for Electoral Promotion and Assistance (CAPEL), a Latin American organization dedicated to the promotion of free and fair elections in the region. The elections projects grew in size and sophistication. In the 1988 plebiscite in Chile on General Augusto Pinochet's continued rule, for example, U.S. involvement ranged from National Democratic Institute assistance for the National Command for the No's campaign against Pinochet to a $1.2 million grant, through CAPEL, to the Chilean Crusade for Civic Participation for voter registration efforts.

Judicial and police reform aid grew even more quickly in this period. Building on the foundations of its experience in El Salvador, USAID established two major regional judicial reform projects, one in Central America and the other in the Caribbean, and a host of bilateral projects around the region. Promoting judicial reform in Latin America became a small but important subspecialty at USAID, one that continued into the 1990s and eventually linked up with new initiatives in that area by the international financial institutions and other donors. Police aid also grew exponentially. When the State Department proposed in the mid-1980s that the United States assist Central American police forces as part of a comprehensive approach to the administration of justice, many USAID officials balked. They recalled the U.S. Public Safety Program in the 1960s and early 1970s in Brazil, Uruguay, Vietnam, and other countries, which led to the U.S. government being associated with police forces engaged in torture. They also pointed to the legislative restrictions on police aid passed in response to the Public Safety Program. The State Department persisted, however, carving out an exception to the legislative prohibition and pushing successfully for the creation in 1986 of the International Criminal Investigative Training Assistance Program. ICITAP was initially funded by USAID and affiliated with the Department of Justice (USAID was subsequently removed from the loop and the program was brought fully under the Department of Justice). ICITAP developed projects to build up the investigative skills of Central American police forces and later spread its work to South America and, eventually, other regions.

Along with these two main areas of attention, smaller initiatives contributed to the growth of U.S. democracy-related assistance to Latin America in the second half of the 1980s. Career USAID officials kept alive a modest group of human rights assistance projects begun in the late 1970s, despite the hostility of Reagan appointees who viewed legal aid and human rights education as politically suspicious areas for U.S. involvement in Latin America. The USAID officials recast these projects as democracy projects to match the new prodemocracy rhetorical line coming from the top. USAID also developed a range of projects under the heading of democracy that focused on training journalists, strengthening legislatures, and improving civil-military relations in the region. The Republican Institute provided support for conservative political parties in several Latin American countries. The AFL-CIO, with funding from both USAID and the NED, continued its decades-old aid for Latin American trade unions, increasingly basing these efforts on a democratic rationale.

Moving Beyond Latin America

Democracy made less progress in the 1980s outside of Latin America. In other parts of the developing world, few democratic transitions were occurring and the Reagan policy was generally the familiar cold war line of supporting anticommunist allies, whether dictatorial or democratic. A partial but important exception was Asia, where several countries held transitional elections in the latter half of the 1980s and the United States provided electoral assistance and diplomatic support.[31]

The Philippines was the crucial first case. Facing rising domestic dissent and eroding U.S. support, President Ferdinand Marcos called in 1985 for "snap elections." These brought to a head a bitter debate in the U.S. government between some senior career diplomats who believed Marcos had outlived his usefulness to Washington and White House and Pentagon officials, including President Reagan, who were reluctant to give up on America's longtime "friendly tyrant" in Manila. The United States sent two delegations to observe the 1986 elections, an official one led by Senator Richard Lugar (R-Ind.) and Representative John Murtha (D-Pa.) and a delegation jointly sponsored by the newly formed National Democratic Institute and International Republican Institute. The observer teams' criticisms were a crucial factor in the Reagan administration's subsequent decision to dump Marcos and to support Corazon Aquino, the rival presidential candidate from whom Marcos had stolen the election.

Although the aid bearing directly on the Philippine transition was limited to these electoral efforts, it was nonetheless a crucial boost to the emergence of democracy aid generally. The Philippine experience did much in U.S. policy circles to establish the credibility of election observing, helping separate it from the controversies in Latin America over whether observers were merely part of a U.S.-staged show to put political favorites in power. The NDI-IRI mission to the Philippines was the first election observation project for both those organizations and launched them into what would, by the early 1990s, become an enormous area of activity. More broadly, the Philippine transition took democracy aid out of the anticommunist context of Latin America policy, showing that it could be used against a traditional anticommunist U.S. ally. This accomplishment fostered increased democracy initiatives in Asia in the second half of the 1980s.

In 1987 the Reagan administration played a quiet but important part in advancing a democratic opening in South Korea. When President Chun Doo Hwan began to backpedal on his stated commitment to political liberalization and elections, Reagan sent a personal letter to him calling for a peaceful transfer of power, the release of political prisoners, and fair elections. As James Lilley, U.S. ambassador to South Korea, delivered the letter, he warned Chun that the threatened reimposition of martial law would greatly strain U.S.-South Korean relations. Chun allowed elections to proceed, resulting in a peaceful transfer of power.[32] In Taiwan, NDI carried out activities in the late 1980s to support the slowly unfolding democratic transition. NDI sent an observer team to the 1988 National Assembly elections in Pakistan, elections that helped move the country away from military rule. Also during these years, the Asia Foundation, a nonprofit organization that operates primarily with U.S. government funding, quietly began to direct some of its assistance work toward democratic development, in areas such as the rule of law, media development, and human rights.

Although the U.S. role in these Asian countries undergoing political transitions was important, it did not represent a major shift in policy toward Asia or on democracy promotion generally. With other Asian countries, such as Indonesia and Malaysia, the United States was content to maintain warm ties to nondemocratic, anticommunist regimes. And official U.S. aid (as opposed to NED funds, which were used for the Asian electoral aid initiatives) did not generally take up the democracy theme. The same was true in Africa and the Middle East, two regions in which the prospect of democracy appeared remote, despite a liberalizing trend in some Middle Eastern countries. One exception was South Africa, where USAID developed substantial human rights programs, as part of the increased U.S. aid in the latter 1980s aimed at helping promote an end to the apartheid system. The human rights aid, approximately $1.5 million a year, included many small grants to nongovernmental organizations working on civic education, grassroots organizing, and rights advocacy.

The Soviet Union and Eastern Europe were not recipients of official U.S. aid in those years and thus not candidates for USAID democracy programs. The NED did support human rights organizations and other potential sources of democratic change in the Soviet bloc. The independent labor union Solidarity in Poland received the most such aid, with NED joining Solidarity's diverse list of supporters that ranged from the CIA to the Swedish labor movement.[33] The NED also backed human rights groups, dissident publications, and other organizations working in or on the Soviet Union, Czechoslovakia, and Hungary.

A Foothold for the Future

The rise of U.S. democracy assistance in the 1980s was concentrated in Latin America, with some small but symbolically important initiatives in Asia and the Soviet bloc and only faint stirrings in Africa and the Middle East. Though both geographically and financially limited (reaching an annual level of between $100 million and $150 million by the end of the decade), it was nonetheless significant. The NED established itself solidly, evolving from inexperience and narrow political views to become a more balanced and effective organization. Democracy promotion was brought within the main U.S. aid agency, USAID. The Latin America bureau of USAID established an office for democracy promotion, and the agency's other regional bureaus began considering whether or when they should do the same. USIA took on democracy promotion as a theme. Congress became engaged, through periodic debates both over the NED and over USAID-sponsored democracy programs in Central America. Though it gained a foothold in USAID, democracy assistance still roused considerable skepticism among career aid officers, many of whom thought that the agency should steer clear of politics and stick to its traditional agenda of social and economic development. In broader policy circles, democracy assistance was still not well understood and was often seen as the tiresome preserve of ideologues and missionaries.

That democracy assistance *arose* in the 1980s as a part of President Reagan's war of ideas but *expanded* as part of the moderation of that anticommunist focus led to much confusion among observers. American liberals associated the democracy line with a Reagan policy they believed to be fatally flawed by militarism, interventionism, and support of unsavory dictators and repressive security forces. This led them to be suspicious of the very idea of democracy policies and programs, a suspicion that lingered long after the Reagan administration was gone and democracy promotion was being pursued by less conservative administrations. American conservatives tried to take full credit for the placing of democracy on the foreign policy agenda, often failing to acknowledge the tensions between the hardline anticommunist approach and the prodemocratic position. It was in reality the reversal and eventual abandonment of the original Kirkpatrick anticommunist approach that led to prodemocratic policies in Latin America, Asia, and elsewhere.

In any event, although limited, the rise of democracy assistance in the 1980s helped set the stage so that when the democratic trend broadened and accelerated at the end of the decade, some of the policy mechanisms and institutions were already in place, allowing a rapid expansion of U.S. democracy aid.

A CORE PRIORITY: THE 1990s

Democracy assistance mushroomed in the early 1990s. With the end of the cold war, the fall of the Berlin Wall, the breakup of the Soviet Union, and the heady acceleration of what enthusiasts were calling the "worldwide democratic revolution," aiding democracy abroad was suddenly of intense interest to U.S. policy makers. U.S. democracy aid extended rapidly in the early 1990s into Eastern Europe, the former Soviet Union, and sub-Saharan Africa, expanded in Latin America and Asia, and crept into the Middle East. More U.S. actors plunged into the fray and onto the bandwagon. By the mid-1990s, U.S. democracy aid was all over both the developing world and the former communist world and was an accepted part of U.S. foreign aid and foreign policy.

Expanding Reach

The largest expansion of democracy assistance in the 1990s came in Eastern Europe and the former Soviet Union. As political revolutions overturned communist governments and the Soviet Union broke up into fifteen successor states, President George Bush adopted a forthright policy of supporting transitions to democracy and market economics. That policy had a strong diplomatic component consisting of high-level U.S. cajoling and pressure to encourage political and economic reforms. It also had an assistance component—one far short of the Marshall Plan some hoped for but significant nonetheless. The Bush administration and Congress reacted quickly to the crumbling of communism in Eastern Europe by establishing the Support for Eastern European Democracy (SEED) program, comprising economic, social, and political components, with funds of approximately $300 million a year. After the breakup of the Soviet Union, they set up several major assistance efforts, including a host of programs under the 1991 Freedom Support Act and the Defense Department's Cooperative Threat Reduction program, averaging about $2 billion a year altogether. In both the SEED program and the aid under the Freedom Support Act, the political component, which is directed at promoting democracy, is only a small part, constituting between 5 percent and 10 percent of the total. Nonetheless, substantial amounts of U.S. democracy aid have gone to both regions, approximately $330 million to Eastern Europe from 1990 to 1998 and $320 million to the former Soviet Union from 1992 to 1998.[34] The NED has also been active in these regions in the 1990s, devoting between $3 million and $5 million per year to Eastern Europe and between $4 million and $5 million to the former Soviet Union. The Eurasia Foundation, established by Congress in 1993, also carries out democracy-related activities in the former Soviet Union, devoting between $5 million and $10 million annually to the task. All told, over the course of the 1990s the U.S. government spent close to $1 billion on democracy programs for the postcommunist countries of Eastern Europe and the former Soviet Union.

For most of the 1990s, Poland was by far the largest recipient of U.S. aid under the SEED Act. Bulgaria, however, has received the greatest share of democracy aid, with Poland next, then Bosnia and Romania. By the tenth anniversary of the SEED program in 1999, eight countries—Poland, Hungary, the Czech Republic, Slovenia, Slovakia, Estonia, Latvia, and Lithuania will have graduated from the program, as the United States, believing its job done, closes down its aid program in most of Eastern Europe. In the former Soviet

Union, close to three-quarters of the democracy aid under the Freedom Support Act has gone to Russia and Ukraine. Kazakhstan and Kyrgyzstan have received modest amounts, and the other former Soviet republics just a trickle.

The other major geographical area of expansion for U.S. democracy aid in the 1990s has been sub-Saharan Africa. Contrary to the expectations of most observers, including seasoned Africa specialists, Africa was strongly influenced by the democratic wave of the early 1990s. Many of the dictators and one-party states that dominated African politics in the 1970s and 1980s were suddenly challenged by opposition movements calling for democracy. Dozens of at least partial openings occurred, often followed by multiparty elections. With the traditional cold war policy framework fading, the Bush administration embraced democracy promotion as a major goal—at least rhetorically—of an Africa policy that lacked much sense of direction otherwise.

USAID was hesitant at first about the new emphasis on promoting democracy in Africa. Over the previous two decades many of USAID's Africa specialists had become disillusioned about the possibility of working productively with African governments in any fashion, and they were skeptical about political aid. Many of the specialists had, consciously or unconsciously, accepted the dogma of African exceptionalism and doubted that democracy was a feasible or even appropriate goal on the continent. But the State Department pushed USAID to support the African elections of the early 1990s. The agency, coming around, established in 1992 a major election aid fund for Africa, the African Regional Electoral Assistance Fund, implemented by the African-American Institute, NDI, and IRI. USAID began to sponsor a range of other democracy programs as well. The Clinton administration built on the Bush administration's line in the region, and aid programs to promote democracy multiplied in the mid-1990s. The NED also increased its work in Africa over the decade. In all, more than forty African countries received U.S. democracy aid in the 1990s, with by far the largest effort in South Africa. Mozambique, Ethiopia, Zambia, Ghana, Mali, Burundi, Rwanda, Kenya, and Malawi have also received significant attention.

In Latin America, the region where the United States most actively pursued democracy aid in the 1980s, the 1990s have seen further diversification and development of such undertakings. With the end of the cold war, and of the civil wars in Nicaragua and El Salvador, U.S. policy toward the region turned a corner at the beginning of the 1990s, leaving behind the decades-old anticommunist framework. The Bush administration adopted, and the Clinton administration has maintained, a policy with the twin goals of supporting democracy and encouraging market reforms. Informing this is a vision of a hemisphere united around common political values and close economic ties, including an expanding free trade area. The most visible expression of the democracy component of this approach has been Washington's diplomatic opposition to threatened or actual coups or self-coups in Peru, Guatemala, Paraguay, Venezuela, Haiti, and elsewhere. At the same time, the democracy component has not always been consistent, because of complicating factors such as hesitance to push the Mexican government on political issues, a drug policy that involves aid to abusive security forces in several countries, and a steep decline in overall U.S. aid to the region. The largest democracy aid effort in the region has been in Haiti. After the U.S. military intervention to restore the ousted president Jean-Bertrand Aristide to power in 1994, Washington poured in more than $100 million in democracy aid in the five years following the intervention.[35] The region's other main recipients have been El Salvador, Nicaragua, Guatemala, Bolivia, Panama, and Peru.

In Asia, U.S. policy in the 1990s has stressed economic goals above all others. At least until the Asian financial crisis of 1997–1998, U.S. officials deferred in many instances to the "Asian values" argument, accepting that the West should not push its political model on countries that were thriving economically under authoritarian or semi-authoritarian systems. Nevertheless, democracy aid to the region increased in the 1990s. The Asia Foundation has intensified its democracy efforts, incorporating at least some attention to the issue in most of the countries where it works. USAID moved gingerly into Asian democracy work, with USAID's Asia specialists frequently skeptical about the idea, preferring a straight economic focus. Cambodia has been the single largest recipient in Asia of democracy aid, as part of the broad U.S. effort to promote a democratic outcome based on the 1991 peace accord. Democracy programs have also been directed at the Philippines, Nepal, Bangladesh, Mongolia, Indonesia, Thailand, Sri Lanka, and Pakistan. The NED has funded programs in Asian countries, including nondemocratic states like China, Burma, and Vietnam.

Finally, there is the Middle East, the region least touched by the global democratic trend. U.S. democracy aid to the Middle East grew only slightly in the 1990s. U.S. policy has emphasized democracy promotion much less there than elsewhere, reflecting the lack of movement toward democracy and continuing, powerful economic and security interests that depend on good relations with several of the region's autocratic regimes. Despite this, some democracy assistance does flow. The extensive U.S. aid portfolio in Egypt includes a large-scale judicial reform program, an effort to strengthen the parliament, and significant aid for civil society. In some countries that have attempted political liberalization, U.S. democracy programs have started up, more often sponsored by the NED than by USAID. They have included elections and parliamentary programs in Yemen, electoral reform work in Jordan, efforts to increase political participation in the West Bank and Gaza, and a program to strengthen Kuwait's parliament. These are generally tentative, small-scale initiatives—minor forays into particularly daunting territory.

The New Democracy Consensus

The upsurge in U.S. democracy aid in the 1990s and in democracy aid from other bilateral and multilateral donors reflects the confluence of three factors: the global trend toward democracy, the end of the cold war, and new thinking about development.

First and foremost, the global democratic trend of the past two decades is itself a major cause. As democracy spread, or at least as more countries attempted democratic transitions, democracy assistance followed. This was the case in the 1980s with Latin America and parts of Asia. It was even more the case in the first half of the 1990s, as the democratic trend reached into Eastern Europe, the former Soviet Union, sub-Saharan Africa, and more countries in Asia. The natural tendency to focus on the effects of democracy aid on democratization in recipient countries overlooks the equally important causal relationship in the other direction—democratization producing democracy aid.

Democratic openings present opportunities for democracy promoters to get involved. Elections are suddenly important, fledgling political parties seek financing and campaign advice, independent newspapers spring up and look for help, new NGOs seek advice and aid. More pointedly, democratic openings challenge the United States and other wealthy, established democracies to respond. It is relatively easy to shrug off democracy promotion in a country that is nondemocratic and shows little sign of changing. When a dictatorial regime falls, however, and a society is struggling to make a nascent democratic system work, the United States cannot as easily ignore appeals for engagement from that society.

Then, too, the end of the cold war created considerable new space for international political aid. The demise of the U.S.–Soviet rivalry greatly lowered ideological tensions in many parts of the world. Although people in developing countries are still sensitive about political interference by the United States or other foreign nations, they no longer reflexively assume that the United States' only political interest in their country is keeping leftists out of power. In Latin America, for example, the 1990s have seen striking changes in attitudes about U.S. political interventions and much greater scope for programs aiding elections, political parties, and other political sectors.

The end of the cold war also contributed to the rise of democracy assistance by doing away with Washington's longstanding habit of downplaying democracy to show support for anticommunist authoritarian friends. A surge of idealism about democracy and its place in U.S. policy rolled through the U.S. policy community in the early 1990s. And policy makers decided that democracy was not just an idealistic interest but often a pragmatic one, stressing the idea that democracies do not fight each other as well as various other favorable attributes of democratic partners. Officials in both the Bush and Clinton administrations declared that with the cold war now history, America's ideals and interests were no longer divided.

In reality, democracy promotion increased in importance in U.S. policy in the 1990s only unevenly across the map. In more than a dozen countries, particularly in the Middle East, Asia, and the former Soviet Union, U.S. interests from oil to air-force bases have led the United States to support less than democratic regimes, proving that interests and ideals still collide. Democracy promotion has become a more regular, accepted element of U.S. policy than in previous decades, engendering greater democracy aid, but democracy is hardly an interest that trumps all others.

Finally, new thinking about development helped spur democracy assistance. During most of the 1970s and 1980s, aid providers from the United States and elsewhere conceived of development largely in social and economic terms. Consideration of a country's form of government was conspicuously absent. This was both because most developing countries were dictatorships and showed little sign of change, and because of the still-powerful legacy of the failure of modernization theory. In the latter half of the 1980s, however, the accumulated economic consequences of the corrupt, stagnant, often incompetent dictatorial regimes in many countries, especially in Africa, prompted donors to begin considering the economic value of openness, accountability, transparency, lawfulness, and other features of good governance. The World Bank took a widely noted step in this direction in 1989, citing bad governance as a key factor in Africa's abysmal record on development.[36] In the 1990s, the donor community accepted the idea that a country's political development could have major impact on its socioeconomic development. The World Bank and other international financial institutions, wary of an overt ideological stance, limited themselves to a growing focus on governance. The United States and many other bilateral donors incorporated democracy as a part of their overall developmental agenda, even though their aid programs remained in relatively separate political and social-economic categories.

The trend in economic development policy in the 1980s toward market economics, or neoliberalism, fortified the new nexus of economic and political goals. American conservatives in the 1980s saw an organic connection between what they termed economic freedom (market economics) and political freedom (democracy). Market reform policies, they said, would strengthen democratization in developing countries by increasing economic growth (thereby raising socioeconomic levels and empowering individuals), shrinking "bloated" government and creating new centers of power outside governments. Democratization, in turn, was held to support market reforms by increasing government accountability and transparency, promoting the rule of law, and fostering respect for citizens' rights and other limits on government power.

Appealing as it is, the notion that market economics and democratization are mutually embracing was by no means uncritically accepted by all. Some partisans of market reform policies, particularly economists at the international financial institutions, quietly questioned whether fledgling democratic governments can carry out the hard tasks of structural adjustment and withstand the political fallout. Many harbored the belief that a strong hand is usually necessary for a transition to free-market economics. The economic progress in Chile under General Pinochet and the various cases of economic success in East Asia under authoritarian rule loomed large in this line of thinking.

On the Left, some opponents of neoliberalism saw the democracy connection in a sinister light. In this view, Western powers push elections and other formal aspects of democracy on developing countries because they believe weak, floundering pluralist regimes will comply with Western demands for low tariffs, liberal investment laws, and other mechanisms that permit Western economic dominance. According to critics of neoliberalism, the political solution for good economic development is not democracy but a "developmental state"—a strong, autonomous state capable of concentrating the authority and capacity to achieve developmental objectives. As Adrian Leftwich writes, "from a developmental point of view, it is the primacy of politics and the character of the state that has to be the focus of our attention, not the form of government (democracy or not)."[37]

Although the multi-faceted consensus underlying democracy assistance is persuasive, it is certainly not absolute. In U.S. policy circles, many still see democracy as no more than a nice extra that does not go to the heart of America's interests abroad. And even among those who put stock in democracy promotion, doubts whether democracy aid itself is really of any consequence are common. Similarly, in the U.S. aid bureaucracy the commitment to democracy promotion is much shallower than the official strategy documents would indicate. In USAID, democracy assistance has been carried out by a fairly small number of people who specialize in it and form a discrete subculture within the organization. Many members of the career bureaucracy there, especially specialists in Asia and the Middle East, remain attached to the idea of USAID as a social and economic development agency, and are privately skeptical about their organization's work in the political sphere. A different leadership team at USAID could choose to de-emphasize democracy promotion significantly. Or if USAID is merged into the

State Department, diplomats impatient with the long-term developmental character of democracy aid could sharply reduce such programs. More broadly, if democratization suffers not just retrenchment but some major reverses in the world in the coming years, democracy aid may be slashed as part of a shift toward a more realist foreign policy. The new consensus on democracy promotion is, in short, an important development with significant underpinnings. As with any policy consensus, however, its self-evident quality of today is no guarantee of longevity.

Multiple Actors

As democracy assistance from the U.S. government has increased, the number of institutions involved in such aid have multiplied. By far the largest source is USAID. In recent years the agency has devoted between $300 million and $650 million annually to democracy programs, as Table 1 shows. USAID divides its democracy programs into four categories: rule of law, governance, civil society, and elections. Table 2 shows the breakdown in spending among these categories from 1991 to 1999. This breakdown highlights the growth across most of the areas of democracy aid, except electoral aid, which, contrary to what many people think, is the smallest of the major categories of USAID's democracy programs. A breakdown of spending by region appears in Table 3, showing a shifting balance among the various regions with a surge of funds in the latter 1990s for programs in Eastern Europe and the former Soviet Union.

Along with USAID, a raft of other federal agencies have become active in democracy assistance. The U.S. Information Agency, which took up the democracy theme in a substantial way in the 1980s, places considerable emphasis on democracy-related subjects in its visitor exchanges, education programs, speaker tours, and other activities. In many countries, USIA supports USAID democracy programs by harnessing its educational and exchange programs to particular democracy projects. Thus, for example, as USAID has carried out a judicial reform project in Guatemala, USIA contributed by sponsoring study tours in which groups of Guatemalan judges spent several weeks in the United States learning about judicial administration. USIA also extensively supports democratic civic education abroad, both in schools and through informal educational methods.

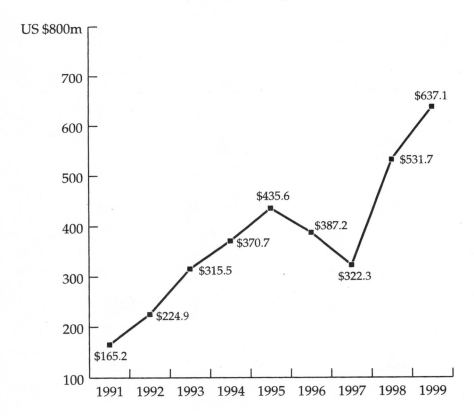

Table 1

USAID Funding for Democracy Assistance

Fiscal Years 1991-1999
(millions of dollars)

*1999 figures are budgeted expenditures rather than actual expenditures.
Source: USAID Democracy/Governance Information Unit

Table 2

USAID Funding for Democracy Assistance by Subsector

Fiscal Years 1991-1999
(millions of dollars)

	Rule of Law	Governance	Civil Society	Elections and Political Processes	Other
1991	$ 46.7	$ 14.4	$ 56.1	$ 9.8	$38.2
1992	70.2	23.6	92.5	38.5	0.0
1993	101.0	28.3	118.1	68.1	0.0
1994	74.6	60.8	151.2	84.7	0.0
1995	139.3	68.5	164.7	64.0	0.0
1996*	—	—	—	—	—
1997	64.0	110.3	106.2	28.7	13.0
1998	99.0	190.0	181.7	62.0	0.0
1999**	146.9	203.2	230.8	58.9	0.0

*1996 data not available.
**1999 figures are budgeted expenditures rather than actual expenditures.
Source: USAID Democracy/Governance Information Unit

Table 3

USAID Funding for Democracy Assistance by Region

Fiscal Years 1991-1999
(millions of dollars)

	Latin America	Eastern Europe and the former Soviet Union	Sub-Saharan Africa	Asia and the Middle East	Global
1991	$ 83.5	$ 22.0	$ 30.6	$ 27.7	$ 1.4
1992	101.2	43.1	55.3	22.0	3.2
1993	132.8	68.6	72.3	30.4	11.4
1994	75.4	156.4	102.9	25.6	10.3
1995	110.0	136.8	70.8	80.0	38.0
1996	67.3	119.8	85.9	83.2	31.0
1997	65.9	107.3	67.4	64.2	17.4
1998	82.2	216.3	96.9	112.4	23.9
1999*	86.8	288.4	123.4	111.5	27.0

*1999 figures are budgeted expenditures rather than actual expenditures.
Source: USAID Democracy/Governance Information Unit

The State Department's part in democracy promotion is concentrated on the policy side rather than the aid side—deciding when to apply economic or diplomatic carrots and sticks to discourage democratic backsliding or to reward democratic progress. The department nonetheless weighs in on questions of aid programming in many situations. It has a special role in aid to Eastern Europe and the former Soviet Union, with aid programs there directed by two offices in the department set up for that purpose. These coordinator offices pass most of the actual dollars for democracy aid through to USAID but exercise oversight and help set priorities. The Bureau of Democracy, Human Rights, and Labor at the State Department houses a small group of aid programs that for various legislative or bureaucratic reasons ended up there rather than at USAID, including, for example, the effort to bolster the Iraqi opposition. That bureau also helps coordinate the overall U.S. government budget for democracy programs and attempts some interagency coordination of the different U.S.-funded efforts within specific countries. The Africa bureau of the State Department has overseen a pot of aid funds amounting to several million dollars a year that is used for democracy and human rights programs.

The Department of Defense increasingly emphasizes democracy promotion in its training programs for foreign militaries. In 1991 Congress mandated that the International Military Education and Training Program (IMET) be expanded to address the needs of new democracies. "Expanded IMET" gives greater emphasis than before to civilian control of armed forces, human rights, and other democracy-related topics. The Department of Justice has also gotten into the democracy field, primarily through training programs for foreign judges, prosecutors, and police. Its International Criminal Investigative Training Assistance Program, which got started in the 1980s in Latin America but now operates around the world, has explicit prodemocracy goals.

In addition to the many initiatives that the government runs directly, three organizations primarily funded by the U.S. government but operating as private, nonprofit organizations are also heavily involved in democracy assistance. The National Endowment for Democracy has survived recurrent doubts in Congress about its continued value and has operated continuously throughout the 1990s with an annual budget of approximately $30 million. The Asia

Foundation has stepped up its involvement in democracy-related activities and does such work in almost all countries in which it operates. Finally, the Eurasia Foundation incorporates democracy-related efforts, such as local government reform, NGO development, the rule of law, and media development, as an important part of its program.

The total amount in dollar terms of these many efforts surpassed a half billion dollars annually by the mid-1990s. Table 4 sets out approximate figures by institution and by region for fiscal year 1998.

For the most part, these different agencies and organizations operate relatively autonomously in dispensing democracy aid, especially the three government-funded private foundations. In some countries the U.S. embassy effectively coordinates the U.S. agencies concerned with democracy programs; in others the USAID mission, State Department officials, Defense attachés, and Justice Department representatives all go off in their own directions on democracy issues. In Washington, the Bureau of Democracy, Human Rights, and Labor is trying to strengthen top-down coordination of U.S. democracy activities, using the newly fortified annual strategic planning process that each U.S. embassy must go through. Greater coordination would generally be desirable although it is unlikely that the various U.S. agencies will work in any greater unison than they do on most other foreign policy issues. It is also important that the coordinating process not impose an artificial regimentation in a domain where certainty about a single best strategy is usually a dangerous illusion and where there is value in attempting and learning from different approaches.

REPEATING THE PAST?

U.S. efforts to use aid to promote democracy abroad have come in two major waves over the past four decades: political development aid that began in the 1960s and receded in the 1970s, and democracy assistance that began in the early 1980s and continues today. Though products of very different periods of history, the two waves are clearly related, both institutionally and intellectually. The question nags but is rarely addressed: is the recent enthusiasm for democracy assistance merely a reenactment of the 1960s?

Looking through aid documents from the 1960s, one has a strong sense of déjà vu, reading about the importance of increasing participation, strengthening local governments, building community-based advocacy groups, training women civic leaders, and the like.

Table 4

U.S. Government Democracy Assistance

Fiscal Year 1998
(millions of dollars)

	Sub-Saharan Africa	Asia	Eastern Europe	Former Soviet Union	Latin America	Middle East	Misc.	TOTAL
USAID	96.91	51.78	127.72	88.60	82.17	60.58	23.92	531.68
USIA	15.40	12.01	17.42	8.80	18.56	6.39	0.00	78.58
State Dept.	0.00	5.00	7.00	.08	.10	5.00	0.90	18.08
Defense Dept.	2.90	2.02	4.01	7.12	3.01	1.11	0.00	20.17
Justice Dept.	.75	0.00	10.75	5.78	11.40	.57	0.01	29.26
National Endowment for Democracy	3.72	5.79	4.54	4.68	3.43	3.38	3.02	28.56
The Asia Foundation	0.00	6.00	0.00	0.00	0.00	0.00	0.00	6.00
The Eurasia Foundation	0.00	0.00	0.00	7.08	0.00	0.00	0.00	7.08
TOTAL	119.68	82.60	171.44	122.14	118.67	77.03	27.85	719.41

Sources: Democracy and Governance Information Unit, USAID; USIA; Bureau for Democracy, Human Rights and Labor, Department of State; Program Management Division, Department of Defense; Criminal Division, Department of Justice; National Endowment for Democracy; the Asia Foundation; and the Eurasia Foundation. See note 38 for detailed information on sources and methods of calculation.

And from time to time in Washington or in the field, one hears career aid officials and other development veterans react to an enthusiastic, optimistic presentation by democracy promoters in their twenties or thirties with the bemused, or sometimes weary comment, "This is modernization theory all over again."

It is certainly true that some of today's democracy programs strongly resemble programs of decades past. Some important differences do, however, separate the two eras. To start with, the overarching motive behind the U.S. entry into political development aid three decades ago differed from the motives at work today. In the 1960s, U.S. political development aid was all about anticommunism—it was spurred by worries about Soviet influence in the third world and the belief that greater prosperity and political participation would head off the possibility of leftist revolutions in less developed countries. Although the current wave of democracy assistance initially grew out of the Reagan administration's anticommunist policies, it grew to full size in the 1990s after the end of the cold war. Democracy promotion is now linked to some strategic ideas—such as "democratic peace" theory—but democracy is now very much a foreign policy goal in and of itself, not merely a means to or a cover for underlying anticommunist ends.

Another difference is the changed political state of the developing world. In the 1960s, democracy was in retreat in Latin America, Africa, and Asia. In the past two decades, by contrast, democracy assistance has expanded in parallel to an important global wave of democratization. Whereas in the 1960s political development assistance faced the daunting task of generating movement toward democracy where none existed, in recent years the primary mission has been furthering democratic transitions that are already under way. This difference partly explains why the political development assistance of the 1960s focused on bottom-up methods of fostering participation—through community groups, leadership training, municipal development, and rural associations—whereas the current wave began with an emphasis on top-down institutions and processes (although the rise of civil society assistance in the 1990s has changed that balance).

It is also possible to compare the two eras from a different angle, by examining the controlling assumptions about democratization and democracy promotion that have informed much of the work.

In this light, elements of both continuity and discontinuity appear. In his masterful study of U.S. policies toward the developing world in the 1960s, *Liberal America and the Third World* (1973), Robert Packenham identified four key assumptions of the U.S. approach. These assumptions derived from the broader American liberal tradition, he argued, and often misled Americans unfamiliar with societies that did not share such traditions.

The first "inarticulate assumption of the liberal tradition" that Packenham underlines is that "change and development are easy." U.S. officials in the 1960s were driven by optimism about the possibility of positive, rapid change in the developing world and the ability of the United States to contribute significantly to such change. The first phase of the current wave of democracy aid, from the mid-1980s to the mid-1990s, was marked by a similar optimism. U.S. officials hailed almost every political opening, no matter how partial or hesitant, as a "democratic revolution." They portrayed the new democracy aid programs as critical boosts to democracy's future in the recipient countries. As in the 1960s, their belief that change and development are easy led democracy promoters to underestimate the difficulties of their work and to fall short of expectations that they themselves had created, damaging their credibility in some cases. Because the democratic trend basically held up in the 1990s, however, they did not suffer the same fall as at the end of the 1960s, when the rosy prospects for democracy in the developing world had come to little. Nevertheless, the slowing down and partial retrenchment of the trend in the mid-1990s pushed democracy promoters toward more realistic views and today it would be hard to find many American democracy promoters who still subscribe to the first of the old liberal assumptions.

The second premise that Packenham highlights is "All good things go together"—the idea that economic, social, and political development are a mutually reinforcing trio, with aid to one contributing positively to the others. This key tenet of modernization theory fell out of fashion in the late 1960s as economic development in many poor countries coincided with the rise of dictatorships. It got a new lease in life in the 1980s with the new development consensus, "Democracy and free markets go hand in hand." The idea was extended in the 1990s as the Bush and Clinton administrations repeatedly asserted that democracy correlated with a dizzying array of good things, such as a disinclination to make war, engage in terrorism, plunder the environment, create refugees, and so forth.

The notable correlation between democracy and economic success in many developed countries, as well as between democracy and other positive characteristics, may demonstrate that over the long run the second liberal assumption Packenham flags has some validity. But democracy promoters have oversimplified the picture by assuming that all good things go together all along the way in complex political and economic transitions. In so doing they have given too little attention to some of the tensions along the road, such as the pressure that the short-term impact of market reform policies can put on fledgling democratic governments, or the fact that democratizing countries may pass through a period in which they are more rather than less conflict-prone than stable authoritarian regimes.[39]

Packenham explains the third assumption, "Radicalism and revolution are bad," as follows: "Radical politics, including intense conflict, disorder, violence and revolution, are unnecessary for economic and political development and therefore always bad." In the 1960s, this assumption was rooted in the fear that radical political change in third world countries would mean leftist change, as well as the underlying belief that America's prosperity and freedom had been maintained so long precisely through the avoidance of radicalism. When U.S. democracy aid got going in Latin America in the 1980s it was based very much on a similar formula of gradualist, moderate change to undercut the political extremes and to avoid the radical route. Yet at the end of the 1980s a shift occurred. Revolutions began to occur in communist countries, revolutions away from leftism, not toward it. U.S. officials delighted in these revolutions and thus for a time at least moved away from the earlier liberal assumption about the evils of radicalism and revolutions. In a number of nondemocratic countries, such as Iraq, Burma, and Sudan, the U.S. government supports efforts to produce radical political change although in others, where it maintains cordial relations with the government, such as China and Vietnam, it prefers the more gradual, nonconflictual approach.

Finally, the fourth assumption Packenham identifies, "Distributing power is more important than accumulating power," reflected the emphasis of political development efforts of the 1960s on broadening citizens' participation. The assumption has been largely operative in recent years as well. Much current democracy aid attempts to foster citizen participation and even the aid directed at state institutions tries to diffuse state power rather than to amass it—by strengthening those parts of the state that may limit the executive power. This assumption led Americans astray in the context of decolonization when the core task for many developing countries was building a coherent state apparatus rather than distributing political power. In the 1980s and 1990s, however, it has been a reasonable approach in many countries that are coming out of decades of over-concentrated political power, though democracy promoters have perhaps been inattentive to the issue of state building in cases of transitional countries that have little coherent state at all.

In short, the liberal assumptions that Packenham blamed for many of the mistakes of the 1960s still make themselves felt in American democracy promotion efforts, though not without some modification from experience. Americans going abroad to foster political changes are still not immune from habits of hubris and oversimplification that grow out of a deep-seated American cultural framework. Yet it would be an oversimplification of a different but equally misleading sort to argue that American democracy promoters today are unchanged from the past or that the political patterns in the world contradicting the liberal assumptions are the same now as they were decades ago.

3
Interlude for Skeptics

Having reviewed the history of U.S. democracy assistance, we can proceed to an introduction of the four cases at the core of this book and the question of strategy. Before doing so, however, I wish to pause briefly for a skeptical interlude. I have noticed that whenever I present an analysis of U.S. democracy assistance, no matter how questioning, some listeners or readers automatically suspect that merely because I treat the subject seriously, I believe such aid is wonderful and that the United States is a faultless champion of democracy on the world stage. They respond with a strong, often bristly skepticism rooted in fundamental doubts about the field, usually including some combination of the following:

- *All the nice phrases about the United States promoting democracy abroad are just so much talk; when push comes to shove, the United States happily supports dictators if they serve U.S. economic or security interests.*
- *Democracy assistance is only a small fraction of U.S. foreign aid and therefore unimportant.*
- *Democracy aid is just a pretty way of packaging illegitimate U.S. intervention in the internal affairs of other countries.*
- *In any case, democracy cannot be exported, it must be grown from within.*
- *Besides, where does the United States get off telling other countries how to run their political systems when its own politics are so full of problems?*

Armed with these beliefs, some observers dismiss the whole enterprise as insignificant, misguided, or sinister without any serious examination of the field. The purpose of this skeptical interlude is not to flatly rebut the skeptics' propositions and then to go on an unfettered idealistic march through the rest of the book. All these fundamental doubts contain some truth. My own views on democracy aid are informed by a considerable amount of skepticism and my perspective is one of constructive critical inquiry. But these doubting propositions are overstatements that if accepted uncritically close off understanding rather than advance it. They are issues for debate, not crushing proof of the senselessness of democracy aid. Let us briefly consider each in turn.

U.S. democracy promotion is mostly rhetoric. U.S. democratic rhetoric of the 1990s does greatly exceed reality. In pursuit of economic and strategic interests the United States maintains friendly relations with many dictatorial or semidictatorial governments, such as those in China, Saudi Arabia, Kuwait, Kazakhstan, Uzbekistan, Azerbaijan, and elsewhere. The hopeful notion, prevalent in the early 1990s, that the traditional divide in U.S. policy between idealistic and pragmatic interests was eliminated by the end of the cold war has not been realized. Nonetheless, U.S. democracy promotion is not merely hortatory.

In the first place, there has been some evolution in U.S. foreign policy since the mid-1980s on the compatibility of democracy promotion with other U.S. interests. Democracy now is more often seen as a pragmatic interest that reinforces other interests than as a purely soft, idealistic interest. In some regions, particularly Latin America, Central Europe, and sub-Saharan Africa, Washington often approaches political, economic, and security interests as a mutually reinforcing set and applies a range of tools to promote democracy. Elsewhere, notably Asia, the United States has more varied interests that still conflict with one another fairly often, yet policy makers still pursue democracy goals in a number of countries.

Second, that the United States fails to push democracy in some countries does not negate its democracy promotion efforts in others. Policy on democracy is inconsistent, but the fact remains that in many countries the United States has genuinely tried in recent years to support democratic transitions. Just because the United States is not promoting democracy in Saudi Arabia does not automatically mean it is not serious when it opposes a coup in Paraguay. Inconsistency detracts from democracy policies, depending on how close by and how similar counterexamples are (U.S. support for a dictator in Peru, for example, would undercut a prodemocracy stance in Paraguay much more than support for a dictatorial regime in the Middle East). But inconsistency does not render such policies meaningless. In denouncing the inconsistency of democracy policy it is easy to forget that all major areas of U.S. foreign policy—whether nuclear non-proliferation policy, trade policy, or support for international law—are inconsistent in important ways. And America is scarcely alone in this regard. One surveys the foreign policies of the major powers in vain for seamless policies on major subjects such as democracy and human rights.

As it is only a small fraction of U.S. foreign aid, democracy assistance is unimportant. Democracy aid is indeed only a small part of the U.S. foreign aid budget—less than 10 percent in the 1990s. Democracy promotion competes for funds in a foreign aid budget that has several well-entrenched priorities (such as population control and economic growth) and that shrank substantially in recent years (in real terms it diminished by approximately 50 percent from the mid-1980s to the mid-1990s). Establishing and expanding a new area of aid in a shrinking budget is extremely difficult; that democracy aid expanded significantly in such a period shows it was a priority for some officials. In addition, democracy aid is relatively cheap. Unlike some types of aid, it rarely entails big-ticket programs costing tens of millions of dollars; most of its costs are expenses measured in the tens of thousands rather than in millions of dollars. The approximately $700 million spent on U.S. democracy aid programs annually thus translates into a great deal of human activity—probably several thousand Americans working in Washington and abroad on a similar number of democracy projects, with the participation of many thousands of people in the recipient countries. This is not to say that the effects of such activities are decisive or earth-shattering—usually they are modest and gradual in nature—but they nonetheless merit attention and analysis.

Democracy aid constitutes illegitimate intervention in the internal affairs of other countries. The question of interventionism is complex and cannot be definitively resolved here. One can start with the general argument of democracy promoters that most democracy assistance is carried out openly, with the permission of the host government, and in pursuit of broad goals, such as a more efficient judiciary or a more competent parliament, that are not usually very controversial within the societies in question. When such aid is clearly oppositional and carried out against the wishes or without the favor of the government in question—which is usually the case in countries with nondemocratic governments—it focuses on fostering basic political and civil rights such as freedom of association or expression and has some or even much the same legitimacy as traditional human rights advocacy.

The end of the cold war, along with the increasing reach of international communications and economic globalization, has lowered barriers to political aid in many places. People and organizations around the developing world and in former communist countries are genuinely interested in, even eager for, the opportunity to learn from people in established democracies about democratic political life. Many countries are surprisingly open to international political cooperation, and a host of formal and informal networks of individuals and groups, both private and public, have arisen to take advantage of that.

At the same time, sensitivities about potential political manipulation and interference from abroad are still there in most countries. The United States carries extra baggage in this regard, because of both its track record of interventionism in others' politics during the cold war and its unusual geopolitical dominance. Many Americans involved in democracy programs are much too quick to assume that what they view as their own good intentions will be accepted as such by people in recipient countries. They also too blithely assume that the negative experiences and images of foreign interventionism lie far in the past for people in other societies and can be easily replaced by positive new ones.

Democracy aid does verge on questionable intervention when it attempts to influence the outcome of elections in other countries. As discussed in chapter 6, U.S. efforts to promote free and fair elections and level playing fields among competing political parties are occasionally exercises in backing political favorites. The legitimacy of such efforts is suspect within the recipient countries and raises complex issues of lines and limits, assistance and manipulation.

Democracy cannot be exported; it must be grown from within. This argument is often delivered with a satisfying fist thump on the table and is greeted by enthusiastic applause at academic conferences. It conveys a certain basic, albeit obvious truth—a country's political system must be its own, rooted in the society and its history, with its own internal logic and legitimacy. Foreign actors, no matter how wealthy and powerful, cannot expect to graft a political system onto another country by training some elites, writing a constitution, supervising an election, constructing some government buildings, and declaring democracy established. But political systems everywhere (like economic systems and cultures) are often greatly affected by external influences. As democracy has spread during the past two decades (and in previous periods of democratic expansion), it has not been a process in which each country discovered democracy on its own, inventing the basic forms and rules from scratch. Instead, influences from abroad, whether the example of neighbors or the appeal of distant exemplars, or the active propagation of political ideas across borders, were usually present and sometimes powerful. Democracy is not exported like a computer chip or a car, but neither is it grown from within in pristine isolation from the rest of the world.

Where does the United States get off promoting democracy when its own democracy is rife with flaws? The sight of earnest Americans traveling to other countries to help legislatures work smoothly or political parties overcome voter apathy may well seem "a curious sight" (the words of a prominent Singaporan skeptic), given the low U.S. public regard for Congress and the low turnout in almost all U.S. elections.[1] Many American democracy promoters are insufficiently troubled by or even unconscious of the fact that they go abroad to promote democracy from a country whose political life has some glaring weaknesses. They operate from the basic idea that the American system is not perfect but is fundamentally sound, and that most transitional countries would do well to get democracy to the point where all they had to worry about were the problems that cloud the U.S. political screen.

The flaws in the U.S. political system should not debilitate Americans so that they do not even try to help other countries achieve more effective democracy. The United States has significant political accomplishments that can be a crucial source of learning for other countries. Democracy promoters, however, need to be more conscious of and more explicit about the flaws of American democracy, and pay more attention to them in aid programs. American efforts to strengthen legislatures in other countries, for example, should acknowledge that Congress is held in low regard by the public and is plagued with credibility problems due to the troubled campaign finance system and other factors. These issues should be built into the training programs just as much as the strengths of the system, so that others can anticipate the problems that arise in democratic systems and learn from American efforts, successful or not, to address them. The same holds for media assistance and the problem of vanishing content on television news in America, for civic education and the problem of low voter turnout, for judicial reform and the problem of skyrocketing litigation. It is also important, as will be discussed in the chapter on strategy, not to create aid programs with the goal of copying the U.S. model. The approach should instead be to provide comparative information as much as possible and to help people in transitional countries make better choices for themselves.

In sum, skepticism about U.S. democracy promotion, and democracy assistance in particular, is certainly warranted. In fact, the profuse democracy rhetoric of U.S. policy makers and the often overbearing, self-congratulatory style of American democracy promoters demand it. To develop a nuanced critical stance, however, one must take a more sophisticated look than the sweeping views that dismiss such aid as a delusion or a fraud. The United States is inconsistent about promoting democracy abroad but nonetheless pursues that goal in dozens of countries. Democracy aid is only a small part of the foreign aid budget but is a substantial body of activity carried out by serious people. The issue of interventionism is always close to the surface, but democracy aid in the 1990s is not simply oldstyle U.S. political interventionism revisited. Democracy cannot be exported wholesale but external factors—including democracy promotion efforts—do affect the political evolution of other countries. U.S. democracy is replete with flaws but democracy promotion does not require perfection in the promoters.

4
Introducing Four Cases

With both some history and some skeptical arguments about democracy aid on the table, the countries of the four case studies can now be introduced. Guatemala, Nepal, Zambia, and Romania are vastly different from one another in most ways, including political history. If one had looked at their political systems at some point in the near past, say, twenty years ago, the contrasts would have been great: one right-wing military dictatorship (Guatemala), one partyless monarchy (Nepal), one single-party "African democracy" (Zambia), and one communist totalitarian dictatorship (Romania). Yet scarcely ten years later, all four were actively seeking to join the global movement toward democracy. All had held multiparty elections, were led by elected governments publicly committed to democracy, and enjoyed substantial political freedom.

U.S. policy toward these countries also underwent a striking change and convergence in the same period. For decades before the late 1980s, U.S. policy toward the four had little or nothing to do with democracy promotion. The United States supported nondemocratic regimes in each of them, mostly for anticommunist reasons, although with Romania the impetus was more precisely anti-Soviet—the United States favored Romania's brutal communist dictator, Nicolae Ceauşescu, because of his relative independence from the Soviet Union. Yet by the early 1990s the United States had shifted gears in all four, and made democracy promotion an important goal.

To introduce the cases I first outline the political character of each country before the late 1980s, then describe briefly the beginnings of their attempted democratic transitions, and finally consider how the transitions fared during the 1990s. For each period I add some analysis of U.S. policy and its relation (or lack thereof) to the democracy issue.

FAR FROM DEMOCRACY

For most of the twentieth century, the political lives of the four countries of the case studies were dominated by diverse forms of nondemocratic rule.

Guatemala: From Repression to Civil War[1]

Guatemalan politics was long a depressing story of harsh dictatorial rule. A wealthy landowning elite, defended by a violent, often vicious military, ran the society according to its wishes from the nineteenth century on, while the majority of the population (over half of which is made up of indigenous people) was excluded from political life and lived in poverty. In the 1940s, a reformist movement arose, part of a larger current of liberal, democratic aspirations in Latin America. The movement gathered momentum in 1951 with the election to the presidency of Jacobo Arbenz Guzmán, a former army major turned populist reformer. Fearing that Arbenz was a communist, the CIA sponsored a coup in 1954 that ousted him. Guatemala reverted to dictatorship; enfranchisement of the indigenous population, unionization, land reform, and other reform measures were halted and undone. In the 1960s, the political ferment turned violent as guerrilla bands made up of disaffected former military officers began operating in the countryside. In the 1970s, these guerrilla groups expanded, forging a leftist revolutionary movement with broad political and military aspirations. The government fought back furiously, employing scorched-earth tactics in the countryside and a systematic campaign of torture and murder of any suspected leftists.

The United States strongly supported the Guatemalan government throughout the 1960s and up to the mid-1970s. Washington provided extensive military aid, particularly counterinsurgency training by Green Berets and other specialized military and intelligence advisers. President Jimmy Carter withdrew U.S. support in the late 1970s, criticizing the Guatemalan government on human rights grounds and shutting off military aid. The new U.S. line angered the Guatemalan military and business leaders, fueling a go-it-alone attitude and scorn for a government they saw as having gone soft on communism.

During the first half of the 1980s, the civil conflict in Guatemala continued to wrack the country. Military repression intensified, with tens of thousands of civilians killed and a climate of terror in much of the country. The incoming Reagan administration saw Guatemala as one of a number of victims of Soviet-Cuban machinations in Central America and sought to rekindle U.S.-Guatemalan ties. Restarting military aid was a priority of the early Reagan policy toward Guatemala, a move frustrated by congressional Democrats leery of aiding the worst violator of human rights in the Western Hemisphere. More quietly, the CIA maintained cozy relations with Guatemalan security forces in the 1980s, based on what both sides saw as their mutual interest in combating communism.

Nepal: Isolated Monarchy[2]

Nepal, a landlocked, mountainous country of approximately 20 million people wedged between two giant neighbors, India and China, is a primarily agrarian society with one of the world's lowest per capita incomes. Unlike most countries in the developing world, Nepal was never colonized by a Western power. It became a state in the late eighteenth century when a Gurkha ruler, Prithvi Narayan Shah, unified a host of small principalities. In the 1840s the Rana family ousted Shah's descendants and established a despotic autocracy and cut the country off from the world. As late as the 1940s, no major roads connected Nepal to the outside world. Cars circulated in Kathmandu, the capital, but only after having been disassembled in India, brought up the mountain paths in pieces, and reassembled in Kathmandu.

Stimulated by India's gaining of independence, a revolution returned the Shah dynasty to power in 1951 and inaugurated a period of political reform and quasi-constitutional rule. Progress toward democracy occurred throughout the 1950s, leading to elections in 1959 and the assumption of power by a democratic government headed by the largest political party, the Nepali Congress Party. In 1960, however, the royal family, led by King Mahendra, ousted the new government, jailed its leaders, suspended the constitution, and reestablished monarchical rule. King Mahendra and his successor, King Birendra (who ascended to the throne in 1972), ruled from the early 1960s to the late 1980s, presiding over the *panchayat* system, a nonparty system of governmental bodies layered from the national to the local. The Nepali Congress Party and various leftist parties operated within the society, banned but nonetheless alive and active. The periodic rise of organized resistance to the monarchy forced various liberalizing reforms, such as direct elections to the National Assembly (though not multiparty elections), especially in the second half of the 1970s and during the 1980s.

Compared with its extensive involvement in Guatemalan politics, the United States was not much involved with Nepal from the 1950s through the 1980s. Washington saw Nepal as a useful buffer between India and China, and got along with its kings, appreciating their opposition to communism and their willingness to walk a carefully independent line between their two neighbors. The United States sent aid to Nepal and basically kept out of internal political matters, its hands full with other political headaches in Asia, above all Vietnam.

Zambia: From Independence to Single-Party Rule[3]

Zambia, a medium-sized, landlocked country in the northern area of southern Africa, with a relatively urbanized population of approximately 10 million, has important copper resources but is nonetheless poor with a per capita GDP of under $400. The territory that is now Zambia was long inhabited primarily by Bantu people. Britain was the dominant colonial power, and the territory formally became a British protectorate in the 1920s, under the name of Northern Rhodesia. In the 1950s, an independence movement, dominated by copper mine workers and led by Kenneth Kaunda and Harry Nkundula, arose. Zambia became independent in 1964, with Kaunda as head of the new state and of the largest political party, the United National Independence Party (UNIP).

Kaunda won reelection in 1968, then in 1972 consolidated near-absolute power, joining the trend in Africa toward single-party democracy, or "African democracy." He banned all other political parties and was repeatedly reelected unopposed in the 1970s and 1980s. Kaunda also nationalized all major sectors of the economy, including the copper mines, thereby ensuring UNIP's complete domination of the society. As copper prices stagnated then declined from the mid-1970s through the 1980s, Zambia sank deeper into poverty and Kaunda's popularity, established at independence, slowly declined. At the same time, he was active on the international stage, seeking a role both as a spokesman for postcolonial Africa and as a leader of the African opposition to apartheid in South Africa.

As with Nepal, the United States had few identifiable interests in Zambia during the cold war beyond a general desire that it not go communist. Throughout most of the 1970s and 1980s, Washington had scant sympathy for Kaunda's international activities but did not consider him anything more than a minor irritant on most matters. It went on paying little attention to the country.

Romania: Balkan Exception[4]

Situated in the northeast part of the Balkan Peninsula, Romania is a Latinate society in a region dominated by Slavic societies. Its population of approximately 23 million is roughly equally divided between traditional farmers and highly educated city dwellers. Romania emerged from several centuries of Ottoman rule in the nineteenth century and began to undertake liberalizing social and political reforms. Romania gained territory after World War I, the most important addition being Transylvania, then lost some of it in World War II under pressure from Germany and the Soviet Union. A partially successful but limited attempt to establish parliamentary democracy in the 1920s and 1930s collapsed soon before World War II, ushering in a short, turbulent period of monarchical and then fascist rule.

In the aftermath of the war, the Soviet Union brought Romania into its sphere of influence, undermining Romania's effort to reestablish parliamentary rule and installing a puppet communist government. After a long, punishing period of Stalinist terror, Romanian communism entered a liberalizing phase in the 1960s. Nicolae Ceauşescu succeeded to the party leadership in 1965 and moved Romania out of lockstep with Soviet foreign policy as well as toward somewhat greater political openness. In the 1970s, Ceauşescu continued his maverick stance in foreign policy but steadily cracked down on his own people, creating the most repressive communist regime in Eastern Europe apart, perhaps, from Albania. Ceauşescu's economic management was equally bad, and from the mid-1970s to the end of the next decade Romania suffered through horrendous repression, grinding economic deprivation, and near-total isolation from the world.

Many Romanians measure U.S. policy toward their country from the starting point of the historic meeting at Yalta in early 1945 between Franklin Roosevelt, Joseph Stalin, and Winston Churchill at which, in the Romanian view, the United States handed over Romania to the Soviet Union. For most Americans, Romania scarcely appeared on the radar screen until the late 1960s, when Ceauşescu gained favor with the United States for his refusal to toe the Soviet line in Czechoslovakia and elsewhere. Congress granted Romania most-favored-nation trade status, and Ceauşescu was warmly received in Washington and other Western capitals throughout the 1970s. By the mid-1980s, however, the stagnant malignancy of Ceauşescu's domestic rule was more and more out of sync with the liberalizing trend in other parts of the communist world, and Ceauşescu's usefulness as a symbol in the superpower competition faded. The United States terminated MFN status for Romania in 1988, and Ceauşescu became an anachronism in a liberalizing region.

TRANSITION FEVER

In the latter half of the 1980s and the first years of the 1990s, all four countries initiated political transitions, with the explicit goal of democratization. The move away from authoritarian or totalitarian rule took different forms in each of the four case study countries, reflecting their different histories.

Guatemala's Hesitant Opening

In Guatemala, the transition from military dictatorship to elected, civilian rule was the military's own project. By the mid-1980s, the Guatemalan military's years of merciless counterinsurgency and massive human rights violations had finally brought the leftist guerrillas under control, although the conflict continued in several parts of the country. The military decided that moving to elected, civilian rule was advisable, primarily to gain international legitimacy and to catch up with the growing trend in Latin America away from military rule. In addition, some segments of Guatemala's powerful business elite became dissatisfied with the military's rule because of its poor economic management, and now supported the idea of civilian rule.

Elections for a Constituent Assembly were held in 1984. A new constitution was drafted and approved in March 1985. Later that year multiparty presidential and legislative elections took place. The Christian Democratic Party obtained a majority in the legislature and its presidential candidate, Venicio Cerezo, was elected president—the first civilian president in Guatemala since the late 1960s. Although the military pushed for this transition, it had no intention of giving up its privileged position as the real arbiter of political power. Civilians would be allowed to rule the government; the military would continue to run the country.

The Reagan administration supported the Guatemalan military rulers in the first half of the 1980s, because of their common hard-line anticommunism. Since the transition to civilian rule was the military's idea, the Reagan administration supported it, too. Reagan officials believed that the transition would help them persuade Congress to renew military aid to Guatemala and would in general be a good thing for that country. The United States talked up the transition in Washington, extended aid to support the 1985 elections, and heralded the election of Cerezo as a major democratic breakthrough.

Nepal's Surprising Opening

Few observers predicted the fall of Nepal's long-standing authoritarian monarchy in 1990. The year before, India had let several critical economic agreements with Nepal lapse, out of irritation over economic and border issues. The ensuing economic crisis fueled the Nepalese people's already considerable anger at the government's economic nonperformance. The powerful, if distant, example of democracy spreading in Eastern Europe also fed political ferment. In late 1989 the Nepali Congress Party assertively called for democracy and shifted to open confrontation with the government. The various communist parties also came out for democracy. In 1990 the Congress Party and a newly united leftist front joined forces to form the Movement for the Restoration of Democracy. The movement almost immediately attracted a huge following and soon persuaded King Birendra to accept an interim cabinet led by the Congress Party. A democratic constitution was promulgated and relatively clean, open elections followed in 1991. The Congress Party won control of the House of Representatives and formed the first government of the nascent democratic era.

U.S. policy makers were preoccupied in 1989–1990 with the startling events in Eastern Europe and the Soviet Union. To the extent that it paid attention to Nepal's transition, Washington was supportive. The Nepalese monarchy had served Washington's cold war purposes but the cold war was ending. The U.S. embassy in Kathmandu threw itself into the transition, attempting to help the political parties work together and to smooth various bumps along the way. Many Nepalese communists interpreted the embassy's politicking as an effort to prevent them from coming out on top in the transition. They were probably correct in surmising that the embassy hoped to see the Congress Party running the new government, but U.S. officials also acted as they did because they believed in promoting democracy. USAID, the Asia Foundation, and the NED scrambled to put together efforts to support the drafting of the new constitution and the holding of national elections.

Zambia Embraces Multiparty Democracy

Zambia's transition to multiparty rule was similarly abrupt and unexpected. President Kaunda had eliminated almost all organized political activity in Zambia outside the direct control of his ruling UNIP. Yet by 1990 the emerging global democratic trend had spread from Eastern Europe to a number of African countries, and Kaunda was suddenly in a much more precarious position than he realized. With little warning, a new political force emerged in Zambia, the Movement for Multi-Party Democracy (MMD), an amalgam of trade unions, business groups, and civic groups, headed by a union leader, Frederick Chiluba. Under pressure from the MMD, Kaunda consented to a referendum on a new government. He soon revoked that consent but allowed the formation of new political parties. The MMD registered as a party in late 1990 and pressed its campaign for a democratic transition. Kaunda relented, met with Chiluba, and the transition became unstoppable. National elections were held in late 1991. The day after voting ended, Chiluba took office, before the ballots were even fully counted. The eventual tally was 76 percent for Chiluba and about 80 percent for the MMD in the legislative elections. Zambians exulted in their swift, decisive political transition.

Like Nepal, Zambia was low on the unusually crowded U.S. foreign policy agenda in 1990. Yet as in Nepal, the United States did support the democratic transition. Kaunda was of no particular value to the United States, while Chiluba promised both political and economic reform and clearly had the backing of most Zambians. The National Democratic Institute helped prepare Zambian observers for the 1991 elections, and with the Carter Center, served as election observers. The U.S. embassy in Lusaka worked throughout 1990 and 1991 to broker negotiations between the political actors and to support a peaceful democratic transition. The United States was welcoming the trend toward democracy in Africa; Zambia was one more case in point.

Romania Starts Over

Romania's transition was also sudden, but in addition it was violent (more than 1,000 Romanians were killed in December 1989) and had none of the sense of the clean break of the Nepalese and Zambian transitions. Ceauşescu's grip on Romania seemed unassailable in the late 1980s. As peaceful revolutions spread in Poland, Hungary, and elsewhere in Eastern Europe, Ceauşescu adamantly resisted change, delivering in November 1989 a no-compromise address to the Fourteenth Romanian Communist Party Congress. Within weeks, however, the bottom fell out of his rule. In mid-December, Ceauşescu's security forces attacked crowds that had gathered in Timişoara, in western Romania, to support a protestant minister, Reverend Laszlo Tokes, against possible eviction from his church for having spoken out on political and religious rights. Protest ignited around the country. Days later, crowds chased Ceauşescu off an outdoor stage in Bucharest, and he fled the capital.

A small group of prominent Romanians led by Ion Iliescu, a party official who had fallen out of favor with Ceauşescu in the 1970s, announced the formation of the Council of National Salvation (later the National Salvation Front) and that they had assumed power. Ceauşescu and his wife were summarily tried and executed several days later, on Christmas Day 1989, by a makeshift military tribunal. Over the next several months the secretive National Salvation Front consolidated its position while many new civic groups, political parties, newspapers, and unions sprouted. Romania hurried into its first postcommunist elections in May 1990. The National Salvation Front exploited its dominance to ensure a commanding hold on the electoral process. Iliescu was elected president with 85 percent of the vote and the National Salvation Front gained two-thirds of the legislative vote. Though Ceauşescu was gone, the links of key figures in the National Salvation Front to the old regime raised doubts about what sort of transition had really occurred. Frequent rumors in Romania that Ceauşescu's ouster was a preplanned putsch by insiders rather than the result of a popular revolt heightened the uncertainty.

The fall of Ceauşescu was so rapid that the United States and others were for the most part bystanders. The Bush administration welcomed the changes in Romania, although it was concerned about the violence during the transition and the murky political character of the National Salvation Front. In early 1990 Bush officials pressed the front to hold elections and permit the growth of new civic and political organizations. Secretary of State James Baker stopped in Bucharest to deliver those messages personally and to meet with fledgling opposition groups. The NED and several other American groups hurried aid to the new independent sector and provided electoral assistance and observers for the May 1990 elections.

THE CHALLENGES OF CONSOLIDATION

After the exhilaration of initial democratic transition inevitably comes the complications of consolidation. In all four countries the path has been rocky; two of the four countries have managed to keep advancing while the two others have run into walls.

To Peace and Beyond in Guatemala

Guatemala's path since the return to civilian rule in 1986 has been painful and precarious. Taking the long view, it represents the most serious try at democratization in Guatemala's history. Seen close up, the shortcomings and problems of the transition are daunting. Two developments in the 1990s, however, have given hope. First, when President Jorge Serrano, Cerezo's elected successor, attempted in 1993 a self-coup modeled after Peruvian President Alberto Fujimori's summary dismissal of democracy the year before, a remarkable collection of Guatemalans—including many business leaders, civic activists, newspaper editors, and politicians—united to defeat it. This was a powerful sign of the breadth and strength of democratic commitment in Guatemala. Second, in 1995–1996, the government and the rebels, aided by the United Nations, finally negotiated an end to the civil war. The peace accords are a comprehensive program for the transformation of Guatemalan society, from the rule of law to ethnic relations. They represent an ambitious plan to move Guatemala beyond the forms to the actual substance of democracy.

Most of the entrenched social and political problems that have marked life for decades are still very much with Guatemalans: a tremendously skewed distribution of wealth in favor of a small, self-protective business class; an indigenous majority that is profoundly marginalized; widespread poverty; incoherent, shifting political parties; a weak civil society; and powerful security forces reluctant to submit to political authority. Nonetheless, democratic rules of the game have gathered force and the amount of political openness is unprecedented. The Guatemalan transition has succeeded to some extent simply by not falling apart.

The United States has supported the transition from the mid-1980s to the present. Washington opposed coup rumblings in the late 1980s, helped mobilize international opposition to the attempted self-coup, and supported the peace process. As described in more detail in the next chapter, U.S. democracy aid projects have multiplied in Guatemala.

In the 1980s, a fundamental tension afflicted U.S. policy toward Guatemala: the anticommunist imperative led the government, especially the Pentagon and the CIA, into a friendly, sometimes intimate relationship with the repressive Guatemalan military, even as the United States supported the democratic transition through diplomatic means and aid. With the end of the cold war, policy makers felt less need to back dubious anticommunist friends in Guatemala (or elsewhere). At the same time, the Guatemalan military improved its human rights behavior substantially. U.S. policy continues to be sympathetic to the Guatemalan business elite and military, but is much more genuinely prodemocratic than before.

Stagnation in Nepal

The optimism and sense of excitement of 1990–1991 about the dawn of a new era in Nepal dissipated steadily over the 1990s. Electoral democracy has stayed on track—many elections have been held and the major parties have traded power back and forth. The country enjoys a respectable level of political freedom. Yet an overwhelming frustration and disappointment with the democratic experiment pervades Nepalese society. One government after another has proved incompetent and unable to inspire the people's trust. The economic situation remains abysmal, and no government has pursued a coherent program to reform it. Grievous social problems, especially in health, education, and housing, are worsening. Most Nepalese citizens have scant sense that the government represents their interests or that they have any meaningful role in political life; the result is apathy and cynicism. Party politics are mired in ritualized, polarized struggles that are often little more than fighting over the spoils of state power. Civil society—including unions, citizens groups, and the media—remains weak and is often manipulated by one party or another for narrow political purposes.

The way forward is unclear. Elections hold little hope or interest for most Nepalese—the entire political class seems to them an ingrown, self-perpetuating circle drawn from a limited stratum of society. A violent Maoist guerrilla group operates in parts of the countryside and seems to be gaining adherents. The profound economic stagnation means that little dynamism is present anywhere in the society and that there are few opportunities to make money outside of milking the state. In sum, the democratic experiment is maintaining the forms but seems neither to be delivering much to the people nor giving signs of how it might improve.

The United States has continued its prodemocratic stance in Nepal, giving diplomatic encouragement and some aid. Washington has weight in Nepalese political life, simply by virtue of America's lone superpower position. Yet the actual level of involvement and interest of the U.S. government in Nepal's democratic transition is low. In Kathmandu, the U.S. embassy and the USAID mission take an active interest, but with little contribution from Washington. The political stagnation has prompted American officials to view democracy promotion efforts in Nepal as a long-term proposition at best.

Zambia Slides Backward

Zambia's attempted democratic transition has proved even more disappointing than Nepal's. Hopes were initially very high. President Chiluba and the MMD firmly committed themselves to democratization and had the solid support of most Zambians. Yet within a few years of taking power Chiluba began to renege on his commitments, and by the end of the 1990s Zambia was a semiauthoritarian system with some political openness but no democratic core. The central problem has been Chiluba's intolerance of opposition. He goes after any political rivals, hounds the few independent news and opinion sources, and bends the rule of law to his needs. The ruling MMD has its tentacles deep in the state apparatus and has shown little sign of any intention to relinquish power.

The 1996 national elections, the first national elections after the 1991 balloting that brought Chiluba to power, laid bare the serious democratic deficit. Chiluba fiddled with the constitution to exclude as a candidate his only serious rival, former president Kaunda. He also insisted on a problematic voter registration process and persecuted domestic observer groups that cried foul. After the voting, Kaunda was arrested on dubious charges of treason and imprisoned for several months. The political opposition remains weak and divided, with Kaunda's party failing to renovate itself and to move away from the past. Independent NGOs are few and not very powerful. Television is state-controlled, and the one independent newspaper limps along from crisis to crisis. The once powerful unions are no longer a force.

Chiluba has carried out economic reforms, particularly privatization. But they have not yet alleviated the harsh poverty afflicting most of the population. Furthermore, the reforms have been accompanied by much corruption. Most of the newly privatized companies purchased by Zambians have ended up in the hands of a closed circle of people with direct or indirect ties to the MMD ruling circle. Advances have been made in a few socioeconomic areas, such as a more marketized health care system. In general, however, patronage politics has again become the norm; public interest in and belief in the possibility of democratic progress is very low.

U.S. policy toward Zambia in the 1990s has centered around two goals—promoting market reform policies and promoting democracy. The two have not always gone hand in hand, and the U.S. government has struggled to balance its favorable view of Chiluba's economic policies with its questioning of his political policies. The basic approach has been a friendly relationship with Chiluba and the MMD, leavened with periodic efforts to exert pressure in response to Chiluba's antidemocratic steps. The most serious test of the relationship came with Chiluba's behavior in the 1996 elections. The United

States and other donor countries criticized the president openly, reduced aid for a time, then normalized relations the next year. The United States has sponsored a varied portfolio of aid programs over the 1990s to support the democracy goal.

Romania's Slow Progress

In the first half of the 1990s, it was not clear whether or not Romania was on a democratic path. President Iliescu and his National Salvation Front showed only a half-hearted commitment to democracy and market economics, and their lingering allegiance to the past was troubling. They continually blurred the line between state and ruling party, failed to carry through on economic reforms, and resisted opening up the communist period to public scrutiny and debate. At the same time, however, opposition parties operated relatively freely (after the miners' brutal rampages of 1990 and 1991), independent media multiplied, civic groups increased in number and reach, and the society hearkened to ideas and exchanges from Western Europe, the United States, and elsewhere.

To the surprise of most observers, Iliescu and his party lost the 1996 national elections. Romanians were angry about the stagnant economy and government corruption; they were also tired of a president who had been in power longer than any other post-1989 Eastern European leader. The assumption of power by the main opposition coalition, headed by Emil Constantinescu, represented for many Romanians the first real break from the old communist system, and generated euphoria and high expectations. Since 1996 those hopes have been only partially fulfilled. The new ruling coalition has wasted large amounts of energy on internal squabbles, has moved only with difficulty to speed up economic reforms, and has not significantly reduced the perception of widespread corruption.

The performance of all governments in Romania since 1989 has fallen far short of expectations, leaving citizens sullen and apathetic. Yet looked at from some distance, Romania's democratic progress has been real. Democratic rules of the game govern the struggle for political power. Genuine alternation of power has occurred. Considerable freedom exists throughout society. Independent civil society has grown substantially. One can cite many defects in the workings of Romania's democracy and lament the tortuously slow pace of the transition. Nevertheless, the direction is positive and the underlying principles are holding.

Since 1989 U.S. policy toward Romania has followed the lines of U.S. policy toward Eastern Europe generally—supporting market reforms and democratization in the service of the vision of a peaceful, secure Eastern Europe that is gradually being integrated into Western political, economic, and security structures. U.S. policy makers gave attention to Romania in the immediate aftermath of 1989 because of the ambiguous nature of the Romanian transition. The Bush administration pressured Iliescu to respect democratic norms, especially to carry through with elections. It provided the fledgling opposition with moral and material support as well. U.S. policy shifted toward normalization after relatively free and fair national elections in 1992, and the pro-opposition stance of U.S. diplomacy and democracy aid faded.

The election of Constantinescu in 1996 produced a warmer relationship, although the Clinton administration did not include Romania in the small group of countries invited to join NATO in the first round of enlargement, to the enormous regret of most Romanians. Romanians continue to consider very important what the United States thinks about Romania and to assume a high degree of U.S. influence in their country. In fact, although the United States supports continued democratization and economic reform in the country, actual U.S. involvement is relatively limited. What high-level U.S. attention goes to Eastern Europe is largely absorbed by the former Yugoslavia. From the policy makers' viewpoint, as Romania has progressed democratically during the 1990s, the need for an active U.S. role in its transition has correspondingly diminished.

THE TRANSITIONS COMPARED

Guatemala, Nepal, Zambia, and Romania are all part of the "third wave" of democratic transitions: in the 1980s or early 1990s they moved from some kind of dictatorship to a political opening featuring multiparty elections followed by attempted democratic consolidation. In both Guatemala and Romania, the shift away from dictatorship was at first only partial. The Guatemalan military maintained informal but powerful control over the new elected government. In Romania, Ceauşescu was dead but the new regime had important links to the ancien régime. In contrast, both Nepal and Zambia initially appeared to have made decisive breaks with the past, starting afresh with new political systems. The four political openings varied along other dimensions as well, including the amount and type of violence involved, the pace, the ideological matters at stake, and the role of organized parties.

At the same time, these openings shared several important characteristics. First, all four were at least partly stimulated by democratization in other countries. The Guatemalan military's decision to return the country to civilian rule was in part due to the desire to keep up with the trend in Latin America away from military dictatorships. The fall of Ceauşescu in Romania was very much part of a domino effect of anticommunist breakthroughs in Eastern Europe. In both Nepal and Zambia, leaders and ordinary citizens felt strongly the example of Eastern Europe's revolutionary year. In Zambia, the sudden movement toward democracy in a number of African countries in 1990 was an additional influence.

Second, long-term economic distress was a major factor undermining the dictatorial regime in all four cases. In Guatemala, the military's failure to manage the economy in the first half of the 1980s weakened the traditional alliance between the military and the elite business class. In Nepal, the economic crisis brought to a head in the squabble with India in 1989 aggravated an already angry populace. In Zambia, the profound economic decline throughout the 1980s did much to undermine Kaunda's popularity. In Romania, Ceauşescu's disastrous economic policies cemented Romanians' hatred of his rule.

Finally, popular pressure from below was also significant in all four cases. In Nepal and Zambia, such pressure manifested itself in the formation of broad-based movements for democracy. In Romania, popular pressure was tightly corked until it burst out in street demonstrations that had a decisive impact. In Guatemala, the popular pressure for change was intense and explosive over decades; the transition occurred only when the Guatemalan military had fought back the insurgency sufficiently to give itself the confidence to open up some political space.

Reflecting the heterogeneous nature of their dictatorial periods, the initial political openings in the four countries varied in important ways. The contours of their initial political openings are not a reliable guide to the evolution over the longer term of these countries' attempted transitions. The two countries that seemed to make decisive breaks with the past, Zambia and Nepal, have fared relatively poorly, with political stagnation in Nepal and backsliding in Zambia. In contrast, the two that had only partial initial breakthroughs, Guatemala and Romania, are advancing toward democracy, albeit slowly and painfully.

No single factor explains the differences in evolution. Democratization is far from complete in any of the four countries, and in general it is far too entwined with the political, social, economic, and cultural conditions of a society to be boiled down to a magic ingredient. It is tempting to highlight, for example, the importance of good leadership for successful democratization. Good leadership is undoubtedly helpful but it is only one of many factors. Romania, for example, has managed to make progress without very good leadership. Neither of Romania's two presidents since 1989 has been especially capable, and one was only marginally a democrat. Guatemala, too, has managed to keep moving forward despite several problematic presidents. Similarly, economic reform is often cited as a key generator of democratization. None of the four countries studied experienced much economic dynamism in the 1990s. Only one, Zambia, had a successful privatization program—or at least one praised by the World Bank and the IMF. Yet Zambia's democratic progress was the least of the four.

All four countries point up a critical difficulty of democratization: transforming state institutions into competent, effective entities. In all four, most of the core state institutions have remained citadels of corruption, incompetence, and inefficiency throughout the process. The four also exemplify a troubling characteristic of many countries struggling to democratize—the tendency of the public to pass quickly from initial high hopes for democracy to disillusionment and political alienation. Democracy promoters often cast this issue in terms of the need for better civic education and promotion of a "vibrant civil society." These, however, as discussed in chapter 8, are far from simple tasks.

Moreover, although the four countries vary in the amount of democratic progress they have made, the differences among their trajectories are not actually all that great. Although their democracies are in better shape, for example, Guatemala and Romania have at times exhibited symptoms of stagnation similar to those in Nepal. The dividing line between Nepal's stagnation and Zambia's retrogression is similarly thin. Nor are these trajectories set in stone. Any number of factors could throw Guatemala or Romania off track. Zambia might find better leadership and a renewed democratic impetus. Nepal could start to move ahead or could slip backward. In all four, the political situation is still far from settled.

Given the ahistorical character of so much of the attention to democratization and democracy promotion in the past two decades, it is important to note that in all four cases the recent transition had strong roots in the country's past. In Guatemala, the democratization of the 1990s represents in some ways the achievement of the movement for liberalization reforms that began in the 1940s. Nepal's democratic experiment of the 1990s is a second try after the failed democratization effort of the 1950s. In Zambia, the surge of democratic aspirations in the 1990s connected to the hopes and ideals of the push for independence in the late 1950s and early 1960s. In Romania, the historical bridge is decades longer but even more vivid. The new multiparty politics of the 1990s draws heavily on the legacy of the failed political structures of the 1920s and 1930s; it even includes the reestablishment of the two main political groupings of that period. These historical continuities underline the fact that democratization is almost always a long-term process and that sudden openings and rapid democratic change are seldom either as new or as decisive as they often appear.

Democracy aid has been part of U.S. policy in all the case study countries, and it has come in a common pattern: little in the period of nondemocratic rule; a burst of interest at the time of the political opening and a rush of aid to support the first transitional elections; and the development of a varied portfolio of democracy programs to support the attempted consolidation after the elections, and then the readjustment of that portfolio as the consolidation process either advances or goes astray. The kinds of programs that the United States sponsored, the strategies employed, the methods of implementation, and the effects achieved are considered throughout subsequent chapters, illustrating the broader inquiry.

PART TWO

The Core Elements

5
The Question of Strategy

Although the United States sponsors democracy aid in all sorts of countries, its approaches almost everywhere are strikingly similar. If one had been told in the mid-1990s that the United States was carrying out democracy programs in a country attempting a democratic transition, yet was told nothing about that country's location, economic level, political past, or cultural traditions, one could still guess the general contents of the portfolio: election assistance around each national election, with growing attention to local elections; aid to the major political parties; a parliamentary strengthening program, judicial reform work, possibly some police aid and small-scale efforts to improve civil-military relations; attempts to strengthen local government; money and training for various NGOs; courses for journalists; and support for independent trade unions.

The explanation for this basic package of democracy programs and the consistency of the package across widely diverse settings lies in a core strategy that U.S. democracy promoters usually follow. The strategy incorporates both a model of democracy and a model of democratization. In other words, it provides answers to the fundamental questions of what political outcomes democracy promoters want recipient countries to achieve and what processes of political change they believe will produce those outcomes.

As I argue in this chapter, the core strategy has certainly served as a guide for aid providers about what to do when faced with the daunting challenge of promoting democracy in a bewildering array of political situations. Whether its adoption has meant that aid providers thereby actually know what they are doing is less certain. The core strategy has several major identifiable flaws, not only many America-specific conceptions that do not always apply abroad but also shortcomings in its ideas about political change and the nature of political sequencing. Democracy promoters are working on the core strategy as they go along, and I devote considerable attention here to the main lines of improvement that are emerging from practice. I close the chapter by examining the application of the core strategy in the four countries of the case studies.

THE CORE STRATEGY

Most U.S. democracy assistance in the 1980s and 1990s has been directed at politically transitional countries—the many countries that have experienced a break from an authoritarian or a totalitarian system and have embarked on an attempt at democratization, or something their leaders claim is democratization. Transitional countries span a tremendous range in the developing world and the postcommunist world of Eastern Europe and the former Soviet Union, from impoverished nations stuck in centuries-old socioeconomic debilities to shattered states trying to recover from conflicts, from relatively well-off countries with past experience in democratic politics to a former superpower struggling to move beyond a legacy of totalitarianism. They encompass transition processes all the way from deep-reaching democratic transformation to the superficial adoption of democratic forms followed by a slide back toward autocracy.

Yet in setting out to support democratization in most transitional countries, U.S. democracy promoters start with the same model of democracy. This model consists of a set list of key institutions and processes that I call the "democracy template" because of the manner in which it is used. The template has three categories: elections, state institutions, and civil society.

Free and fair elections, particularly national ones, are a critical component. Political competition must be open, the campaign process relatively fair, most citizens allowed to vote, and the balloting secret and fairly counted and reported. Directly related to elections are political parties. U.S. democracy promoters consider desirable a party system in which there are a few major parties, thus avoiding one overly dominant party or a fragmentation of politics under many tiny parties. The parties should adhere to democratic values, be organized around preferably moderate ideological affinities rather than on ethnic, religious, or regional lines, and have sufficient internal organizational capacity to reach a significant proportion of the citizenry and represent their interests.

The second category of the template covers the institutions of the state. The starting point is a written constitution that establishes a system of government based on the consent of the governed, the separation of powers, the rule of law, and respect for political and civil rights. The government is to be made up of three branches: a democratically elected, law-abiding executive; a representative and at least somewhat autonomous legislative branch; and an independent judiciary. U.S. aid providers increasingly stress the importance of a local government that is democratically elected and has some genuine authority of its own. Another focus among state institutions is a military that is subordinate to the government.

The template's third category is civil society. The template ideal is a diverse, active, and independent civil society that articulates the interests of citizens and holds government accountable to citizens. U.S. democracy promoters often highlight nongovernmental organizations (NGOs) involved in public interest advocacy, such as human rights or women's issues, as a vital form of civil society. They also emphasize independent media and labor unions.

Alongside this model of democracy, democracy promoters have also relied on a basic model of democratization. This centers on the notion of a natural sequence of political steps. Democratization is assumed to proceed along a relatively set path: It starts, according to the model, when a nondemocratic regime, faced with waning legitimacy and rising popular pressure for liberalization, decides it must permit a political opening. The opening occurs; opposition groups and independent civic actors multiply. These newly mobilized forces press the government to hold multiparty national elections. The elections are held and an elected government takes power. The initial transition achieved, gradual consolidation follows. Consolidation involves top-down change—the rationalization and democratization of the main state institutions. It also includes bottom-up change—the strengthening and diversification of civil society. These two halves of the consolidation process are mutually reinforcing. Democracy promoters often speak of seeking to increase both the "supply" (state institutions) and the "demand" (civil society) of democracy.

The Democracy Template

Sector	Sector Goal	Type of Aid
Electoral Process	Free and fair elections	Electoral aid
	Strong national political parties	Political party building
State Institutions	Democratic constitution	Constitutional assistance
	Independent, effective judiciary and other law-oriented institutions	Rule-of-law aid
	Competent, representative legislature	Legislative strengthening
	Responsive local government	Local government development
	Prodemocratic military	Civil-military relations
Civil Society	Active advocacy NGOs	NGO building
	Politically educated citizenry	Civic education
	Strong independent media	Media strengthening
	Strong independent unions	Union building

Early on in the current wave of democracy assistance, roughly from the mid-1980s through the early 1990s, U.S. democracy promoters emphasized elections and top-down programs. The focus on elections reflected the fact that at the time an extraordinary number of breakthrough elections were taking place in formerly nondemocratic countries. The emphasis on top-down programs grew out of the tendency of Reagan and Bush administration officials to support controlled, step-by-step transitions, particularly in Latin America, and their disinclination to back anything resembling populist mobilization, lest it veer off into violence or leftist revolution. In the 1990s, for a host of reasons outlined in chapter 8, democracy promoters got interested in fostering civil society. U.S. democracy promotion became a synthesis of top-down and bottom-up initiatives.

People working on democracy aid often argue over the relative merits of top-down versus bottom-up approaches. Some insist that reforming state institutions is the most powerful, efficient way to produce real democratic change. Others contend that empowering citizens is the one true path. Officials at USAID and other government agencies tend to reach the bland but bureaucratically lubricative conclusion that democracy promotion requires working simultaneously from the top down and the bottom up.

To develop a set of democracy aid programs for a particular country, U.S. providers apply the three-part democracy template and the natural sequence model. If a country has not yet even begun a political opening and is run by an authoritarian or a dictatorial regime, democracy providers concentrate on activities to foster independent groups and to disseminate the idea of democracy. If a country is in the midst of the initial transition phase—moving toward elections—the democracy aid is usually focused on that, primarily through support for elections and political parties.

If a country is completing the electoral transition and entering the consolidation phase, the democracy template is brought to bear. Each of the institutions in the country corresponding to the template—the legislature, judiciary, media, NGO sector, and so forth—is analyzed to determine its divergence from the ideal form. The aid providers then prescribe assistance programs to help strengthen the various institutions so as to make them fit the template models. Each aid program is usually directed at one institution on the list. For most countries, aid providers deem almost every institution on the list deficient compared to their ideal, so the result is a set of small programs that seek to do at least something with most of the template institutions. This is the approach described at the start of the chapter as the standard portfolio of U.S. democracy aid in most transitional countries—a mix of aid for elections, political parties, the legislature, the judicial system, local government, media, labor unions, and advocacy NGOs.

Built into the two guiding ideas of a democracy template and a natural sequence for democratization is a third critical part of the core strategy—the concept of institutional modeling. In this view, if a society can reproduce the institutional components of established Western democracies, it will achieve democracy. The process of transforming institutions is seen as the process of democratization itself. To a person in a transitional country asking democracy aid workers how democratization can be accomplished, the answer they give through their programs is, "Get your legislature working right, fix up your judiciary, increase the strength of the independent media, unions, and advocacy NGOs, develop stronger political parties, and hold regular free and fair elections." As envisioned in democracy aid efforts, institutional modeling is to be a peaceful, steady process of political change characterized by the progressive habituation and socialization of an ever-widening range of political and other actors in basic democratic norms and practices. Conflicts over power, resources, and other concrete interests are to be managed by the increasingly accepted democratic rules of the game.

The self-assigned role of democracy assistance is to stimulate and speed up such institutional modeling. Each project in the typical U.S. portfolio aims to shape a particular sector or institution along the lines of its counterpart in Western democracies. That is why training is such a common method of democracy assistance—the training of judges, prosecutors, police, parliamentarians, parliamentary staff, politicians, election commissioners, mayors, city councilors, union officials, lawyers, human rights specialists, journalists, civics teachers, civic activists, and many others. Much of this training is founded on the idea that individuals in key institutions can and should be taught to shape their actions and their institutions in line with the appropriate models.

Sources of the Models

Having identified the models of democracy and democratization that underlie the core strategy of U.S. democracy assistance, it is worth asking from where U.S. aid providers initially got them. The source for the democracy template is not mysterious. It is based on the conventional Western liberal democratic model, and, as discussed below, a specifically American formulation of it, and a rather idealized one at that. Although political scientists have spilled considerable amounts of ink defining democracy, the most widely accepted definition emphasizes two features: periodic, genuine elections in which citizens choose their leaders, and political and civil liberties that permit citizens to participate freely and openly in political life.[1] The democracy template that U.S. aid providers employ is more specific about institutions than the standard political science model, specifying types and forms for the institutions of both government and civil society. Nonetheless, the essential similarity of the template applied abroad and the model at home is clear.

In contrast, the model of democratization at work in democracy assistance—the natural transition sequence combined with institutional modeling—is less obviously drawn from the American experience. Aid providers give little sign of basing their approaches on study of how democratization occurred in the United States. Certain articles of faith associated with the establishment of American democracy inform their method, such as the importance of a good constitution and the value of bold, selfless democratizers at the start. The assumptions and strategies of democracy aid, however, have little to do with the history of how American democracy was deepened and broadened over the nineteenth and twentieth centuries. Bumps on the road like the Civil War and the Great Depression fit poorly with the idea of a naturally unfolding sequence. Similarly, the often tortuous paths of democratization in many West European countries, involving embattled aristocrats and landlords, a rising bourgeoisie, and a mobilized working class, seem to U.S. democracy promoters remote in time and of uncertain relevance. With their armed struggles, ideological passions, economic conflicts, and strong class divisions, such histories differ greatly from the technocratic, gradualistic conception of democratization that underlies U.S. democracy programs.

The primary source for the notion of a natural sequence of democratization is not the experience of established democracies but the impressive example of the transitional countries themselves in the 1980s and early 1990s. In those years, one transition after another occurred around the world, seemingly on the same basic pattern—a dramatic collapse of dictatorship, followed quickly by national elections, then by a peaceful period of gradual democratic consolidation. As apparent democratic transitions broke out in places where only a few years before the possibility of democratization had appeared remote, it suddenly seemed that democratization did not depend on any social, cultural, or economic preconditions, but only on the political will of elites or the political demands of citizens. Furthermore, there seemed to be little disagreement about the forms democracy should take. Societies everywhere were embarking on what appeared to be similar projects to achieve Western-style democratic institutions.

These characteristics of what democracy enthusiasts were calling the "worldwide democratic revolution" led Western officials and aid providers to think in terms of a natural sequence of democratization and of institutional modeling. Then, in the mid-1990s, the shine went off the global democratic trend as various transitions—in Cambodia, Albania, Armenia, Kazakhstan, Algeria, Belarus, Peru, the Gambia, Niger, Sierra Leone, Kenya, Gabon, Cameroon, and Côte d'Ivoire, among others—proved hollow, hit rough patches, or went bad. For democracy activists in those countries, and many others looking on, the concepts of a natural sequence and of institutional modeling that had seemed so obvious and right began to lose force. This has led aid practitioners to explore some alternative strategies for use in cases that are not a simple progression from political opening to democratic consolidation.

Similarly, the concept of institutional modeling derives not from American history or any abstract theory but from the experience of aid providers on the ground. When people from established democracies go to other societies that are struggling with democratization and try to figure out how to promote democracy, they tend to take a commonsense approach. They compare the major sociopolitical institutions of the transitional country with those of their own society, identifying the main discrepancies. They then propose projects to bring the various institutions into line with the model. They focus, in other words, on endpoints rather than process. When aid providers go to a transitional country and discover that the legislature passes laws with poor technical grounding, for example, their typical response is to prescribe programs that will build up the legislature's research staff and train legislators to make use of research studies. They will usually give less attention to the much more complex question of how aid might encourage broad change that would result in a legislature made up of better-qualified people more interested in and capable of writing good laws. It should not be a surprise that endpoints dominate over process in the core strategy of democracy assistance. People from established democracies who go abroad to promote democracy are usually somewhat knowledgeable about democracy from having grown up in one, but rarely start out having extended experience with democratization, not having grown up a society that is making a democratic transition.

As an endnote to this initial discussion of the core strategy it is worth commenting on the role of academic theory. The idea of a sequence of democratization from political opening to electoral transition to democratic consolidation certainly resembles some currents of scholarly work on democratization that began to burgeon in the mid-1980s, particularly the work by Guillermo O'Donnell, Philippe Schmitter, and others on the transitions in Southern Europe and Latin America.[2] Aid providers and those scholars sought to interpret and understand the same set of transitions, and thus tended to reach similar conclusions about the basic sequence of democratization. But the actual direct influence of the scholarly work on democratization on the core strategy—or on democracy aid generally over the past fifteen years—has been low. Very few of the project papers, assessments, and reports from democracy programs sponsored by USAID, the State Department, USIA, the Justice Department, or others contain any reference to academic writing on democratization. There has been little borrowing of concepts from the literature, nor has there been that much direct interchange of ideas beyond the occasional lecture by a visiting academic or the input of a small number of political scientists who have served as democracy officers with USAID. To give just one example, a critical element in the "transitology" literature on Latin America is the concept of national "pacts" and "pacted transitions."[3] Yet one looks in vain in the many official documents from the second half of the 1980s dealing with democracy assistance in Latin America for any reference to the concept of pacts. Neither would one have found the concept of pact formation at work in the actual programs.

One major reason for the separation between the worlds of democratic theory and democracy aid is that of differing objectives.[4]

Although academic theorists and aid practitioners may at times work on the same issues, they are engaged in dissimilar enterprises. Academic studies of democratization are generally backward-looking and explanatory. Aid practitioners are concerned with looking ahead. Academic studies attempt to explain the internal causes and dynamics of transition processes. Practitioners are preoccupied with a question that academic analysts rarely explore—how external assistance can be applied to affect a political transition in the real world. Moreover, even when academic studies contain useful ideas for the practitioner, they present competing theories among which the practitioner has little basis for choosing. An aid official perusing the "transitology" literature in the early 1990s to identify the key causes of democratic transitions, for example, might first learn from O'Donnell and Schmitter that such transitions are best understood as complex negotiating processes by state and opposition elites as well as newly mobilizing actors from civil society.[5] Turning to the work of Adam Przeworski from that period, however, the aid official would be instructed to think instead in terms of a strategic choice model focusing on sociopolitical actors responding to perceived social opportunities.[6] But then if he or she consulted *The Third Wave* by Samuel Huntington, the emphasis is on the role of ideology, political culture, religion, underlying socioeconomic structures, and an eclectic collection of other factors. The more the aid official delved into the literature, the more he or she would be convinced that almost every major element of society is important in some way to a democratic transition and that academics have achieved no greater certainty on the subject than practitioners have.

More mundane factors also contribute to the gap between theory and practice on democratization. Practitioners have an understandably low tolerance for the political science jargon that often clogs academic analyses. Ideological rifts between the academy and the government have also played a role. In the 1980s, for example, most academic Latin Americanists were much to the left of the U.S. government and mutual antipathy between academics and officials was frequently high. And finally, most U.S. officials simply do not have the time to keep up with the ever growing academic literature, as their hours are filled with pressing bureaucratic tasks.

Against Authoritarians

Most U.S. democracy aid of the 1980s and 1990s has been directed at countries already in transition to democracy, or at least openly attempting to move away from dictatorial rule. In a smaller number of cases, democracy aid has been aimed at nondemocratic countries, or what U.S. democracy promoters like to call "pretransition countries," such as China, Burma, Cuba, Sudan, Nigeria (before the opening in 1998), Indonesia (before the fall of Suharto the same year), Vietnam, Yugoslavia, Croatia, and several others. The usual array of democracy programs cannot be established because of the political repression and because the country has not started on the standard sequence of democratization. The approach is instead to spread the idea of democracy, to support the development of civil society, and to help open some political space or widen what space does exist.

The National Endowment for Democracy is the most active American organization in promoting democracy in nondemocratic countries. Taking advantage of its status as a private rather than public organization (though financed by the U.S. government), the NED operates in politically sensitive situations, dispersing financial support to human rights groups, independent newspapers and journals, groups of exiled dissidents, fledgling civic activists, and independent civic education efforts. The United States also beams radio broadcasts into nondemocratic countries, via, for example, Radio Free Asia and Radio Martí for Cuba. Such broadcasting is both democracy dissemination and pro-U.S. political propaganda, with supporters seeing it primarily as the former and critics as the latter. USAID has carried out some small-scale democracy programs in a few authoritarian contexts where a certain amount of freedom is allowed. For most of the 1990s in Indonesia, for example, USAID supported NGOs working on human rights and other types of civic activism to strengthen the weak but growing independent civil society. For the most part, USAID has not attempted to promote democracy in harsh dictatorial contexts. In recent years, however, Congress earmarked funds for democracy programs in Cuba, Burma, and Sudan.

The U.S. approach to promoting democracy where autocrats rule is an addendum not an alternative to the core strategy. Its intention is to foster enough political space, acceptance of the democratic idea, and new civic and political actors to edge a nondemocratic country toward a political opening and elections. In other words, the goal is to help move nondemocratic countries to the starting point of what democracy promoters hope will be a subsequent sequence of democratization.

ASSESSING THE CORE STRATEGY

The core strategy has important strengths. Foremost, perhaps, it has a clear, commonsense appeal to Americans. It derives from how Americans think about their own democracy, and therefore seems familiar and feasible both to democracy promoters and to people not deeply involved in democracy promotion. Since democracy providers have to build support for democracy assistance in the U.S. government, the policy community, the media, and with the public, they need a strategy that can be easily explained to a wide variety of audiences. An additional attraction of the strategy, at least in terms of bureaucratic politics, is its inclusive nature. Application of the democracy template usually results in the conclusion that there is need to do some of everything on a long menu of program options. This allows assistance providers to avoid hard choices between different types of assistance, as well as between the well-connected American democracy promotion groups aggressively seeking program funds.

The core strategy also has the useful qualities of certainty and universality. It lends itself to straightforward arguments about how to proceed in dauntingly complex situations. An independent, honest judiciary is critical for democracy, for example, but Country X's judiciary is severely flawed; therefore we will promote democracy by helping to reform X's judiciary. Or, an accountable, competent legislature is essential to democracy, Country Y's parliament is weak, therefore we will promote democracy in Y by strengthening the parliament. Using the strategy, assistance providers can arrive in a country anywhere in the world and, no matter how thin their knowledge of the society or how opaque or unique the local circumstances, quickly settle on a set of recommended program areas. This facile certainty is often misplaced and in many cases proves to be a problem; nonetheless, it has been useful. Given the tremendous variety of countries in which aid providers have sought to provide democracy assistance in recent years, and the time pressure under which the design of that assistance is often carried out, the providers have needed some broadly applicable, easily comprehensible approach. The core strategy has met that need.

Made Only in America

Each of the key components of the core strategy—the democracy template, institutional modeling, and the natural sequence—has serious shortcomings. Consider first the template. U.S. democracy promoters use the template as if it were a general model applicable to any society attempting democratization. In fact, however, almost every item on the template reflects ideas about democracy that are specific to America and whose applicability to other countries is uncertain.

U.S. efforts to strengthen foreign legislatures, for example, invariably attempt to make those bodies more independent of the executive branch, more concerned about exercising oversight of the executive, more engaged in public hearings, more open to outside lobbying, and more well equipped, with a large, powerful staff and a good library. In other words, they seek to help them acquire many of the distinctive features of the U.S. Congress—features that are not shared by legislatures in many other established democracies. Similarly, programs to support NGOs typically stress methods important to certain segments of the NGO world in the United States—maintaining independence from government funding, making legislative lobbying a principal operating method, and avoiding openly partisan approaches. U.S. media programs often teach separating news from editorial comment, private rather than public ownership of electronic media, and vigorous investigative reporting—cardinal features, or at least ideals, of the American media but not necessarily of the media in other democracies. Political party assistance seeks to foster a political landscape defined by broad-based parties organized along muted ideological lines rather than on an ethnic or religious basis, with an emphasis on American-style campaigning and its preoccupation with media relations, polling, and message development.

The model of democracy that U.S. democracy promoters employ is not only America-specific, but also idealized. These confident messengers of democracy punctuate their training courses or consultations abroad with occasional wry remarks to the effect that the American system does have its own problems. On the whole, however, they project a sunny image of the system, akin to an old-fashioned high-school civics version of American democracy in which whatever problems there are will be made right in time with a little American ingenuity and goodwill. As discussed in the "Interlude for Skeptics," serious shortcomings of U.S. democracy, such as chronically low voter turnout, profound corruption in campaign finance, and low public regard for some major political institutions, are not factored into the aid programs.

Many Americans involved in democracy assistance are strikingly unaware of the variety of political structures in other established democracies. Common elements of democratic life in Europe, for example, are absent from or even conflict with the tenets of U.S. programs: overlapping personnel and responsibilities of parliaments and executive branches; civil law rather than common law systems; centralized tripartite (business-labor-government) negotiations on wages and labor relations instead of union-by-union bargaining with management; government rather than private funds for NGOs; public rather than private ownership of television and radio; religion-based political parties (as in the Netherlands); and so on. Unconsciously or consciously, many Americans confuse the forms of American democracy with the concept of democracy itself. Theirs is an unfortunate combination of hubristic belief that America's political ways are the most democratic in the world and lack of knowledge about political life in other democratic countries.

Pursuing assistance programs based on American attributes of democracy frequently leads to problems. Many of these attributes have grown out of particular aspects of America's social makeup and history—whether the immigrant character of society, the "frontier" mindset, the legacy of suspicion of central government authority, or the high degree of individualism—that are alien to other societies. Pushing programs that rely on political models based on these features results in poor fits with the local context or simple irrelevance. Specific examples are far too frequent to enumerate, from programs that seek to foster independent legislatures where the constitution makes the legislature subordinate to the executive to judicial training courses that teach American-style legal activism in civil law countries where judges do not have scope for such an approach.

Although they may do so with more exuberance and less self-doubt than others, Americans are hardly the only aid providers to base their democracy programs on their own national model. Germans working for the *Stiftungen*, the German political party foundations, instinctively strive to reproduce in other countries the contours of the party system in Germany, as well as the German social-market political economy. Dutch officials say in private that a Dutch-style political system, with a large number of political parties and an emphasis on tolerance and cooperation, is of particular value for transitional countries. British party representatives working in other countries quietly but confidently refer to the Westminster model as *the* model for new democracies. Aid officials from all over the West insist that their programs are based on careful listening to and learning from the recipient societies and are designed to conform to the local environment. Yet when one looks at their programs' content, Western aid providers promote what they know best and admire most, which is almost always their own country's approach to democracy.

Some criticize U.S. democracy assistance not just for using a model that is too America-specific but for using Western liberal democratic models of any kind. In this view, democracy promoters should embrace non-Western forms of democracy. One hears this most often regarding Africa, Asia, and the Middle East.[7] It is rare anymore in Latin America or Eastern Europe, where the overwhelming desire is to catch up with the established Western democracies economically, politically, and otherwise and most political elites are insulted by the suggestion that their goal should be something different from what the successful democracies of Europe and North America have achieved.

The argument that Western political models are not appropriate for non-Western countries is an easy criticism to make, one that gains applause at academic conferences in the West and is invoked by commentators in non-Western countries unhappy with the role of Western powers in their countries. Yet even within Africa, Asia, and the Middle East, the utility and legitimacy of Western-style democracy is as vigorously defended by some as it is decried by others; Westerners who assert that Western models should not be applied to the developing world are not, as they sometimes seem to think, in solidarity with whole continents of non-Westerners, but are taking one side in a debate among non-Westerners.

Moreover, there are few working examples of non-Western democratic models from which assistance practitioners could learn. What democracies there are outside the West, whether in India, Taiwan, the Philippines, Botswana, or South Africa, are based on the principles of Western liberal democracy, in spite of many local particularities. There is of course "Asian-style democracy," but its main adherents, the leaders of Singapore and Malaysia, are not actually democrats—they do not subject their rule to the consent of the governed through free and fair elections. One can theorize, as some political scientists do, that non-Western societies that are more communal and less individualistic than Western ones either have or are developing democratic systems that are not liberal in the Western sense. Yet it is hard to find any such systems that actually allow genuine periodic elections or any other form of systematic expression of consent from those governed.

American and other Western aid providers should be open to non-Western versions of the institutional forms within a democratic system. Justice programs should take account of local forms of justice, such as the tribal councils in many African countries for resolving disputes in villages. Strengthening efforts for local government should be responsive to traditional local authorities. Programs to develop civil society should not assume that such development takes the form only of Western-style NGOs. In addition, as discussed below in the examination of sequences of democratization, democracy promoters must assume that non-Western countries in transition may travel very different paths toward democracy than do Western ones. The key issue for U.S. democracy promoters with regard to models of democracy is to learn to be open to different institutional manifestations and different paths without jettisoning basic democratic principles.

An overarching critique of the model of democracy embodied in U.S. democracy programs comes from the academic Left. In this account, the United States and other Western countries are guilty of promoting "elite democracy," in which a small elite rules over the majority using democratic forms to legitimate its power. The Western states push elite democracy abroad, the argument runs, both because they practice the same flawed system at home and because the cultivation of elite rule in developing countries allows Western countries to exercise political hegemony more easily and to better exploit them economically. Getting beyond elite democracy apparently requires getting beyond capitalism: "Democracy is an historical view which begins under capitalism but can only be consummated with the supersession of capitalism." Such critiques employ vague palliatives that sound rather like the calls for socialism of decades past but avoid the actual term, such as "the democratization of social and economic life."[8] They issue bracing condemnations of all Western democracies, from Sweden to Spain, as "incomplete" and "elite-based" but are unable to name a single example of a "complete" democracy. And they are noticeably weak when it comes to sketching out a specific vision of true democracy. All this gives little aid to the democracy promoter open to adopting a more enlightened path.[9]

The Missing Link of Power

A second fundamental problem with the core strategy has to do with the concept of institutional modeling. Much too often, aid to reshape institutions in transitional countries is a self-contained effort, disconnected from the society in which the institutions are rooted— the structures of power, authority, interests, hierarchies, loyalties, and traditions that make up the dense weave of sociopolitical life. Assistance providers proceed as though they can bring about major changes in the ways institutions operate—transform a rubber-stamp parliament into an effective body, help a cowed, ineffectual local government assume large new responsibilities, or wean the media from government dominance—without confronting or changing those structures.

A different way of stating the problem is that democracy programs frequently treat the symptoms rather than the causes of democratic deficits. U.S. aid providers responding to the lack of formal justice in a country assess the judicial system, for example, and conclude that it falls short because cases move too slowly, judges are poorly trained and lack up-to-date legal materials, the infrastructure is woefully inadequate, and so on. The aid providers then prescribe remedies on this basis: reform of court administration, training and legal materials for judges, equipment for courtrooms, and the like. What they tend not to ask is *why* the judiciary is in a lamentable state, whose interests its weakness serves, and whose interests would be threatened or bolstered by reforms. The assistance may temporarily alleviate some of the symptoms, but the underlying systemic pathologies remain.

The disconnection of aid from the local context has been especially noticeable in programs targeting state institutions. Many U.S. programs treat judicial systems, for example, as though they were somehow separate from the messy political world around them. Such programs have been slow to incorporate any serious consideration of the profound interests at stake in judicial reform, the powerful ties between certain economic or political elites and the judicial hierarchy, and the relevant authorities' will to reform.[10] Similarly, efforts to strengthen legislatures frequently focus on narrow technical issues, such as the staff's ability to research issues, the number of public hearings the legislature holds, the extent to which it uses committees, and whether MPs have offices in their home districts. The aid aims at the technical level—training staff researchers, instructing MPs in how to hold public hearings, supporting the use of committees, and underwriting constituent offices—while taking too little account of the forces molding the institution, such as the interests and intentions of the party that controls the legislature, or the patronage networks in that body.

It is not only with state institutions that the problem of disconnection arises. Media aid programs sometimes seek to correct the media's lack of political independence by training journalists, while deeper, more influential factors, such as ownership patterns, may not even be considered. Efforts to aid NGOs sometimes assume that with the right advocacy training and a few fax machines, a band of small groups will be able to exercise powerful influence, while paying no attention to the actual social base from which the organizations supposedly draw their support.

By giving short shrift to underlying structures of power and interests, U.S. efforts at institutional modeling take on an artificial technical quality. Aid providers treat political change in a pseudoscientific manner as a clinical process to be guided by manuals, technical seminars, and flowcharts specifying the intended outputs and timeframes. They assume that local actors will adopt democratic goals because democracy is inherently desirable. They are then surprised and disappointed when local people and groups refuse to change their ways, to work for the common good, or to give away power out of respect for principles. The truth that politics involves harshly competing interests, bitter power struggles, and fundamentally conflicting values—not to mention greed, stupidity, and hatred—is downplayed until it asserts itself, unwanted, at some later stage. Democracy projects often fail then, their formal frameworks splintered when they smash up against the obdurate foundations of the local scene.

Setbacks on the Sequence

A third major problem with the core strategy relates to the idea of a natural sequence of democratization. At the height of the democratic trend, in the early 1990s, it did seem that countries by the dozens were marching along a single path from political opening to first-time elections to democratic consolidation. By the late 1990s, however, enough of the once-exciting democratic transitions had gone off track or stopped—especially in the former Soviet Union, sub-Saharan Africa, and the Middle East—to raise serious doubts about the sequence. Many of the original political openings turned out not to be what they seemed. They were not moves by dictatorial regimes to accept a democratic process but feints intended to relieve domestic pressure for change and to impress Western audiences. In some cases, promising first-time elections were manipulated by entrenched powerholders who had no intention of ceding power. In others, breakthrough elections came too soon in a highly fluid situation and locked one set of actors into power. Even when elections came off successfully, consolidation often proved not to be a peaceful process of top-down and bottom-up reform. In some countries, consolidation broke down, resulting in a relapse into either civil conflict or authoritarianism. In quite a few others, consolidation stagnated, leaving countries stuck in the unsatisfactory condition of having the forms of democracy while enjoying little of the substance.

Where the sequence of democratization goes awry, the core strategy of democracy assistance unravels. Electoral aid is of little use if a supposedly democratizing regime is holding elections merely to legitimate its power and has taken steps to ensure it cannot lose. When consolidation collapses, the standard menu of democracy programs suddenly seems as out of place as a good seat at a barroom brawl. Stagnation of consolidation calls into question the ability of either top-down or bottom-up aid to make much difference. The peaks and valleys of some transition processes make any effort to plan long-term strategies seem futile. The democratic transitions of the 1990s undermine the notion that democratization naturally proceeds in any regular or orderly sequence.

IMPROVING THE CORE STRATEGY

The core strategy has been an intrinsic part of U.S. democracy assistance for about two decades. Nevertheless, by the mid-1990s, accumulated experience in the field and the mixed fortunes of the global democratic trend increasingly led democracy promoters to try to improve on the strategy. Here and there they have sought to move beyond a static template, to broaden the concept of institutional modeling, and to explore other sequences of democratization. The evolution is still just beginning, but its main lines merit attention.

From Model to Models

Basing their programs on the American model of democracy is probably the deepest instinct of American democracy promoters. When asked about it, Americans involved in democracy promotion will insist they are not pushing an American model on anyone. Yet when one looks closely at the choices they make about people, institutions, training approaches, and other aspects of aid projects, there are often telltale signs of the model. Nevertheless, aid is starting to evolve. A growing number of democracy programs are using non-American trainers, consultants, and experts. In some cases these people are culled from other established democracies, often Great Britain, Canada, Ireland, or Australia. In other cases, they are from new democracies, particularly from some that democracy promoters like to think of as their success stories, such as Chile, the Philippines, South Africa, and Poland. The National Democratic Institute has long been a leader in this regard, regularly sending successful activists from new democracies to other transitional countries to share the lessons of their experience. U.S. judicial reform projects in Latin America have used many Latin American and European experts, mindful of the dissimilarities between the U.S. and the Latin American legal systems. Non-American experts do not automatically avoid the problems involved in transferring political know-how to foreign settings. Nonetheless, they can bring a wealth of comparative democratic experience and help foster in U.S. programs the important sense that democratization is a venture common to many societies, not the special preserve of the United States. Many American groups, however, still primarily use American experts, whether out of habit, ignorance about the benefits of using non-Americans, U.S. aid restrictions, or lack of contacts with good foreign experts.

Forward-looking designers of democracy programs are building comparative perspectives in their programs' basic design. Some legislative strengthening programs, for example, explain to foreign parliamentarians the workings of different legislative models and help them make informed choices for their countries. Similarly, electoral programs are becoming more sophisticated in presenting information about choices in electoral systems, such as between proportional representation and majority systems. The trend is starting to appear in most areas of democracy programming and represents an important area of potential development.

U.S. democracy promoters are sometimes doing more than offering comparative information; they are trying to bring democratic principles and methods to non-Western social and political institutions. In Nepal, for example, the Asia Foundation is training rural women in basic legal rights and rights advocacy by working directly with informal women's groups in villages, groups that do not fit the Western NGO mold. In Yemen, NDI is exploring how tribal chiefs can be incorporated in a legislative development undertaking. Efforts to develop rule-of-law programs in Africa are addressing rather than ignoring traditional justice mechanisms. Creative initiatives of this sort are still few but are beginning to multiply.

Confronting Power and Interests

Aid providers are learning to look for the missing link of power in the societies that they seek to change. They are starting to pay closer attention to the interests of all those touched by their interventions and the kinds of power those actors have to retard, advance, or otherwise affect reform.

Interests and power are almost always complex, even for programs with straightforward purposes. An undertaking to promote greater parliamentary transparency where the legislature normally operates behind closed doors, for example, may anger parliamentary leaders who fear a loss of control and perquisites. The opposition may favor greater transparency as a way to gain access to a process they are usually shut out of. Some officials in the executive branch may worry that they will lose privileged influence over the parliament if light is shed on that body's workings. Businesses that have cozy relationships with key members of parliament may be concerned about losing the ability to get their favors carried out quietly. NGO advocacy groups are likely to support increased transparency for the leverage it may give them. In short, some people will badly want reform to fail and some, equally determined, will want it to succeed, for reasons ranging from political interests to money, control, influence, personal reputation, or pure bullheadedness.

The power behind the interests may derive from a person's official position or role, from personal relationships and contacts, from money and the willingness to use it to achieve political ends, from the ability to mobilize publicity, civic action, or other forms of pressure, from the actual or possible use of force or violence, and on through a long list. In the case of a parliamentary transparency program, the parliamentary leaders may be able to use their control over the institution's agenda to block the reform. Opposition parliamentarians may appeal to public opinion. Officials in the executive branch who are against the reform can call on their executive branch leaders to weigh in with counterparts in parliament. Businesses can lobby on their own behalf or simply bribe key parliamentarians. Advocacy by NGOs may get the media interested and mobilize public pressure.

As democracy aid providers pay more heed to the interests and power relationships in play in different program areas, they should not expect to find cut-and-dried answers. They may look to formal methods of interest analysis or power mapping, as proposed by consultants or borrowed from the scholarly literature. These are not magic keys but merely organized ways of thinking about those issues, methods that must be carefully adapted to a particular sector, not mechanically applied. Factoring in the relevant interests and power relationships requires, above all, close, thoughtful analysis of the local scene by people who both know that scene well and understand the critical tensions that an aid program in its midst will provoke.

Good project managers in the field instinctively incorporate such perspectives into their work. Yet many projects reflect little hard thinking on these points, and rely on simplistic ideas about institutional modeling—teaching judges and politicians that corruption is bad will substantially cut bribe taking, teaching citizens about the importance of voting will overcome their political apathy, and on and on. Some democracy promoters cling to what one critic calls the "Walt Disney view of democratization" in which the endings are always happy and no one ever gets hurt.[11] They have trouble moving toward a grittier worldview, one that does not assume entrenched concentrations of political power will melt away in the

sun of training and workshops, that deeply rooted habits of patronage and corruption will subside in the face of Western technical aid,
that people from mutually hostile socioeconomic or ethnic groups
will work cooperatively because visiting Western experts have
patiently pointed out how much better off they would all be if they
did so.

But just because an aid provider understands the underlying interests and power relationships does not give him or her the means
to shape those factors. Often aid cannot substantially modify an
unfavorable configuration of interests or counteract a powerful contrary actor. Nevertheless, a thorough understanding of these factors
helps an aid provider decide what is feasible and where to concentrate the aid efforts. Aid can sometimes affect interests and power
in minor but worthwhile ways by changing the perceptions and
knowledge of particular actors. Realizing that officials of the central
government are likely to oppose decentralization because they fear
loss of control, aid providers can design a training program that
helps those officials understand their options, rather than simply
training local government officials to be more competent. Similarly,
a scrutiny of interests and power may prompt aid providers to
consider how to bring together actors that have complementary
stakes in a reform process, to encourage new alliances and cooperative efforts.

A focus on interests and power inevitably pushes aid providers
to think more in terms of process than endpoint, about how to
stimulate and help along processes of sociopolitical change rather
than merely to reproduce forms. Institutions are conceived of in
relation to their contexts, not as things than can be worked on and
developed separately. A legislative program should not aim to produce a legislature with a library of a certain size, for example, or
staff of certain types, committees of a certain form, and so on. It
should instead aim to help a legislature become a place in which
certain processes and principles are valued, such as the ability of
different political factions to work constructively together and to
take account of citizens' views. And legislative programs should
often entail working with many related institutions—the executive
branch, the political parties, diverse elements of civil society, and
others—as well as with the legislature itself.

Building the underlying interests and power relationships into
democracy aid programs requires much deeper knowledge about

the recipient society than most aid providers have or want to take the trouble to acquire. Moreover, truly grappling with the local context shows providers that aid efforts are likely to be much slower, difficult, and risky than they had probably figured from a distance. Such knowledge is unpleasant to face and often frowned on by head offices determined to portray democracy aid in the most optimistic light possible.

Confronting interests and power is also hard because it lays bare local political sensitivities and dilemmas of interventionism that aid providers usually wish to avoid. Few hackles are raised by an outside assessment that says that a particular legislature lacks books and staff. Powerful people in the country are likely to be upset, however, by any study that identifies the clan that controls the legislative process and which other groups have a realistic chance of breaking its hold. This problem points to a central paradox of democracy assistance: Much democracy assistance is overly formal and suffers from a disconnection to the local context. Yet when donors attempt explicitly to take account of the real power relations and interests in a particular context, the aid becomes much more overtly political, risking a negative reaction from host countries and causing aid officials themselves to question the appropriateness of their own role.

Multiple Sequences

Finally, aid providers are starting to reach beyond the attractive but simplistic notion that democratization follows a natural sequence. In a dozen or so transitional countries, mostly in Central Europe and South America, such a sequence—from opening through transitional elections to consolidation—is in fact holding together, although shortcomings abound in the consolidation phase. In those countries, U.S. aid providers have been able to follow their standard menu of democracy programs until, in their opinion, the country has progressed enough to be "graduated" from democracy aid.

For many countries the "natural" sequence does not hold. As the global democratic trend slows and shakes out, democracy promoters are identifying a growing list of transitional trajectories and searching for strategies to match. One important category in this list is that of the democratic backsliders. These are countries that launched what appeared to be a democratic transition, held breakthrough elections, but then over time fell back into strongman rule. Zambia, Kazakhstan, Azerbaijan, Armenia, Cambodia, and Peru all fit into this category to some extent. Their backward slide or drift has been not to outright dictatorship but to semiauthoritarianism of one kind or another. Leaders of the regimes in these countries pay enough deference to the forms of democracy and allow enough political space to hold onto some international credibility. Yet they maintain enough control over political life to ensure that their power is not seriously threatened. Many transitional countries ended up at the end of the 1990s in this problematic no-man's-land between democracy and dictatorship.

In such situations, electoral aid is of questionable value, since strongmen hold elections with no intention of allowing a fair contest. Helping reform parliaments, judiciaries, or other state institutions is usually unrewarding for aid providers because the governments are not interested in deep-reaching changes. Frustrated by the results of their usual methods, U.S. aid providers in backsliding societies have begun to try several different approaches. They have focused in some countries on support for civil society, aiding those groups that are still able to preserve room for dissent and debate and possibly push the regime to widen it. Often they give up on working with central institutions and instead concentrate on strengthening local government and grassroots citizens groups to build a local base for democracy. They sometimes forgo the idea of systemic political change but keep working with state institutions, supporting whatever pockets of reform exist within the state—a human rights commission whose director is trying to carve out some real authority to challenge governmental wrongdoing, a parliamentary anticorruption committee that is taking on some vested interests, or a supreme court chief who manages to maintain some independence and wants to foster at least limited judicial reform. Finally, in particularly bleak situations they may give up on democracy aid altogether and instead concentrate on fostering economic growth and social development in the hope such progress may result in democratization down the road.

Another category of transition also involves semiauthoritarian rule, but one emerging in a different fashion. In partial transition countries, a nondemocratic government undertakes a long, gradual process of political liberalization, opening up some room for opposition forces and independent civic groups, but stops short of putting its own power up for grabs in free and fair national elections. Egypt, Jordan, Morocco, and Algeria are Middle Eastern examples. Uganda and Ethiopia fit this description, depending on where their governments lead them in the next several years. Mexico might end up in this category as well if the long-time ruling party undercuts the electoral process in 2000 out of a fear of losing power. The transitions in such countries remain partial for different reasons, such as fear that further democratization will lead to political radicalization, or the unwillingness of rulers to take the final step of risking the loss of power. In such situations, many kinds of democracy aid only spin the wheels of reform. Aid providers have struggled to try to find points of entry that can make a difference. Legislatures in partial transition countries are sometimes the most pluralistic part of the political system, and aid providers have bolstered legislatures that appeared to be playing a leading role in the attempt at multiparty politics. Development of long-term civil society has been another focus of aid in such countries, with aid providers hoping that fostering peaceful, moderate civic participation will make the final stage of democratization less threatening to nervous rulers. Supporting local elections—for municipal governments, town councils, and other institutions of local government—is another approach, intended to accustom the society to multiparty politics from the bottom up.

Stagnant transitions constitute yet another category of transition sequence. These are cases where a country makes real progress in the conventional sequence of democratization, making it through genuine elections to reach the consolidation phase, but then the transition stalls. The consolidation effort does not seem to deepen; it is characterized by persistently feeble state institutions, weak civil society development, and citizens' low or diminishing belief in the value of democracy. Nepal in the 1990s epitomizes such stagnation. In Latin America, Honduras may also be an example, and Ecuador as well. Kyrgyzstan and Georgia are post-Soviet cases. Many transitional countries live close to stagnation as institutional strengthening proves harder than expected, civil society development plateaus after the first big dollop of assistance for NGOs runs out, and the public's hopes, raised by the break with dictatorship, fade. Democracy providers have not settled on any approach to stagnation. In some cases they persist with the standard template programs, hoping they will gradually make inroads. In other cases they try the "go local" approach, working with local governments and community-based NGOs to get around feckless central institutions.

Postconflict societies have emerged as a distinct category of transition, and a distinct challenge for the democracy agenda. When some countries emerged from civil conflicts and appeared to join the wave of democratization in the late 1980s and early 1990s, democracy promoters assumed that since the shooting was over, national elections would propel the countries into the natural sequence of democratization. Difficulties in several cases, however—the breakdown of the postelection settlement in Cambodia, the relapse into war in Angola, and the continuing political friction in Nicaragua—have pushed aid providers to look at the specific tensions and demands of democratization in countries recovering from conflicts. Relatively positive experiences in El Salvador and Mozambique have added to the mix.

The special features of postconflict elections have received considerable attention, including the danger of holding elections too early in a peace process, the need to blend them with broader negotiations setting the political rules, and the importance of avoiding winner-take-all scenarios.[12] Aid providers are also focusing on reconciliation as an essential element of democratization in such situations, one that should be supported by aid efforts that consciously combine democracy and conflict resolution methodologies.[13] In addition, postconflict countries in which the civil conflict was especially devastating, such as Liberia, Sierra Leone, and Rwanda, or in which it came on the heels of a long period of decay, such as the Democratic Republic of Congo, find themselves with a shattered state incapable of keeping order, repairing the economy, or providing for citizens' most basic needs. Rebuilding the state is critical in such situations, yet the relationship of state building to the promotion of democracy is still only starting to be explored. Pushing a fragmentary, barely functioning state toward high levels of citizen participation may not be feasible. Yet helping a state rebuild without giving attention to democratic norms in the process is dangerous. Finding a constructive middle path in such situations will be a challenge for aid providers in the years to come.

Finally, new thinking about promoting democracy in authoritarian states is starting to percolate. As discussed earlier in the chapter, where dictators reign, democracy promoters have supported democratic opposition groups, incipient civil society, and educational efforts to spread the idea of democracy, trying to nudge or push these countries toward a democratic breakthrough. Catharin Dalpino, formerly responsible for democracy policy at the State Department, takes issue with this approach in her recent book, *Opening Windows*.[14] She argues that in nondemocratic countries that are carrying out some degree of liberalization, democracy promoters should conceive of their task as helping to encourage the advance of liberalization, not as promoting democracy per se. Rather than concentrating on democracy groups and democracy education, she contends, aid providers should give attention to liberalization processes such as increased intraparty pluralism in ruling parties, efforts to extend law into elite circles, and other low-profile but important building blocks for greater openness and pluralism.

The question of whether an approach based on what Dalpino calls a liberalization framework is really different from a democracy framework has not yet been settled. And there is danger of handing aid providers and diplomats a new reason to give up on democracy in China, Vietnam, Burma, and other hard cases. Nevertheless, Dalpino has, at a minimum, usefully pointed out that democracy promoters have given too little thought to the pretransition stage of democratization—the gradual liberalization by which some nondemocratic regimes move toward democratization.

The various categories outlined above by no means make up a formal list that aid providers acknowledge. Rather, they are based on my own observations of the different routes that political transitions are taking and of how aid providers are reacting. This list is intended to be suggestive, not definitive. One might want to include additional categories, for example, dominant-party democratizers—countries with political systems that are largely dominated by one party but still seem to be democratizing, such as South Africa and Namibia (and for many years, Taiwan). Or one might sort the many countries that have ended up in the gray area between democracy and dictatorship into categories such as personalistic regimes, neopatrimonial systems, bureaucratic semiauthoritarian systems, liberalizing authoritarians, and others. The typology nonetheless reflects the complex state of democracy in the real, rather than the ideal, world at the close of the 1990s. As such, it represents a necessary evolution beyond the "natural" sequence that underlay the earlier dream of a "worldwide democratic revolution."

A NOTE ON PRECONDITIONS AND A LOOK AT THE CASES

If they are not to act haphazardly, aid providers intent on trying to promote democracy in other countries need a guiding strategy. Throughout the 1980s and 1990s American aid providers relied on a core strategy in democratizing countries that rests on a democracy template, an assumed natural sequence of stages of democratization, and the belief that aid can foster institutional modeling that will advance transitional countries along the sequence toward the template. All three concepts upholding the core strategy have serious shortcomings. They are all simplistic, more based on hope rather than reality, and too well-suited to mechanical application. With experience, aid providers are improving the core strategy on all these fronts. The template is being made less America-specific and aid programs are drawing from comparative ideas about what democracy may look like in different contexts. Aid providers are more openly addressing the structures of interests and power that shape political institutions and processes rather than trying to mold institutions in isolation from their context. The idea of a natural sequence of democratization is giving way to an appreciation of varied political paths, each requiring different approaches for democracy aid.

The unifying element of these strands of changing strategy is a shift from a focus on forms to a focus on process. This includes process at the level of specific institutions. A legislature or a judiciary or a local government or a media sector does not become democratic by taking on the forms of legislatures or other counterparts in established democracies. Deeper kinds of change must occur in the institution's overall relationship to the society, the political forces that dominate it, and other basic factors. Similarly, at the national level, merely reproducing a certain set of institutions does not mean a democratic system exists. Many relational elements—the establishment of formal and informal democratic rules of the game, the actual involvement of citizens in the process, and other significant but often elusive features—are necessary. The growing concern with process at all levels is a major challenge for democracy aid. It requires democracy promoters to move from the surface to the deeper waters of the societies in which they work. And there are far fewer clear-cut ideas about process than there are about institutional templates of democratization.

More attention to process is related to bringing back the idea of preconditions of democracy, although no one likes to use this phrase. In its initial form the core strategy embodied the tantalizing notion that any country, no matter what its political traditions, economic level, or current political state, could make a rapid transition to democracy if its political elites embraced democratic values and adopted the right institutional forms. The dramatic outbreak of democratic transitions around the world at the start of the 1990s fed this view. The mixed experience of those transitions over the 1990s, however, has brought democracy promoters back to earth. It is clear that countries with no history of democracy, with desperate economic conditions and powerful internal divisions, are having a much harder time making democracy work than countries with some pluralistic traditions, a growing economy, and a cohesive social and cultural makeup.

Those in the democracy community are understandably reluctant to talk about such issues, because it can sound as though one is saying that certain countries simply cannot become democratic or that certain cultures are inherently antidemocratic. The term "preconditions" is misleading in this regard. A better, albeit inelegant, term might be "nonpolitical factors of democratization." One cannot say with certainty, for example, that a certain average educational level is a prerequisite for democracy, but one can say that, in general, a more highly educated populace makes democratization more likely. Analyzing the prospects for democracy in a country without reference to economic conditions, educational levels, historical traditions, social and cultural divisions, and other basic aspects of the society is clearly inadequate. Democracy promoters are just beginning to relate democracy aid to the full range of factors bearing on democracy beyond the political institutions and immediate problems of political life. The potential deepening of democracy through attention to those many factors is an element of a greater focus on process.

To give a sense of how some of the issues of strategy have played out in specific countries, I return briefly here to the four case study countries. For each country I outline the application and evolution of the core strategy.

Guatemala: A Study in Patience[15]

When U.S. democracy promoters went into Central America in the mid-1980s, they talked about the need for a long-term stay—as much as ten years. Fifteen years later, U.S. democracy aid to Guatemala and other countries is still in mid-course, having been adapted continuously to fit the difficult local circumstances. Democracy promoters now measure the distance to the horizon in decades rather than years.

The first U.S. democracy assistance for Guatemala targeted the 1985 national elections that marked the return to civilian rule. It included financial support for the Guatemalan electoral tribunal charged with overseeing the polling and certifying the vote and a training program for poll workers and poll watchers. After President Cerezo took power, USAID launched programs to help reform the judiciary and strengthen the national legislature. When the Guatemalan government created the office of human rights ombudsman in the late 1980s, USAID supported it as well. The newly established U.S. police aid organization, ICITAP, began training Guatemalan police in investigative methods. The Republican Institute funded a research and analysis service for center-right Guatemalan legislators.[16] With NED funds, the AFL-CIO supported voter education activities of an anticommunist Guatemalan trade confederation (Confederación de Unidad Sindical de Guatemala).

The largely top-down focus of this first phase of democracy aid reflected the desire of U.S. policy makers to encourage in Central America carefully controlled political change, and their fear that any mobilization of citizens could overwhelm the fragile new governments with demands and potentially veer off into leftist radicalism. A USAID strategy document on Guatemala from the late 1980s, examining the "constraints to the consolidation of democracy in Guatemala," cited Guatemalans' lack of belief in democracy, the war-ravaged country's economic woes, and the weak state of government institutions.[17] It did not even mention the all-important fact that Guatemalan political and economic life was dominated by entrenched business elites and military forces, both with a long record of antidemocratic behavior. This sort of formalistic analysis, avoiding any examination of underlying power structures and interests, characterized the first phase of U.S. democracy aid in Latin America—and elsewhere as well.

In the early 1990s, the U.S. aid providers shifted gears in Guatemala, scaling back programs aimed at state institutions and creating new efforts to strengthen civic education, to train journalists, and to improve civil-military relations. This change reflected frustration with the top-down programs because of the Guatemalan government's apparent lack of real interest in change, and the de-emphasis of anticommunism after the cold war's end, which made Washington more willing to try bottom-up aid. After the historic peace accords of 1996, U.S. aid providers anticipated greater governmental commitment to reform and new latitude for civil society. They pursued a synthesis of top-down and bottom-up approaches: rejuvenated attempts to nurture judicial and legislative reform, continued work with the national police, a new local government strengthening project, and a more ambitious effort to foster civil society development through aid to NGO advocacy groups.

Nepal: Responding to Stagnation[18]

When Nepal unexpectedly experienced a political opening in 1990, the United States quickly put into place a small but varied set of democracy aid programs to bolster the initial transition. It included technical assistance and voter education for the 1991 elections, support for the drafting of a new constitution, parliamentary aid, judicial strengthening, media training, and support for some NGO advocacy groups. After an elected government took power in 1991, USAID carried out a strategic review to establish longer-term priorities for democracy programming. Out of this came a planned three-year portfolio, begun in 1993, that primarily emphasized a top-down approach through judicial and parliamentary aid. This approach reflected the view of aid officials that the weakness of Nepal's government institutions was the most glaring obstacle to democratization. The portfolio also included smaller efforts aimed at media strengthening, advocacy development for NGOs, labor union strengthening, and support for the next elections.

Only two years into this set of programs the USAID mission changed tactics, dropping the democracy objective and replacing it with a major women's empowerment project. This shift was partly driven by bureaucratic factors. Overall reductions in U.S. foreign aid meant the budget for Nepal was shrinking, forcing cuts in the number of objectives and programs.

The change also stemmed from trouble with democracy programs in the field. U.S. aid officials had become frustrated with the tepid response of Nepal's judiciary and parliament to external aid. They concluded that the political elite was uninterested in deepening democratization and that top-down approaches to democracy aid were futile. So they decided to try a wholly bottom-up approach, focused on women's empowerment and linking economic, social, and political objectives. State Department officials in the U.S. embassy in Nepal disagreed with USAID's decision. Reflecting a common division between the State Department and USAID over democracy aid strategy (see chapter 9), they argued for a continued explicit focus on democracy promotion, targeted at the top levels of government. After some bureaucratic skirmishing, the aid mission prevailed.

The women's empowerment project aims to reach a large number of rural women (the target figure is 100,000) with training in basic literacy, legal literacy, and economic literacy. Thus USAID hopes to provide the women with skills that will enable them to improve their social and economic situation, to gain greater control over their lives, and to become more participatory citizens. As an example of an effort both to work around the stagnation of democratization at the center and to integrate the democracy goal with social and economic objectives, the women's empowerment project represents an evolution of the core strategy of democracy aid. NDI complemented that project with a training campaign of its own aimed at women— designed to prepare women candidates for the 1997 local elections.

Zambia: In Search of a Strategy[19]

As with many attempted democratic transitions of the 1980s and 1990s, U.S. democracy aid to Zambia began with the first multiparty elections. The National Democratic Institute trained domestic observers for the 1991 elections and, together with the Carter Center, sent an international observer team. In the optimistic climate following the election of President Frederick Chiluba, the United States decided to make Zambia one of its major democracy aid recipients in Africa. After an extensive strategy assessment, USAID put together a five-year, $15 million program. The assessment identified two principal concerns: whether the new government would be able to respond adequately to the heightened expectations of the citizenry and whether the citizenry would be able to articulate its interests effectively. To address the former concern, USAID created a legislative strengthening project, a project to bolster policy making in the cabinet, and support for the constitutional reform. For the latter concern, USAID established a major civic education effort and a media strengthening project. The Zambia assessment was carried out by an unusually knowledgeable set of experts and was couched in sophisticated political terminology. Nonetheless the strategy it recommended—a mix of institution-building programs and some civil society work—was none other than the familiar core strategy.

The central dynamic of the Zambian transition turned out, however, not to be an earnest balancing act between a fragile but democratizing government and an expectant, increasingly engaged citizenry. Instead, it has been the gradual descent into semiauthoritarianism and brought about by a politically intolerant president and a ruling party with the apparent goal of holding power indefinitely. The portfolio of democracy programs designed for a positive environment did not fare well in this negative one. As the political situation deteriorated further in 1997 with the imprisonment of former president Kenneth Kaunda and as the five-year set of programs ended, USAID set out to rethink its approach. An assessment team sent to Zambia from Washington recommended de-emphasizing top-down programs and concentrating on civic advocacy, to help preserve the limited political space and to exert greater pressure for change on the government. The USAID mission in Zambia, however, took a less pessimistic view than others of the state of Zambian politics and rejected turning away from the government. Instead, it assembled a new set of projects that basically followed the same mixed strategy as before: some work with state institutions, the cabinet, legislature, and judiciary, and some minor civil society efforts, including NGO support and training for journalists. The mission argued that this approach would support pockets of reform in the government while contributing to long-term development of civil society as a base for democratization. From the outside it appears that the USAID mission was aware that it could do little about the negative direction in Zambian politics and decided simply to keep trying a range of small democracy projects and see if anything positive might be accomplished.

Romania: From Opposition to Partnership[20]

In the first six months after the fall of Ceauşescu in Romania, the United States moved with alacrity to support the first elections and also the newly emergent groups and associations that represented the seeds of a new independent sector in the country. From 1990 to 1992, the United States (through both NED and USAID) supported the main opposition political parties, the largest new trade union confederation, the main opposition newspaper, the first private television station, the most prominent students organization, the leading group of independent intellectuals, the most active civic education group, and the most visible human rights organization. Publicly, U.S. aid providers described the U.S. democracy aid strategy as a civil society approach—helping build an independent sector in a country in which fifty years of communism had decimated civil society. In fact it had a sharper political edge. The thrust of much of the aid was to help create a viable political opposition and to oust the former communists from power.

When U.S. policy toward Romania moderated somewhat after the 1992 presidential and legislative elections there, the democracy programs evolved correspondingly. Aid to civic groups began to emphasize nonpartisanship rather than pro-oppositional stances. Aid to the opposition parties was reduced. USAID developed projects directed at the reform of state institutions, including the judiciary, parliament, and local government. Some American groups, particularly the Republican Institute and the AFL-CIO, maintained an openly oppositional line, but they no longer set the tone. By the mid-1990s the portfolio of U.S. democracy programs tracked the core strategy closely, with programs corresponding to almost all items on the conventional democracy template.

The surprise victory of the pro-Western, reform-oriented opposition in the 1996 presidential and legislative elections prompted U.S. aid providers to reinvigorate their democracy aid to Romania. They felt strongly that the new government would be much more committed to political and economic reforms yet also face a lack of capacity when it came to actually governing. Accordingly, they expanded efforts to strengthen state institutions, not only the parliament and the judiciary but also the prime minister's office and various government ministries. They de-emphasized the civil society domain and moved away from the earlier focus on nurturing the independence of NGOs vis-à-vis the government, toward fostering new NGO-government partnerships.

As the euphoria in Romania over the new government quickly dissipated, the bloom also went off the new democracy assistance efforts. The inability of aid initiatives to do much to alleviate the government's obvious weaknesses and failure to push reforms forward became manifest. In the second half of 1998, the USAID mission in Romania, with an active push from the U.S. embassy, began to reformulate the democracy aid strategy once again. Its officials decided to back away from efforts intended to augment the central government's policy-making capacity and to give renewed attention to other sectors, such as political parties, unions, and local government.

Variations on the Core Strategy

U.S. democracy aid in each of the case study countries has followed the core strategy. Democracy promoters initially concentrated on elections, then shifted to a mix of top-down and bottom-up approaches over time, drawing in each case from the standard template of program areas. They operated on the assumption, or hope, that the political transitions would follow a basic sequence from transition through consolidation and that the reform of key institutions would cement democracy into place. In all four cases aid providers made improvements in their basic approaches, moving beyond the simplistic exportation of U.S. models, grappling with the internal complexities of target institutions, and shifting emphases in response to changing circumstances. Nevertheless, the evolution of strategy was slow and halting; the overall portfolios of democracy aid in each country still conveyed a sense of the mechanical application of a predetermined approach to highly divergent settings.

The size of the U.S. democracy assistance programs varied in the four countries. Guatemala had the largest programs, with several million dollars of USAID programs a year from the late 1980s through the late 1990s plus similar amounts for ICITAP police aid, for a total of between $60 million and $80 million worth of programs from all U.S. sources for those years. For Romania, U.S. democracy assistance from USAID, the NED, and other sources ranged from

$2 million to $4 million per year, adding up to between $30 million and $40 million for the 1990s. Democracy programs in Zambia were somewhat smaller, with between $1 million and $3 million a year devoted to the portfolio, primarily from USAID, for a total in the 1990s of between $15 million and $25 million. Nepal received still less, on the order of $1 million to $2 million annually, for a total of between $15 million and $20 million since the 1990–1991 democratic opening there. The amounts of U.S. democracy aid in these countries were fairly typical for transitional countries, falling in the medium-large to medium-small range relative to U.S. efforts elsewhere.

The main substantive differences among the programs in the four countries came in the varied emphasis on top-down versus bottom-up initiatives. In Guatemala and Romania, aid providers tilted first toward one side, then synthesized top-down and bottom-up elements. In Romania, the aid initially emphasized civil society and political opposition and then eventually added top-down programs. In Guatemala, the reverse occurred; U.S. aid first focused on top-down programs, then built in a civil society dimension over time. These contrasting paths reflected the ideological differences between the two contexts. In Guatemala, the United States was at first friendly to a liberalizing rightist elite and wary of leftist popular organizations. In Romania, the United States was suspicious of a liberalizing former communist elite and friendly to anticommunist civic and opposition groups.

In Nepal and Zambia, aid providers responded to the apparently propitious initial transitions with a balanced mix of top-down and bottom-up programs, then struggled with whether and how to change that mix as the countries failed to progress along the hoped-for sequence of democratization. In Nepal, aid providers responded to democratic stagnation by shifting to a primarily bottom-up approach, focused on women and integrating social and economic goals with the democracy objective. In Zambia, aid providers had trouble coping with backsliding. They tried to put the best light possible on the government's dubious political stance, continuing to search for pockets of reform in the state institutions while simultaneously looking for some way to generate genuine sources of civic advocacy.

In all four countries, adjusting aid portfolios to the continually changing circumstances was an uncertain and sometimes seemingly haphazard process. The main impression the core strategy conveys after more than ten years of its use is that it provides some degree of direction in contexts where democratization is advancing relatively smoothly, but that democracy promoters are still largely groping in the dark when transition processes depart from script.

6
Basic Steps: Elections and Political Parties

If there is one area of democracy assistance that has gained broad visibility, it is elections assistance. The ubiquitous international observers at the many high-profile, first-time elections in countries launching democratic transitions over the past two decades have lodged elections assistance in the consciousness of people around the world. Elections assistance (of which election observing is just one component) has been part of international life off and on throughout the twentieth century. Until the 1980s, however, it was an exceptional practice, applied in cases of UN trusteeships or U.S. interventions like those in Central America and the Caribbean in the 1920s and 1930s. In addition to giving aid that directly promotes free and fair elections, the United States and other aid providers have responded to the wave of electoral activity around the world in the 1980s and 1990s with increased aid to political parties.

This chapter examines the basic features of elections assistance and aid to political parties, as well as some of the lessons of recent experience. Given the widespread use of the findings of election observers by the international community, I pay particular attention to election observing. I also consider a critical question often raised about U.S. elections aid, namely, whether the United States is overdoing elections around the world. Turning to aid for political parties, I focus on an equally sensitive issue—whether it is possible, or necessarily desirable, to be strictly nonpartisan in such work.

ELECTORAL AID

As discussed in chapter 2, aid for transitional elections (elections that are part of a movement away from a nondemocratic regime toward democracy) in Latin America and Asia was a central element in the rise of U.S. democracy assistance in the 1980s.[1] Such aid grew rapidly in the early 1990s. As dozens of transitional elections took place in Eastern Europe, the former Soviet Union, Africa, and Asia, American election observers and technical aid experts raced around the globe keeping pace. Several nongovernmental organizations, usually operating with USAID or NED funds, came to dominate American international election-observing, notably the International Republican Institute, the National Democratic Institute, and the Carter Center, though many others participated. The International Foundation for Election Systems, an American NGO financed mainly by USAID, has carried out many of the U.S.-funded technical aid efforts for election commissions and election administrators abroad.

U.S. electoral aid has been considerable, but it is only one source of a swelling sea. Many international organizations support elections in transitional countries. The United Nations has become one of the leading actors, upgrading its election promotion significantly, especially in postconflict situations such as Cambodia, El Salvador, and Angola. The Organization of American States (OAS) and the Organization for Security and Cooperation in Europe (OSCE) are also extensively involved in mounting observer missions and assisting election administrators in their regions of focus. Other international institutions, from the Council of Europe to the Commonwealth Parliamentary Association, as well as other Western governments and some private Western organizations, play a role. Almost every election in a transitional country in the 1990s saw some form of international involvement. For high-profile elections, observers arrive in droves. To cite just one example, more than eighty international groups observed the 1996 presidential elections in Nicaragua.[2]

The rapid growth of U.S. and other electoral aid reflects both the prevalent Western belief that free and fair elections are fundamental to democracy, and the fact that many transitional countries embraced elections to mark the break with dictatorship and to choose new governments, presenting a plethora of opportunities for international electoral assistance. Certain features of elections make them an attractive focal point for international actors seeking to support a democratic transition in a particular country. Elections are highly visible, tangible events with a clear endpoint, in contrast to more amorphous elements of democratization that have no time limit, such as the fostering of democratic values or building of responsive government institutions. Electoral aid fits naturally for donors into short-term efforts with a built-in exit strategy. In addition, more than most elements of the democracy template that democracy promoters utilize, elections pose a relatively consistent set of technical challenges across very different contexts. Thus aid providers can draw on the same toolbox in many different places.

Five Ways to Help

Electoral aid has grown into a multifaceted domain, with five major categories.[3] The first is helping a transitional country with the *design of the electoral system*.[4] One of the most important choices is voting methods. Legislative elections may use a majority system, proportional representation, or some kind of mixed (or semiproportional) system. For presidential elections, a major choice is that between a single round and two rounds. Many other issues may also need to be settled, such as the size and shape of legislative districts, the vote threshold for parties' entry into parliament, the registration requirements for political parties, whether to allow independent candidates, and the length of campaigns. In some democratic transitions of recent years, such as those in many Latin American countries, the fundamentals of the electoral system have not been up for grabs, since a system was already in place from previous periods in which elections were held. In such cases, external aid providers do not get much involved with system design. In other transitions, particularly in Eastern Europe and the former Soviet Union, old electoral systems were discarded and new systems designed as part of the transition process. In some of those cases, the United States and other countries offered information and advice about the range of available choices and the experience of different established democracies. American and other aid providers do sometimes attempt to push a particular system—single-member districts rather than proportional representation, for instance. They usually do so simply on the basis of what they know best—the system in their own country—not because of any conscious policy of favoring one system over others.

The second category of electoral aid is intended to ensure *good administration of elections*. Election administration includes elements of electoral system design, those bearing on the mechanics of an election. There are highly specific technical issues to be decided, such as the necessary number of polling stations, the method for distributing and collecting ballots from polling stations, and the procedures for checking in voters on election day. There are also more qualitative, and politically sensitive, issues, such as regulations on candidates' access to the media and campaign spending for political parties. And once these many difficult decisions are made, there is the election itself to run—a mammoth undertaking in almost any country, often nearly overwhelming in countries with little electoral experience, empty government coffers, inadequate roads, and other major infrastructural shortcomings. Election administration is almost always a concern in transitional elections, and has become a major area of electoral aid. The United States has sponsored countless programs of training and technical advice for election administrators in transitional countries, often donating equipment, such as ballot boxes, ballot papers, or computers, as well.

The third category is *voter education*. In many transitional countries, citizens have little or no experience voting in democratic elections and scant knowledge of either the political significance of elections or the basic procedures. Moreover, in some countries embarking on democratization, particularly those in the former communist world, citizens previously participated in regular elections, but the elections were sham. Thus people must unlearn most of what they already know about elections. The United States and numerous other donors have sponsored many voter education programs around the world to support elections in transitional countries. These programs usually provide advice on materials and methods, as well as financial support, to organizations in the country organizing voter education, whether the elections commission itself or citizens groups. Although voter education is a form of election assistance, it also falls under civic education assistance, a category of aid discussed in chapter 8.

Election observing, the fourth category of electoral aid, has become a huge industry. It includes international and domestic observation efforts, both of which encourage everyone in a country to conform to the practices of a free and fair election and also to gather the information necessary for an accurate report on the elections. Most international observation efforts are carried out either by teams sent by one or more governments, by nongovernmental organizations such as NDI, IRI, or the Carter Center, or by intergovernmental organizations like the United Nations, the OAS, or the OSCE. The United States has sent official delegations to dozens of transitional elections, but the majority of American observers have been nongovernmental (though usually funded by USAID or the NED). Intergovernmental observer efforts, sometimes with twenty or thirty different governments taking part, are also numerous and are sometimes part of comprehensive peace missions, as in Cambodia and El Salvador.

Many of the NGO and the intergovernmental observer efforts have evolved far beyond the weekend missions and instant reports that characterized some early undertakings.[5] They often start months before voting day with analysis of the country's electoral law and periodic assessments of the campaign period and of the administrative preparations for the elections. They conduct an extensive examination of the voting process, from the distribution of the ballot boxes and ballots, through the actual voting and the vote count (though their coverage of vote counting remains a weak spot). They sometimes continue past election day, taking in the vote tabulation and announcement as well as the post hoc resolution of electoral disputes. The early stages of the missions are typically staffed by election specialists. The larger observation teams that arrive for voting day are a mix of people, including not only a core of election experts, but for NGO-sponsored missions, often also several prominent Western politicians, some Washington insiders friendly to the NGO, and a board member or two of the NGO, a few country or regional specialists, and various others.

Domestic election observing is carried out by people from the country holding the election, who may be representatives of political parties or of NGOs dedicated to elections monitoring or human rights. Domestic observers sometimes number in the thousands and, when especially well organized, may cover every polling station in the country and carry out a parallel vote count using sophisticated sampling techniques. NDI has played a leading role in supporting the creation of domestic election monitoring groups and, more broadly, in spreading the idea of domestic nonparty monitoring and in developing a method for such activities.[6] Donor support for domestic monitors has been much more limited than for international observer missions, both because donors still often doubt the ability of domestic observers to be nonpartisan and because they prefer to spend their money on sending their own teams on what are usually popular, interesting trips to foreign locales.

In some transitional elections, international election observers may engage in the fifth category of electoral aid, what may be called *election mediation*—working directly with the major political actors to help hold a fragile electoral process together and to ensure that the losing party obeys the result. Election mediation may be considered an additional function of election observing or a separate function that is more hands-on and more concerned with political negotiation. Former president Jimmy Carter has been a prominent mediator in at least a dozen elections in the past ten years, including the 1990 Nicaraguan elections that ended Sandinista rule and the 1989 Panamanian elections that were stolen by General Manuel Noriega.[7]

Learning the Limits

The early U.S. elections aid work in Central America in the mid-1980s was a problematic start for a type of assistance almost inevitably fraught with political sensitivities. The first U.S. elections programs in El Salvador, Honduras, and Guatemala were amateurish, heavy-handed, and politically stacked. The observation missions were brief visits by hastily assembled teams of Washington politicos. They issued ringing endorsements of what were in reality deeply troubled electoral processes—endorsements that seemed either precooked sales efforts or naïve assertions of faith inspired by the sight of thousands of Central Americans waiting long hours in the hot sun to vote. The technical aid for election administration often lapsed into equipment dumps or a "we'll just do it for you" approach. U.S. officials attempting to help the Honduran electoral commission in 1985, for example, responded to the commission's difficulty producing voter lists by printing out the lists in the American embassy.[8] Moreover, these elections were part of a U.S. policy that pursued the contradictory goals of promoting credible electoral processes while also influencing the outcome of the elections through political influence or covert aid, to ensure results useful to the United States.

These defects soured many Americans (and many Latin Americans) on the idea that the United States should engage in electoral aid abroad. Opponents of the Reagan administration's Central America policy, particularly those from the American human rights community, quickly concluded that U.S. elections aid was merely about public relations and political manipulation.[9] But as elections aid moved beyond Central America—to the Philippines in 1986, Chile in 1988, and around the world in the late 1980s and early 1990s— the aid improved and gained credibility.

Technical aid to improve the administration of elections in transitional settings has become more adept. Aid providers have developed an elaborate arsenal of tools to address the many challenges of organizing elections in countries with little experience of them. Voter education programs have grown in subtlety and size. The main organizations in the United States that carry out election observing eschew simplistic in-and-out missions for more comprehensive efforts. A well-elaborated method for fostering domestic monitoring groups has been built from the experience in many countries. Aid providers have drawn a clear line that they usually respect between efforts to promote a free and fair election and efforts to influence the outcome.

U.S. and other international electoral aid has improved many elections since the mid-1980s. Facing tremendous adversity in some cases, with obstacles such as land mines, ongoing civil conflict, and economic ruin, as in Haiti in 1990, Mozambique in 1994, and Liberia in 1997, international electoral aid brought off elections against heavy odds. In many less dramatic and visible cases, aid has strengthened transitional elections. The improvements are usually difficult to measure or to attribute wholly to external influences but are nonetheless real: improved election administration, increased public understanding of the electoral process, powerholders made aware that observers will be checking every step, and more information collected and disseminated internationally on the shortcomings of campaigns and elections. In Latin America and Eastern Europe in particular, the quality of the average election has dramatically improved in the past ten years, to the point where reasonably free and fair elections are common. More generally, international electoral aid has helped establish and spread the ideas that there are basic standards for electoral practices and that it is increasingly difficult for a government to violate those standards without a great many people hearing about it.

It is important, however, not to paint too bright a picture. Many highly flawed elections are still held in transitional countries, including countries that receive electoral aid. In the former Soviet Union and sub-Saharan Africa, electoral aid has not prevented many instances of substantial unfairness, haphazard administration, or outright fraud. Aid providers are confronting the real limits of their interventions. To start, if a government or an electoral commission does not take the task of election administration seriously, well-designed training courses, savvy external advisers, and generous donations of sophisticated equipment will not solve the problem.

Romania's elections during the 1990s are cases in point. With USAID funds, the International Foundation for Election Systems provided successive doses of intensive, generally well-conceived technical aid on election administration. Despite frequent urgings from the United States, however, the Romanian government failed to establish a permanent electoral commission, relying instead on temporary commissions set up for the three sets of national elections. These temporary commissions accumulated little technical skill or capacity. Each election ended up an administrative scramble with the same serious problems affecting the process. There have been many other such cases. El Salvador and Haiti are two glaring examples where repeated technical aid dissipated because the election commissions and the various governments lacked commitment to good election administration.

Moreover, if a leader is determined to undermine or compromise an election to stay in power, aid can do little to stop it. Technical undertakings to strengthen election administration can be nullified by a regime's decision to manipulate the process. Observers may be able to document the ways in which an electoral process is deformed by the ruling powers but often such publicity does not stop strongmen from doing so—largely because the United States and other countries have rarely exacted much punishment, economic, diplomatic, or otherwise, for electoral wrongdoing.

The 1996 national elections in Zambia vividly exemplify this problem. The United States and other major donors, concerned about the backsliding in Zambia's transition, established a full range of aid programs to support the election. President Frederick Chiluba, however, was determined to run the elections his way, doing everything necessary to ensure his continued rule. He manipulated the drafting of constitutional amendments to exclude his only major opponent, insisted on using a controversial foreign company to handle the voter registration system despite widespread lack of confidence in that system, treated state television as his personal campaign tool, and persecuted domestic observer groups that dared to criticize. The many international aid programs bearing on the election—the voter education programs, the technical aid and equipment donations for the election commission, the support for the constitutional revision process, and the aid to the domestic observer groups—did not stop Chiluba from doing what he pleased with the elections. Neither did the fairly serious diplomatic pressure from donors. After the voting, the donors imposed some reductions of aid to punish Chiluba. These were soon lifted, however, because the donors did not want to jeopardize the economic reform program they heavily supported or to seriously aggravate the already desperate economic situation of ordinary Zambians.

Not only are many bad elections still held in transitional countries, despite the impressive development of elections assistance, but even when an election does come off well it often results in less significant democratic gains than the providers of electoral aid hoped for. The 1990s have seen many successful first elections fail to fulfill their promise as launching pads for democratic transition and consolidation. Several dozen transitions have moved from exciting breakthrough elections into stagnation, backsliding toward authoritarianism, or even breakdown into civil conflict. Democracy promoters often regard elections aid as a key that will help open the door to broader democratization. Once the door is open, however, the remaining challenges are often overwhelming.

Observing the Observers

Although election observing has made great strides, it still suffers from significant shortcomings.[10] Policy makers, journalists, and others who base their analysis of transitional elections on observers' reports often do so too uncritically. They should take into account several flaws of many observer missions. First, observers generally devote too much energy and attention to the events of election day relative to the campaign and the postballoting period (vote counting, tabulation, resolutions of electoral dispute). The major American observer organizations have evolved toward more comprehensive approaches, but even they still concentrate too much on the actual voting. It is hard for organizations involved in election observing to avoid the allure of high-profile short-term observer missions as opposed to the slow, often unexciting work of covering an electoral process from start to finish.

The continued imbalance of attention is a particular problem because of a trend in elections in some transitional countries. As noted in the discussion of alternative transitional sequences outlined in chapter 4, many transitions have produced semiauthoritarian leaders who pick a clever path between dictatorship and democracy. The way these leaders approach elections is a key element of their strategy. They have learned that as long as voting day is relatively peaceful and orderly, they can commit serious wrongdoing in the preelection period—harassing opposition parties, restricting the opposition's media access, commandeering state funds, vehicles, and other resources for their campaign—and still get acceptable marks from most of the international observers. The tendency of the international press covering such elections to focus heavily on voting day only compounds the problem.

In 1998, for example, strongmen leaders in Armenia, Azerbaijan, and Cambodia manipulated electoral processes yet were let off fairly lightly by at least some of the international observers. The Council of Europe, for example, found only minor problems with the first round of the Armenian national elections of spring 1998, elections that were later heavily criticized by the OSCE.[11] In Cambodia, Prime Minister Hun Sen, having forcibly ousted the previous elected government, strong-armed the June 1998 elections. Security forces loyal to him murdered several dozen people in the wake of the coup, intimidated the opposition throughout the campaign, and employed the state-controlled media as a campaign tool.[12] Yet election day went off with few incidents, and the largest international observer group, a joint mission coordinated by the United Nations, declared the elections free and fair.[13]

The second problem is that of partiality. International election observers present themselves as politically neutral, but sometimes they have political motives that lead them to act as partisans. In some cases the motives come from the same place the funds do. The U.S. government finances observers for some transitional elections because it wants to convince the policy community that a favored government is successfully democratizing.

Observers may at times inject their own biases. In Romania in 1992, for example, IRI served as an adviser to and a supporter of the main Romanian opposition parties in the run-up to the national elections, then cosponsored, with NDI, an observer team—at least one member of which was one of the political consultants working directly with the opposition. Not surprisingly, the Romanian government gave little credence to the observers' claim to impartiality. For the 1995 Haitian elections, the polarized views in Washington on policy toward Haiti (the Clinton administration straining to defend huge investments in Haiti's political reconstruction and a Republican Congress sharply critical of that effort) clearly influenced the observer efforts. The official U.S. observers praised the elections as "a significant breakthrough for democracy," while on the same day the IRI delegation lamented "the nationwide breakdown of the electoral process."[14] Which was closer to the truth is not clear; but the divergence of views demonstrates that the impartiality of observers is not always assured.

A third problem concerns the "free and fair" standard. A common assumption about election observing is that the observers' job is to decide whether the election in question is free and fair. There is indeed a set of good electoral practices that covers all aspects of an electoral process, from voter registration through the vote count. Reaching a definitive conclusion about whether a particular election is free and fair, however, is not always possible. Cases at either end of the spectrum—very good or very bad elections—are easy to judge. But many elections in transitional countries fall into a gray area— they have a number of flaws but are not outright fraudulent—and so are difficult to label either "free and fair" or "not free and fair." If, for example, an election is marked by moderately unequal media access and sporadic but serious incidents of harassment, yet the voting is relatively orderly and the vote count accurate, is the election free and fair? As one analysis of the standard concludes, "The phrase 'free and fair' cannot denote compliance with a fixed, universal standard of electoral competition: No such standard exists, and the complexity of the electoral process makes the notion of any simple formula unrealistic."[15]

With experience, observer groups have learned to avoid the magic words "free and fair" in their reports, except in clear-cut cases. In the many in-between cases, they increasingly limit themselves to describing the positive and negative aspects of the electoral process and leaving it to others to draw what conclusions they wish. Nevertheless, those who use observers' reports, especially the media, hunger for thumbs-up or thumbs-down verdicts on elections and are liable to press observer groups to supply them. Less experienced groups, not having grappled with the complexities of applying a single threshold to highly diverse situations, tend to offer the sound-bite judgments that journalists and others seek, and these judgments dominate the reporting on the elections.

A final problem with election observing is that it is sometimes overdone. When transitional elections are big news, as in South Africa in 1994 and in Bosnia, Russia, and Nicaragua in 1996, too many foreign observers crowd into the country. They needlessly duplicate each other's work, take up too much of the time of election commissioners and politicians, and create a zoo-like atmosphere. Among so many groups, some inevitably are amateurish ones that deliver superficial judgments (which distract attention from the more serious reports) and engage in unprofessional behavior, hurting the reputation of all observers. This surfeit is not a problem of U.S. election observing per se but of the world of international electoral aid. Nevertheless, the U.S. government sometimes contributes to the problem by unnecessarily sponsoring multiple observer groups for the same election. In the 1996 Nicaraguan elections, for example, USAID could not bring itself to say no to the various organizations politically well-connected in Washington that wanted to send observer delegations, and ended up funding five different observer missions.

Postconflict Elections

Postconflict elections—elections held as the capstone to a resolution of a civil war—present special challenges for providers of electoral assistance. Ideally, such elections serve several purposes. They are a means of selecting a new government in the wake of conflict. They provide the contending political forces with a peaceful, orderly domain of competition. And they help begin a long-term process of political reconciliation and rebuilding. In the 1990s, instances of such elections have multiplied, particularly in Central America (El Salvador, Nicaragua, and Guatemala) and Africa (Namibia, Angola, Mozambique, Liberia, Ethiopia, and elsewhere).

The international community is often heavily involved in the administration and monitoring of postconflict elections, its involvement usually growing out of its participation in the peace negotiations. The setting for elections in countries emerging from conflict is often highly challenging due to the physical devastation that has taken place and the lack of trust on all sides—the UN, as well as U.S. and European groups, have accomplished remarkable logistical feats in many of these cases. Moreover, the political results of such processes have sometimes been significant. In El Salvador, for example, the 1994 elections that represented the culmination of the UN-brokered peace process constituted a major step in that country's transition toward democracy. Against formidable odds, the 1994 elections in Mozambique helped complete the peace settlement and start a pluralistic system that although shaky, was still functioning five years later. At the same time, some such elections have gone sour, either quickly, as in the breakdown of the 1992 Angolan elections, or over a longer period, as in the 1997 coup in Cambodia that shattered the political bargain forged after the 1993 elections.

Recent postconflict elections have taught aid providers several major lessons.[16] The first is about timing. The international community tends to pressure leaders of postconflict countries to move quickly toward elections, sometimes because of the belief that a postconflict society needs to get a legitimate government in place quickly or risk disorder. It also reflects the tendency of the international actors engaged in aiding the conflict resolution to view elections as a strategy for an early exit. Yet at least sometimes, early elections can be a recipe for failure. They may come when the two sides have not yet really stopped fighting and thus easily lapse back into conflict. Or they may preempt protracted but necessary negotiation about the political rules of the game and so force what Marina Ottaway has called "premature closure" of a transition.[17] It is noteworthy how late elections came in the Salvadoran peace process and in the South African transition to majority rule—they followed years of arduous negotiations. The United States and other international actors must be wary of reflexively pushing countries emerging from conflict into immediate elections, and should explore the kinds of extended transition processes that can foster gradual confidence-building before plunging opposing forces into a difficult national election.

A second issue is design. When warring parties to a civil conflict are persuaded to stop fighting and compete peacefully in an election, they are frequently concerned that losing will mean being shut out of power. It is essential for aid providers to help foster a conviction that a postconflict election will not be a winner-take-all process. Election aid specialists have been arguing in recent years that the right kind of electoral system, one using proportional representation to ensure power sharing, can solve this problem. It is indeed important to pay close attention to the implications for power distribution of different possible electoral systems. Yet designing an electoral system is at best a first step and does not guarantee success. All elements of the postconflict political reconstruction process, from the design of state institutions to decisions on social and cultural issues such as national education and language policy, must be developed with a view to avoiding a winner-take-all society.[18]

Finally, the issues of resources and sustainability are also often relevant. The international community has repeatedly demonstrated a willingness, even a decided tendency, to spend huge amounts of money on postconflict elections and to develop relatively sophisticated technical systems for elections in poor, physically devastated societies. None of these societies is likely to come up with the resources to sustain such systems in future elections.[19] Yet the international community's interest usually plummets after the first breakthrough elections, making dispensers of aid much less willing to spend a similar amount again. The sustainability of the electoral systems being created is thus open to doubt.

Overdoing Elections?

The most common criticism the American policy community levels at U.S. democracy promoters is that they overdo elections. Democracy activists are portrayed as "election nuts" who equate elections with democracy and blithely assume that any country can benefit from voting anytime. This criticism came to the fore in the latter 1990s as the shine wore off the many breakthrough elections of the early 1990s and doubts about the value of elections in transitional countries grew. The criticism has several parts.

To start, election naysayers accuse democracy promoters of pushing transitional countries into holding elections, almost against the better judgment of decision makers in those countries. U.S. and other Western aid officials and policy makers do indeed often hope or expect that a country coming out of dictatorship will proceed directly to multiparty elections, and they sometimes exert diplomatic pressure to this end. The external pressure is the decisive factor only in a limited number of cases, however, when international actors have been deeply involved in the settlement of a civil war and they push for elections as a means of closure, as in Cambodia, Angola, and Mozambique in the early 1990s or Bosnia in 1996. Most transitional elections have come about due to internal factors—either popular pressure for elections or the decision of the major contending political forces that elections are the best way to recut the political pie after a dictatorship falls. The popular pressure for elections that often erupts when an autocratic regime is losing or has lost its grip cannot easily be ignored. In Nigeria, for example, one can argue that the country was really not ready for the 1999 elections that followed the death of dictator General Sani Abacha, given the ethnic tensions and profound political uncertainty. Yet any other path would have risked an explosion—Nigerians were demanding their right to choose their leader. The same was true for Indonesia after the ouster of President Suharto.

The four countries of the case studies are fairly typical in this regard. Guatemalan military leaders' decision to return their country to civilian rule was very much their own. It was influenced by the surge of elections elsewhere in Latin America, but very little by U.S. officials, to whom the Guatemalan military was not in the habit of listening carefully. In Nepal and Zambia, the broad-based movements of 1990–1991 that brought down the dictatorial regimes had elections as one of their central goals. The United States and other outsiders applauded and offered support, but were peripheral players. In the months after Ceauşescu's ouster, Washington did pressure Romanian leaders to hold elections. But with the wave of elections in Eastern Europe, those leaders already knew they would have to call elections to satisfy the popular appetite for democracy. The only questions were how soon they would take place and how open they would be.

A second part of the critical view of elections—that the United States gives too much aid to elections relative to other respects of democratization—is also less of a problem than it may appear. Election-related aid, especially election observing, tends to stand out because of the high visibility of elections. This creates the misleading impression that democracy aid is primarily focused on elections. In recent years, however, less than one-third of USAID's democracy aid has gone to elections. An even lower figure holds for the NED.

The bulk of U.S. democracy aid goes toward transforming state institutions and strengthening civil society. Postconflict countries are a partial exception. As noted above, the international community sometimes spends enormous sums to pull off elections in a country after a civil war, then devotes far fewer resources to the challenges of the postelection period.

Democracy promoters are also accused of overdoing elections by putting too much stock in them. This was certainly a major problem in the 1980s. The Reagan administration loudly declared El Salvador, Honduras, Guatemala, and other Latin American countries democracies because they had held one shaky election. U.S. officials were not just overstating for effect; many policy makers watching the new wave of elections were carried away by enthusiasm and simplistically equated elections with democracy. But events in transitional countries since the late 1980s have made it abundantly clear that elections are only one step in a long process of democratization.

Although democracy promoters today do not equate elections with democracy, they still tend to expect too much from elections. Even in unpromising circumstances they pin significant hopes on transitional elections, imagining they will give new legitimacy to a troubled government or bring real reformers to power, engage citizens in meaningful political participation, foster party development, and reduce political tensions and divisions. Yet elections in transitional countries with little history of democracy often do little of this. They produce a government of fragile legitimacy that is quickly dissipated by persistent social and economic problems. The citizen participation that goes into the election is often a one-time act followed by a dispiriting lapse back into political cynicism and apathy. The elections spawn a clutch of opportunistic "briefcase" political parties that develop few real ties to the citizenry. The campaign aggravates political tensions and social divisions as parties gravitate toward sharp messages and methods that will distinguish them from the rest of a crowded field. Elections in transitional countries thus often end up disappointing aid providers, even those who profess a realistic view of such exercises.

Some critics take the argument about overdoing elections a large step further and assert that many countries moving away from dictatorship would be better off not having elections until some time well into the future. Fareed Zakaria, for example, contends that too many elections are held in countries that have not developed the basic elements of Western liberalism, particularly the rule of law.[20] This leads, he says, to elected regimes that violate human rights and overstep their political boundaries, regimes he labels "illiberal democracies." He recommends that the international community concentrate on promoting rule-of-law development first and leave democratic participation for a later phase that will be built on a working system of laws and rights. Robert Kaplan holds that elections in poor countries with no democratic experience often end up causing civil conflict and chaos, the weak state torn apart by the divisive forces unleashed by the balloting.[21] He presents an updated form of the argument familiar from decades past, "Development first, democracy later," and asserts that development is best accomplished by enlightened authoritarians, not fledgling democrats. These two critics distrust elections in transitional countries for different reasons—Zakaria because he believes they produce overly strong, unbounded states, Kaplan because he fears they produce weak, incapable states. Yet the two critics converge on their preferred alternative—a long period of soft authoritarianism and development, to be followed only much later by elections and democratization.

A necessary period of enlightened soft authoritarianism before democratization is a tempting vision but a dubious one. Only a few authoritarian regimes (of varying degrees of softness) have actually led sustained periods of development in the past fifty years, primarily in East Asia. The history of the developing world is littered with dictators who started off professing enlightenment and promising a developmental path but then descended into corruption, cronyism, and incompetence, and dragged their country down. In Latin America, the "Pinochet model" is not a model but an exception—scores of other dictators in the region promised moral austerity and a steady economic hand but delivered nothing of the kind. Moreover, the notion that fledgling democratic regimes are incapable of implementing tough economic reform policies has been proved wrong in the 1990s in a number of countries, including Poland, the Czech Republic, Hungary, Brazil, Argentina, Thailand, and South Korea. In fact in the past ten years some of the most economically dynamic parts of the developing world have been among the most democratic parts.

It is true that a rush to elections is not always advisable in transitional countries. In postconflict situations elections may be more successful if they represent the culmination of a series of negotiating processes and confidence-building measures. In some cases where dictators fall, or a country gains independence from a large, political entity, state building is the highest priority and elections should follow only once basic authority and institutions are stabilized. Sometimes when ethnic divisions are at a boiling point elections should be delayed. In all these cases, however, elections should rarely be put off more than three to five years and should be announced as an eventual goal early on to prevent the ruling forces from settling into power for an indefinite stretch. Elections can be problematic, but a long period without elections is usually worse.

POLITICAL PARTY ASSISTANCE

Complementary to and often integrated with electoral assistance, aid to political parties is the other major kind of aid intended to contribute directly to a democratic electoral process in transitional countries.[22] Before the mid-1980s, the United States did not engage in extensive or systematic efforts to foster political party development in other countries. As discussed in chapter 2, during the 1950s and 1960s the CIA funneled money covertly to political parties in numerous countries in Western Europe and the developing world. The aim was not party development, however, but fighting communism—the funds were given to tilt elections in favor of pro-U.S. or anticommunist parties. Such activity dropped off after public exposure in the late 1960s and early 1970s of some of the CIA's political operations, though it continued at lower levels during the rest of the cold war years (for example, in the 1984 Salvadoran elections) and may still continue today.

A new current of political party assistance from the United States, carried out overtly rather than covertly and with a prodemocracy rationale, began in the 1980s with the establishment of the NED and of the two party institutes, IRI and NDI. NDI got involved gradually in programs to strengthen parties in the latter 1980s. The IRI carried out a substantial party strengthening program in those years in Latin America. Concerned that right-of-center parties were ill prepared to compete in the new era of multiparty politics in the region, IRI extended technical aid and training to conservative parties in Guatemala, Colombia, Costa Rica, Bolivia, and elsewhere.

U.S. political party assistance grew rapidly in the 1990s as part of the general expansion of democracy assistance. USAID began funding party-related projects (implemented by IRI and NDI) and by the middle of the decade was devoting more than $10 million a year to them, more than NED's total grants to the party institutes for all their activities. The emphasis in the 1990s was on Eastern Europe, the former Soviet Union, and Africa. The party institutes threw themselves into the task of supporting new political parties in the former communist world, spurred by the goal of frustrating the efforts of former communists to hold onto or regain power. In Africa, the reopening to multiparty politics across the continent offered many opportunities for the institutes to work with fledgling political parties. The institutes found fewer opportunities in Latin America, Asia, and the Middle East, where parties were less in flux and often not open to change. Nonetheless, they did some work in these regions, including in Cambodia, Nepal, Yemen, Morocco, Haiti, Paraguay, and Nicaragua.

U.S. aid is only one slice of assistance to political parties, which comes primarily from West European actors. West Europeans have been active for decades in strengthening political parties in the developing world, and since 1989 they have extended their efforts to the former communist countries. The Germans are the heavyweights in this field with their large, well-funded political party foundations, or *Stiftungen*. Each of the party foundations is tied to one of the main political parties in Germany and seeks to promote both the interests of that party, and a set of core democratic values at home and abroad. The Konrad Adenauer *Stiftung*, for example, associated with the Christian Democratic Party, has an annual budget in the neighborhood of $130 million and offices in more than eighty countries. The *Stiftungen* carry out various kinds of democracy-related assistance, including work with media, NGOs, and policy research institutes, but political party development has traditionally been one of their main areas of concentration. Each *Stiftung* targets parties it considers fraternal, that is to say, with the same ideology. Thus the Christian Democratic *Stiftung* seeks to promote Christian Democratic parties in other countries, the Social Democratic *Stiftung* works with Social Democrats, and so forth.

The Germans are by no means the only players. British, Dutch, Danish, Austrian, Italian, Swedish, Belgian, and other West European parties engage in international cooperation. The party internationals—such as Liberal International and Socialist International—are also important vehicles for international party cooperation. The Democratic and Republican Parties of the United States stand somewhat apart from this active European circuit of party cooperation. The Europeans view them as relative newcomers and as parties that tend to go it alone internationally rather than conforming to the ideological alliances and networks to which many of the European actors belong. This apartness is an advantage for the U.S. party institutes in that it has helped them avoid some of the entrenched flaws of the European aid: dogmatic efforts to teach party ideologies, an overemphasis on ritualized exchange visits and conferences, and the often forced method of identifying and cultivating ideological partners. Some European parties have begun to revise these methods in response to obvious program failures (such as the enormous but largely unsuccessful effort by the German Christian Democrats in the 1970s and 1980s to build up Latin American Christian Democratic parties), but change has been slow.[23]

Party-Building Methods

American practitioners of political party assistance generally assert a straightforward rationale for their work: no existing democracy functions without political parties, therefore political party development is an essential element of democracy promotion. Political parties, they assume, should play at least three essential roles in political life: 1) aggregating and articulating the interests of citizens; 2) structuring electoral competition and shaping the political landscape; and 3) providing coherent political groupings to run the government. In this view, not just any kind of party will do; democracy requires parties that are representative organizations subscribing to basic democratic values.

Beyond these general ideas, most American practitioners of party assistance operate from more specific ideas about what a democratic party system should be: The parties should be organized around political ideologies rather than ethnic, religious, or regional identities. Their ideological differences should be distinct but not too sharp; extreme ideologies are dangerous. The parties should not be personalistic vehicles for the self-aggrandizement of charismatic leaders but organizations with democratic internal structures that seek a constituency among citizens and strive for openness, account-ability, and lawful behavior. They should cultivate relations with other social and political organizations and be willing to work in coalitions when circumstances require.

U.S. party assistance aims to foster party systems that conform to the above profile. The boundaries of political party aid are not always easy to specify with precision. Some such aid strives to bolster the capacity of parties to govern once in office, usually legislative pro-grams that train politicians to operate in a democratic legislature. It may take the form of election aid initiatives, such as efforts to train party pollwatchers or to bring parties together to negotiate the elec-toral rules.

The core area of party aid—party strengthening—breaks down into assistance relating to a particular election campaign and assis-tance for party development between campaigns. The former seeks to help parties learn to be effective at the gamut of tasks that a campaign involves: message development, issue analysis, media relations, fund raising, voter mobilization, candidate selection and training, volunteer recruitment and deployment, coalition building, and general campaign strategy and management. Such aid usually consists of training provided by the American organization but sometimes takes a more direct, active form. IRI, for example, has inserted itself directly into some electoral campaigns abroad, such as in Romania and Bulgaria in the first half of the 1990s, where IRI representatives designed campaign strategies, attempted to broker opposition coalitions, and generally served as campaign consultants for selected parties.

A new focus of some political party aid is increasing the number of women candidates in legislative and local elections and, it is hoped, in office as well. These programs offer training to women who are considering running or who are already candidates. NDI trained women candidates competing in the 1997 local elections in Nepal, for example.

Party aid between campaigns focuses on organizational develop-ment over the long term. It usually emphasizes the reform of a party's internal management and organization, policy analysis (often by building up research wings within parties), bolstering the role of women in the party, beefing up youth programs, and strengthening membership recruitment, public outreach, and fund raising.

Although somewhat distinct, programs directed at campaigns and those directed at institution building between campaigns frequently overlap. Significant parts of campaign-related aid fortify a party's basic organizational capacities for the long haul. And party-building work not tied to a particular campaign nonetheless will help a party campaign more effectively when the time comes. The majority of U.S. party aid since the late 1980s has been related to campaigns. Campaigns stimulate the attention of the aid providers. As with most types of democracy assistance, it is more difficult for implementing groups like the party institutes to persuade the funding sources to support quieter projects less driven by events and to stay with them over the longer term.

The Perils of Partisanship

All areas of democracy assistance raise the fundamental question of political interventionism: whether it is legitimate for an outside actor to seek to shape the internal political life of another country. Yet it is political party aid that touches this nerve most directly, given that political parties are the means by which citizens compete for political power. In providing aid to a party or parties, are outsiders influencing the chances of particular parties to win, and are they are doing so in a selective, purposive fashion? The two U.S. party institutes publicly state that they are not in the business of trying to influence foreign elections, that their work is multipartisan and serves the general goal of promoting democracy, not specific political outcomes. Yet in practice they sometimes take a partisan approach, provoking debate about the legitimacy and value of such work.

IRI's first efforts in party building, its activities in Latin America in the latter 1980s, were explicitly partisan—the institute sought to strengthen only like-minded conservative parties. In the early 1990s, IRI dropped these efforts and said that it was no longer going to take a partisan line. In Africa, Asia, and Latin America, IRI has generally worked with at least several major parties in each target country or with one party when NDI or other U.S. groups were helping other parties. At the same time, however, in former communist countries including Russia, Ukraine, Mongolia, Bulgaria, Albania, and Romania, IRI has pursued a distinctly partisan line, seeking to strengthen parties that oppose former communists. IRI also took a partisan approach in Haiti in the latter 1990s, supporting parties that opposed those political groups associated with Jean-Bertrand Aristide, reflecting IRI's ideological discomfort with the former president. Much of IRI's partisan aid has been campaign-related and has been tied in with IRI's own active role in the campaigns. It has thus clearly been intended to influence electoral outcomes—to weaken the showings of former communists, or other left-leaning political forces.

IRI plunged into the 1992 presidential election in Romania, for example, sending experienced American political consultants to energize and direct the opposition's campaign against President Iliescu. IRI's aggressive, openly partisan approach created waves in Bucharest, especially after a high-octane strategy memo written for the opposition by a resident IRI consultant leaked to the press and was published in a national newspaper. Many Romanian political elites, not surprisingly, assumed that since IRI's efforts were funded with U.S. government dollars and IRI represented the political party that controlled the White House, IRI's partisan line reflected official U.S. policy. The U.S. embassy's insistence on U.S. neutrality in the election seemed to many Romanians hollow rhetoric belied by the open U.S. support for one side in the contest.[24]

NDI has adopted a multipartisan approach for its party work in many countries, but there have been important exceptions. In Russia, NDI has worked only with certain parties, the two small reform-oriented parties, Russia's Democratic Choice and Yabloko, and, to a lesser extent, "Our Home is Russia," the party led by former prime minister Viktor Chernomyrdin. In Croatia, NDI has worked in recent years only with some of the political groups opposed to President Franjo Tudjman. In Chile in the late 1980s, NDI worked on the "No" side of the 1988 plebiscite on General Augusto Pinochet's continued rule. In some countries, NDI has started out not intending to favor one side but has ended up doing so for situational reasons, usually that one party proves to be much more receptive than others. In Poland, for example, NDI's extensive political party aid, though initially intended to be multipartisan, goes mostly to the center-right parties. Aid from both NDI and IRI sometimes ends up favoring one party over others, not because of a specific political agenda but because of the particularities of personal contacts and relationships.

In general, U.S. political party assistance is intentionally partisan in one of two contexts: supporting fledgling political opposition groups against an autocrat, as in Chile (prior to 1989) or Croatia; or in former communist countries, supporting political forces that oppose parties led by former communists (or, in the unusual case of Russia, current communists).

When IRI and NDI involve themselves in a partisan manner in foreign elections, they insist they are not trying to influence the outcome of the election in question. First, they may argue that they have excluded only antidemocratic parties and are not being partisan but merely prodemocratic. Second, they may say that they are just trying to "level the playing field," to counterbalance the advantages the ruling party has in the way of access to state resources, control over television and radio, greater experience, or other factors. Behind the scenes, however, IRI and NDI representatives working on partisan party programs often make no bones trying to help the "good guys" beat the "bad guys," and they judge their own success in part by counting the electoral gains of the parties they are aiding. Each of these rationales nonetheless deserves attention.

Clearly political party aid should not go to antidemocratic forces (at least campaign-related aid; it may sometimes be appropriate to invite officials of antidemocratic parties to participate in seminars or to exchange visits to expose them to the idea of democracy). Yet deciding in a particular political setting which political parties are antidemocratic and which are prodemocratic is not always straightforward. IRI's approach in Eastern Europe of simply treating all parties led by former communists as antidemocratic is questionable. Former communists in the region have in some cases evolved, accepting and playing by democratic rules of the game. Even in Romania, where the break with the communist past was less complete than elsewhere, it was an oversimplification for IRI to portray the political scene of the first half of the 1990s as sharply divided between democrats in opposition and nondemocrats in power. The president and his party had many defects, including serious levels of corruption and incompetence. Though they had an instinctive dislike of all opposition, they did not systematically violate political and civil rights. They held several reasonably free and fair elections at the national and the local level and respected the results of the elections when they lost. Simply labeling ideologically undesirable parties antidemocratic does not solve the problem of partisanship.

Similarly, reflexively excluding ethnic-based parties, religion-based parties, and nationalist parties as antidemocratic forces, which the party institutes sometimes do, raises hard questions about criteria. Nationalistic parties, for example, can be unappealing to Americans but not necessarily antidemocratic. The line between democratic nationalism and antidemocratic nationalism is often blurred. Inevitably, highly subjective and often unexplained judgments are made. The danger is that the American party institutes will label as antidemocratic any party they do not like for one reason or another.

Leveling the playing field is an appealing idea to get around the charge of partisanship but raises many issues. A basic question that tends not to trouble American democracy promoters much but is often asked of them in countries where they so involve themselves is, "Who appointed you responsible for leveling playing fields?" The idea that it is America's job to go around the world leveling political playing surfaces is not widely shared outside the borders of the United States. Such a role assumes a deep political neutrality and a freedom from other political interests that the U.S. government does not have with regard to most countries. Selectivity is also a problem—why choose to level some but not others? Most electoral situations involve inequality to some degree. In some cases of seriously tilted fields, such as Mexico and Egypt, the United States has not aided opposition parties directly. It appears that the United States goes after unlevel playing fields when the ruling party is one the United States (or a political party institute) does not like. The appeal to neutral principle often seems a tacked-on explanation rather than a driving motivation.

One approach to the problem of partisanship is simply to reject political party assistance flat out as a violation of the fundamental principle of political sovereignty. One could note how sensitive the United States is about foreign involvement in its own elections and ask how most Americans would react to foreign (say, Chinese or Japanese) government-sponsored training and donations of equipment for the Democrats or Republicans. Allegations of Chinese government money going to the 1996 Clinton campaign created a major scandal for the administration. Yet there is a plausible case for partisan assistance in political contests where both rationales clearly apply: a fledgling opposition of obvious prodemocratic intentions is up against an entrenched, clearly antidemocratic regime, and the playing field is profoundly unlevel because the ruling power is abusing its access to state resources and putting obstacles in the way of the opposition. The 1988 Chilean plebiscite fit that description, and many people in the U.S. policy community who typically oppose Washington's political intervention abroad were happy to see the U.S. aid the opposition forces. Some of the first post-1989 elections in Eastern Europe and the former Soviet Union substantially fit the description, such as the 1990 balloting in Romania. Few people in the United States or elsewhere raise doubts about the appropriateness of U.S. aid to the political forces attempting to oppose Balkan dictators such as Tudjman in Croatia and Milosevic in Yugoslavia (except for the supporters of those regimes). The argument for partisan aid becomes steadily less persuasive, however, when the antidemocratic nature of the ruling forces is less clear-cut and the tilted playing field is more due to the opposition's own incompetence and inexperience than to wrongdoing by the government. One enters into gray area situations, such as Romania, Bulgaria, and Albania in the mid-1990s, where the political playing field is unlevel but still open to real competition and the competing political forces cannot be described simply as antidemocratic on the one hand and prodemocratic on the other. It is easy for democracy promoters to have a political preference in such situations but harder to make a good case that external actors are justified in trying to influence the outcome of elections.

In policy guideline documents, USAID asserts a firm adherence to a nonpartisan approach in all political party work: "USAID must be particularly scrupulous in avoiding even the perception that it is favoring a particular candidate or party through the provision of financial or technical assistance."[25] USAID officials simply try to ignore the fact that a number of USAID-funded party programs are partisan, sometimes openly so. But the issue occasionally erupts. In Romania in 1995 for example, the U.S. ambassador, Alfred Moses, decided that it was inappropriate for IRI to continue its partisan efforts on behalf of the opposition (since the Clinton administration by that point had a friendly relationship with President Iliescu). He ordered IRI to open its programs to Iliescu's party. IRI refused and left the country. Representative Frank Wolf (R-Va.) wrote Secretary of State Warren Christopher protesting that IRI "was not able to offer political party training to level the playing field for the opposition." (As evidence for the unlevel playing field, he noted that "the

Iliescu government has, reportedly, been able to hire 16 political consultants from the United States to run their campaign.")[26]

IRI and NDI representatives generally prefer that USAID, the State Department, and the NED leave to them decisions about which parties they should work with in particular settings and whether they should adopt a partisan approach. They habitually underestimate, however, the political sensitivities raised by such work. They are often surprisingly incapable of imagining how local political elites will react to well-organized groups from the most powerful country in the world working with or against particular parties in their country. Sometimes those forces not favored by U.S. assistance develop a siege mentality, fueling whatever tendencies they have to use state resources for campaign purposes and allowing them to justify themselves by saying they are only counteracting the meddling by the United States. They may also assume that all elements of the U.S. democracy aid portfolio—NGO programs, media aid, parliamentary programs, and other nonpartisan efforts—have the same partisan purpose. Moreover, partisan interventions feed the tendency of citizens in many transitional countries to believe that their political system is controlled by powerful, obscure outside forces and thus devalue their own role in choosing or influencing their government.

At the same time, providers of party assistance tend to overestimate their ability to bolster the performance of political parties. Theirs is a can-do attitude, often developed from their experience on U.S. political campaigns, and they assume that any negative side effects of their partisan work will be outweighed by the accomplishment of giving the "good guys" a boost. Yet as discussed in the next section, political parties in problematic transitional countries are difficult organizations to assist. Thus, underestimating the unintended negative consequences and overestimating the intended positive consequences, providers of political party aid tend to decide on a partisan course in some situations where a more realistic weighing of the advantages and disadvantages would point toward staying clear.

The United States is not the only country to engage in partisan political party aid. Many of the programs of the West European parties and party foundations are partisan as well, in the sense that they try to strengthen parties that follow their ideology. The British

Conservative Party, for example, works in transitional countries to strengthen conservative parties, while the British Labour Party supports left-of-center parties. Although the basic issue of interventionism is the same, the partisanship of European assistance tends to cause less of a flap within recipient countries than that of U.S. efforts. European aid is usually focused more on long-term party building than on specific campaigns, reducing the impression that the foreign aid provider is trying to influence a particular electoral outcome. In addition, the fraternal approach of European party aid is a blanket philosophy, applied all over, not just where former communists are a force. Moreover, the West European parties tend to balance each other's efforts out—if the German Christian Democrats are working with a conservative party in a country, the German Social Democrats will likely be there aiding the main left-of-center party. Finally, European actors typically provoke fewer local political sensitivities than U.S. actors. Because of America's superpower status, people in transitional countries are quick to assume that U.S. political party organizations are acting in the service of U.S. geostrategic interests, whereas they are less preoccupied with hidden motives of Belgian, Danish, Dutch, and other European parties.

Aiding versus Transforming

Attempting to be nonpartisan, however, is not without its own problems. In many transitional countries, especially ones in Africa, the Middle East, and the former Soviet Union, a single party controls the bulk of power while a few weak parties operate at the margins. Offering aid to all parties risks aggravating the already skewed political balance. The dominant party will likely have many more activists able to make use of whatever training is offered and the resources to implement whatever they have learned. Aid providers interested in party building are thus faced with a difficult choice: favoring the small parties and taking on the risks of partisanship, adopting a multipartisan approach that may strengthen the dominant party, or doing nothing.

In Zambia in the mid-1990s, for example, the ruling party, President Chiluba's Movement for Multi-Party Democracy, had achieved dominant-party status and was marginalizing the already weak opposition. NDI wanted to try to work with political parties in

Zambia, but faced a difficult choice—to work only with the opposition and risk antagonizing the MMD or to include the MMD and risk strengthening a party of dubious democratic intentions? NDI opted for an inclusive approach, providing training on party building and political communication for the MMD and the two largest opposition parties in 1995. President Chiluba and the MMD bullied their way through the 1996 elections, excluding former president Kenneth Kaunda, the main opposition candidate, and using their party organization at all levels, national and local, to tighten their grip. The opposition parties were unable to make much headway in the difficult political atmosphere and ended up boycotting the election to protest Kaunda's exclusion. At best, the U.S. aid bounced off a troubled political scene. At worst, it may in small ways have helped an antidemocratic party, the MMD, strengthen its grip.

The dilemmas of dominant party situations are just some among many that arise in trying to assist political parties in countries with weak or nonexistent traditions of multiparty politics. One of the greatest shortcomings of the many attempted democratic transitions in the developing world and former communist world in the 1990s is political party development. Most countries are stuck in one of two unpromising scenarios: either they have several well-entrenched political parties that have been around a long time, operate through long-established patronage networks, and have little interest in reform (as in much of South America and parts of Asia); or political life is dominated by several recently formed parties that are essentially personalistic power structures with little connection to the citizenry, few internal democratic procedures, and little coherent ideology beyond the immediate views of the party leader (as in many countries in Africa and the former Soviet Union).

In either situation, the prospects for the positive development of political parties are clouded by two factors of contemporary political life. First, the rapid growth of mass media has altered the way politicians garner support and mobilize constituents. Politicians now need only money, not institutional bases, to mount direct appeals to the people. This encourages the rise of demagogues and populists, vividly demonstrated by the 1998 presidential elections in Venezuela, in which a populist figure, Lt. Col. Hugo Chavez, trounced the traditional parties.

Second, the left-right ideological spectrum that has long defined political party systems has been dealt a double blow by the end of the cold war and by the rise of a single economic model, the market model. In Argentina, for example, the fading of the ideological wars of the 1960s and 1970s and the acceptance of the neoliberal model have left the two main political parties with little clear ideological division between them. Parties in many parts of the developing world still cling to traditional left-right labels. Yet the public in many countries is profoundly uninterested in ideological positioning. Instead, people judge politicians by their level of honesty, technocratic capacity, charisma, or entertainment value. Parties can no longer coast on old ideological claims to provide raisons d'être or guideposts for party action.

Despite the formidable obstacles to party development in transitional countries, providers of political party aid are often able to help parties learn to use more sophisticated or effective campaign methods. Such methods are in the interest of parties seeking to gain power and thus are naturally attractive. The party institutes have amassed considerable expertise in delivering such assistance and do not hesitate to take credit for gains they see in the field. In 1995, for example, NDI assessed its impact on its Russian political partners as follows:

> NDI has observed markedly different behavior among the parties with which it is working. These parties are targeting their communication to voters based on demographic and geographic information from the previous elections; conducting research on voter attitudes through focus groups and polling; contacting voters through small meetings, coalitions with civic groups, door-knocking, organizing phone banks, and public leafleting; organizing more sophisticated press operations that attempt to create news and respond to events; and relying on party activists who consider party organizing their full-time jobs. Much of this change can be attributed to NDI training.[27]

It is certainly true that political parties in many Eastern European countries and in some former Soviet republics, as well as in other parts of the world, have in the 1990s strengthened their campaign methods considerably (although it is worth noting that the parties NDI principally assisted in Russia have done poorly in successive elections, despite their transformed campaign methods). The U.S. party institutes have played a role in these developments, as have party assistance from other countries and for-hire Western political consultants, who are increasingly common in transitional countries.[28] The assumption, however, that the adoption of modern campaign methods necessarily advances democratization provokes a certain queasiness. It is difficult to observe most American political campaigns without wondering whether the sophisticated techniques—candidates adopting positions based on advanced polling methods, putting forward highly crafted media messages, and pursuing fund raising as a fine art—are really furthering democracy. It is natural, consequently, to wonder about teaching those methods to personalistic political parties in transitional countries with weak civic traditions. The party institutes argue that they are attempting to help parties become democratic through the use of active outreach and communication. Nevertheless, the enthusiasm for aggressive American methods that verge on the superficial and manipulative is evident, even just from the passage quoted above with the references to "press operations that attempt to create news" and other tricks of the contemporary campaign trail.

The issue underlying most party aid is whether external providers can have much effect on the basic nature and values of political parties in transitional countries. In many countries, the parties cannot be understood as simply underdeveloped or weak; they are fundamentally different kinds of organizations than Western ones. They are political cabals or clubs whose principal goal is achieving or maintaining power and perquisites for a small, closed circle of party leaders whose methods of operation are a mix of opportunism and patronage, and which have little interest in serving constituents or pursuing any larger agenda. It is certainly possible to help such groups learn more sophisticated campaign methods, but it is exponentially more difficult to transform their basic structures, interests, and goals.

The U.S. party institutes have been grappling with this challenge in many countries, and they pursue several kinds of efforts to promote basic institutional change: encouraging parties to democratize their internal structures through the use of internal primaries and other techniques; training party workers and leaders in the value and methods of building active constituent relations; attempting to stimulate the greater incorporation of women and youth into party activities; and introducing new fund-raising techniques to expand parties' financial bases. These are all logical methods, but the resistance to change within parties is high. Party leaders often have little interest in democratizing their parties' internal structures, and the whole institutional culture is different. Many parties are in the pocket of a handful of wealthy sponsors who, similarly, have little interest in broadening the party's base. Party leaders may make pleasing noises about the need for a greater role for women, but block the path to any real change in that direction.

This is not to say that efforts to transform problematic political parties are always futile or that aid efforts have not sometimes made progress. It is to underline how profound the challenge is and how often the task is to produce a fundamental change of course rather than to help parties move farther in a direction they are already headed. Examples of the difficulty of such work abound. In Cambodia, for example, the U.S. party institutes worked extensively with the two main political parties during and after the 1993 elections. The institutes reported success in building the parties as democratic actors. Yet in 1997, the leader of one of the parties, Hun Sen of the Cambodian People's Party, launched a coup and a course of political repression involving the murder of dozens of activists in the opposing political camp. Despite NDI's party training efforts, Chiluba's Movement for Multi-Party Democracy in Zambia continued the backward slide to semiauthoritarianism. NDI's work in Côte d'Ivoire during the same period made similarly little dent in the authoritarian drift of the ruling party. IRI invested considerable effort building up Sali Berisha's Democratic Party in Albania, only to watch him and his party drag the country into misrule and eventual political collapse. NDI's and IRI's efforts to solidify Haiti's parties did little to change the fetid political environment in that country. The negative developments in these various countries are by no means the fault of the party assistance programs. The point is just how often attempts to change the nature of political parties in transitional countries fall short.

It is not just particular parties in many transitional countries that are problematic—the entire party system is rife with personalism, patronage, and corruption. Merely attempting to strengthen specific existing parties is unlikely to change their basic role and risks entrenching more deeply a system that is a primary obstacle to democracy in the country. External aid providers in some countries must think about how new parties may emerge and take on the existing ones. That challenge clearly will be met only over decades or generations; it is not one that aid providers concerned with short-term impact are equipped to do much about.

7
From the Top Down: State Institutions

My first exposure to promoting democracy through the reform of state institutions included an incident that has stayed in my memory. On assignment from the State Department to USAID, I traveled to Haiti in 1986 to assess the judicial system as part of an effort to develop democracy programs there after the ouster of longtime dictator Jean-Claude Duvalier. I visited judges, lawyers, government officials, and others who might help me diagnose the infirmities of Haiti's barely functioning judicial system and come up with ideas about what the United States could do to help. I met with a warm reception almost everywhere I went, although also with a certain puzzlement about the U.S. government's intentions, since the Haitian judicial system had never been a focus of the quite extensive U.S. assistance to Haiti under both Jean-Claude Duvalier and his even more repressive, cruel father, "Papa Doc."

Late in my stay, I talked one afternoon with the head of Haiti's labor court, an institution that for years had done little to uphold workers' rights. I discussed the state of justice in Haiti with the genial, corpulent judge, who was attired in a heavy black robe despite the 100-degree heat in the dilapidated court building. After some time he pressed me about the purpose of my visit, listened carefully to my explanation, then repeated my answer carefully in his own words. So you are here, he said, to find out how the American government can help make our courts work properly? I nodded brightly, pleased that I was getting through. He looked at me wide-eyed for a moment, then burst out laughing, tipping back his head in unrestrained hilarity, laughing until the tears ran down his cheeks. As I slipped out the door he was still laughing.

Given the highly problematic experience of aid to reform the judiciary and other state institutions in Haiti from 1986 through the present, the judge's reaction was not far off the mark, or at least closer to it than the many optimistic reports and projections issued by aid providers along the way. Nevertheless, at least in some contexts the task is not futile and progress can be made. This chapter examines assistance for state institutions, the largest of the three main categories of democracy aid. It concentrates on the key challenges aid providers face in this area and the ways they are responding to those difficulties.

The chapter covers the five principal targets of such aid: 1) *constitutions*, which are institutions not in the sense of buildings with people working inside but in the sense of agreed sets of rules that govern specific areas of behavior in a society; 2) *judiciaries*, the leading focus of democracy programs oriented toward state institutions; 3) *legislatures*, the second largest such focus; 4) *local government*; and 5) *civil-military relations*, an area that does not fall neatly into the major categories of democracy aid but that primarily concerns militaries, which are state institutions.

In considering this broad category of democracy aid—assistance to state institutions—it is important to start with an idea of the character of such aid. It is not, for the most part, about state design. That is to say, it does not generally entail U.S. democracy promoters helping officials in transitional countries craft the structure of their states, such as choosing whether to have a presidential over a parliamentary system, or a bicameral legislature over a unicameral one. Here we run into the previously mentioned gap between scholarly work on democratization and the world of democracy assistance. The issues that have inspired considerable research by scholars—the interesting questions of different state designs and their effects on democratization, such as the much-debated topic in academia of parliamentary versus presidential systems—have not generally been accessible to democracy aid, because the transitions have not entailed the redesign of the state or powerholders have not opened redesign processes up to foreign involvement.

Democracy aid for state institutions is also not accurately characterized as state building. Aid for state building refers primarily to helping a country build from scratch the institutions of government necessary for a functioning state. Democracy programs that strive to strengthen judiciaries and legislatures may be seen in part as state-building activities, but they differ from classic state-building efforts such as those carried out by the European colonial powers in Africa in the first half of the twentieth century. They generally do not involve constructing institutions from scratch, except in the case of some especially devastated postconflict societies; instead, they reshape existing institutions. Additionally, they do not deal much with the executive power of the state—the governing functions of the president, prime minister, and executive ministries.

It is striking how little democracy aid is targeted at the executive branch of governments. Most democracy programs directed at state institutions are for the judicial or the legislative branch, or for local government. This is not by chance. U.S. democracy promoters in the past two decades have acted on the assumption that a key obstacle to democratization in countries coming out of long periods of authoritarian or totalitarian rule is an overly strong executive. They have oriented their work so as to strengthen the other parts of the government and thereby counterbalance the executive. Thus the thrust of most U.S. democracy aid for state institutions is best characterized not as state building but as state reform (reforming existing institutions) and state rebalancing (bolstering nonexecutive parts of the state to balance the power of the executive).

In chapter 5, I argue that aid providers are gradually learning from experience that merely reproducing other democracies' institutional forms is a simplistic and usually futile approach to democracy promotion. They are realizing that they must confront the underlying interests and power relationships in the sectors in which they wish to help bring about change. That involves identifying and understanding the interests that different actors have in particular sectors, the power that they can bring to bear to advance or retard change in those sectors, and the ways external aid can and cannot affect the interests and power. Such an approach is necessary in all areas of democracy aid but especially for work on state institutions, which—perhaps because of their size and formal structure—most seem to tempt democracy promoters into formalistic, technocratic methods. In this chapter I chart the learning by democracy promoters along these lines for each of the five main areas of work with state institutions.

CONSTITUTIONS

Next to election observing, aid to help other countries write or rewrite their constitutions is probably the form of democracy assistance best known to Americans. The image of an American constitutional scholar heading off to foreign lands with copies of the U.S. Constitution in his or her briefcase, to help constitutionally underdeveloped foreigners, is somehow a familiar one. Americans rewrote the Japanese Constitution after World War II, in a hurry but with some success, and assisted various decolonizing states in the 1950s and 1960s draft their constitutions.

The democracy wave of the 1980s and 1990s has included a good deal of rewriting old constitutions in transitional countries and writing new ones for new states. The fall of communism in Eastern Europe and the breakup of the Soviet Union provoked the largest surge of activity, but political transitions in Latin America, Africa, and Asia contributed as well. The U.S. government has responded with many constitutional aid projects. USIA has been a major actor, with USAID also taking part. Most such projects have sought to transfer knowledge about the American constitutional experience by sending U.S. experts abroad to advise constitution drafters, hosting conferences on constitution writing, bringing foreign constitution drafters to the United States on study tours, and sending books and other materials on the U.S. Constitution to other countries. In addition to providing information and expert advice, the projects sometimes support the mechanics of constitutional reform processes: underwriting the expenses of a constituent assembly or review commission, providing support for a constitutional referendum, or paying for the printing and distribution of a draft or finished constitution.

Constitutional assistance is tremendously appealing to U.S. aid providers, but its promise of great bang for the buck is seldom fulfilled. In theory, a single short visit by an American constitutional expert could steer a draft constitution in a particular direction and thereby profoundly affect a country's political direction. In practice, however, most constitutional aid is very much on the sidelines when the writing or rewriting is going on. The state design element of a constitution—deciding the basic structure of the government and the powers of the different branches—is not something the major political actors in a country are likely to be willing to turn over to foreign advisers. Such issues are usually worked out in intense negotiations between the major players in the country. In Eastern Europe, for example, the state design issues opened up by the fall of communist systems were usually hammered out in complex roundtable negotiations between representatives of the government and the opposition. In Africa in the same years, large-scale national conferences took responsibility for such decisions. As one U.S. constitutional scholar with much experience in constitutional reform in Eastern Europe has noted:

> A constitution is, after all, not just a legal document. It is primarily a social and political construct of past troubles, current conflicts, and aspirations for the future. Only those who have lived, suffered, and survived within that society can, should, and will write it. Americans, on the other hand, usually don't even know the language; many of us can barely find these countries on a map; and we certainly don't know their legal systems. In addition, we come from a common-law background, and these are generally civil-law countries with very different judicial structures and legal frameworks.[1]

Occasionally, an American adviser does gain the trust and respect of key figures in a constitution-making process and ends up having significant influence on at least some of the final document. The reports of such occurrences greatly exceed their actual number, however, as advisers often mistake for real influence a warm welcome and a deferential attitude toward the visiting foreign expert.

As discussed in chapter 5, all areas of democracy assistance tend to emphasize endpoints at the expense of process, and constitutional assistance is no exception. Aid providers are drawn by the prospect of helping a transitional country craft the ideal constitution. Getting certain provisions included in the document—and other provisions taken out—becomes a natural focus of attention. The equally important question of how the society in question participates in the constitution-making typically receives much less attention from aid providers, beyond the assumption that some sort of public referendum will be held at the end to approve the new document. If anything, aid providers' desire to mold a draft constitution through highly specific technical advice works against an interest in sponsoring an open, deliberative process of constitution-making. The more the constitution-drafting is kept within a small circle of technicians, the more likely that Washington or another external actor can wedge in an influential adviser.

Another shortcoming of U.S. democracy assistance, the tendency toward the artificial application of American models, is especially common in constitutional assistance. Most Americans have a special pride in their constitution and instinctively believe that it is a valuable example for others. In fact, the Constitution's relevance for other societies varies considerably. Many Latin American countries did copy the U.S. Constitution to a significant degree when they established their republics in the nineteenth century. Accordingly, American constitutional jurisprudence is often relevant to those countries. In contrast, in postcommunist Eastern Europe and the former Soviet Union, those molding the legal and constitutional systems have looked much more to Western Europe for models. In the words of an American scholar who has extensively studied recent constitutional processes in Eastern Europe, "The Constitution of the United States has been marginal."[2]

Finally, although aiding constitutions has a technocratic appeal—one imagines disinterested constitutional experts sitting calmly around a table burnishing a draft constitution to a state of finished perfection—it can be as politically treacherous, messy, and frustrating as any area of democracy aid. U.S. constitutional aid to Zambia is a case in point. Soon after taking office in 1991, the government led by President Frederick Chiluba decided to undertake a constitutional review to develop amendments to the constitution that had been adopted just before the elections of that year. USAID and other donor agencies offered to pay most of the costs of a newly established Constitutional Review Commission. They negotiated extensively with the government on the process that was to be followed for the adoption of amendments, securing promises that the draft would be widely distributed and a public referendum held.

The commission did its work in 1994 and 1995 and produced a series of proposed amendments. With elections approaching in 1996, however, Chiluba imposed a provision designed to disqualify his main political rival, Kenneth Kaunda, from the contest. He also insisted that the draft constitution be approved by the National Assembly, which Chiluba's party dominated, rather than by the Review Commission and by referendum. The result was a revised constitution that served Chiluba's own interests and that the Zambian people had no say in. The United States and most other major Western bilateral donors reacted angrily to Chiluba's manipulation of the constitution and for a brief period reduced and even eliminated some aid programs. Nevertheless, Chiluba got the constitution he wanted and all the pressure, negotiations, and money the donors put into the constitutional review process came to little. That did not prevent USAID, ever determined to claim success for its democracy work, from subsequently citing the constitutional review process as one of several "quiet but important D/G [Democracy and Governance] Project accomplishments."[3]

JUDICIAL REFORM AND THE RULE OF LAW

The first wave of U.S. aid directed at legal systems in other countries, the law and development programs of the 1960s and 1970s, attempted to reshape legal education and the role of the lawyer. When U.S. aid providers took a new interest in law-oriented aid, starting in Central America in the mid-1980s, they focused instead on the administration of justice, or more specifically, the administration of criminal justice. They attempted to help Latin American countries reshape their criminal law systems, through a shift from a partially inquisitorial to a fully accusatorial system, the introduction of oral rather than purely written proceedings, the expansion of due process protections, the general strengthening of the basic institutions of criminal justice, and other systemic reforms. The criminal law focus of the U.S. aid efforts reflected U.S. policy makers' hope that they could improve the human rights situation in the region by helping Latin American security forces and judicial institutions operate in accordance with legal norms. The highly top-down approach—as opposed to, say, strengthening legal aid groups and nongovernmental groups pressing on the agenda of popular justice—reflected the policy context of the time, the U.S. desire to foster tightly controlled, gradual processes of democratic reform and to bolster besieged anticommunist governments friendly to the United States.

Law-oriented aid grew significantly in the early 1990s, as part both of the expansion of U.S. democracy aid and of U.S. efforts to bolster market reform processes around the world. In Eastern Europe and the former Soviet Union, U.S. programs have supported the many efforts at de-Sovietization of the judicial and legal systems, encompassing the wholesale rewriting of many laws, attempts to establish judicial independence, and major institutional changes such as the reintroduction of appellate courts and reduction of the autonomy of once all-powerful prosecutors. In East Asia, U.S. groups have supported governments' attempts to renovate the legal frameworks, to advance both economic and political reforms.

As they have expanded the reach of law-oriented aid from Latin America to all regions in which they work, U.S. aid providers have also broadened their operative concept, from strengthening the administration of justice to promoting the rule of law. Effective, efficient administration of justice is a part of the rule of law, but not the entirety. Rule of law rests on other important features: laws that are publicly known, clear, and applied equally to everyone; respect for political and civil liberties, especially due process in criminal matters; and the subordination of government power to legal authority.[4] Aid providers draw a close connection between advancing the rule of law and promoting democracy. The fundamental elements of the rule of law, especially the equal, consistent application of laws, respect for political and civil liberties, and subordination of political power to law, are, they argue, all essential to democracy.

An economic rationale for rule-of-law assistance is often close by the political one. Aid officials assert that the rule of law is necessary for a full transition to a market economy—foreign investors must believe that they can get justice in local courts, contracts must be taken seriously, property laws must be enforceable, and so on.[5] Not only do political and economic rationales dovetail, but many transitional societies confront growing government corruption and ordinary crime, and the United States and other donors now prescribe strengthening the rule of law for those ills as well. In short, the rule of law appeals as a remedy for every major political, economic, and social challenge facing transitional countries. It has joined civil society as a new element of donors' conventional wisdom, an ideologically nonaligned concept, rarely invoked in previous decades, that is suddenly considered indispensable for democracy, economic success, and social stability.[6]

The result is an explosion of rule-of-law assistance all over the developing world, Eastern Europe, and the former Soviet Union. Many other bilateral donors, as well as the World Bank and the regional development banks, have plunged into the field. At least in some countries, this new consensus on the importance of rule-of-law aid produces congestion on the ground. Guatemala is a vivid example. As the country's leaders have struggled to implement the ambitious 1996 peace accords, donors have gravitated toward rule-of-law strengthening as the solution to the challenges of deepening democracy, furthering human rights, advancing market reforms, reducing corruption, and fighting crime. Rule-of-law aid programs are multiplying: the U.S. government, the Inter-American Development Bank, the World Bank, the Swedish government, the UN Development Programme, the Spanish government, and the Dutch government are all sponsoring rule-of-law aid activities in the country. The various donors have commissioned more than thirty separate diagnostic studies of Guatemala's legal and judicial system in recent years. The rather small set of Guatemalan institutions responsible for the rule of law is overrun with aid programs.

A Multifaceted Domain

Attempting to change the status and function of law in another society is a daunting task. Law is not a circumscribed institutional domain such as labor unions or the military. Many different institutions in a society, both governmental and nongovernmental, contribute to the making and use of law. Law is also very much about relationships between individuals and between institutions and individuals, as well as about norms and values affecting all different parts of life. Aid providers interested in promoting the rule of law have not, for the most part, agonized much about the complexity and even ineffability of the concept. They have concentrated on two of its most tangible manifestations—the state institutions that play a central role in the enforcement of law and the written laws themselves.

The most important institutional focus is usually the judiciary. (Assistance to strengthen legislatures can be considered a form of rule-of-law aid since legislatures are law-making bodies. Aid providers, however, have generally conceived of legislative strengthening work as a domain of its own, one related to a wider set of political goals including representation, accountability, and executive branch oversight). Judicial reform aid seeks to make a court system work more efficiently, armed with better knowledge of the law, applying the law more consistently and appropriately, and with greater independence from political authorities or other powerful actors in society who would interfere. It may include programs for:

- rationalizing and strengthening overall management of the judiciary
- increasing the judiciary's budget
- renovating the physical infrastructure
- reforming judicial selection and judicial career laws
- training judges and other court personnel
- increasing the availability of legal materials for judges
- strengthening case management and other internal administrative tasks.

U.S. judicial reform aid usually consists of a mix of most of these elements, with one exception. U.S. aid providers have stayed away from large-scale physical infrastructure projects in the judicial realm, due both to a lack of funds for such high-cost efforts and a general view that building buildings does not solve developmental problems. Other aid providers, including European donors and the World Bank, have provided aid for the renovation of courthouses, the furnishing of vehicles to judges, and other infrastructure items.

An area of aid directly related to judicial reform that has gained currency in some regions, particularly Latin America, is alternative dispute resolution, usually through mediation and arbitration. Programs to foster its use hold out the possibility of keeping some kinds of disputes out of problematic judicial systems and easing the burden of courts choked with backlogs.

In a country trying to reform its criminal law system, other state institutions are often the targets of U.S. rule-of-law aid, including prosecutors, public defenders, and police. Work to revitalize or otherwise reshape the role of prosecutors and public defenders has been a complementary element in many judicial reform assistance programs in Latin America. Police aid has been a staple of U.S. democracy portfolios in Latin America since the late 1980s and is becoming common in other regions, especially in postconflict countries like Bosnia, Rwanda, and Somalia. Only a small portion of U.S.

police aid programs abroad—primarily the International Criminal Investigative Training Assistance Program with its focus on strengthening police investigative capacities and rebuilding police forces under civilian control—are democracy-related. The rest—including programs sponsored by the FBI, the Drug Enforcement Agency, and the State Department's Bureau for International Narcotics and Law Enforcement—are law enforcement efforts with an uncertain and sometimes contradictory relation to democracy goals.[7]

Prisons have not been a target of U.S. rule-of-law assistance, despite the horrendous state of prisons in most transitional societies and governments' interest in receiving external aid to improve them. Such work is extremely politically sensitive and the potential for criticism at home from Congress or human rights groups has scared away most U.S. officials. Other public and private donors have begun venturing into this field in Latin America and Eastern Europe, and it is likely to grow, given the enormous need for better prison conditions in so many countries.

Aid for law reform, the other major component of U.S. rule-of-law assistance, provides support for the revision of existing laws and regulations or the writing of new ones. It typically consists of expert advice on drafting, including information on models from other countries. Law reform encompasses any number of substantive areas. A tremendous amount of donor-supported law reform in the 1990s has targeted the commercial domain in transitional countries—banking regulation, taxation, antitrust, bankruptcy, foreign investment, and the like—as part of economic reform programs. In Latin America, the United States has pushed for the drafting of new criminal codes. In the former communist countries, the United States and other Western nations have supported the rewriting of all types of laws—commercial, criminal, civil, and others—as part of the attempt to decommunize whole systems.

Although rule-of-law assistance concentrates on institution building and law reform, they are not the entire picture. Aid providers sometimes attempt to bolster the legal profession, primarily through strengthening bar associations, in the hope that the associations will become more active advocates for judicial reform and for stricter ethical and professional standards applicable to lawyers. Legal education is also sometimes a focus, although U.S. aid providers have not emphasized it in most of their programs, believing it to be too

Rule-of-Law Assistance Standard Menu

Reforming institutions

> Judicial reform
> Legislative strengthening*
> Retraining prosecutors
> Police and prison reform
> Bolstering public defenders
> Introducing alternative dispute resolution

Rewriting laws

> Modernizing criminal laws
> Updating civil laws
> Introducing new commercial laws

Upgrading the legal profession

> Strengthening bar associations
> Improving legal education

Increasing legal access and advocacy

> Stimulating public interest law reforms
> Supporting advocacy NGOs that use law to pursue social and economic
>   goals
> Aiding NGOs that promote judicial and legal reform
> Training journalists to cover legal matters
> Underwriting legal aid clinics

*Legislative strengthening relates to rule-of-law change but also serves political process goals; accordingly, it is often treated by USAID and other donors as a separate category of aid.

indirect a way to effect change. Such aid may target legal education at universities through curriculum reform, professorial exchanges, the establishment of clinical law programs to give students hands-on experience, and the updating of law libraries. Or it may concentrate on informal legal education, such as adult education on basic legal rights.

Finally, in recent years U.S. aid providers have been trying bottom-up approaches in response to their frustrations with many of the initial top-down efforts. The goal is often the same institutional reforms the top-down programs pursue; the difference is where the reform impulse is expected to come from. These efforts, which overlap with the category of civil society assistance discussed in the next chapter, include support for:

- nongovernmental organizations that work for public interest law reform—changes in laws and the application of laws bearing on matters of public interest such as political and civil rights, government transparency, and the environment[8]
- law-oriented NGOs that seek to help groups of citizens, such as a group of farmers or tenants, overcome problems through legal advocacy directed at local government officials, judges, and other authorities[9]
- NGOs whose explicit goal is to stimulate and advance judicial reform, police reform, or other institutional reforms directly related to the rule of law
- media training to teach journalists about legal and judicial reform and how to cover legal and judicial matters
- legal aid clinics to help disadvantaged people or groups gain access to the legal system.

Some people in American nongovernmental organizations committed to promoting human rights or socioeconomic equity in developing countries contend that bottom-up approaches should not be merely supplements to top-down methods but the main thrust of rule-of-law aid. In historically unjust societies, they argue, justice will not be handed down by reformed state institutions; it must be won by people asserting their rights and demanding their due. They are wary of the technocratic line that many donors take on judicial reform, warning that creating administratively efficient courts is no guarantee of the quality of justice. They concentrate their law-oriented aid on advocacy groups that pursue public-interest law reform or particular sociopolitical goals, and on legal aid programs and other methods to widen legal access.

The Difficulty of Reform

Judicial reform constitutes a whole realm with its own dynamics, rules, and logic, and the same is true of reform of police, legal education, public interest law, and the other major components of rule-of-law work.[10] In each of these realms, lessons from experience are accumulating. Just with respect to aiding judicial reform, for example, an extensive body of knowledge is taking shape, one that incorporates many specific issues, including methods and structures for improving judicial selection, the effects of raising judicial budgets, options for streamlining case management by courts, the benefits and limitations of establishing judicial training schools, the shortcomings of bar associations as agents of reform, how to foster acceptance of alternative methods of dispute resolution, and many others. It is beyond the scope of this book to review all these many lessons about rule-of-law aid. Instead, I wish to highlight an overarching conclusion: what stands out about U.S. rule-of-law assistance since the mid-1980s is how difficult and often disappointing such work is.

In Latin America, for example, where the United States has made by far its largest effort to promote rule-of-law reform, the results to date have been sobering. Most of the projects launched with enthusiasm—and large budgets—in the late 1980s and early 1990s have fallen far short of their goals. They have had some positive effects, yet have made only a dent in the grievously flawed situation of rule of law around the region. In particular, countries have made little progress on the key issues of increasing judicial independence and overcoming the de facto legal impunity that military and economic elites in many Latin American countries enjoy. Writing in a 1998 Inter-American Development Bank report on judicial reform in Latin America, Edgardo Buscaglia portrays a troubled realm that shows few signs of improvement after more than ten years of rule-of-law aid:

> Mounting delays, case backlogs, and the uncertainty of results have diminished the quality of justice throughout the region. Among the obstacles facing the judiciary are dysfunctional administration of justice,

lack of transparency, and a perception of corruption. Delays and corruption in the judicial systems in Latin America have reached unprecedented proportions.[11]

Linn Hammergren, who worked extensively on USAID judicial reform programs in the region, takes a more positive view. Since the mid-1980s, she asserts, the situation of justice systems in Latin America "has been altered dramatically, probably irreversibly, and generally for the better," featuring higher budgets, greater professionalization of staff, rationalization of procedures, new laws, the establishment of monitoring systems, improved quantity and quality of output, greater access, and better adherence to written procedures.[12] Yet she acknowledges many shortcomings: reforms have often worked on superficial elements rather than fundamental structures; aid providers have often chosen clients or allies with a vested interest in the status quo; attempts to expand judicial access and to ensure fairer treatment of the majority of citizens remain incompletely realized, and in some countries not achieved at all; corruption, excessively vertical structures, clientalistic appointments, and inadequate organizational missions persist; public confidence in judicial systems remains low; crime continues to escalate; many businesses still prefer to settle conflicts extrajudicially; and increases in the productivity of courts have not kept up with demand.

Probably the most significant accomplishment of U.S. rule-of-law assistance in Latin America since the mid-1980s has been to help push the issue onto the agendas of governments in the region. The goal of improving courts, police, and other basic law-related institutions now stirs up public debate and galvanizes officials' attention. The reasons for this agenda shift are many—citizens' frustration over skyrocketing crime is one major factor—but the U.S. emphasis is certainly one of them. Getting the issue onto the agenda is much less than what aid providers have sought to accomplish, but in the long run it may prove an important contribution if Latin American governments and societies are able to sustain their efforts and make some lasting progress.

In other parts of the world where the United States has invested significantly in rule-of-law aid, disappointment is also common. In Russia, an array of rule-of-law assistance was one element of the rush of U.S. political and economic aid in the optimistic aftermath of the breakup of the Soviet Union. Yet some ten years later, the lack of rule of law in Russia is an open sore and many of the U.S. and other Western programs in this field have little to show.[13] The other cases when the United States has concentrated on rule-of-law aid, including Cambodia, Egypt, and Haiti, have been similarly frustrating.

The experience in three of the case study countries is fairly typical in this regard. In Guatemala, as in many Latin American nations where the United States rushed in with hefty amounts of judicial aid in the 1980s, the first wave of judicial and police programs came to grief over the lack of local support for reform and the powerful resistance to reform within the targeted institutions.[14] In the early 1990s, USAID pushed hard to get the Guatemalan government to adopt a new criminal procedure code, a code written by USAID-sponsored consultants from other parts of Latin America. The government adopted the code but had made few preparations to persuade resistant prosecutors and judges to implement its new requirements for defendants' rights. In the mid-1990s, USAID launched a new rule-of-law program, with one component designed to teach prosecutors about the new code and another to create several pilot centers to help judges, prosecutors, and police learn to work together productively. This project was better designed and implemented than previous initiatives and unfolded in a more conducive political environment. Nevertheless, its positive effects were modest at best, and represented only a few points of light in a still troubled system.

In Romania, USAID sponsored a program run by the American Bar Association to strengthen a judicial training school set up by the Romanian government after the fall of Ceauşescu. Although the opening of the school represented a genuine spark of interest in reform, kindled chiefly by a particular minister of justice, that spark flickered out (and the minister left) and several years of U.S. support to the school were undermined by Bucharest's profound uninterest in judicial reform.[15] After the arrival to power of President Constantinescu in 1996, and the return to office of the same reformist minister of justice, the possibility of progress increased notably. The recent small U.S. rule-of-law efforts in legal education, law reform, and judicial training have contributed in minor ways to a gradual improvement of the judicial and legal environment, but major institutional reforms are still only just starting to get under way. In

Nepal, the Asia Foundation set up a judicial assistance program after the 1991 democratic transition, as part of a set of new top-down democracy programs. The various aid efforts to improve the administration of the courts sank almost without a trace into a judiciary riddled with corruption and mismanagement.[16]

With aid for law reform, the reasons for less-than-expected effects are often obvious. Merely sponsoring the writing of new laws, especially by copying models from the United States or other donor countries, barely scratches the surface. The shiny new drafts are often not enacted into law, or if they are, the relevant state institutions usually lack the capacity to implement or enforce them and no budgetary provisions have been made to pay the costs of implementation.

The story of why so much judicial reform assistance has proved disappointing is more complicated. One reason is the gap between the enormity of the problems facing many judicial systems and the modest scale of the assistance response. This gap exists with all areas of democracy assistance but is especially glaring in the realm of state institutions, where the problems are often gargantuan. The judicial systems in most transitional countries are beset with fundamental shortcomings, including a lack of infrastructure, inadequate salaries for judges and other personnel, insufficient operating budgets, weak support personnel, and poor training, not to mention the lack of a tradition of judicial independence, political elites used to forcing the judiciary to serve their interests, and entrenched government corruption. Merely offering some training for judges and some technical assistance on new administrative methods is unlikely to do much to renovate a system debilitated by these severe financial and political problems.

The shortfall between the scale of the problems and of the aid is aggravated by the inherent difficulties of aiding judiciaries. They are relatively decentralized institutions, with multiple sub-units run by independent-minded people (judges) who by training and usually by temperament are inclined to do things their own way. At the head of the judiciaries is often a supreme court chief or a minister of justice who has considerable power and who frequently proves difficult for aid providers to work with, again for reasons of training and temperament. Most judicial systems in transitional countries (and those in a number of established democracies as well) are poorly managed and administered, with archaic practices such as clerks wielding special wax stamps and presiding over filing systems of a Dickensian nature. Assistance, therefore, cannot simply be poured in at the top with the expectation that it will reach the bottom. Yet neither are most heads of judiciaries eager to decentralize control over how the aid enters the system. Moreover, management of the judicial system is often contested by the executive and judicial branches, with the ministry of justice and supreme court fighting for control—a fight that frequently spills over into and frustrates judicial reform programs.

Not only are judiciaries unwieldy institutions, but a will to reform is hard to find in them, or among the political leaders. Politicians may speak about the need for judicial reform in their country, but they rarely devote much energy to what is inevitably a long-term process with only a distant political payoff. Public pressure for judicial reform may build up enough to motivate political leaders to undertake real reforms, although this has not happened often. It is rare for citizens' unhappiness to coalesce around the rather technical issue of judicial reform; when faced with spiraling crime rates, for example, citizens tend to demand stiffer punishments for criminals rather than systemic reform. Even when popular pressure for judicial reform becomes a factor, as in Argentina in the latter 1990s when citizens called loudly for the Menem government to clean up the corrupt, inefficient Argentine courts, politicians tend to carry out superficial bureaucratic reforms without dismantling the underlying patronage networks that are a prime source of problems for the courts.

The occasional minister of justice or supreme court chief turns out to be a real reformer—whether out of a desire to make a name or simply out of conviction. Such reformers are often able at least to stir things up and get some initiatives under way, but they are usually very much on their own. They encounter powerful resistance from within the target institutions. Moreover, often they are not supported by the other parts of the government and are gradually ostracized for threatening entrenched interests. To the chagrin of the international aid providers who have rushed to support these beacons of hope (often inadvertently contributing to the local resentment toward them with a too-warm foreign embrace), the lone reformers are often gone in a couple of years.

Some rule-of-law reforms in Latin America have been led by small groups of lawyers or law professors who push from inside the system for new laws, or even a whole new criminal procedure code, or some other change. These reformers are often younger technocrats who have been exposed to foreign models. Such informal groups of reformers can be important but they also face significant limitations. Often they have little connection to the public, so there is no popular base they can mobilize when they encounter resistance. Then, too, they are apt to favor changes in laws and procedures that are conceptually sophisticated but not necessarily geared to producing useful changes in practice.[17]

Even where the desire for reform does exist and judicial reform begins, resistance to reform often surfaces at different levels. In the first place, those responsible for the management of the judiciary, whether at the ministry of justice, the supreme court, or elsewhere, often believe they have much to lose from real reform. They may lose power if hierarchical, ingrown management systems are rationalized; they may lose control if outsiders start recommending and designing changes; and they may lose money and perquisites if corruption is reduced and transparency instituted. The possible benefits to them of a better-functioning judiciary—greater pride in their job, possibly greater professional prestige and the satisfaction of knowing that society as a whole is better off—are diffuse and distant by comparison. Self-interest frequently leads them to resist reforms, whether actively or passively.

Judges and other court personnel throughout the system run through similar calculations. For many judges who have spent their careers in dysfunctional systems, the vision of a reformed judiciary may well be unappealing: judges, no longer able to rule their courts as personal fiefdoms, they reason, will likely have to work harder, forego the income from corruption, sit through frequent training sessions, and accept the dictates of outside advisers on how to run their courts. Thus judges often engage in foot-dragging in the implementation of reforms. Lawyers also resist. Although quick to offer withering critiques of the judiciary in their country, many of the more successful and powerful lawyers benefit greatly from cozy relationships with senior judges and an insider's knowledge of how to make a dysfunctional system work to a client's advantage. Moreover, lawyers are reluctant to support reforms that will mean major new laws and procedures for them to learn and that will render worthless much of their accumulated knowledge about the peculiarities of the existing system. Even the public, despite a clear general interest in a strong rule of law, may at times oppose certain changes. In some Latin American countries, for example, revisions of criminal procedures to better protect citizens' basic rights were criticized by some of those citizens as "soft" on crime.

Learning from Experience

The difficulties of judicial reform work have become evident in recent years as the same patterns crop up in projects in different parts of the world. U.S. aid providers, however, still tend to underestimate the challenges, reluctant to give up their assumptions that judicial reform will advance naturally once a country enters a democratic transition and that strong internal resistance to reform is the exception rather than the rule. As aid providers attempt judicial reform work in previously uncharted regions, they seem determined to repeat mistakes made in other places. The spate of U.S. judicial and legal aid to Russia in the first half of the 1990s, for example, was designed with little attention to the failures and hard knocks in Latin America a few years before, which hammered home the need to avoid applying U.S. models and to make sure of some genuine local will to reform before one started. The extensive judicial aid to Cambodia in the mid-1990s was similarly unencumbered with learning from either the Russian or the Latin American experiences.

Nonetheless, some learning is occurring, particularly among aid officials and consultants working in Latin America, the region in which the United States has labored most intensively on rule-of-law aid. As mentioned earlier, many specific relatively technical lessons are being learned about the individual elements of judicial and legal strengthening. At a more general level, aid providers are confronting the need to move from the surface to the internal working of the institutions they want to help reform. They are also grappling directly with the question of will to reform. As discussed in this chapter's concluding section, these broader shifts are by no means easy.

A second form of learning has been the gradual broadening of approach to institutional reform. Rather than assuming that training and technical assistance efforts directly focused on judiciaries, police, and other law-related institutions are the only way to help produce significant changes in those institutions, aid providers are adding bottom-up initiatives. They are drawing in public interest law groups, human rights organizations, and judicial and police reform NGOs, and sponsoring training for the media and other citizens-oriented projects, sometimes as alternatives to institution-oriented efforts and sometimes as an additional avenue of approach for stimulating change. In other words, aid providers are learning not to treat the target institutions as self-contained entities that can be tinkered with as though they are machines that run on their own. Rather, they are beginning to work with them as institutions connected in manifold ways with the societies of which they are a part, and to make those connections focal points. For rule-of-law work this means seeing justice not merely as something that courts and police deliver but as a set of values, principles, and norms that define the relationship of citizens to their government and to each other.

LEGISLATIVE ASSISTANCE

Programs to strengthen national legislatures in other countries are another major form of democracy assistance directly aimed at state institutions.[18] Like most other areas of U.S. democracy aid, legislative assistance has followed the wave of democratization around the world: several projects were established in Central America and various parts of Asia in the 1980s, followed by a burst of new projects in Eastern Europe, the former Soviet Union, sub-Saharan Africa, and the Middle East in the 1990s. The Asia Foundation has served as the principal provider of such aid in Asia. The Congressional Research Service, which is the policy research arm of the U.S. Congress, has been the most active U.S. player in Eastern Europe and the former Soviet Union. The two political party institutes and private consulting firms have carried out most of the legislative projects in the other regions, as well as some of the efforts in the former communist countries.

American democracy promoters gravitate toward legislative assistance, largely because they are accustomed to a political system in which the national legislature—the U.S. Congress—is unusually powerful. To them, it seems obvious that a strong, capable legislature is a key element of a democracy. In almost all countries coming out of authoritarian or totalitarian rule, national legislatures are extremely weak. They are usually subordinate to the executive branch; poorly funded, equipped, and staffed; lacking law-drafting capacity and political experience; and enjoying only minimal public respect. Helping such legislatures to get on their feet, to become more efficient, effective, and representative, is therefore assumed essential to furthering democratization.

The clear prodemocratic rationale is not the only attraction of legislative assistance. Reform work with a major institution at the core of the political system holds out the promise of producing significant changes in the recipient society with just one project. In addition, some of the traditional forms of legislative assistance, such as study tours for legislators and computers and fax machines for legislative offices, buy goodwill with the legislators, something that is useful and appealing to the U.S. embassy in the country and the State Department generally. Moreover, aid providers know that legislative assistance is likely to be an easy sell to Congress, the original source of U.S. aid funds: U.S. congressmen and congressional staffers are naturally sympathetic to the argument that strong legislatures are essential to democracy.

The United States is by no means the sole player in legislative assistance. Numerous European parliaments sponsor parliamentary exchanges, training sessions, and technical assistance for parliaments in the developing world and former communist states, often overlapping with U.S. programs. The Inter-Parliamentary Union carries out legislative assistance in many parts of the developing world. There is a busy circuit of visits, exchanges, and goodwill missions, largely funded by European parliaments and international institutions, among parliaments around the world. These activities go under the label of parliamentary aid but many serve social and diplomatic goals more than anything.

Goals and Types of Legislative Assistance

Although they often insist that they are not seeking to export the U.S. model, Americans involved in legislative assistance abroad usually hope to see the legislatures they aid become more powerful vis-à-vis the executive branch. They want the legislatures to play a larger

Legislative Assistance Standard Menu

Building the capacities of legislators

Training legislators
    On substance: nature of democracy; specific political and economic topics; comparative legislative systems
    On methods: legislative process; use of parliamentary committees; value of public hearings; constituency outreach; transparency; accountability

Building the capacities of legislative staff

Training legislative staff
    On substance: budget analysis; policy analysis
    On methods: legislative research; bill drafting; media relations; constituent relations

Strengthening infrastructure

Stocking libraries
Underwriting new buildings
Providing office equipment
Developing new information systems

Bolstering input and scrutiny from NGOs and media

Supporting NGOs that promote parliamentary transparency and accountability
Training journalists to cover legislatures
Aiding advocacy NGOs that provide technical input on bills

role in law-making rather than rubber-stamping laws written in ministries, to exercise more oversight of the executive branch, and in general to challenge the executive's predominance. Along with this central goal, legislative programs usually have two other goals: increasing the effectiveness of the legislature in question, and making it more representative. The concept of effectiveness has both substantive and procedural elements: first, helping legislatures pass better laws, laws that reflect a genuine understanding of the policy issues and of the interests at stake; and second, promoting greater legislative efficiency, that is, coherent internal procedures which allow a legislature to handle its agenda effectively. Making a legislature more representative is usually taken to mean enhancing the legislature's ability to factor in the views of the citizenry. This may involve fostering more contact between legislators and citizens through greater use of constituent offices, more public hearings, increased transparency of the legislative process, and more interaction with interest groups and advocacy organizations.

In the pursuit of these goals, four types of activities are common in legislative assistance programs. The first is training and technical assistance for the members of a legislature. Such support may be focused on general democratic education—instructing legislators on what democracy is and the role of a national legislature in it—or it may be seminars on issues of social or economic policy that legislators face. Much training and technical assistance focuses on legislative methods—rationalizing the legislative process, fortifying the role of committees, holding more public hearings, increasing transparency, and widening constituency outreach—in the service of the different aspects of the goals of efficiency and better representation. Such work is sometimes carried out in the recipient country itself but is frequently complemented by the perennially popular study tours for members of parliament—all-expenses-paid visits to Western capitals to see the workings of Western legislatures firsthand.

U.S. legislative aid programs often direct training and technical assistance at the professional staff of legislatures, drawing again on the U.S. model (the staff of Congress is unusually powerful and numerous, with more than 15,000 employees). Such aid may focus on substance—understanding budgets, learning about privatization, social safety nets, or other policy issues. Or it may concentrate on methods—how to do policy analysis, legislative research, or legislative drafting, for example. All this is intended to help legislative staff play a substantial role in the law-making process, providing the research, analysis, and drafts that go into effective legislation. Training may extend to media relations and public outreach and the setting up of a public affairs office in the legislature.

Infrastructure support constitutes a third category of legislative assistance. Parliamentary libraries are a favorite target of U.S. aid providers, who often cite to foreign legislators the example of the Library of Congress and the need to build a knowledge base for legislative action. In some countries, aid projects have helped establish sophisticated information centers, using the Internet and other communications technologies to make available to legislatures much information about laws in other countries. Aid programs also often provide at least some office equipment, especially computers and fax machines. Legislators in many transitional countries have learned that visiting U.S. aid providers are swayed by the argument that democracy is impossible without a healthy number of computers in the legislature. Through one project, the Frost Committee Program, sponsored by the U.S. Congress, the United States provided more than 1,200 computers to parliaments in former communist countries.[19] In some cases (usually involving European donors, not the United States), infrastructure support extends to the refurbishing of offices or even the construction of a new building for the legislature.

These first three categories all represent top-down approaches to legislative strengthening; they entail working directly with the legislatures. As with judicial reform, U.S. aid providers have only gradually come to develop bottom-up approaches in this domain. These have included support for watchdog NGOs that monitor legislatures, with particular concern for transparency and accountability; teaching journalists how to cover legislatures and the legislative process; and aid to policy institutes or other NGOs that can offer substantive advice to legislatures on the drafting of legislation. Bottom-up legislative assistance aims to help citizens hold their legislature accountable, to increase their knowledge about legislatures' activities, and to increase the input into the legislative process of technical policy advice and information from outside the government.

Reform Roadblocks

If asked to name the area of democracy assistance that most often falls short of its goals, I would have to point to legislative assistance.

Its record is riddled with disappointment and failure. That is not to say that it is always futile. In a handful of transitional countries where leaders have seriously sought to reform the state institutions, legislative aid from abroad has helped make possible significant improvement. Legislators who have received training have become more effective representatives. Legislative staff have gained new skills and equipment transfers have been put to use. In the context of rapid overall democratic progress, the legislatures of several East European states, including Poland, Hungary, and the Czech Republic, made reasonably good use of U.S. and West European legislative assistance in the first half of the 1990s. The Salvadoran national assembly clearly benefited from U.S. and other aid that it received after the end of the civil war in that country.[20] In the 1990s, the Philippine Congress improved relations with citizens and became more transparent and accountable partly because of assistance from and pressure applied by the Center for Legislative Development, a U.S.-funded Philippine NGO.[21]

All too often, however, legislative aid efforts have barely scratched the surface in feckless, corrupt, patronage-ridden parliaments that command little respect from the public and play only a minor role in the political process. Legislators emerge unchanged from repeated training seminars. The training sessions for legislative staff do not deal with the facts that the trainees are beholden to powerful political bosses and are not given much of a role. Shiny new computers sit unused on legislators' desks or disappear. New parliamentary committees are formed at the urging of outside advisers but end up as fiefdoms of the senior legislators who are the root cause of the parliament's poor performance. More public hearings are held, again on the advice of aid providers, but they are mostly for show. Anticorruption committees are set up but corruption continues. The drafting and negotiating of laws continue to take place in a few key government offices or behind closed doors at meetings of select members of the ruling party.

The story of U.S. legislative aid in the case study countries is fairly representative of the overall pattern. Officials of Nepal's parliament happily accepted U.S. and European aid in the early 1990s, participating in study tours, receiving computers, engaging in extensive staff training exercises. Parliament did take on some of the trappings of a more professional body, but made little progress in overcoming the corruption, inefficiency, and isolation from the citizenry that have long defined its operating style. In Guatemala, the first U.S. program to aid the National Assembly, implemented in the late 1980s, foundered on a lack of real interest among assembly leaders and on the Assembly's unimportance within the country's governing structures. An effort begun in the mid-1990s in a more favorable climate has gained greater traction, but change for the better is still painfully slow. A range of U.S. parliamentary aid initiatives in Romania in the first half of the 1990s, including the writing of a guide to parliament, donations of equipment, efforts to strengthen committee structures, and training for parliamentarians, had little effect on the deeply corrupt, stagnant institution. New projects after the change of government in 1996 have failed to make much headway in a body still dominated by partisan deadlock and profound inefficiencies. In Zambia, a planned U.S. legislative assistance project in the early 1990s never got off the ground because the parliamentary leadership opposed it. Many other such cases could be cited.

Some common deficiencies of legislative aid programs are partially responsible for the frequent failures. These include aid providers' lack of knowledge about the political and personal dynamics of the institutions they are trying to reshape, a determination to apply models that fit poorly with the local situation, and a focus on technical solutions—such as new rules of order or Internet access for staffers—for deeply political problems. By far the biggest obstacle, however, is the paucity of interest in reform among the main power-holders in the legislatures of many transitional countries. Even ardently prodemocracy leaders may not consider strengthening the legislature a priority on an agenda loaded with difficult items. They may believe that a dominant executive branch is necessary to get their slate of reforms enacted quickly and that a stronger legislature, even one their party dominates, will only slow them down. Then, too, they may worry that legislative strengthening will give more of a voice and role to the opposition, further complicating their plans.

Moreover, as in judiciaries, legislatures often have built-in motives that spell quiet but strong resistance to reform. Rationalizing the legislative process, for example, usually means reducing the power and control exercised by the ruling elite within a legislature. Increasing transparency and accountability reduces the perquisites and sources of corrupt revenue to which legislators in many countries have grown accustomed. Professionalizing the legislative staff may mean a loss of patronage opportunities for legislators as well as a redistribution of capacity, and potentially, therefore, of power in the institution. The fact is that the people at the top of poorly functioning legislatures are likely benefiting from some of their institutions' inadequacies. In some cases they may be committed reformers who wish to sacrifice those benefits to help create a better institution, but many times the avowals of reform melt away.

This cautionary view may seem overly harsh, but it should be noted that built-in resistance to reform is by no means peculiar to political systems outside the established democracies. Consider, for example, the stubborn refusal of the U.S. Congress in recent years to reform campaign finance laws and the role of money in the legislative process, despite the glaring abuses and the broad public support for reform. The standoff is a clear demonstration of resistance to prodemocratic reforms within a key institution in a well-established democracy based in large part on legislators' concern about a possible loss of power for themselves or their party.

Some of the configurations in legislatures in countries attempting democratization mean a weak reform impulse within those institutions. Dominant-party situations—in which one party holds 80 percent or 90 percent of the seats in the legislature—are common, especially in sub-Saharan Africa, Central Asia, and the Middle East. Even though the leaders of such legislatures may be happy to work with donor programs to upgrade the technical capabilities of the body, they will likely have little incentive to open up the legislative process significantly or to increase pluralism. Merely avoiding a descent into rubber-stamping the pet projects of the executive branch is a difficult challenge. A converse problem is a legislature divided fairly evenly between factions that engage in such intense partisan conflict that the institution is polarized and paralyzed. In such situations, external aid not only lacks the power to change an unhelpful political dynamic but is itself one more thing for the sides to fight over.

The regular turnover in the membership of many legislatures also complicates the task of legislative assistance. After costly, time-consuming investments in training MPs, the next elections may end up removing many of those trained and bringing in a whole new bunch. In Guatemala, for example, turnover in the National Assembly in 1990 removed most of the people who had previously participated in a U.S.-sponsored training program. A USAID project paper highlighted the problem aid officials faced with the new legislature: "Following the 1990 elections, conversations were initiated immediately with the Guatemalan Congress as part of the project design. Since there had been a 90% turnover in the representatives, there was little memory of the activities carried out by The Center for Democracy . . . from 1988 to 1990."[22] This sobering report contrasted noticeably with an evaluation in early 1990, which enthused about the earlier project's many "major accomplishments."[23]

Yet a further complicating factor is the political sensitivity of such work; while almost all areas of democracy assistance are politically sensitive, legislative assistance is one of the touchiest. The prospect of a powerful foreign actor working directly to help shape the internal workings of a country's highest law-making body is, understandably, unsettling for many people in that country. Furthermore, in legislatures that house a range of viewpoints, at least one faction may harbor anti-U.S. or anti-Western views and will oppose foreign involvement in their institution. In Zambia, the U.S. legislative assistance program planned in the early 1990s, as mentioned above, never got off the ground. This was not simply due to a lack of will to reform in the institution but to the specific suspicion of the speaker of the parliament that U.S. involvement in "his" institution was hostile to the interests of his country or at least his party.

Broadening the Approach

Although a lack of genuine impetus for reform is a central problem that plagues many legislative assistance efforts, a deeper limitation is also often at work: the institutional weaknesses aid providers hope to help remedy are caused by factors outside the legislature. The dominance of legislatures by executive branches, for example, is often rooted in the country's constitution. When examining the functioning of a weak legislature in a transitional country, American democracy promoters almost reflexively insist the legislature should play a major role in initiating laws, even if it is part of a parliamentary system where many laws originate in the executive branch. Similarly, they often push for greater oversight of the executive branch by legislatures, even when the legislature has few formal powers that would allow it such a role and is part of a parliamentary system in which the same leaders dominate both the executive and the legislature. Even where the executive's dominance is the result of habit rather than law, aid to the legislature is unlikely to cause the executive to cede much power. Aid providers' hope may be that a more capable legislature will wrest power from the executive, but this is by no means assured, and the executive will likely resist any such move.

Similarly, training and technical assistance may improve the knowledge of legislators, but much broader factors shape the human content of legislatures—the rules for choosing candidates, the type of electoral system (especially the list system versus direct election of members), the underlying political culture and level of voter education, and the campaign finance laws. The nature of the political parties is a major determinant of the way a legislature functions. Where parties are patronage-dominated machines, those politics will be replicated in the legislature. Instructing legislators to act certain ways or to subscribe to certain values is unlikely to have much effect on the deeper patterns of incentives, informal rules, and power principles that guide political life.

The point is not that weak, troubled legislatures can never change. It is, rather, that treating legislatures as self-contained entities that can be fixed by repairing internal mechanisms is unlikely to get very far. Rather than seeing the task as legislative assistance per se, it is more useful to think in terms of helping a society develop the capacity to enact laws that incorporate citizens' interests and reflect sophisticated knowledge of the policy landscape. Ultimately, helping bolster this capacity will mean working with many people and groups outside the legislature, including political parties, citizens groups, the media, officials from the executive branch, jurists, and others.

U.S. aid providers have begun to move in this direction in some cases. To help stimulate an interest in parliamentary reform in situations where the interest within the parliament is obviously low, aid projects sometimes support NGOs that seek to mount pressure campaigns for particular reforms. A group of Romanian NGOs, for example, oversaw a U.S.-funded transparency campaign in the mid-1990s that managed to provoke the notoriously opaque, sluggish Romanian Parliament to adopt at least some basic reforms in that department. More generally, much of the aid for civil society from U.S. organizations encourages citizens advocacy efforts, which are often directed at legislatures. Political party programs now sometimes include efforts to help parties learn to operate in legislatures.

The broadening of legislative work does not mean that the many obstacles to a better law-making process will be readily overcome. It is, however, at least a useful corrective to the aid providers' habit of designing legislative assistance programs as narrowly focused institutional repair packages.

LOCAL GOVERNMENT ASSISTANCE

In the late 1980s, USAID began adding projects labeled "democratic local governance" or "local government strengthening" to its standard portfolio of democracy assistance. The first of these projects unfolded in Central America in the late 1980s and early 1990s, where the transitions to elected civilian governments prompted efforts to decentralize what had long been highly centralized, authoritarian systems. Local government initiatives multiplied in the 1990s, especially in Eastern Europe and the former Soviet Union, where reversing the stultifying centralism of the communist era was at least a declared priority of most post-1989 governments. As U.S. democracy assistance got under way in sub-Saharan Africa, USAID launched democratic local governance projects in various countries, including Ethiopia, Côte d'Ivoire, Guinea, and Mali. A modest number of such projects were established in Asia, by far the largest in the Philippines (more than $50 million) and much smaller efforts in Nepal, Bangladesh, and Mongolia.[24]

The increasing attention to local government in the 1990s grew out of U.S. democracy promoters' focus on aiding the reform of state institutions. They viewed strengthening local governments as a natural next step after tackling judicial and legislative reform. It was another element of their "state rebalancing" strategy—attempting to lessen the dominant power of the executive authority of the central government by fortifying other institutions of the state. It also reflected growing frustration with the difficulties and limitations of aiding institutions at the center. In this way, local government assistance connects with the rise of aid to civil society and the desire of democracy promoters to get more directly at the links between citizens and governments. USAID's New Partnership Initiative, a policy initiative launched in the mid-1990s, encourages USAID missions to take a tripartite approach to promoting both democracy and economic development from the bottom up: simultaneously working to promote more effective democratic local government, more active local citizens advocacy groups, and small business development.

This surge of local government projects within democracy portfolios is only part of a much larger set of aid efforts aimed at promoting decentralization. Since the 1980s the United States and other Western donors have sponsored an enormous number of decentralization projects in nearly all countries receiving foreign assistance. A bibliography on decentralization work prepared in 1983 lists more than 500 studies of such projects around the world.[25] The first wave of donor interest arose in the 1960s. The United States and others pushed governments of developing countries to give a greater role to local authorities, in the belief that increasing local participation in what many expected would be rapid economic development would help ensure more equitable, stable socioeconomic change. A new round of decentralization programs began in the late 1970s, part of the heightened attention in those years to poverty alleviation, community-based development, and basic human needs generally.[26] This second wave continued through the 1980s and into the 1990s, eventually joining up with the recent wave of decentralization programming established under a prodemocracy rubric.

The programs of the first two waves differ from the more recent group in one important respect. The earlier efforts concentrated on two forms of decentralization—*administrative* (transferring functional responsibilities) and *financial* (transferring responsibility for government spending). The programs under a prodemocracy rationale incorporate these two goals but go beyond them to include the goal of *political* decentralization—transferring accountability and representation to the local level, through local elections and other political processes.

In practice, the distinction between these three types of decentralization is not always sharp. Administrative decentralization, for example, often involves making local officials more responsive to citizens' demands, causing it to resemble elements of political decentralization efforts. Nonetheless, there have been dividing lines. Many of the decentralization projects over the past several decades promoting administrative and financial decentralization have been carried out in nondemocratic countries. By far the largest recipient of U.S. decentralization aid since the 1980s is Egypt, a country that is only marginally democratic. Indonesia under President Suharto was another major recipient. In these cases and many others in Asia, Africa, and the Middle East, decentralization assistance flows in for years with little reference to and little apparent effect on democratization. Of the almost $7 billion that the United States spent on decentralization projects from the late 1970s to the mid-1990s, only about $1 billion was for projects that explicitly incorporated political decentralization.[27]

The Many Types of Local Government Aid

As outlined above, decentralization projects may focus on any or all of three types of decentralization—administrative, financial, and political. The projects range from efforts that strive to restructure completely the way a government provides services and exercises authority, to minor efforts bolstering a few dozen village councils. The term "local government" itself is capacious in meaning; it is used to describe almost any form of government authority not part of the central government, from provincial governments with authority over millions of people to village councils with responsibility for a few hundred. Whichever types of decentralization they foster, and whatever their magnitude, aid projects to promote decentralization (or local government strengthening, or democratic local governance, or the various other formulations in this domain) generally consist of some mix of three kinds of assistance.

The first type of aid is structural—intended to bring about the legal changes necessary to increase the formal power and authority of local government and in some cases to revamp the manner in which the government is selected, possibly including the introduction of direct local elections. Such changes may require a constitutional amendment, though more often a new decentralization law is the object, or even just new regulations under an existing law. Aid providers often furnish model laws or constitutional provisions, as well as other forms of technical assistance relating to the legal measures. They may also stimulate officials' interest in embarking on decentralization by jawboning, sending government officials on study tours to observe local government in action in other countries, and sponsoring studies and policy conferences on decentralization. Supporting associations of municipal officials that articulate the interests of local government officials and lobby central governments for greater decentralization is another means of encouraging system-wide change.

The second type of aid—the core of many decentralization projects—is training and technical assistance for local government officials and institutions. This aid may cover any or all of the many technical skills that go into local government work, including service delivery, budgeting, accounting, resource mobilization, project planning and implementation, and management. Particularly in decentralization projects with explicit democratization objectives, the training may also instruct local officials on how to be responsive to citizens and how to expand contact with citizens through means such as town meetings, citizens boards, and drop-in centers. In previous decades, training was often carried out through national centers for such work run by the central government of the recipient country. In the past ten years, the United States and other donors have developed training programs that reach local officials directly, bypassing what often proves an inefficient, unhelpful central bureaucracy.

The third category of decentralization assistance, which has become increasingly common due to the rise of local government aid with a democracy thrust (though it was by no means always absent from earlier decentralization efforts based only on administrative and financial decentralization), seeks to encourage citizens to work more with local governments. As U.S. aid officials are fond of saying, such work bolsters the "demand" side of the local government equation. Most often, it entails training for locally based NGOs on the importance of a local government focus and on ways to make their case to local government. Such efforts represent an area of fusion between civil society assistance and local government assistance. Similarly, media assistance now sometimes trains journalists in the investigation and reporting of local government activities, both to get journalists to recognize the growing importance of local government and to increase media scrutiny of what local government is up to.

The Hard Road

The appeal of strengthening local government as a means of fostering democratization is powerful. It is enough to hear an enthusiastic

Local Government Assistance Standard Menu

Fostering system-level change

Advising or pressuring government on decentralization policy
Helping redraft the basic national law on local government
Aiding the introduction or strengthening of local elections
Supporting associations of local government officials

Building the institutional capacities of local governments

Training local government officials
    Service delivery
    Budgeting and accounting
    Project planning and development
    Resource mobilization
    Citizen outreach
    NGO relations

Supporting local government infrastructure development
    Providing office equipment
    Underwriting construction or rental of offices
    Supplying vehicles

Increasing citizen input

Aiding citizens councils that work with local government
Training local-level advocacy NGOs to work with local government
Training journalists to cover local government

proponent of democratic decentralization enumerate its virtues—bringing government to the people, engaging citizens in the political process on issues that touch their everyday lives, developing a training ground for a new generation of national leaders, bringing the provision of government services into line with actual needs, increasing transparency and accountability, and so forth—to understand why in the 1990s democracy promoters have embraced decentralization. Yet the "discovery" of decentralization is built on what seems almost willful ignorance of the long record of efforts at decentralization in the 1960s, 1970s, and 1980s. Assessment studies and bidding requests for democratic local governance projects glisten with the sense of excitement of something new and promising, almost never delving into failed initiatives and wasted aid in the long, murky past of this domain—often in the very country for which new decentralization aid is being proposed.

The record of decentralization programs in the developing world in past decades is weak.[28] Many of the projects from the 1960s through the 1980s brought about improvement in the technical capacities of local government bodies and officials. Nevertheless, the bulk of countries in Africa, Latin America, Asia, and the Middle East entered the new global environment of the 1990s with highly centralized states. A few countries, especially the Philippines and El Salvador, have made notable progress in strengthening local government in the past ten years, thanks in part to large U.S. decentralization aid projects. So far, these remain exceptional cases, although Latin America at least boasts a number of other countries that are making local government stronger.[29]

To the limited extent that they confront the problematic past of local government aid, current enthusiasts argue that a fundamental difference divides the present from previous eras—today the push for strengthening local government is primarily in democratizing countries, whereas before most such efforts took place in autocratic contexts. Authoritarianism is intrinsically hostile to decentralization, they argue, accounting for the failure of many past efforts. A context of democratization is fundamentally more hospitable, making for greater chances of success. It is true that the new interest in decentralization in many parts of the world is related to democratization, and therefore has greater promise. Nonetheless, several pitfalls of decentralization and decentralization assistance are still extremely relevant.

Although decentralization raises manifold economic, administrative, and social issues, it is above all a political issue. It is about power—about whether those holding most of it in a society are willing to give significant portions of it away, whether for the sake of democratic principle or for specific instrumental objectives, such as greater efficiency in the allocation of public resources. Even when a country is in a democratic transition, the leading power-holders, and the civil service bureaucracy, are usually reluctant to devolve real authority to local government. Central governments' overwhelming tendency, for decades throughout the developing world and since 1989 in the postcommunist states, has been to resist decentralization despite the blandishments of donors and pressure from citizens:

> Most politicians everywhere are mainly preoccupied with maintaining and enhancing their own influence. Few are able to grasp the subtlety that even though their decentralization deprives them of some powers, it can reinforce their influence in more important ways. . . . Unfortunately, most politicians fix on the influence they will lose through devolution. This . . . has wrecked many promising experiments. . . . There is not much that can be done about it, other than to try to prepare high-level power holders for the loss of powers which will attend decentralization, and to explain the more subtle and substantial gains that will accrue to them if they can tolerate those.[30]

Resistance to decentralization resides not only in the executive branch, but also in the legislature, at least within the ruling party. Influential members of parliament are often virtual barons in their districts, doling out patronage and having a hand in all major business matters. Decentralization thus holds little appeal for them. Often the opposition favors decentralization, hoping it will allow them to strengthen their local bases of power.

Politicians' tendency to resist decentralization is not always rooted in the desire to hold power for power's sake. It may stem from unselfish concerns about national unity and ethnic division. In ethnically divided societies, decentralization raises loaded questions about the balance of power among the different groups. Even relatively narrow technical elements of decentralization can become symbols of the ethnic issues at stake, preventing even minimal progress on what donors may view as unquestionably useful initiatives.

Donors' attempts to persuade politicians that giving away power is the right thing to do are uphill struggles. A good example is the experience of the United States and other donors, including the European Union and the World Bank, trying to strengthen local government in Romania in the 1990s. The overcentralization of Romania's post-1989 political system—a dual legacy of French-inspired statist administrative models of the early twentieth century and the Stalinist model of the communist years—was manifest. In the early 1990s, the donors identified decentralization as a priority for both democratization and socioeconomic development, and they sponsored various efforts to strengthen local government. Yet the Iliescu government steadfastly resisted steps toward decentralization, to the point of turning down a major World Bank loan rather than comply with the attached requirement of a certain degree of administrative decentralization. The government simply did not want to give up the power that the centralization helped ensure. After Constantinescu's election as president, the donors anticipated that a more reformist government would finally move on decentralization. Yet progress remained slow for more than a year, with decentralization stuck on the question of the appropriate degree of autonomy for the ethnic Hungarian minority in Transylvania. In 1998 the government enacted a new law on decentralization that at least set in motion some administrative and financial decentralization, although the devolution of power remains at an early stage.

Even if a country's leaders are persuaded to engage in genuine decentralizing, the problem often arises of what one analyst calls "local elite takeover": entrenched vested interest groups and elites at the local level take over and manipulate for their own purposes whatever local institutions central governments empower with new responsibilities and authority. As Harry Blair, an expert who has examined numerous decentralization programs, has written, "National policy intentions to empower the weak through decentralization may be noble, but the traditional dynamics of political economy at the local level inevitably skew things to the benefit of the locally powerful."[31] In Nepal, modest steps in the 1990s toward decentralizing a highly centralized political system immediately ran into powerful local patronage networks and often impossible to untangle controlling loyalties based on clan and ethnic group. Local governments began to receive regular grant funds from the central government, but in many areas of the country such funds did not work to change dysfunctional local political structures or habits but to reinforce them. Only in places where donors' presence was strong and funding of local NGOs was heavy was it possible to ensure some transparency and accountability in the use of local government resources.

Local elite takeover is one part of a broader syndrome. Donors' dreams of decentralization are born from the idea of starting anew, setting aside central governments' pervasive problems and building up more responsive, cleaner government practices at a manageable local level. The reality, however, is often that decentralization exports the pathologies of the center to the periphery. A national political culture of patronage, corruption, and dishonesty does not somehow stop at the outer edges of the capital city. If anything, it is often more intense at the local level, where the educational and socioeconomic level of the main political actors is lower, media scrutiny is weak, and civil society is thin. The experience of the United States, where corruption and patronage in many state and city governments is much higher than at the federal level, is fairly clear in this regard.[32]

Often local government assistance also faces a problem of scale. Unlike aid to a national legislature, or even to a judicial system, local government aid almost always involves a large number of potential recipients, scattered throughout the country. For most U.S. local government assistance projects, a maximum of only a few million dollars is available over several years. Such amounts do not go far when trying to reach many different localities. As a result, the assistance projects often consist of a handful of pilot projects in a few provinces. Even if these are successful they rarely have much impact beyond their bases. The funds necessary to "take the project to scale"—a favorite donor concept—are almost never forthcoming, and the projects end up falling into the classic foreign aid syndrome of being short-lived oases of change that fade away once the aid stops flowing. There are rare exceptions, such as the unusually extensive U.S.-supported decentralization project in the Philippines in the early 1990s.[33] But much more common is the example of Nepal, where the USAID-funded local government project of the early 1990s reached only a few provinces. Although the project was well-received in those provinces and addressed the critical issue of relations between local government bodies and citizens, it was never expanded and left almost no trace after funding dried up in the mid-1990s.

At the heart of debates over decentralization in many countries is the question of whether decentralization can take place when the existing structures of local government are so weak. On the one hand, governments say that they cannot decentralize much because the local government lacks the technical capacity to handle increased responsibilities; on the other hand, local authorities say they are unable to develop their technical capacities without some genuine transfer of authority. The approach of the United States and other donors in such situations is often to provide at least some local government assistance, in the belief—or more accurately the hope—that the aid will encourage the central government to decentralize. Many local government assistance projects thus end up being carried out in relatively unfavorable circumstances and produce few benefits because the assistance alone is not enough to overcome the resistance to decentralization.

The chicken-and-egg debate over capacity and decentralization has a much broader form. The question can legitimately be raised whether democratic decentralization is possible in countries where national political parties have little presence in the countryside and civil society is weak outside the major cities. Yet at the same time, without active, capable local government, it is hard to foster the grassroots development of political parties and civil society. As mentioned above, the response of U.S. aid providers to this conundrum and to the difficulties of local government strengthening generally is to pursue an approach combining work on local government with aid to promote local-level civil society development, political party development, and small-scale business development. This is a useful direction, but one that takes on four difficult challenges simultaneously, making clear that change will occur only very slowly at best.

CIVIL-MILITARY RELATIONS

An additional area of democracy aid that merits at least brief mention in this chapter is civil-military programming. Such aid is normally carried out in countries that have undergone a transition away from military rule or from an authoritarian regime upheld by a military establishment. Even after the armed forces have gone back to the barracks, much usually remains to be done to establish genuine civilian control over the military, to foster democratic values in the military, and to reintegrate the military into society on a new footing. Civil-military aid straddles two of the three main categories of democracy assistance. It concerns a state institution, although militaries are not institutions of government in the way that parliaments, judiciaries, and local governments are and democracy promoters are not trying to strengthen militaries, as they are doing with the other state institutions. Civil-military aid is also closely tied to civil society, homing in on the important relationship between civilian actors and military ones.

Reflecting the dual nature of the task, the U.S. government supports two different types of aid to improve civil-military relations. U.S. civilian agencies and nongovernmental groups, especially USAID, USIA, and the NED, have funded some civil-military programs in transitional countries. These have focused on opening up lines of dialogue between militaries and civilians. They also often involve instructing government officials and legislators in military budgeting and military policy to give them the technical knowledge necessary both to deal intelligently with matters of military policy and to assert control over military financing. Most of these programs have operated in Latin America, reflecting the major role played by Latin American militaries in the political life of their countries in recent decades. Some efforts in this domain have also been carried out in Africa, Eastern Europe, and the former Soviet Union.

In addition to these civilian-run programs, the Defense Department also works in this field. In the 1990s, the Pentagon added courses on democracy and human rights, military-media relations, and other aspects of civil-military relations to its extensive programs to train military personnel in countries around the world. (The International Military and Education Training Program [IMET] administered by the Pentagon has an annual budget exceeding $50 million and sponsors military training programs in approximately 100 countries.) The inclusion of these elements came after harsh domestic criticism of the U.S. military's long history of support for military forces involved in human rights abuses and military dictatorships.

It also reflected the end of the cold war and the Pentagon's search for new missions. Moreover, the U.S. military expanded its training programs for foreign military personnel to take in foreign civilians, offering them training in military oversight, budgeting, and other facets of civil-military relations. The topic of civil-military relations is also included in other cooperative programs in which the U.S. military is involved, such as NATO's Partnership for Peace in Eastern Europe and the former Soviet Union.

These efforts to foster more open, productive, and prodemocratic civil-military relations in transitional countries are useful, but change is slow and difficult in militaries that for decades played a repressive, antidemocratic role. As do other state institutions targeted by democracy programs, militaries resist change. They are typically even more self-contained than judiciaries, legislatures, and other civilian institutions, and operate on the notions that a certain separation from society is necessary and that openness to influence from the outside is a sign of weakness. Often they interpret the positive-sounding idea of "improving civil-military relations" as implying a loss of control over their budgets and even their operational policies to civilian politicians for whom they have little respect, or open contempt.

Improvements in civil-military relations are nonetheless possible, even in countries with a catastrophic record in this area. They have, for example, improved in most of Latin America over the past twenty years. The aid efforts sponsored by the United States and other nations have made a modest contribution. But the issue is still fraught with tensions and problems, not just in the Central American states that only recently emerged from civil war, such as Guatemala, Nicaragua, and El Salvador, but in South American ones like Colombia and Peru. As a recent USAID report on civil-military aid noted:

> Civilians in Latin America still remain unschooled on security issues. Creating a role for civilian expertise, developing the mechanisms necessary to train civilians, and guaranteeing that those trained will become the planners for the next generation are all necessary steps. . . . Military experts who are part of the armed forces continue to call the policy shots in the ministries.[34]

Assessing the value of the U.S. military's efforts to train foreign military personnel in democracy and human rights is especially difficult and has been a subject of considerable controversy for years. U.S. military officers have long argued that bringing foreign military personnel in contact with the U.S. military will have powerful demonstration effects in terms of professionalization and change in values. They are fond of recounting what they believe are anecdotes showing the benefits of bringing foreign military officers to the United States. To cite just one example:

> Secretary of Defense William Perry likes to tell the story of how he recently visited Albania and saw the success of IMET firsthand. There he met an Albanian battalion commander who, thanks to IMET, had gone through Ranger training at Fort Benning, Georgia. When the commander got back to Albania, he immediately set up his own American-style training program. Secretary Perry was extremely impressed by the level of discipline his troops exhibited and their respect for civilian authority.[35]

Such anecdotes, though appealing, are hardly proof of the deep impact of U.S. exposure, given the historical record. The U.S. military has had extremely close ties for decades with its Turkish counterpart, for example, and countless Turkish military personnel have been trained in the United States and Turkey by American military personnel. Despite this sustained, far-reaching contact however, the Turkish military has for years committed grave human rights abuses in its battles with the Kurdish minority in Turkey and shows no sign of stopping. Similarly, the Pentagon resisted criticism throughout the 1990s of its friendly relations with and training of the Indonesian military, arguing that it was instilling good values in that institution and gaining the United States an important channel of influence. That rationale rang hollow in the first half of 1998 when in the growing crisis over President Suharto's slide from power the Indonesian security forces killed several civilian demonstrators, resisting U.S. appeals to avoid doing precisely that. The list of such cases is long. That does not mean that it is useless for the U.S. military to include democracy and human rights in its training courses for foreign military personnel. It means that its claims for the transformative effects of such efforts—"Expanded IMET has changed the nature of civil-military relations in many countries"[36]—must be greeted with considerable skepticism. As with all democracy-related assistance, training courses, no matter how well designed and salutary, do not by themselves reshape entrenched, often badly flawed foreign institutions.

CHALLENGES OF AIDING THE STATE

U.S. democracy promoters gravitate naturally toward aid designed to help reform the basic political institutions of transitional countries. When they look at these countries they see poorly functioning institutions at the top and decide that democracy will never take hold until those entities are fixed. The tasks are tangible, the targets large and visible. Despite this clarity of aim, the record of democracy aid directed at state institutions over the past fifteen years is cause for caution. Hundreds of millions of aid dollars have been expended, but most programs have produced modest results at best; in many cases, there is little to show. The appealing goals of state reform and state rebalancing that lie behind much of this work are largely unrealized in most democratizing countries. The state institutions of most of these countries remain corrupt and inefficient. They carry out their basic functions poorly and command little public respect.

Although the different kinds of institutions present specific challenges, democracy promoters have discovered that state institutions, as a general matter, are hard to change. Each institution is an entrenched subculture of its own, and resistance to reform is common to most of them. As discussed throughout the different sections of this chapter, this fact crops up again and again, in judiciaries, police forces, prosecutors offices, parliaments, executive branch ministries, local government bodies, and militaries, and for the same reasons: people working in the institutions perceive proposed reforms as potentially involving a loss of their own political and bureaucratic power; the giving up of licit or illicit perquisites, especially extra income from corruption; bigger workloads (when efficiency measures are implemented); the need to retrain and to master new areas of knowledge; acceptance of criticism and advice from foreign advisers; and in general, the loss of a protected, insular situation. The resistance may reside at the top levels of the institution but often it is present more quietly but just as stubbornly at the middle and lower levels.

Democracy promoters have stumbled frequently over the lack of embeddedness of their undertakings, the tendency of aid programs to fail to get truly inside the target institutions. As should be evident in reading this chapter, aid to state institutions, more than any other area of democracy assistance, often goes for formalistic activities that float on the surface of the recipient societies. State institutions present democracy promoters with tempting targets for over-designed, technically elaborate projects that make sense only in an idealized plan. Training courses and seminars reach countless employees of state institutions yet often fail to have much lasting effect. Administrative reforms are achieved through concentrated technical assistance but end up negated by persistent managerial failures. Oases of excellence flourish temporarily in troubled institutions, but dry up once the aid ends.

At times, the most basic elements of the assistance context, such as the psychological outlook of the people being helped, elude aid providers and subvert their programs. The Danish government, for example, has been sponsoring visits to Copenhagen by Nepalese parliamentarians so they can observe a democratic legislature at work. The idea of such visits is commonplace among aid providers from many countries. Yet when I asked a senior staff member of the Nepalese Parliament what he saw as the effects of these trips, a different view emerged. With every trip to a foreign parliament in an affluent country, he said, the members of Nepal's parliament are more impressed by the luxurious offices, cars, and fancy equipment, and they return to Nepal yet more determined to increase still further their own perquisites and benefits—or simply to steal more money—so that they can live like "real" parliamentarians.

Democracy promoters are discovering that not only do many state institutions harbor resistance to reform, but political leaders often fail to supply much positive impetus. Democracy promoters entered the fray in the late 1980s and early 1990s assuming that transitions to elections and multiparty politics would naturally stimulate the reform of state institutions, by bringing democratic reformers to power and subjecting governments to pressure for improved performance from engaged, scrutinizing publics. It turns out, however, even where the new leaders of transitional countries are genuine democrats—which is only sometimes the case—they often do not have a real interest in, or capacity for, the grudging task of institutional reform. Moreover, although publics are now able to vote governments out of power, the achievement of fine-grained institutional reform is rarely a key criterion when ballots are cast. People are likely to look to more immediately visible issues, such as economic results, that may well not correlate closely with progress on judicial reform, legislative strengthening, decentralization, or the other items on the democracy promoters' list. The average citizen in most transitional countries typically lacks the information necessary to make definitive judgments about the progress of institutional reforms, even if he or she is so inclined.

Democracy promoters' trying experiences in the realm of state institutions, though a process of discovery for them, correspond to the findings of political scientists and aid providers examining or working in social and economic domains for decades. There exists a well-established literature, which emerged in the 1970s as part of the renewed attention in academic circles to institutions under the rubric of the "new institutionalism" or the "new political economy," on the problematic public sectors of developing countries, and the difficulties of reform. These writings emphasize the same symptoms and causes that democracy promoters have been encountering in the institutions themselves. They also stress how hard it is to foster citizen-led impetus for change, even in democracies. Barbara Geddes, for example, highlights what she calls "the politician's dilemma"—the fact that politicians "have good reason to spend the resources they control in the distribution of individual benefits to important supporters rather than the pursuit of public goods to benefit external constituents."[37] She also identifies the collective action problem impeding citizen engagement for state reform: "Since individuals cannot be excluded from enjoying public goods such as bureaucratic reform, whether or not they helped organize movements to achieve them, ordinary citizens have no incentive to take the risks and expend the resources needed to organize."[38]

Democracy promoters have evidenced little awareness of this literature. They proceeded through the 1990s discovering the obstacles to institutional reform on their own. The disconnect is sometimes jarring. For example, in *Rediscovering Institutions*, a widely cited book published in 1989, James March and Johan Olsen make the following observation: "The political difficulties in changing political institutions are well documented. For example, the major deliberate reform of legislatures is rare, and virtually unknown in many Western democracies.''[39] This conclusion came just as democracy promoters were launching dozens of programs to strengthen legislatures around the world, fully believing that major institutional progress was in their grasp.

The gap between the literature on institutional reform and the work of democracy promoters is another part of the general gap between democracy promoters and academics mentioned in chapter 5. And to the extent democracy promoters were aware of this body of writings, they tended to discount its relevance to their work on two grounds. First, much of it focuses on the executive branch function of public administration rather than the nonexecutive branch institutions to which democracy promoters devote their attention. Second, the literature grew out of the experience of developing countries in the 1970s and 1980s, before democratization spread widely (though the Latin America–oriented works dealt with democratizing contexts); democracy promoters believed, as noted above, that much would be different in the context of democratization.

With the accumulation of experience, aid providers are beginning to respond, or at least adapt to, the challenges of aiding state institutions. To start with, aid providers are learning to ratchet down optimistic projections and are revising their notion of long-term change from five to ten years to several decades at a minimum. Embedding aid undertakings in the actual workings of the target institutions is never easy, but democracy promoters are at least becoming more aware of the need to try. Some are shifting to participatory design methods, or turning over the onus of designing reforms entirely to the people in the institutions, rather than bringing in outside experts or utilizing blueprints from abroad. As part of this process, some are learning the internal politics of the institutions, the unwritten rules, and the realities of who calls the shots. They are finding roles as long-term, low-profile internal management consultants who try to stimulate change from within, rather than recommend it from the outside. Such approaches force aid providers to invest more labor per aid dollar, to accept a slower pace of program implementation, and to cede control over projects to people in the target institutions—all changes that go against the bureaucratic grain.

After frequent encounters with resistance to reform inside state institutions, U.S. democracy promoters now speak readily about "political will" or "will to reform" and its crucial role in institution-building projects. Recognition of the importance of will to reform is overdue, yet democracy promoters are still learning what they can and cannot do about it. They must avoid a mechanical application, as though political will were easy to assess in a particular governing institution, either present or absent, like a switch that can only be on or off. A leader of an institution—a supreme court chief or speaker of a parliament—may intend to carry out broad institutional reforms but lack the support of either key colleagues, such as the minister of finance who must approve the funds for the reform program, or of the rank and file in the institution in question. Moreover, "will to reform" misleadingly implies that the meaning of "reform" is clear and widely agreed on. But in any institution there are likely hundreds of different ideas about what reforms would be desirable, how deep they should reach, how quickly they should be implemented, and who should lead them. Thus many individuals within an institution may have a will to reform in a general sense but disagree strongly over particular reforms and determinedly frustrate each other's reform efforts.

If the political will for reform within an institution is weak, staying away is sometimes the best response, but this depends on the reasons for the weak will. If the will to reform reflects simply a lack of interest by top politicians in working to improve an institution, well-crafted aid interventions may awaken an interest in change. Providing aid in such circumstances requires considerable tactical skill, as well as the avoidance of falling back on the too-easy assumption that just by being engaged, aid providers will generate support for reform. If the lack of will to reform reflects the active desire of powerholders to prevent or co-opt changes in an institution for their own narrow benefit, aid providers are unlikely to be able to do much about it.[40]

In reaction to the problem of lack of will to reform and the generally hard road of top-down approaches to promoting institutional reform, aid providers have increasingly supported work from the bottom up. With each of the institutions reviewed in this chapter, aid providers started with a focus on aiding the institution itself, then over time began supporting NGOs that seek to pressure institutions for greater accountability and to stir up citizen interest in state reform. As discussed in the next chapter, aid for civil society has wrinkles of its own, and fostering broad, sustained citizen interest in state reform is in most cases extremely difficult. Nonetheless, this expanded focus is a positive development. By working with state institutions' connections to the public rather than just the institutions' internal processes, aid providers are getting beyond the tendency to treat state institutions as self-contained entities and increasing the democratic character of such work.

In closing this chapter, it should be noted that the World Bank and the regional multilateral development banks, and even the International Monetary Fund, are now taking an interest in institution building in the countries where they work. In the mid-1990s, some influential economists articulated the view that institution building was central to the second stage of market reform, the first stage having focused on macroeconomic measures to achieve fiscal stabilization and liberalization. Developing market economies cannot do without the state altogether. They require efficient tax collection, banking supervision, antitrust enforcement, customs services, and other regulatory and administrative functions.[41] The Asian financial crisis of 1997–1998 reinforced this view by highlighting weak banking regulation and other deficient institutional functions as central elements of crony capitalism.

The multilateral development banks previously concentrated their institution-building work on executive branch functions, but they are now also taking on judicial reform, legislative strengthening, and decentralization. Their aim is to promote improved governance, not democracy; the World Bank emphasizes that it is not allowed to pursue explicit political objectives. Yet the core attributes they support—greater transparency, accountability, and efficiency— overlap substantially with the goals of democracy programs targeting state institutions. For bureaucratic reasons, the two worlds of institution building—those of the democracy promoters and of the market reformers—have been somewhat separate. Yet as the two groups proceed, they are starting to coordinate their efforts in particular countries and even to combine forces. The multilateral development banks have no silver bullets for institution building. If anything, they have an even greater tendency than democracy promoters to sponsor elaborate institutional designs created by external consultants and to rely on formalistic, top-down methods. Nonetheless, they are confronting the same obstacles as democracy promoters and responding with the familiar elements of greater attention to the politics of reform and the need to involve nongovernmental organizations. This convergence on institution building by democracy promoters and market reformers can work to their mutual benefit if both sides recognize the opportunity and make additional efforts to work together and learn from one another.

8
From the Bottom Up: Civil Society

Before the 1990s the term "civil society" was rarely used by U.S. aid providers and policy makers. Since then however, it has become a fashionable concept whose invocation is nearly obligatory in any document or discussion about democratization. Aid programs explicitly directed at "strengthening civil society" have grown more and more common, and are now part of U.S. democracy aid portfolios in most countries. The United States is scarcely alone in this regard. Many other donor countries, as well as private aid organizations, have embraced the concept and established corresponding programs. On the other side, in the transitional societies, agile seekers of aid funds have learned to cast themselves and their ambitions in terms of civil society.

THE "DISCOVERY" OF CIVIL SOCIETY

The rise of civil society assistance as an element of U.S. democracy aid has several causes. The first, and possibly most important, is the growing persuasiveness of the idea of civil society itself. The current keen interest in this venerable but for many generations almost forgotten concept was stimulated by the dissident movements in Eastern Europe in the 1980s, particularly in Poland and Czechoslovakia. The rise of these movements, and their triumph in 1989, fostered the appealing idea of civil society as a domain that is nonviolent but powerful, nonpartisan yet prodemocratic, and that emerges from the essence of particular societies yet is nonetheless universal. In the same decade, the idea of civil society gained currency in South America also. In Chile, Brazil, Argentina, and elsewhere in the region, civil society—especially as expressed in the human rights movement—came to be conceived of as both a special preserve of democratic values in the face of authoritarianism and an alternative to the dead ends of Marxist revolution and right-wing dictatorship. With the fall of the Berlin Wall, the resurgence of democracy in Latin America, and the explosion of democratic transitions world-wide, civil society catapulted to a new prominence. Western academics and commentators embraced the concept, producing an out-pouring of conferences, seminars, books, and articles exploring every aspect of the subject. Aid practitioners began to familiarize themselves with it, exploring how to go about promoting civil society and adding it to the checklist of core features of democracy making up their template for democracy programming.

The experience of democracy aid in the late 1980s and early 1990s reinforced the newfound interest in civil society promotion. When they first sought to bolster democratic transitions, U.S. democracy promoters focused on elections. After breakthrough elections in many countries had been held, their second instinct was to turn to the reform of state institutions. Yet as chapter 7 argues, many democracy aid efforts directed at state institutions have been frustrated by the magnitude of the problems encountered and the lack of interest in reform within the target institutions. This experience prompted democracy promoters to turn to civil society assistance both as a way of stimulating external pressures for reform on stagnant state institutions and as an alternative, more accessible, and welcoming target for aid than state institutions.

The arrival in office of the Clinton administration bolstered this inclination toward civil society work. Conservatives in the Reagan and Bush administrations had been friendly to the concept of civil society in the context of anticommunist struggles in Eastern Europe and the Soviet Union. They had been wary of it in developing countries, where the idea of "people power" was often closely associated with leftist political movements. American liberals, in contrast, were much more comfortable with the general idea of bottom-up political development in all parts of the world. Many of the people who entered the foreign policy bureaucracy in the Clinton years, particularly at USAID, themselves came from the NGO community, and they gravitated instinctively toward an NGO focus for democracy assistance.

A final factor, banal but significant, also contributed to the rise of civil society assistance. The major reduction in the overall U.S. foreign aid budget in the first half of the 1990s created intense pressure on aid officials to do more with less. Civil society assistance generally entailed smaller budgets than projects involving the reform of major state institutions. And funding citizen activism seemed to hold out the promise of a low-cost way to achieve large-scale effects. Thus civil society programs grew as aid budgets shrank.

As a concept, civil society represents a broad domain—the space in a society between individuals and families, on one hand, and the state or government, on the other. Although scholars debate the exact definition of the concept, there is a fair amount of consensus around a view of civil society that excludes private business and the formal political sector (what some call "political society") but is otherwise fairly inclusive. Gordon White defines it as

> an associational realm between state and family popu-
> lated by organizations which are separate from the
> state, enjoy autonomy in relation to the state and are
> formed voluntarily by members of society to protect
> or extend their interests or values.[1]

Incorporated in this definition are a wide range of groups, associations, and networks that span many dualities, including those between

> 'modern' interest groups such as trade unions or pro-
> fessional associations and 'traditional' ascriptive orga-
> nizations based on kinship, ethnicity, culture or region;
> between formal organizations and informal social net-
> works based on patrimonial or clientalistic allegiances;
> between those institutions with specifically political
> roles as pressure or advocacy groups and those whose
> activities remain largely outside the political system,
> between legal or open associations and secret or illegal
> organizations such as the Freemasons, the Mafia or the
> Triads; between associations which accept the political
> status quo or those who seek to transform it.[2]

Given the breadth of the concept, efforts to support the development of civil society in transitional countries could in theory reach across quite a number of organizations, associations, and collectivities. In practice, however, they have not. U.S. civil society programs carried out under a democracy rubric have focused on a limited part of the broad fabric of civil society in most recipient countries: nongovernmental organizations dedicated to advocacy for what aid providers consider to be sociopolitical issues touching the public interest—including election monitoring, civic education, parliamentary transparency, human rights, anticorruption, the environment, women's rights, and indigenous people's rights.[3] Three other areas of U.S. democracy assistance—civic education, media assistance, and aid to labor unions—also represent efforts for the development of civil society, though when U.S. aid providers use the term "civil society assistance" they are usually referring specifically to their work with advocacy NGOs.

U.S. civil society assistance that is part of democracy promotion portfolios typically does not reach a number of significant parts of civil society: 1) major established social or socioeconomic organizations such as churches and labor unions (U.S. civil society aid goes to some religious organizations, but only sporadically; unions are often targets of democracy aid, but under different programs than civil society assistance); 2) social and cultural groups such as sports clubs, nature clubs, music societies, sewing clubs, and the like; 3) informal groups based on social identity, such as clans, ethnic associations, tribal groups, peasant associations, and others; and 4) the large class of NGOs in most transitional societies that provide socioeconomic services or that seek to promote socioeconomic development, such as volunteer health clinics, agricultural cooperatives, tenants associations, community development organizations, child welfare societies, and many others.

Aid officials have in fact begun to call the advocacy NGOs they support under civil society programs "civil society organizations," misleadingly implying that these few, usually rather new and specialized organizations represent the core or even the bulk of civil society in the countries in question. It has become common for U.S. aid officers in transitional countries, describing the activities of the few NGOs they are funding, to say grandly, "Civil society has decided to do this" or "Civil society disagrees with the government on that." Thus, as few as one or two dozen people who happen to have close relations with the donors are thus characterized as deciding and acting for the entire civil society of the country.

This chapter primarily examines aid to advocacy NGOs, the main form of U.S. assistance to civil society, although it includes analyses of the three other main types of democracy aid that flow to civil society—civic education assistance, media assistance, and aid for labor unions. The focus throughout is on the frequent gap between the expectations of aid providers and the realities of civil society development in transitional countries. This is an issue of special importance in this domain because aid providers and others have puffed up civil society into a gleaming ideal, investing it with unusually high expectations in the role they have assigned it, that of a key to democratization. The chapter also stresses issues previously highlighted in discussions of other areas of democracy aid, including the export of particular institutional models, the difficulty of changing underlying interest structures and power relationships, and the gradual incorporation of lessons from experience.

ADVOCACY NGOs

The tendency of U.S. civil society assistance to concentrate on advocacy NGOs from among the many other elements of civil society in transitional countries is based in part on the belief that they can serve critical prodemocratic functions. They are supposed to articulate citizens' interests, serving as the proverbial "transmission belt" between the populace and the government. Aid providers hope such groups will increase citizens' participation in public affairs and themselves be models of democratic methods and values. They are also supposed to provide an impetus for better government performance—by holding the state accountable to norms and standards, pushing specific reform ideas, and supplying the government with technical advice and help on designing and implementing particular policies. U.S. aid providers generally see these various functions as a mix of good things that complement each other and that should be pursued in most situations to the greatest extent possible.

Advocacy NGOs also appeal to U.S. democracy promoters because of the character of their work and their culture. They stimulate public participation yet channel it around discrete issues, such as anticorruption or human rights, that are not necessarily linked to any one partisan ideology. This presumed nonpartisanship is critical—it allows donors to feel that they are engaging deeply in the political life of the recipient society without engaging in party politics. Among other traits endearing advocacy NGOs to U.S. and other Western donors, they highlight technocratic knowledge rather than bombastic propaganda, seek dialogue rather than confrontation, and are typically staffed by young, up-and-coming, Western-oriented professionals rather than older, well-entrenched pols of the political parties and unions. Aid providers often imagine the advocacy NGO sector as a pristine domain, free of the murky ties and tensions of ethnicity, class, clan, and political partisanship that make the political fabric so messy and difficult to deal with.

Moreover, many of the other types of organizations of civil society in most transitional countries are difficult for U.S. aid providers to support. Churches or other religious organizations are tremendously important actors in civil society in many countries, but not ones the U.S. government can easily aid in many cases due to sensitivities about the U.S. government funding religious organizations and the hesitancy of those organizations about taking U.S. government funds. Tribal associations and clan groups are apt to be nebulous, have unclear purposes from Washington's point of view, and often do not want U.S. backing. In short, it is not just that advocacy groups have clear links to processes of political change; they are the easiest for donors to fund. They are more likely to be willing to accept foreign support, to have professionalized organizational structures that match funders' bureaucratic needs, and to articulate their goals in terms funders can understand and accept.

Although the idea of nonpartisanship is a common guiding notion behind U.S. civil society programs, such assistance clearly often reflects the application abroad of the basic U.S. domestic liberal agenda—support for human rights, the environment, women, indigenous people, and so forth. Rarely within such programs does one find aid going to a women's group that opposes abortion, a citizens group working to have the death penalty instituted, or a business association seeking relaxed environmental laws. Aid providers say that the advocacy NGOs they support are pursuing the public interest, but the public interest is interpreted very much in accordance with the worldview of the U.S. NGO community from which come most U.S. enthusiasts of civil society promotion abroad.

The emphasis on advocacy in U.S. civil society assistance differs from the concept of "social capital" developed by Robert Putnam in his seminal work on civil society in Italy, although boosters of civil society aid often cite Putnam as support for their approach.

Social capital, according to Putnam, refers to "features of social organization, such as trust, norms, and networks, that can improve the efficiency of society by facilitating coordinated actions."[4] Putnam does not emphasize advocacy groups in his examination of the kinds of associations in civil society that generate social capital, but rather civic associations that entail "intense horizontal interaction," such as "neighborhood associations, choral societies, cooperatives, sports clubs, mass-based parties, and the like."[5] Although U.S. aid providers have nothing against choral societies, sports clubs, or other forms of civic association that do not do much advocacy work, they are not inclined to devote aid funds to them, in the belief that such groups are a less direct route to strengthening democracy than advocacy organizations.

Two forms of aid dominate assistance to advocacy NGOs. The first is technical assistance—training, advice, and information about organizational development and management, advocacy methods, fund raising, issue analysis, and media relations. Advocacy training has become a minor subculture in the aid world, with legions of young Americans, usually with experience of doing civic activism in the United States, going off to the four corners of the globe to teach foreigners how to frame a policy issue, plan an advocacy campaign, write grant proposals, generate a publicity campaign, marshal the necessary policy analysis, draft laws, and make a persuasive case to government officials. They convey more than just a set of specific tools, but rather a broader sense of mission about public interest advocacy.

The second form of support for advocacy NGOs is direct funding, including the provision of equipment, particularly computers, fax machines, and photocopiers. USAID provides both types of assistance although it has emphasized training and technical assistance over direct grants. The private groups operating with U.S. government funds, the NED, the Asia Foundation, and the Eurasia Foundation, have put much more emphasis on direct grants.

U.S. providers also pursue other aid methods. Sometimes they try to organize coalitions of NGOs in recipient countries to tackle particular issues with a broad front. In Romania in the mid-1990s, for example, U.S. advisers to some of the human rights and civic groups pushed for the formation of a coalition to advocate for greater parliamentary transparency. In Nepal in the late 1990s, an in-country

NDI representative tried to build a coalition of NGOs to lobby against corruption. They also attempt to strengthen the legal frameworks within which NGOs operate. Many countries began their transition with restrictive legal frameworks for independent associations, hold-overs from the nondemocratic past designed to prevent the establishment of independent NGOs. A whole new body of civil society assistance has developed around this issue, with the elaboration of model NGO laws and a great deal of information-sharing about the subject across countries and regions.

Development versus Democracy Groups

The recent "discovery" of NGOs by democracy promoters is by no means donors' first encounter with NGOs. With the rise of the basic human needs approach to development aid in the 1970s, donors began emphasizing concepts such as participatory development, community development, and local development, and channeled increasing amounts of aid through both international and local NGOs. Donors' growing emphasis on these issues continued in the 1980s and 1990s, fueling an enormous growth in service NGOs and development NGOs in developing countries. It also stimulated a growing body of analysis and writing about NGOs and their role in development and in development aid.[6] Donors and international NGOs working with local NGOs on development projects did not initially push an advocacy or democracy role for such groups. The view rather was that in societies with dysfunctional, usually authoritarian governments, it was often better simply to try to go around government and to pursue self-help methods. For the social and economic side of development, working with NGOs was thus often a means of avoiding governments rather than engaging them.

When U.S. democracy promoters began in the early 1990s to focus on civil society development through politically oriented NGOs, they proceeded independently of the larger world of NGO development and assistance that had unfolded in preceding years. If one visited a USAID mission in the mid-1990s and received a briefing from the democracy officer on the agency's civil society work in that country—usually involving a small circle of advocacy NGOs and civic education organizations—he or she would likely have made no reference to the many NGO-related projects being carried out by other parts of the aid program, relating to health, agriculture, and population, for instance. The two NGO worlds—democracy NGOs and development NGOs—were treated as separate domains. But as discussed in the section below on the current trend among U.S. civil society promoters to "go local," these different worlds of NGO assistance are slowly beginning to intersect.

NGO Boom

Some transitional countries, primarily in Latin America, have had an active NGO sector for many years, even before their transitions to democratic rule. In both South America and Central America, groups known as popular organizations—farmers organizations, community associations, unions, teachers organizations—mobilized resistance to autocratic governments. With the advent of democracy in the region these groups have been adapting to the new political context, attempting to shift from the tactic of *denuncia* (condemnation) to that of *propuesta* (proposal). As U.S. democracy promoters have turned to civil society aid in the 1990s, they have entered NGO sectors in some recipient countries that are already populated with many groups, and that have complex political histories.

In many other transitional countries, however, in Eastern Europe, the former Soviet Union, sub-Saharan Africa, and Asia, independent advocacy NGOs were scarce during the periods of nondemocratic rule. In these countries, aid from the United States and other Western donors in the 1990s has fueled an NGO boom. Despite the huge social and economic differences among these countries the basic patterns of these booms have been strikingly similar. At the time of a country's initial political opening and first-time elections, a burst of development occurred. In the capital, dozens of small but intense and active groups sprang into being, focusing on issues such as election monitoring, human rights advocacy, and civic education. Soon hundreds, even thousands, of groups emerged, the array of their concerns broadening to include many social and economic issues alongside political ones.

Today, some ten years after the initial transitions, the multiplication of NGOs has plateaued. At the core of the NGO world in most countries is a small, relatively ingrown circle of several dozen advocacy groups focused on human rights, civic education, women's issues, the environment, media monitoring, and other democracy-related themes. They are almost entirely funded by donors. Their leaders are young and Western-oriented persons who speak English and are also fluent in the new international lingo of civil society. These leaders have some ties to political parties but are not part of the traditional class of political party leaders and have weak ties to the unions, the national professional associations, churches, and the other more traditional nongovernmental organizations. Among them are a few stars who have become well-known figures on the national scene and are darlings of the Western donors. The much larger set of NGOs beyond the inner circle is a more heterogeneous collection of smaller groups involved in civic advocacy and civic education outside the capital, with much less access to foreign funding, weaker organizational structures, and agendas dominated by issues of local rather than national concern. With support from donors, the privileged NGOs from the capital are engaged in training and other assistance to help the second circle strengthen its advocacy skills and organizational structures.

In most transitional societies, the NGO boom has had a number of effects that have worked to advance democracy. Election monitoring organizations, for example, have helped discourage electoral fraud and have provided reliable information about the manner in which various elections were administered. Human rights groups have kept up the pressure on government to respect political and civil rights and helped ensure that human rights protections are incorporated into new laws as they are drafted. Media watchdog organizations and groups focusing on corruption, government transparency, and judicial reform have forced some officials to pay attention to these issues and have raised the awareness of at least some citizens.

Above and beyond their accomplishments in the specific issue areas on which they work, the advocacy NGOs have usually contributed to democratization in broader ways. They have been a channel for talented young people who wanted to become involved in public affairs but were alienated from political parties dominated by entrenched factions and stale partisan debates. NGO work has provided hands-on leadership and management training for many— skills that are transferable to many other domains. The local NGOs have linked up with international NGO networks—such as those for human rights, women, and the environment—bringing new ideas and resources into the country. They have given donors new points of entry into their society, alongside the more familiar but often routinized contacts with state institutions.

Women's NGOs are often the most impressive sector of the advocacy NGO world in transitional societies. They have multiplied with particular rapidity across many different regions. The commitment of their leaders and members is often strong, especially compared with those at some advocacy NGOs, who seem to learn their lines from donor instruction manuals. Women's NGOs often seem better able to connect to an extensive constituency than most other NGOs, and to bridge the urban-rural gap so common in the NGO world. They take up issues of immediate interest to their constituents, and their agenda naturally synthesizes economic, political, and social concerns. It is still difficult to predict the results of the extremely widespread but still nascent consciousness-raising that they are fomenting in newly democratizing societies around the world. But it is clear that many democratic openings, no matter how partial or problematic, have opened the door to changes in the role of women that may have profound positive consequences over the long run.

Corruption, Sustainability, and Other Problems

Though a positive sign, the rapid increase in advocacy NGOs in transitional countries has many limitations as a form of civil society development. For starters, in many countries the flood of Western funds for such organizations has produced too much or the wrong kinds of growth. The money attracts many opportunists and sharks alongside the genuine activists. NGO work becomes a lifestyle for some, rather than a cause. And in transitional societies where the economic situation is bleak it is often a relatively comfortable lifestyle compared with alternatives. Corruption within NGOs sometimes occurs, a fact that U.S. and other donor representatives working directly with NGOs allude to frequently in private.[7] Some NGOs pad expense reports, carry fictitious employees on the books, draw multiple salaries from multiple funders, and generally take advantage of the often overrich funding environment. Such corruption is bad in and of itself but it also breeds resentment of NGOs within the government, political parties, and the public. NGO workers are often seen by others in the country as an arrogant, overpaid, and self-interested sector. In Nepal, for example, bad NGO practices growing out of too many donor funds chasing too few worthwhile organizations in the capital have led many Nepalese to hold NGOs in contempt.

European donors, especially the Nordic countries, inspired by the idea of North-South solidarity, often require little accountability with the money they give NGOs. When, occasionally, they look carefully at how the funds are used, the picture is often not pretty. A Danish aid representative in Nepal, for example, told me how an audit of a large (approximately $1 million) grant to a Nepalese NGO discovered that the funds had been seriously misused, mainly to line the pockets of the NGO leaders. He expressed shock that the Nepalese involved had been so greedy with the grant their organization had received. But when asked about the outcome of this incident, he replied that his organization had given a new grant to the same NGO but that this time they were going to watch more carefully.

U.S. groups on the whole keep a closer eye on the money given to local groups than do most European donors, both because of stricter auditing practices and for fear of aid scandals that would supply congressional skeptics with ammunition in their battle to cut foreign aid still more. Yet problems arise, even so. Just one example: a USAID-funded American organization working on the women's empowerment project in Nepal hired eight Nepalese NGOs to carry out some of the training and insisted on auditing all eight groups afterwards. Every one was found to have misused funds, some seriously. In this case, all the groups involved were taken off the list for future projects.

A second problem is participation. Aid providers like to think of advocacy NGOs as groups that foster a great deal of citizen participation, but in practice that is often not the case. Many of the newly formed advocacy NGOs based in the capitals of transitional countries have a weak popular base. They are "of civil society," but are actually elite associations formed by small circles of people possessing expert knowledge. Their advocacy often relies much less on public mobilization or involvement than on expert-based persuasion directed at government officials. Exceptions exist, such as environmental groups that carry out broad public campaigns, but even groups concerned with civic education often attempt to educate the public without involving it in the work of the organization. The notion, therefore, that merely by supporting the proliferation of advocacy NGOs donors are fostering much greater participation in transitional societies is less true than donors usually think.

One illustration of the artificiality of the putatively participatory work of U.S.-funded civil society groups is the case of the Foundation for Democratic Progress in Zambia. FODEP was formed in the early 1990s as an outgrowth of U.S.-supported domestic election monitoring efforts. It became the central element of USAID's strategy for building civil society in Zambia in the 1990s, receiving hundreds of thousands of dollars worth of training and direct financial support. Despite intensive financial, managerial, and administrative aid from the United States, FODEP failed to become the community-oriented, activist civic education group that the U.S. aid providers felt Zambia needed. A USAID evaluation of the foundation concluded in 1997 that there was no evidence that FODEP "has served in any serious way to provide civic education at the community level."[8] The evaluation critically analyzed FODEP's basic method:

> Another weak point in FODEP's operation is that it cannot run successful workshops for its "volunteers" unless attendees receive a sitting allowance, a per diem, and a transportation subsidy. The total payments are approximately $8.00 a day excluding transportation. In many cases, the workshop participants earn more from FODEP events than they earn for a day's work. FODEP staff are not happy about these payments but indicate that this was the general pattern for most so-called 'advocacy' organizations in Zambia. USAID provides the funds by which these payments are made. If USAID decided not to fund workshops, FODEP would collapse as an organization. This patronage in the form of sitting allowances and per diems creates the active membership. In essence, the agents of democratic change must operate within the same patrimonial political culture within which the politicians operate: provide gifts to your clients for their support.[9]

A further concern about U.S. civil society assistance is the issue of sustainability, lately much discussed in the world of donors and recipients. A large percentage of the NGOs that the United States and other donors have funded in the name of strengthening civil society are almost entirely dependent on foreign financial support and would fold if it became unavailable. In their rush to provide civil society assistance in the wake of democratic openings, U.S. aid officials tended not to think much about sustainability. They were intent on getting the aid going and nurturing groups into being, not worrying about how those groups would support themselves in the long run. As the field matured, with NGOs multiplying and aid money beginning to level off or dry up, sustainability emerged as a pressing issue, at a very late stage for some groups.

In Zambia, for example, only in the final six months of its five-year aid commitment did USAID sponsor a workshop for FODEP staff on methods of self-sustainability. Shocked FODEP leaders were unwilling to believe that USAID was ending its support, having concluded from the constant references by USAID representatives to the agency's "partnership" with FODEP that their funding was secure. After USAID stopped the aid, FODEP shrank considerably. It managed to obtain some money from Scandinavian donors but still has not developed any significant domestic source of funds. FODEP officials now harbor a deep bitterness toward USAID; despite the five years of extensive support, FODEP leaders ended up feeling mistreated by the United States.

The reaction of U.S. aid officials to the problem of NGO sustainability varies. Some believe that the democracy-oriented NGOs are part of the initial political transitions and are not "meant" to last long. Or they say flatly that sustainability is not their concern, that it is the up to the NGOs to take care of themselves once the donors move on. Some aid providers talk a great deal about helping local NGOs "diversify funding sources," but what they actually mean is getting other donors to pick up the tab. The underlying problem of long-term sustainability is merely deferred.

Some aid officials, as well as both international and local NGO specialists, have explored the methods by which NGOs in transitional countries can raise money within their own society. The difficulties are usually great: membership fees or personal contributions are difficult to collect or attract; corporate sponsorship is often not available due to lack of incentives, traditions, or sources; charging fees for services or publications usually proves a limited source. Success stories do exist and "local resource mobilization," as it is called, can sometimes at least partially replace funding from outside donors.[10] Yet the NGO model pushed by U.S. civil society assistance simply may not be appropriate as a generalized approach to building civil society in many transitional countries. The professionalized NGO model comes out of a society that has wealthy, private grant-making foundations, a large middle class with considerable discretionary income, and a corporate world with a tradition of philanthropy. The model does not do well in societies with none of those characteristics.

The Illusion of Nonpartisanship

The issue of nonpartisanship among advocacy NGOs is also difficult. In authoritarian and semiauthoritarian countries or where Washington does not like the government, support for advocacy NGOs is often given with the expectation that those groups will play an oppositional role. This oppositional approach to civil society assistance is dealt with in a separate section below. In countries where a transition to democracy is advancing and genuine multiparty politics seem to be getting under way, U.S. civil society aid frequently emphasizes the value of nonpartisanship. Advocacy NGOs are expected to be politically *engaged*, in the sense of tackling issues that concern government policies, but *nonpartisan*—that is to say, not affiliated with or working to advance any particular political camp. Aid providers do sometimes cite as a benefit of civil society assistance that NGOs can be a training ground for new politicians, but the hope is that the NGOs themselves will not be narrow vehicles for the political agendas of particular parties or politicians.

The emphasis that U.S. democracy promoters put on nonpartisanship reflects their view that the advocacy issues favored by U.S. civil society programs, such as human rights, anticorruption, and government accountability, are universal values rather than partisan issues. It also stems from the somewhat mythic conception of nonpartisanship they often bring from the NGO world in the United States: the notion that there is a clear line between nonpartisan advocacy and partisan politics. U.S. aid providers shake their heads disapprovingly when NGOs in transitional countries turn out to be linked to political parties or when NGO leaders turn out to have what aid providers disparagingly call "a personal agenda"—as though U.S. groups working to promote civil rights, the environment, or women's rights never involve themselves in party politics, support candidates, openly take sides, or serve as vehicles for the advancement of their leaders.

Nonpartisanship is indeed difficult to achieve in advocacy NGOs and other types of groups in civil society in transitional countries. In many countries embarking or reembarking on multiparty politics, elites are intensely politicized (even while the general public quickly slides into deep apathy about political life). Parties compete ferociously to distinguish themselves, to capture resources and levers of influence, and to line up local elites on their side. There is little room for neutrality under such circumstances. And when the political parties are bound together by densely woven loyalties based on personal allegiances, clan networks, and ethnic divisions, neutrality becomes elusive. In Nepal, for example, posttransitional politics have been marked—many would say hobbled—by frantic politicization in which the three main parties fight constantly over everything, no matter how small. All NGOs in Nepal, not just advocacy groups but also NGOs that provide services (such as those running health clinics or child welfare programs), are under intense pressure in this charged environment to develop party allegiances. A few manage a certain independence, but most do not. In Guatemala, the advocacy NGO sector developed in the 1980s as one form of resistance to the military dictatorships, and was part of the deep struggle in that country between Left and Right. With the end of the civil war and the advance of multiparty politics, the NGO sector is becoming less overtly political, but it is a slow process, given the powerful legacy of ideological struggle.

The Benevolent Tocquevillean Vision

Serious questions can also be raised about the benevolent Tocquevillean vision underlying U.S. assistance to civil society: a society in which ordinary citizens are engaged in all sorts of cross-cutting civic participation, with thousands of earnest, diligent civic groups working assertively but constructively to help ensure that a reluctant government gradually becomes responsive to citizens' needs and sheds its habits of indolence and corruption. In the first place, it is an inordinately American vision: it is not even widely shared by other established democracies. The structure and role of civil society in some continental democracies, particularly France, is very different from the Tocquevillean ideal, with much more government funding of NGOs and much less advocacy work by independent NGOs than American civil society enthusiasts think proper or normal. And, with developing countries, one doubts the possibility of creating high levels of civic participation and thousands of active advocacy groups in societies in which the bulk of the people are mired in poverty and powerful sociopolitical forces work to keep them marginalized. It is also hard to imagine the profoundly flawed states of many developing countries, especially in Africa but also in much of Latin America and parts of Asia, undergoing anytime soon the profound reforms that would allow them to deliver the response envisioned with the notion of mass civic participation.

Moreover, the vision's assumptions about advocacy—that it is a benign expression of interests by citizens, and that the more advocacy the better—are questionable. There is no assurance, as aid providers seem to think, that training legions of people as advocates (the words "lobbyist" and "lobbying" are never used in such programs) and ensuring that the national and local governments are fully open to advocacy will lead to the predominance of wholesome public interests. A lobbying culture is just as likely to reinforce the dominance of powerful private interests that learn to use the paths opened by civic activists and then outweigh those activists by dint of resources and persistence. Again, mythic thinking about the United States appears to be at work. It seems almost as if aid providers are willfully denying the fact that the U.S. Congress, whose openness to influence by interest groups serves a model in U.S. aid programs, is influenced most by powerful business interests, not public interest NGOs. Paradoxically, U.S. aid providers hold out as truth around the world that advocacy by citizens will help correct government's deficiencies in accountability and representation. Yet in the United States, the distortions wreaked by lobbyists on the accountability and representativity of Congress and state legislatures provoke calls for deep-reaching reforms.

As NGO development proceeds in some transitional countries, NGOs representing business interests are clearly becoming more powerful relative to public interest NGOs. The most effective part of the NGO sector in Romania is the growing set of NGOs that represent businesses, such as the National Council of Small and Medium Enterprises. Unlike the public interest NGOs, these groups have their own domestic sources of funding (membership dues from businesses), a pool of talented, organized, energetic people to carry out their work, and above all, advocacy methods with teeth, such as member businesses pressuring the government on an issue by refusing to pay their taxes. Similarly, in Zambia, the NGOs that have most influence on government policy and the legislative process are not the human rights and democracy NGOs but the National Association of Manufacturers and other business groups. In some countries USAID supports business NGOs as part of civil society programs, in the hope that they will become advocates of anticorruption, governmental reform, and rule-of-law development. The advocacy agenda of business groups in transitional societies is less high-minded in many cases, however, concentrating instead on measures specifically favorable to business, such as a low minimum wage, weak environmental laws, and minimal labor rights.

A Study in Contrasts

The mix of positive aspects and limitations of the U.S. approach of promoting civil society through support for advocacy NGOs plays out differently in different settings. The cases of Romania and Nepal present revealing contrasts. In Romania, the U.S. government actively assisted the fledgling advocacy NGO sector after the fall of Ceauşescu. Examining the development of that sector, the limits of such aid are readily apparent. Particularly in the early 1990s, many of the newly formed advocacy groups were elite operations dominated by intellectuals who had little feel or inclination for working with the public. The number of NGOs grew exponentially, with a tendency toward the creation of NGOs for the wrong reasons—the easy availability of donor funds, faddishness, and opportunism. The problem of sustainability haunts the sector, and few substantial NGOs have managed to find a strong domestic base.

At the same time, however, the advocacy NGO sector in Romania has played an important role in the democratization of the country. Despite a dominant party with weak adherence to democratic norms in the first half of the 1990s, advocacy groups, especially human rights organizations, helped keep open and expand the possibility of free expression. They voiced democratic values and principles, especially the right to question authority. Throughout the postcommunist period the advocacy NGOs have been a haven for energetic, talented people who want to help open up the country but prefer not to work through the troubled, divisive political parties. Many of these people have gained substantial leadership and organizational skills through their work, skills they have applied in increasingly sophisticated advocacy endeavors and in other domains, such as the media, business, and government. None of these effects was dramatic, and all were frequently overstated by NGOs eager to believe themselves central to Romania's democratization. Moreover, the U.S. aid to advocacy NGOs was but one contribution among many; assistance came from quite a few European public and private donors, as well as private U.S. foundations. The balance sheet for U.S. aid was nonetheless clearly positive.

Nepal is a different story. It also experienced rapid, unprecedented NGO development in the years after the 1990–1991 democratic opening. The U.S. government, in addition to the European donors active in Nepal, supported the burgeoning realm of advocacy groups in Kathmandu with the intention of helping build Nepal's civil society. Yet the accomplishments of these groups scarcely go beyond input into a few new laws and a good deal of nebulous "consciousness-raising" of the public.

Some of this weakness can be blamed on the various governments that have ruled Nepal since the transition. These, on the whole, have been ineffective and lethargic, which renders difficult NGOs' task of bringing about positive change through pressure on or cooperation with the government. The NGO sector itself, however, is clearly problematic. Far too many advocacy NGOs have been formed, many of them shells established for the primary purpose of absorbing the rich flow of funds for NGOs from donors that followed the transition. The sector as a whole has poor relations with all other major sectors of political life including the government, the parties, the media, business, and the donors, who have grown cynical about their own creations. The NGO sector is widely seen as overpaid, corrupt, and self-interested. Sustainability is a major issue. The sector depends almost entirely on foreign funding, and domestic sources of income that could support the nice offices, up-to-date computers, and well-paid staffs of the many NGOs are hard to identify in such a poor country. In less then ten years, a whole new sector of organizations—this low-performing set of advocacy NGOs—has sprung into being and established the same unhealthy aid dependency that afflicts the Nepalese government and society as a whole.

The Opposition Approach

As mentioned above, a variant of U.S. civil society assistance is support for advocacy NGOs as a form of opposition to a government that the United States believes is not committed to democracy—one that is either stagnating politically or actively sliding back toward authoritarianism. Such an approach may supplement a partisan stance involving support to opposition parties, as in some East European countries and former Soviet republics. Or it may be an alternative to a party-oriented partisan approach: aiding advocacy NGOs is less directly challenging to a government than aiding opposition parties and in some backsliding countries there are no viable opposition parties that can be supported.

The U.S. aid to Romanian advocacy NGOs in the first half of the 1990s was an example of supplementing a partisan approach with support to an NGO sector that aid providers believed was largely pro-opposition. The U.S. assistance to human rights groups, independent newspapers, democracy foundations, associations of intellectuals, press monitoring groups, and other independent organizations was key in the strategy of challenging the Iliescu government's rule and ensuring that political space widened rather than narrowed. In Zambia, U.S. (and European) aid to the scattering of democracy-related advocacy NGOs that sprang up after the 1991 transition became a lifeline for democracy promotion in the mid-1990s as President Chiluba reversed his democratic path and slipped into strongman rule. Aid providers hoped that these groups would serve as a source of organized resistance to the government and would preserve at least a modicum of political space on which others might eventually build. USAID followed the same approach in other backsliding African countries in the 1990s, such as Ethiopia and Kenya, as well as elsewhere in the world, including Central Asia and Southeastern Europe.

Where the problem is stagnation and indifference to democracy on the part of the ruling forces, aid to advocacy NGOs can make a positive contribution, as in Romania. Where the problem is backsliding led by entrenched political forces determined to subvert democracy and preserve their rule, however, the oppositional approach of civil society assistance is usually of limited utility. In Zambia, for example, President Chiluba has ridden roughshod over independent

NGOs that have tried to advocate democratic principles, such as when he persecuted those election monitoring groups that reported the shortcomings of the 1996 national elections. Some independent advocacy groups continue to operate, but they have not been able to counteract the negative trends in political life.

Advocacy NGOs generally face fundamental limitations that render them unable to make much headway against strongman rulers: they are small, usually fairly weak organizations; their advocacy tactics are based on the supposition of a rational government and do little against corrupt or closed workings of government; they typically have a limited popular base and scant ability to mobilize citizens against repression; and their near-exclusive reliance on foreign funding leaves them open to attack as agents of foreign influence. If the United States or other donors wanted to craft civil society programs that could actually produce powerful resistance to budding authoritarians, they would have to focus much more on social and political movements, an unpredictable, complex enterprise entirely different from the safe, rational world of technocratic NGOs. Such an approach would necessitate a depth of involvement in social and political life that would be extremely interventionistic, a long-term perspective completely unlike the short-term focus of most aid, and a probability of failure or unintended consequences far above that normally tolerated by donors.

Going Local

In the mid-1990s, U.S. aid providers began broadening their approach to civil society assistance, following a new one that can be characterized as "going local." They increasingly directed aid at advocacy groups outside the capitals of recipient countries, to what are usually smaller, sometimes less formalized groups that operate in provincial cities, towns, or villages. At the same time, they widened the ambit of advocacy issues from directly democracy-oriented topics to social and economic ones ranging from public health and social welfare to landlord-tenant relations and small business conditions. The local approach to civil society ties in with the increasing emphasis on local government on the state institution side of U.S. democracy assistance. The more local NGOs focus on local government as the natural arena for their advocacy, while U.S. aid programs increasingly focus on helping such groups and local government institutions work productively together. The previously mentioned New

Partnership Initiative at USAID, launched in 1995, pushes within the agency for a three-part "go local" approach in which USAID missions are encouraged to develop programs that simultaneously foster stronger local government, more active local advocacy NGOs, and small-business development.

The "going local" trend in U.S. civil society assistance reflects a natural evolution in U.S. aid methods. As democracy promoters engage with civil society, they confront the limitations of working with only a small set of national organizations. They respond by seeking to reach a wider range of groups on a greater number of issues. In most transitional countries, the gap between the political elite and the majority of the population is huge, and it quickly becomes obvious that a civil society development program must span the divide if it is to have lasting meaning. Although this broadening of civil society assistance involves a wider range of both issues and organizations, the attachment to advocacy remains: aid goes to NGOs that are smaller, based outside the capital, often pursuing social and economic goals rather than political ones, but that are still advocacy groups. As a result of its expanded reach, civil society assistance is beginning to converge with other aid programs, such as those relating to health, population, agriculture, and small-business development, where local development NGOs are engaged. A democracy promotion program helping build the advocacy skills of a tenants association may find itself doing similar work as an aid program concerned with housing development. The convergence occurs not just between U.S. democracy programs and U.S. social and economic development programs but with the work of international NGOs such as Oxfam and ActionAid working on grassroots development. Representatives of such groups often regard U.S. democracy aid with suspicion or disdain (assuming it is superpower neo-imperialism in action) and are surprised when they discover that the local organizations they are working with on poverty alleviation and community development are also taking part in U.S. democracy assistance programs. Such convergence is not yet extensive, but it is growing.

A look at the four case studies highlights some of the ways the "going local" approach in U.S. civil society programs is manifesting itself in different parts of the world. In Romania, the first phase of U.S. civil society assistance peaked in the mid-1990s. U.S. aid providers came to believe that Bucharest-based NGOs were saturated with donor funds and that civic development should be extended to the other parts of the country. A second phase more oriented toward the provinces got under way with the establishment of the Democracy Network Program, a regional effort funded by USAID to support local forms of civil society development across Eastern Europe. In Romania, the Democracy Network Program offers training and technical assistance to small Romanian NGOs working in smaller cities and towns on a range of advocacy areas, as well as groups involved with delivery of basic social services.

In Nepal, U.S. assistance for civil society also moved in the mid-1990s away from NGOs based in the capital to a much more local approach, focusing on women's empowerment. Under the program, Nepalese NGOs (overseen by American NGOs that receive the USAID funds) are providing training to tens of thousands of Nepalese women in small towns and villages. The training reflects a multifaceted approach to advocacy and empowerment. Each participant receives training in basic literacy, legal rights and advocacy, and economic rights and skills (particularly ones related to micro-enterprise development), the idea being that individual empowerment is rooted in both basic education and advocacy skills and that those skills must cut across social, political, and economic life. The evolution of the U.S. approach in Nepal reflects the tendency in several Asian countries for U.S. civil society assistance to go to the local level, to take on social and economic themes, and to link the democracy and the development agendas.

In Zambia, the first phase of U.S. civil society assistance, which was one component of the five-year democracy aid program launched in 1992, was a civic education program, run by FODEP, the Lusaka-based NGO discussed above. As the program developed, the USAID mission in Lusaka gave small grants to other Zambian groups, including ones outside the capital and urged FODEP to extend its work around the country as much as possible. When the mission formulated a second phase of democracy programs in the late 1990s, it attempted to broaden its civil society work to encompass advocacy on social and economic issues rather than the earlier emphasis on voter and civic education.

In Guatemala, USAID's civil society efforts have evolved from a badly executed phase in the mid-1990s in which a U.S. contractor whose knowledge of the country was poor oversaw some superficial civic education programs to a much more sophisticated undertaking to aid major Guatemalan advocacy NGOs working on women's issues, indigenous people's rights, and human rights in general. The program remains focused on the national organizations; attention in the democracy aid portfolio to NGOs at the local level is coming only as part of a local government program. The slower movement in the "going local" direction in Guatemala is typical of U.S. aid in Central and South America and reflects the fact that in Latin America, U.S. democracy assistance has been dominated by the top-down approach (a result of its origins in the politically polarized 1980s and U.S. officials' fear of empowering radicalized popular movements).

The "going local" trend has much to say for it. By moving away from the world of elite NGOs based in the capital into different levels of the social fabric of recipient countries, aid providers run less risk of sponsoring activities with little connection to the majority of the population. Taking on social and economic matters rather than keeping to a narrow range of often abstract "democracy issues" gets at the concerns that are of more immediate interest to people. Engaging local and municipal governments rather than just the national government can tie citizens to the government much more directly. In general, the local approach holds out the possibility of encouraging widespread participation in public affairs.

Despite these advantages, the local approach faces challenges and problems. Working at the local level is difficult for USAID and other aid organizations. Such work requires a more detailed, nuanced knowledge of the recipient society than aid projects directed only at the national level, knowledge that few people in the aid organizations are likely to have. The work also requires a much greater degree of bureaucratic flexibility. Giving assistance to small, informal civic groups requires greater nimbleness with small amounts of money and greater tolerance of the risk of misspent funds—qualities that are in short supply in the U.S. government.

The problem of sustainability does not go away just because the assistance moves to local rather than national NGOs. Whether the Western advocacy NGO model is well suited to poor societies remains an open question. The lack of domestic resources for such organizations is even more acute in villages than in capital cities, requiring aid providers to look harder for alternatives to the professional NGO model. Similarly, the assumption that heightened advocacy means wholesome public interests will predominate is just as suspect at the local level as the national. A system of local-level interest groups advocating their interests to local government institutions can easily be captured by powerful local elites, either large landowners or local business owners, unless considerable thought about local power structures goes into the design of aid efforts.

Finally, and perhaps most important, can locally oriented efforts to promote civil society actually change society? Many small, dedicated efforts to build civil society in the countryside are encouraging, and heartwarming, but it is far from certain that such efforts can add up to a powerful force for change. Many grassroots and community-based programs of the past twenty years in the development field have created oases of change that never connect with the society around them. It is logical to expect that the same may occur in the democracy field. A local approach to civil society assistance calls for greater modesty among aid providers about their ability to bring about large-scale change—a useful but difficult dictum for aid providers to accept.

CIVIC EDUCATION

Civic education has been a common element of U.S. democracy aid portfolios worldwide over the past fifteen years. The idea is to teach citizens of democratizing countries basic values, knowledge, and skills relating to democracy, with the objective of those citizens understanding how democracy works, embracing democracy as a political ideal, and becoming participatory citizens. Many civic education efforts have centered around elections in recipient countries, with teaching concentrated on the purpose of elections, the mechanics of voting, and the candidates and issues involved. These programs are usually one component of larger election assistance programs. Other civic education efforts focus more broadly on general democracy education, typically including information on human rights, constitutions, democratic procedures, and civic values. Some civic education is classroom based, incorporating new or revised civic education materials into primary, secondary, or adult education. Other programs use nontraditional or informal methods of instruction, which may consist of dramatization, role-playing, group forums, and other kinds of exercises. Still others are electronically based—television and radio shows that convey civic education messages.

Civic education has a strong appeal for Americans, because of the American idea that it is the collective democratic attitudes and values of the citizenry that are the bedrock of a democratic system. American aid providers and consultants frequently return from assessment missions in transitional countries with the accurate though not especially penetrating observation that people in the country "just don't understand democracy." The almost reflexive response is to set up civic education programs, in the belief that people can fairly rapidly be taught to understand democracy and that once they understand it they will embrace it and this will significantly advance democratization. That the American electorate exhibits often astonishing levels of civic ignorance—a recent survey revealed for example that 40 percent of American adults could not name the vice president—does not somehow shake the confidence of U.S. civic educators operating abroad.[11] The appeal of civic education also stems from the sustained efforts in cold war years to expose citizens of communist countries to the idea of democracy. Such efforts assumed that knowledge of democracy was a powerful agent that could produce large-scale resistance and uprisings against the communist governments. For believers in civic education as a tool of democratic revolution, 1989 confirmed their conviction. In the 1990s, U.S. democracy promoters pushed for civic education on democracy in Africa, Latin America, Asia, and elsewhere with the same conviction that knowledge about democracy could be an agent of transformation.

Although the appeal of civic education assistance is strong, the results are often disappointing. In many transitional countries, even in those parts of Latin America and Eastern Europe where democratization has gone relatively well, public belief in democracy stagnated during the 1990s, despite countless foreign-sponsored civic education projects. The experience of many civic education efforts points to one clear lesson: short-term formal instruction on democracy that presents the subject as a set of general principles and processes generally has little effect on participants. Such information is too abstract and usually too removed from the daily lives of most people. In many former dictatorships, people are deeply suspicious of anything that smacks of political propaganda, which some crudely designed democracy education programs do.

Moreover, civic education in many transitional countries is negated by the actual practice of politics. It is hard for people to accept that a national legislature is a valuable body with the important charge of representing their interests when they see every night on their televisions endless squabbling sessions of a corrupt, feckless parliament. Teaching them that elections are essential to democracy has little effect if the only elections they know are manipulated by a dominant party to entrench its power still further. When democracy promoters disseminate information about democracy to people in authoritarian countries, they are asking people to embrace an ideal that almost always compares favorably with the political realities at hand. When they operate in fledgling democracies, however, their challenge is in some ways more difficult: they are trying to sell the concept of democracy to many people who are disillusioned with the struggling democratic system they already have. In transitional countries where the new democratic system is doing well this is not so much of a problem, but in such circumstances new forms of education about democracy usually seem less needed.

The generally poor results of conventional civic education efforts were highlighted by an in-depth study, commissioned by USAID and carried out by a group of social scientists, on the impact of civic education programs in two countries, Poland and the Dominican Republic.[12] The researchers used a sophisticated sampling method to compare like groups of people either exposed and not exposed to a variety of typical U.S. civic education programs and to evaluate their levels of democratic participation, skills, and values. The study found limited impact on levels of political participation and knowledge (and even that limited effect faded markedly over time), and almost no effect on participants' values and skills. Similarly, a study of the effects of U.S. civic education activities in Zambia, by scholars who helped design and oversee the implementation of those activities, found that, "Civic education's effects are marginal, partly contradictory, and socially selective" (having no measurable impact except on relatively wealthy, well-educated Zambians).[13]

Better methods of civic education are gradually supplementing the conventional, formalistic methods that dominated U.S. civic education assistance from the mid-1980s into the early 1990s. The teaching materials now increasingly stress the practical application of civic values and knowledge rather than abstract principles. They are tailored to the realities of the societies where they are being used. Furthermore, active teaching methods, especially role-playing and group exercises, are employed more often. Thus, for example, the subject of police brutality might once have been addressed in a lecture on the legal rights of citizens in a democracy. In a more up-to-date program, it would be covered by presentation of some specific recent cases of police brutality in the local community, a discussion with a visiting police officer and a human rights activist, and possibly some role-playing exercises in which participants act out the different roles and learn strategies to minimize abuse. As civic education methods become more hands-on and applied, they become similar to training for advocacy that is a component of most aid programs for advocacy NGOs.

The cases of both Guatemala and Zambia exemplify many of the fundamentals of U.S. civic education assistance. In Guatemala, USAID has funded several undertakings since the mid-1980s, taking contrasting approaches to the subject. From 1987 to 1989, Guatemala was one of three Central American countries receiving civic education aid as part of the USAID-sponsored "Program of Education for Participation." Despite being an early undertaking relative to the overall wave of democracy assistance, this project had features of a later-stage civic education effort. It was intended for grassroots Guatemalan organizations, especially ones concerned with women; it sought to convey not abstractions about democracy but "a participatory nonformal education program that enables community organizations to define their problems and design action strategies;"[14] and its methods were hands-on rather than classroom instruction. The relatively evolved form of this project reflected its origins with some USAID officers in Washington who had experience in civic education stretching back to the 1960s, as well as their choice of an American intermediary with similarly extensive experience.

Several years after the end of that relatively small project (approximately 1,000 Guatemalans participated), the USAID mission in Guatemala initiated a new, larger civic education program. That program, which also lasted about two years, was quite different. The education was specifically designed "to motivate the people of Guatemala to participate in the electoral process." The instruction relied heavily on formal written materials, with titles seemingly drawn from a Chinese reeducation campaign of the 1960s—"All Guatemalans are Equal and Free," one pamphlet declared and another promised to show "How the State and Government is Organized to Protect

Our Lives and Work for the Development and the Good of All."[15] This project was viewed largely as a failure by the USAID mission due to the superficiality of the American intermediary's understanding of the local scene and the too-formal nature of both the basic message and the teaching methods.[16]

The USAID mission in Guatemala attempted to incorporate lessons from that bad experience when it designed further efforts to strengthen civil society in the late 1990s. Its new program focused on the development of advocacy NGOs, emphasizing educational content of relevance to local advocacy groups rather than abstract democratic ideology, and practical, learn-by-doing methods rather than the printing of many pamphlets and texts. The mission also strove to find an American project team with a commitment to immersing itself in the local milieu.

In Zambia, USAID geared up a major civic education project after the 1991 elections—which was primarily a five-year struggle to teach Zambians about the importance of voting and about the principles and practices of democracy in general. The project, carried out by FODEP, suffered at first from the artificiality of trying to teach abstract democracy lessons to a population of mainly poor and poorly educated citizens with little experience of political participation. It also faced the problem of a local environment that worked against it. Much of the teaching about the value of elections was intended to encourage citizens to participate in the 1996 national elections, but those proved a troubled event marked by the exclusion of the main opposition presidential candidate and an opposition boycott. Thus the elections themselves contradicted the lessons of the civic education programs—they ended up teaching citizens that elections are sometimes shabby affairs in which the value of citizens' participation is doubtful. Over time, FODEP developed more interactive teaching methods, attempting to relate the question of democracy to the everyday concerns of villagers. Nonetheless, given the tremendous disconnection between the life of most rural Zambians and the formal political system, the task of civic education remains extremely difficult.

MEDIA ASSISTANCE

Media assistance—aid to strengthen independent television, radio, newspapers, and magazines—has also become an important area of U.S. democracy assistance. It is one of the items making up the democracy template, on the civil society side, and media programs are now part of most U.S. democracy aid portfolios. In the 1980s, such efforts were small and scattered. They included some programs in Asia carried out by the Asia Foundation, a USAID-sponsored regional training program for Central American journalists, and initiatives sponsored by the National Endowment for Democracy to bolster independent publications in Eastern Europe and the Soviet Union.

Much new U.S. media assistance arose after the fall of the Berlin Wall and the breakup of the Soviet Union. Numerous U.S. organizations, including USAID, USIA, the NED, and later the Eurasia Foundation, set up media programs in the former communist countries, USAID often working through private American groups specializing in media work such as the International Media Fund, the International Center for Journalists, Pro-Media (run by the International Research and Exchanges Board), and Internews. In the 1990s, USAID and USIA also increased the number of media projects in Asia, expanded previously established efforts in Central America, and started programs in Africa.[17] The growth of U.S. media assistance abroad was part of a surge of such aid from many sources, including private Western foundations, European aid agencies, some international institutions, and even the World Bank.

The Media Model

Being from an unusually media-oriented society, in which the media play an enormously influential role in political and cultural life, U.S. democracy promoters often take to media assistance with gusto. They tend to be certain that media development is critical to democratization and that the United States has much to offer in this domain. American print journalists brought in as program consultants often believe they are a special breed—the most aggressive, skilled, and influential anywhere—and that they are therefore natural models for journalists in other countries. As for electronic media, Americans tend to see their country as the leading global force in television and film, and to assume that they have a natural authority for working with television and radio in other countries.

A consequence of these attitudes is that the use of American models, a tendency in all areas of U.S. democracy assistance, is particularly marked in media assistance. Across extremely different cultural and political contexts, U.S. media assistance programs emphasize a few core principles: the importance of nonpartisanship and objectivity, the value of investigative reporting, and the preferability of privately owned to publicly owned media. These are cardinal features of the American media world (although whether the news reporting of the major television networks and the major newspapers is actually nonpartisan is often debated), and ones that Americans instinctively feel media in all countries should pursue.

As in most areas of democracy assistance, the U.S. model for media differs in important ways from the models drawn from other established democracies. The anathema against state-owned television, for example, contrasts with the belief in some parts of Europe in the value of state-owned television. Similarly, the faith of many U.S. politicians and American media people that more television—more channels broadcasting more hours each day—is basically good is not automatically shared by people in other democracies. The insistence of many American journalists that a good newspaper is one with no overt political line and with a sharp separation between news stories and editorials is not consistent with the practice of at least some major newspapers in Great Britain, France, Italy, and elsewhere.

The Range of Media Assistance

The types of media assistance are many and their usage depends on the political situation in the recipient country. Many of the attempted democratic transitions in Latin America, Asia, and Africa present the most common context—a media sector that is opening up due to the increased political freedom but is not fundamentally restructuring. In these regions the media are typically a blend of state-owned and private: television is usually state-owned; radio is a mix of public and private; and newspapers and magazines are largely privately owned, although their owners often have close ties to or are actual members of the ruling elite (except in Africa, where state-owned papers are often still dominant).

Media assistance in these regions typically works with what is already there, emphasizing the professionalization of journalists and improving the quality of news coverage. The core of most media aid in these countries is training of journalists. That usually revolves around basic tradecraft—fact collection, story writing or show production, editing, and the like—stressing the importance of accuracy, objectivity, ethics, and investigative reporting. Efforts to stimulate the establishment or strengthening of journalists associations sometimes complement the training initiatives. Aid providers hope journalists associations will push to advance the professional interests of journalists and to foster the exchanges of ideas and information among journalists. Aid providers may also provide assistance to spur the creation of nongovernmental media watchdog organizations that encourage higher professional standards by analyzing the political content and accuracy of news coverage.

Much U.S. media aid also goes to the former communist world, where it pursues a more far-reaching agenda. In the 1990s, the media of most East European countries and some former Soviet republics have been undergoing a transformation from being completely state-dominated to systems with a substantial private component. Supporting such transformations has been the goal of most U.S. media aid to these countries. Training journalists, establishing journalists associations, and supporting new media watchdog groups are important tools. The aid goes further, however, in two ways. It concentrates on organizational development—helping the new independent media begin publishing or broadcasting and then learn to operate successfully as business enterprises. A frequent starting place is material aid—either donations of equipment, from a few fax machines to an entire printing plant, or grants or loans of money. U.S. aid providers follow up with training and technical assistance to help new radio stations, newspapers, magazines, and television stations learn the business, including how to attract advertisers, manage accounts, analyze markets, and develop business plans. In addition, aid in this context often attempts to help modify the legal and regulatory framework in which the media operate. Aid projects often include technical assistance for the writing or rewriting of the basic media law to ensure that it provides the protections and freedoms for the strong development of private media.[18]

Media aid is inevitably more limited in semiauthoritarian or backsliding situations, in whatever region, where the media are not becoming more politically open and the media sector is not transforming. What few independent media exist—usually a handful of newspapers and a few radio stations—are under siege by the government. In such cases, media aid focuses on ensuring the survival of the independent media. That may include funds and equipment. Equally critical is diplomatic support and the willingness of senior U.S. officials to speak out forcefully when the government in question throws journalists in jail or moves to close down a publication. Media aid in such a context is not merely the task of public and private donors; it is also the work of human rights groups, international journalists associations, and other organizations working to promote press freedom. The efforts by various public and private Western groups to support the embattled independent media in Serbia during much of the 1990s was probably the most visible and concentrated such attempt.

Finally, media aid goes to postconflict societies. The Office of Transition Initiatives at USAID has developed media programs in countries coming out of civil conflict including Rwanda, Burundi, Angola, and Bosnia. Those programs help support the establishment of publications and broadcast programs that will advance the reconciliation process, and often are part of larger civic education efforts.

Successful Scenarios

Positive effects of media assistance are most obvious in two kinds of situations. First, when a repressive leader is trying to squeeze a small, struggling independent media sector out of existence, external aid, combined with diplomatic pressure, can help keep the sector alive. Relatively small amounts of money can make a fundamental difference to newspapers or radio stations under siege. International attention to their plight and diplomatic pressure on the repressive leaders can raise the political costs of shutting down the independent media. This support can be highly useful but it is not a guarantee of survival. The case of Serbia demonstrates both the value and limits of media aid in authoritarian contexts. For much of the 1990s, Western aid, including both public and private support from the United States, helped keep open at least some independent media outlets. Nevertheless, when NATO went to war against Serbia in 1999, President Slobodan Milosevic closed down or intimidated into conformity the independent media.

Second, when the political and economic transformation of a transitional country is deep-reaching and involves a genuine restructuring of the media sector, external aid can help advance it. Such situations have arisen in some former communist countries, primarily in

Eastern Europe and the Baltic States although to some extent in Russia and Ukraine as well. State monopolies in electronic and print media have given way to the establishment of some private television stations, a great deal of private radio, and an explosion of private newspapers, journals, and magazines. Remaining state-run media have often opened up politically and revamped their internal structures and management. Media laws have been rewritten to provide a much stronger legal and regulatory foundation for independent media. Western media aid programs have been able to insert themselves productively, offering technical advice, training, business know-how, funds, and equipment that help facilitate the transformation of the media sector.

Romania is one example. Despite the slow, partial nature of Romania's transition away from communism in the early 1990s, the media sector experienced considerable change from the start. Independent newspapers and magazines sprang up in large numbers, and enjoyed significant freedom from censorship. Television and radio opened up more slowly. The Iliescu government kept a tight hold on national television and radio but permitted the establishment of some private radio and television stations with less than national reach. In the latter 1990s, the role of private electronic media, including cable television, grew until Romania had a media sector of considerable diversity.

Despite some setbacks—such as a failed effort in the early 1990s to create the country's first private television station—U.S. media aid has contributed meaningfully to the transformation. Grants in the early 1990s helped various independent newspapers get up and running. Training courses all during the decade helped supply the growing demand for new journalists in both print and electronic media. Technical aid has helped improve the business skills of many media organizations. The U.S. media aid has been just one portion of a pool of such assistance to Romania from external private and public sources, especially the Soros foundations network and the European Union. This external aid has been at most a facilitating agent alongside changes initiated by the Romanians themselves. Nonetheless, it has helped advance the restructuring of the media sector.[19]

The extensive U.S. media aid efforts in former communist countries bring greater potential risks as well as potential benefits. Giving significant amounts of money or equipment directly to new media ventures is often risky. They may fail outright or go off the tracks into sensationalism, extremism, or other dead ends. When aid providers give direct grants to local media operations and, more generally, actively involve themselves in the transformation of a country's media, the issue of sovereignty often arises. No society likes to see its television, radio, and newspapers dominated by foreign advisers and foreign funds. At the same time, the people of many East European countries and some former Soviet republics have been willing to tolerate a high degree of Western influence in their media, both because of an interest in Westernization and with the supposition that the Western advisers and aid are part of a transition period, not a permanent feature. When asked whether a particular newspaper or magazine is tainted or discredited because it receives money from the West, many East Europeans shrug and say that they are used to such things. What bothers them more than foreign funding is poor quality and any sign that foreign funding is propping up anticommunist publications or broadcasting as one-sided and crude as the communist publications of old.

The U.S. push in the former communist countries to promote private ownership of electronic media also raises complicated questions. The assumption behind this push is that private control is fundamentally better than state control, above all because private ownership permits political independence. But that assumption is simplistic. To start, broadcasting by state-owned media does not have to be politically tendentious, as evidenced by the BBC. Other forms of public ownership, such as the model offered by the U.S. Corporation for Public Broadcasting, produce high-quality programming. In addition, some postcommunist countries pass rapidly from an environment in which fledgling media enterprises are struggling just to stay afloat to one where significant amounts of foreign and domestic capital are flowing in, especially to private television companies. In some cases, privately owned media can be captured by powerful domestic business interests—often linked to the government—that manipulate them as much as the old government did. The control that Russian business moguls exert over the new private Russian press, for example, is hardly salutary, and the ability of President Yeltsin to influence and even manipulate that press during the 1996 presidential elections in Russia was discouraging. Moreover, private ownership does not guarantee high-quality content.

Local television news in the United States, with its sensationalism and almost total lack of serious news reporting, has become a significant cause for concern. The same negative tendencies can and do appear in private media in transitional countries, especially where educational levels are low.

In many transitional countries, especially in Latin America, Asia, and Africa, the media are not under attack from an overreaching strongman, yet neither are they rapidly transforming themselves for the better. Instead, they enjoy a fair amount of freedom but are plagued by corruption (such as government payoffs to newspapers), low professional standards, risk-averse and politically collusive owners, and an insufficient local economic base for growth or change. As mentioned above, most U.S. media aid in such contexts goes to training for journalists, given the lack of other entry points. Such training often does less than aid providers hope or expect. To some extent this is because of weaknesses in the training programs themselves. Almost all training under democracy programs has shortcomings, but training in the media domain gives rise to an unusual number of complaints from trainees. Many of the U.S. training programs, especially early on, have consisted of short-term courses led by American trainers who have little knowledge of their trainees' society and who emphasize methods suited specifically to the United States. A frequent complaint is that journalist training courses are too basic, with the trainers assuming that the low level of media development in the country must be the fault of journalists' ignorance. Moreover, in countries where journalists are being persecuted and sometimes killed for daring to question the official line, visiting Americans lecturing on the rigors of investigative reporting frequently command little respect.

Even when journalist training is well-designed, it does little to change the conditions at the root of the problems. With the media sector, these conditions usually include persistent state dominance of television, ingrown structures of ownership in what private media does exist, rising pressure for sensationalism with increased commercialization of the sector, and an inadequate advertising base due to the country's economic troubles. Training courses may make journalists more knowledgeable and skillful but they will not ameliorate these negative factors.[20]

U.S. media aid to Guatemala exemplifies this problem. Some 1,000 Guatemalan journalists received training in the 1990s through a

USAID-funded project that provided training to more than 6,800 Central American journalists. Yet the results of this huge effort were highly circumscribed. Television, which remains primarily state-controlled, continues to do a mediocre job of providing informative, balanced news coverage. The diversity and quality of radio broadcasting is still poor. Although newspapers have become freer to publish criticisms of the government, the quality of reporting and writing also remains low. The owners of the major newspapers continue to oblige their papers to defer to the interests of the business elite. What improvements there have been in the openness of the media have come about largely because of the end of the civil war and the improved human rights situation, rather than because of external aid.

Similarly, in Nepal, the many training courses for journalists sponsored by the United States and other donors have not had many apparent effects. Given the low literacy rate, newspapers have small circulations, although they are influential in elite circles. A few newspapers are independent and fairly high quality, but journalists at those papers do not cite the training programs as having any part in that. Although political power has alternated between the three main parties, none of the many post-1990 governments has reduced the high levels of state control and politicization of television and other media. Specifically, they have refused to grant licenses for new radio stations or to permit the establishment of private television stations.

In Zambia, a relatively sophisticated, well-run center for the training of journalists, the Zambian Institute of Mass Communication, was established with U.S. support. Yet as the director acknowledges, his center has trained many television, radio, and newspaper journalists, yet not improved the disastrous state of the Zambian media. The government-controlled outlets continue their mediocre ways. And the country's handful of independent establishments—the Zambia *Post* and a few others—seem to make little use of the training. Features the training has stressed—professional journalistic methods and the importance of objective, fact-based reporting—remain noticeably absent from all publications. Asked about the value of such training, the *Post*'s editor, Fred Mmembe, says that what his paper needs above all is money and protection from persecution, since it is always on shaky financial ground and its writers and editors are always in danger of being locked up. Training, he says, addresses neither of those needs.

In short, in most transitional countries, journalists' lack of knowledge and skills is only one of many causes of the weakness of the media. It is the most amenable to donor intervention, which leads to its becoming the major focus of media assistance. But unless significant changes occur in the other factors that hobble the media, training alone will not change much.

LABOR UNIONS

For decades the AFL-CIO, using U.S. government funds, has aided labor unions around the world, training union activists in union-building, negotiating, labor law, and fund raising; underwriting salaries of union officials and other union expenses; contributing equipment and other materials; advising on management and strategy; fostering contacts with U.S. unions; paying for study tours in the United States for foreign union officials; and sponsoring union-related research. The fundamental purpose of this aid has been to strengthen labor unions abroad, reflecting the AFL-CIO's belief that strong, independent labor unions are good for any country. From the early days of the cold war into the 1970s, the AFL-CIO's international work was in the service of the organization's ardent anticommunism. The AFL-CIO worked determinedly in Western Europe and the developing world to support unions that fit its political criteria and to oppose leftist unions. Its efforts were often closely tied to U.S. government efforts to prevent left-leaning regimes from coming to power or to subvert those that did. The CIA often financed or used AFL-CIO activities as part of its anticommunist covert action campaigns. In Latin America in the 1960s and 1970s, for example, the AFL-CIO, through its affiliate, the American Institute for Free Labor Development (AIFLD), mobilized its client unions to support CIA-backed efforts to destabilize governments in the Dominican Republic, Chile, El Salvador, Guyana, and Brazil.[21]

In the 1980s and 1990s, the AFL-CIO moderated its international line somewhat, more openly embracing prodemocratic values and moving away from support of right-wing, anticommunist dictatorships. As the U.S. government began to develop democracy assistance programs in the 1980s, the AFL-CIO claimed a place in that domain, arguing that strong, independent labor unions are an essential part of democracy. The AFL-CIO was one of the main forces behind the creation of the National Endowment for Democracy and in the first ten years of the NED's existence, the AFL-CIO's international affiliates, taken together, received by far the largest share of NED funds. USAID also regularly gave the AFL-CIO funds for international work throughout the 1980s and 1990s.

Although the AFL-CIO began moderating its political approach in the 1980s and early 1990s, it still tended to see politics in black and white and to devote itself in many countries to battling what it believed to be dangerously leftish labor unions. A USAID-sponsored evaluation of the AFL-CIO's activities in El Salvador in the latter 1980s, for example, praised them on the grounds that without them, "a number of organizations would have affiliated with or lost considerable membership to the leftist, extremist oriented Union Nacional de Trabajadores Salvadorenos."[22] Similarly, in Nicaragua, well after the end of the cold war and the fall from power of the Sandinistas, the AFL-CIO was still working hard to weaken the Sandinistas. In the mid-1990s, AIFLD provided $3 million worth of administrative support and training to unions affiliated with one union federation, the Congreso Permanente de Trabajadores, "to counterbalance Sandinista labor."[23] After 1989 in Eastern Europe, the AFL-CIO, through its affiliate the Free Trade Union Institute, moved quickly into most of the countries of the region (it had been aiding Solidarity in Poland for much of the 1980s), openly choosing political sides in labor sectors undergoing major changes.

In the mid-1990s, Lane Kirkland, long-time head of the AFL-CIO and the person most responsible for the hard-line anticommunist line with foreign unions, stepped down. New leadership came to power and the moderating trend on the international side of the AFL-CIO's activities accelerated. The organization disbanded its regional affiliates and replaced them with a single new group, the American Center for International Labor Solidarity. The leadership stated its intention to organize the international work clearly around the goals of democracy promotion, worker rights, and social and economic justice. The degree to which the AFL-CIO has actually changed some of its deeply engrained habits is not yet clear.

Despite the shift in the past two decades partially away from the hard-line cold war interventionism of earlier decades, the AFL-CIO's international activities have nonetheless been the most aggressively partisan and politicized in the U.S. democracy assistance portfolio. The organization has often been heavy-handed, anointing friends and trying to advance their fortunes over rival union groups. The AFL-CIO often seems to have little regard for the local sensitivities and unintended consequences involved when a powerful U.S. actor behaves in such a partisan fashion in the highly politicized realms that union sectors tend to be. Its partisanship has resulted in cozy relationships with particular unions in other countries, breeding bad aid practices all too reminiscent of the corruption scandals that frequently erupt on the labor scene in the United States. Furthermore, the AFL-CIO uses the crudest of aid methodologies—reflexively attempting to export its own model wherever it goes. To mention just one example, an evaluation of the work of the AFL-CIO-affiliated African-American Labor Center in Egypt in the early 1990s cited as an indicator of success the fact that a recipient organization, the Egyptian Trade Union Federation, "appears to have adopted the AFL-CIO as the model to emulate."[24] The AFL-CIO has consistently opposed efforts by unions around the world to develop other forms of labor-government relations than the AFL-CIO's arm's-length, confrontation-oriented model. Basing democracy aid on the stubborn reproduction of a single model is almost always a mistake. When the model does not even seem to work well at home—the U.S. labor movement has been in serious decline for decades—such an approach makes particularly little sense.

Some of the difficulties of the AFL-CIO's partisan approach were highlighted by the experience of the Free Trade Union Institute (FTUI) in Romania in the early 1990s. FTUI arrived in Romania after the fall of Ceauşescu determined to strengthen new independent unions against the old union groups linked to the communist past. FTUI embraced a newly emerged union confederation, Fraţia, and its outspoken leader Miron Mitrea, rapidly channeling aid in their direction and making clear to other labor activists that U.S. labor believed Mitrea to be the future of Romanian labor. Labor politics in post-Ceauşescu Romania ended up being more fluid and murky than the AFL-CIO's litmus tests provided for. Within a few years Mitrea and Fraţia turned markedly pro-government while the union confederation that FTUI initially criticized as being a bunch of hold-overs from the communist era gradually became the most outspoken, pro-opposition part of the labor scene. FTUI shifted its aid away from Fraţia and Mitrea, but only after antagonizing many Romanian labor activists and highlighting U.S. labor's overactive partisan style.

In the second phase of its work in Romania, FTUI carried out some innovative activities that highlighted the new side of the AFL-CIO's international profile. FTUI worked with many Romanian union officials and members, for example, to help them learn about privatization and how Romanian unions could develop an informed and productive response to a phenomenon few understood. For this effort FTUI brought Romanian unionists together with some Polish union officials who had experience in this domain, taking advantage of intraregional expertise.

Though it is part of the U.S. government democracy assistance portfolio, aid to labor unions is something of a world apart from the rest. The AFL-CIO operates more independently than most U.S. organizations that receive U.S. government funding to promote democracy abroad. Some NED and USAID officers who fund AFL-CIO activities comment in private that they often receive only sparse information from the AFL-CIO about its programs, that it describes its activities to them in generalities and is reluctant to share details of what it does. In addition, USAID staff commonly believe that the AFL-CIO has strong congressional protection and thus that it is unusually difficult to question its activities without a major political fight. Both in Washington and in the field, U.S. labor representatives express the firm view that labor union work is their special domain, that no one else has the knowledge or experience to work in it. The AFL-CIO's combatively partisan, often divisive approach abroad increases the defensiveness and secrecy that surrounds the aid at home.

In many transitional countries, unions are potentially among the most important civil society actors. Unlike many of the groups reached by aid programs expressly aimed at civil society development, labor unions have genuine ties to large numbers of citizens, are able to mobilize people for forceful civic action, and have the ability to come up with domestic funding. Yet when U.S. aid providers talk about aiding civil society and developing programs, labor unions are not part of the picture. The focus instead is on advocacy NGOs, civic education, and media. Labor sits alone as its own category, in its own private world. Thus a dual paradox exists: the most important form of civil society organization is not generally part of programs labeled as civil society development. At the same time, the basic values of U.S. civil society assistance—nonpartisanship, openness, cooperative methods—are not characteristic of the aid to those organizations, labor unions, that are often critical to civil society.

BEYOND CIVIL SOCIETY ROMANTICISM

The recent surge of attention among democracy promoters to strengthening of civil society is a positive, necessary development. It serves as a useful corrective to the initial, overly narrow emphasis in U.S. democracy aid on elections and the top-down reform of state institutions. Civil society is the connective tissue that transitional countries need to join the forms of democracy with their intended substance, to ensure that new democratic institutions and processes do not remain hollow boxes and empty rituals. The civil society domain offers democracy promoters many points of entry into democratic transitions and often contains many dedicated and skillful people committed to advancing democracy. Moreover, it offers the possibility of useful projects of all different scales, from modest support for a few activists working together on a single project in one locale, to huge, national reform campaigns involving the mobilization of thousands of volunteers.

As they have rushed to embrace the fashionable notion of civil society, U.S. democracy promoters have often subscribed to romantic, stereotyped, or limited versions of this attractive, even mesmerizing concept. They have overemphasized one particular sector of the complex domain of civil society: the rather specialized set of policy-related nongovernment organizations that carry out advocacy work and civic education directly relating to what aid providers consider to be core democracy issues, such as election monitoring, government transparency, and political and civil rights. In related fashion, democracy promoters have held to a denatured, benevolent view of civil society's role in political life as town hall politics writ large— the earnest articulation of interests by legions of well-mannered activists who play by the rules, settle conflicts peacefully, and do not break any windows.

This romanticization of civil society has roots in Americans' rather mythicized Tocquevillean conception of their own society, but it entails a gross oversimplification of the makeup and roles of civil society in other countries around the world. American democracy promoters have made few efforts to understand civil society on its own terms in complex traditional societies in Africa, Asia, and the Middle East. They basically ignore the many layers of clans, tribes, castes, village associations, peasant groups, local religious organizations, ethnic associations, and the like as essentially unfathomable complexities that do not directly bear on democratic advocacy work. Democracy promoters pass through these countries on hurried civil society assessment missions and declare that "very little civil society exists" because they have found only a handful of Westernized NGOs devoted to nonpartisan public-interest advocacy work on the national scale.

Democracy promoters keen to foster civil society development have generally given little thought to the relationship between particular forms of civil society and the socioeconomic conditions of the target countries. They like advocacy NGOs and assume that every country can and should support thousands of them. Through their funding programs they try to jumpstart the development of NGO sectors, fueling the proliferation of NGOs with little attention to the questions of when the society is likely to develop the resources to integrate and sustain them. They end up, ironically, falling into the same trap of institutional modeling that plagues so much top-down democracy aid and that partially prompted the push toward civil society work in the first place: they approach civil society development as a matter of getting certain institutional forms (advocacy NGOs) in place, elevating form over content, process, or underlying sociopolitical reality.

Following the pattern that has occurred with aid for elections and for the reform of state institutions, democracy promoters are beginning to pass through the initial enthusiastic, boom phase of aid for civil society development and to enter a phase of lower expectations and more sophisticated programming. The emphasis on advocacy NGOs is still strong but democracy promoters are starting to pay greater heed to the key issues of representativity and sustainability. They are looking more carefully at the actual ties that NGOs have to the sectors on whose behalf they claim to act, and are trying to encourage the development of more representative, rooted organizations. Similarly, they are increasingly introducing the issue of sustainability at the beginning rather than the end of relationships with recipient NGOs, and investing more resources in helping NGOs find local sources of money.

Two major areas of evolution in civil society aid are the dual push to "go local" and to support NGOs involved in advocacy of social and economic issues rather than just explicitly democracy-related issues. As discussed earlier in the chapter, the move toward greater support for NGOs at the village, town, or municipality level allows democracy promoters to begin helping to build the basic fabric of a democratic culture. Broadening the scope to social and economic concerns helps connect the rather abstract idea of civic advocacy to issues about which citizens are directly concerned. In addition, by working at the local level on nitty-gritty issues of daily concern, democracy promoters begin to come into contact with and to support a broader, often more deeply established range of civil society groups, such as community organizations and informal citizens associations.

As they accumulate experience, civil society aid programs are also taking more account of the necessity of a responsive, effective state for civil society to be fully useful. The early, heady temptation to view civil society as an alternative to or something existing in only distant relation to the state has faded. Civil society programs at both the national and local level in transitional countries now typically seek a productive dialogue with state institutions and view state and civil society as partners more than opponents (except in authoritarian contexts where civil society plays a more oppositional role). Just as programs aimed at reforming state institutions have progressively incorporated a civil society approach to the task, civil society aid has adopted the idea of a symbiotic relationship of the state and civil society. In this important way, a natural synthesis between the original dualism of top-down and bottom-up approaches to democracy promotion is occurring.

These various lines of positive evolution of civil society assistance are still only just solidifying. As they advance, civil society programs will improve, but they will not gain the ability to cause major effects on the entire civil society of any given country. Although the domain of civil society is often more accessible and responsive to external aid than that of state institutions, it is even more vast and more rooted in underlying socioeconomic, cultural, and historical conditions and patterns. Democracy promoters are starting to learn more what they are doing in this complex domain, but a central element of their self-education is realizing just how inflated their expectations have been and how limited their capabilities to produce broad-scale change really are.

PART THREE

On the Ground

9
Making It Work: The Challenges of Implementation

On a cold January day in Bucharest several years ago, I met with a visiting American consultant who was working on a small project funded by USAID to improve Romania's court administration. The consultant, a state court administrator from a small U.S. state, was halfway into a six-week trip to identify the administrative problems of Romania's courts, to come up with some solutions, and to interest some Romanian court officials in those solutions. His diagnosis, reached after visiting several courts, was that the root cause of the obviously flawed administration in the courts—the chaotic record-keeping, the tremendous delays and inefficiencies, and the general lackadaisical attitude about delivering justice—was Romanian court personnel's lack of understanding of basic filing methods. He was particularly struck by the many different sizes of the different official forms. If the experts only had a standard size of paper for their forms, he explained to me, their filing problems would be solved. His proposed solution was to order a three-year supply of paper from the United States—he knew just the right company in his home state—and persuade several Romanian courts to use it for their forms, replacing the odd-sized paper they were using. Once Romanians see how well it works in a few courts, he told me, they will realize how valuable a well-run court can be and will use the new paper nationally.

This earnest consultant, determined to do his best on a difficult assignment, had no idea who his interlocutors were in the court system or who his potential local partners might be. He was just turning up at the courts wherever someone had scheduled him and talking (through an interpreter) with whichever officials met with him. Though experienced in court administration in the United States, he had never been to Romania before, or in fact to any country on a similar assignment. His previous international experience was limited to vacation trips to Britain and Mexico with his wife, although he felt he had quickly learned some basics about Romania—most important, that the country "just doesn't work very well." His assignment was a follow-up to a visit the year before by a different American expert, who had written a 100-page single-spaced report (in English) on the shortcomings of Romanian court administration, with detailed suggestions for corrective measures. Although that report had been sent to many judges, the new consultant was finding that few in the courts had read it or even remembered it.

Later that week, I spent some time with another American working on a different USAID-funded project, this one for civic education. He was a young political activist halfway through a multi-year assignment in Romania as a field representative for an American organization that promotes democracy, and was serving principally as an adviser to a Romanian civic education group formed in the early 1990s with significant U.S. funds and technical support. The group was still largely financed from abroad, but had broadened its base of funders and was now staffed and run entirely by Romanians. The group had a presence nationwide in Romania and was active in monitoring elections, educating voters, and advocating the principle of free and fair elections. The consultant was well informed about the political environment in Romania, had learned some Romanian, and had a nuanced appreciation both of what he could offer the Romanian group in the way of assistance and the limits of his role. He was also realistic about the possible impact of one civic education project and the challenges of trying to change the country's political culture.

Those two projects, though operating in the same country at the same time, both using intermediary American organizations and American consultants, nevertheless differed enormously in their operating methods. They took contrasting approaches to key issues such as the duration and role of external consultants, involvement of local partners, application of outside models, and the likely rapidity of broad-scale change. Such issues of implementation are critical in democracy assistance, as in all areas of foreign assistance. Strategy, conception, and design are all of great importance. In the end, however, the manner in which an aid project is implemented does much to determine whether or not the project does any good. What a project can accomplish is often a question of the mundane details of day-to-day operations. These details are at the heart of how the project is perceived and experienced by people in the recipient country.

This chapter explores the methods of implementation of democracy assistance. It focuses on the main approach to implementation, what I call the external project method, tracing its bureaucratic roots and pointing out its major shortcomings. It also examines some of the corrective steps that democracy promoters are taking in response to criticism of their implementation, particularly their efforts to incorporate a more active role for people and organizations of the recipient countries. The chapter concludes by considering some of the differing roles and approaches of the major institutions in U.S. democracy assistance, including the U.S. Agency for International Development, the State Department, and the National Endowment for Democracy.

THE EXTERNAL PROJECT METHOD

Much U.S. democracy aid is developed and administered in accordance with a method familiar in foreign aid, in which people from the country providing the aid dominate every step of the process. Schematically, it works as follows:

- The aid organization assesses the needs and opportunities for democracy assistance in a chosen recipient country.
- Once a particular need or opportunity has been identified, the aid organization designs an aid project (using either its own staff or American consultants); or the aid organization asks for proposals for projects from American groups, either democracy promotion groups or for-profit consulting firms.
- The aid organization gives funds to a U.S. intermediary organization—usually either a nonprofit democracy group or a for-profit development consulting group—to carry out the project.
- The intermediary directs and carries out the project, often placing an expatriate project manager, or a whole project team, in the recipient country and bringing in expatriate experts for training and technical assistance. The intermediary works in collaboration with one or more local partners—organizations in the recipient country.

- The project ends after two or three years. The intermediary organization leaves the country. The aid organization hires a different American consulting group to do a brief retrospective evaluation.

USAID has long relied heavily on the external project method. Other federal agencies that sponsor democracy-related activities, such as the Justice Department and the Defense Department, use an external method but skip the intermediary—their own personnel often design the projects and even provide the training and technical assistance themselves. The NED's grants to its four core grantees utilize substantial features of the external project method, although the majority of the Endowment's discretionary grants, which currently amount to approximately half of NED grants, go directly to organizations in recipient countries (the direct grant method is discussed later in this chapter).

U.S. democracy aid providers rely on the external project method because they hope that giving aid dollars to American intermediary organizations rather than directly to groups or people in the recipient countries will allow them to keep close track of the funds. U.S. aid givers, especially USAID, live in fear that even the smallest misuse of their funds abroad will become the subject of congressional inquiry or media attention, threatening the already tenuous support for foreign aid. U.S. intermediary groups know the accounting rules and administrative regulations for funding recipients. U.S. funders tend to believe—though not to say aloud—that American intermediary groups are less likely to commit fraud than are people or groups in the transitional countries.

The American intermediary groups push for the use of the external project method, not just in democracy assistance but in foreign aid in general. A whole community of American development consultants depends on U.S. aid funds. In the field of democracy promotion, some of the groups that receive U.S. funding, such as the political party institutes, the American Bar Association, and the AFL-CIO, have their own political backers in Congress and in different parts of the executive branch. They call on them when needed to zealously defend what they regard as their fair share of the democracy pot. Both in Washington and in the field, USAID officers refer at times to the more politically connected American recipients of democracy funds as "sacred cows" whose projects they do not always think are good but whom they believe cannot be challenged because of their clout in Washington.

There are substantive reasons for using the external project method as well as the bureaucratic and political ones. In some cases, assessment teams and project design specialists sent in on short-term missions can see a complex transitional situation afresh and make useful recommendations for the establishment of democracy promotion programs. American consultants, trainers, field representatives, and aid experts who travel to recipient countries to oversee or directly participate in the implementation of projects do sometimes contribute valuable knowledge and experience. They help spread ideas across national lines and sometimes add comparative experience from previous assignments in other countries. Particularly in Eastern Europe and parts of the former Soviet Union in the early 1990s, the mere presence of Western experts seeking to help advance democratic transitions was exciting at first for many people since they had long been isolated from the West. That excitement wore off fairly quickly, however, and by the mid-1990s had been replaced by almost equally automatic resentment of the outside experts whom people felt soaked up funds that should go directly to their countries. In the developing world, where Western aid representatives and consultants have been a fact of life for decades, the arrival of Western democracy experts in the late 1980s, continuing into the 1990s, was never much of a cause for enthusiasm.

Systematic Shortcomings

It would not be difficult to present a harshly critical, even lurid, view of the implementation of democracy assistance projects. Some scathing accounts have appeared in recent years, some of them by disillusioned former aid practitioners. They paint a tragicomic picture of democracy promoters as arrogant fools forcing simplistic schemes onto societies they do not understand, all the while preaching hollow homilies about the wonders of democracy.[1] The implementation of democracy projects has indeed often been problematic and one does not have to scratch very deep to find examples similar to those set forth in the harsh critiques cited above.

Democracy assistance in Eastern Europe and the former Soviet Union appears to have been particularly troubled in this regard.

Democracy promoters—along with aid providers of many sorts—rushed into the former communist countries in the early 1990s, armed with especially strong hubris yet usually lacking any significant experience in the region. Moreover, these societies were fundamentally unlike those in most other places in which aid providers operated—in their educational levels, political histories, social and cultural backgrounds, and other ways. The result was a large number of troubled programs and rapid aid fatigue on the part of the recipients.

Although the problems of implementation in democracy aid vary tremendously from project to project, it is possible to identify five key shortcomings that regularly arise. The first is the frequent *lack of local ownership* of the aid projects. Assistance projects that are funded, designed, managed, and evaluated by foreigners are only occasionally backed by much real commitment or attachment from people in the recipient countries themselves. When assistance providers go to target countries and propose activities—"We will be working on judicial reform, would your ministry like to be part of our project?" or "We will be strengthening independent media, would your institute like to help provide training?"—the answer is often "yes" even though the local participants may have little interest in the project. They agree in the hope that participating will bring at least some benefits, whether computers, cash, a trip to the United States, or simply the association with a powerful foreign friend. Local partners often have refined to a high art the technique of putting on a show of great interest in projects launched by donors. And many aid providers are remarkably quick to believe them. "The minister of justice has told us he is deeply committed to reform." "When I asked the president if we should keep working in his country, he said we have been crucial to democracy there." "Our project is highly valued—I know that because our local partners told me it would be a major mistake not to continue it."

Although the problem of ownership is endemic in all areas of foreign aid, it has been acute in the democracy domain. This is partly because many democracy promoters plunged into their work with no experience in the basic dynamics of aid-giving, a point developed more extensively below. It also has been aggravated by the hurry in which much U.S. democracy assistance has operated. When countries have unexpected political openings, U.S. aid providers often rush to get democracy programs under way, believing that the democratic moment must be seized or it will be lost. That attitude was especially prevalent in the early 1990s in Eastern Europe and the former Soviet Union, where some Americans feared that communism would come back if they did not dive in with support for the new political forces. Attempting to get assistance funds out the door as rapidly as possible tempts aid providers to pay little attention to the actual local commitment to the projects and to put can-do consultants and organizations uninterested in the nuances of local realities in charge of the work.

This is not to say that groups and people in recipient countries are only going through the motions when they participate in assistance projects developed through the external project method. In some cases the local participation is dedicated and diligent. Yet lack of ownership is a fundamental shortcoming of much foreign aid over the past four decades. With democracy assistance, it is most evident in projects involving state institutions, where (as discussed in chapter 6) the problem of inadequate will to reform is paramount, and where aid providers are often tempted to unfurl complex blueprints developed by expert consultants from the outside. Yet it dogs civil society projects as well. With donor dependence so high among NGOs in most transitional societies, donors invariably find an enthusiastic response to almost any line of activity they propose. Such NGOs are hard put *not* to show interest, even if it is something in which they are not really interested. The United States and other donors habitually insist that in funding NGO work in transitional societies they are responding to local initiatives and demand. Even the most superficial look at the explosion of NGO sectors in the 1990s makes clear that NGOs in transitional societies everywhere are following the leads of donors in both subject area and project style and that local ownership of much civil society assistance is still very partial.

The second major problem with the external project method is that it often produces activities based on *a shallow understanding of the society being assisted.* Aid projects are built primarily using ideas brought from abroad, blended with limited knowledge about the local setting. At each stage, from assessment to design to implementation to evaluation, the understanding of the local scene by outside consultants, managers, and technical experts is sharply limited.

Short-term assessment teams may, for example, be able to identify which of the major state institutions have the most glaring flaws and what improvements are most needed. Often they are not able, however, to learn much about how amenable the key people in those institutions really are to an aid project, who is likely to oppose reforms and how they will do so, and what actually happened with previous reform efforts.

The resident project managers who implement or oversee the implementation of the project do accumulate knowledge about the local scene. The learning process is not, however, automatic or assured. These expatriate managers or field representatives sometimes have previous experience in the country but are usually starting from scratch. They frequently do not speak the local language. If they are in a managerial role, much of their time is spent dealing with the bureaucratic demands of the funding institution, giving them less opportunity to immerse themselves in local currents. Often the most important decisions in a project, such as choosing the local partners, have to be made early on, when expatriate managers know least about the local scene. Moreover, once they are exercising authority over a project, their access to needed information actually becomes more limited as people begin telling them what they want to hear and hiding from them critical information that may be damaging to particular local actors.

As with the problem of ownership, the problem of knowledge of the local context has been endemic in all foreign aid but is especially common in democracy assistance. Unlike aid sectors such as public health and agriculture, democracy programs target people and institutions that few people in the United States or other donor countries have had direct contact with. Aid projects working with, for example, Latin American judiciaries, African legislatures, or Eastern European local governments could not, at least in their start-up phase, draw on an established community of expatriate experts with intimate knowledge of such institutions in those regions.

The third problem with the method is its *lack of flexibility*. The external project method typically entails a great deal of upfront planning and design based on what the assessors and the aid organization say the project should accomplish and their ideas about how it should reach its goals. This planning may cover what activities are to take place, who the local partners and participants will be, what kinds of training, equipment, and study tours are to be provided, and so forth. Yet once the project is under way, those working on it frequently discover that the real needs and possibilities are different from what the initial studies indicated. Changing tracks can be difficult, depending on the internal policies of the funding institutions. USAID's bureaucracy is notoriously rigid, a problem that seems only to be worsening as the agency steps up its efforts to manage and monitor its projects. At times the rigidity is especially severe in the democracy domain, where more elaborate upfront design is required to convince the still skeptical aid bureaucracy that democracy programs are not vague, unscientific gambles. Smaller, nongovernmental or quasi-governmental funders such as the NED and the Eurasia Foundation permit greater flexibility in the design and implementation of projects, because of their smaller size, shorter history (thereby being less bureaucratically sclerotic), and greater self-confidence about the value of democracy work.

To choose just one of countless examples, the project to strengthen local government in Nepal in the first half of the 1990s suffered greatly from both too much and the wrong kind of design, as well as the difficulty of shifting gears once under way. A team of outside consultants designed a project to train local government officials how to plan and implement local-level development projects. Another consulting group was contracted to implement the project, and it sent out an American consultant to be the in-country manager. In less than a year that consultant left, for unspecified reasons, stopping the project in its tracks. A new manager was sent out, who quickly decided that the project design was misguided, that the work to date had been futile, and that a redesign was necessary to focus on building citizen participation in local government. The manager expended enormous energies persuading the USAID mission in Kathmandu and USAID in Washington to accept a new plan. During the third year the project finally got going in earnest and made some promising advances in the three districts in which it was based, stimulating citizens groups to work together with local government officials. The project was not renewed when its three years were up, because USAID decided to shift to other priorities, despite local government officials' energetic lobbying of the USAID mission. In short, a tremendous amount of bureaucratic energy was devoted to a project that barely got under way and was terminated just as it was finally taking shape.

A fourth problem, highlighted in the above example, is that of *duration*. Under the conventional project method, democracy projects rarely last more than three years. Projects take a year to get going, spend a year at normal functioning, and then their managers worry for the last year about sustainability and close-out. The relatively short duration of most projects increases the pressure to make the most important decisions about implementation during the period of least familiarity with the local setting. It results in the abandonment of many opportunities for significant learning, building of trust, and investment in human resources just when they are beginning to solidify. Successful projects can sometimes be extended or act as a foundation for new ones, but this occurs less than might be expected. At USAID, for example, personnel in the field missions tend to be reassigned approximately every three years, and staff have their own ideas about what projects to sponsor and are often disinclined to continue their predecessors'.

The final major shortcoming of the external project method is its *high cost*. Using American intermediary organizations drives up costs enormously at every stage. Assessments by fly-in teams cost tens of thousands of dollars in airfares, hotel bills, and fees. Expatriate project managers often draw salaries and benefits of more than $100,000 a year, in countries where highly qualified professionals may be earning less than one-tenth that amount. Visiting trainers, technical consultants, and other experts further drive up costs. Volunteers from the United States can add thousands of dollars to a project's budget, for airfare, hotels, and meals. Even when an American intermediary is present only to oversee activities carried out by local partners or to administer direct grants, the proportion of administrative costs can still be high. In Zambia, for example, the U.S. university managing the USAID civil society project incurred administrative expenses equal to 40 percent of the aid dispersed.[2]

Local participants are often acutely aware of this phenomenon and deeply resentful of it. A local NGO may have to cajole and negotiate with the USAID mission for weeks to get a fax machine included in its project budget. The NGO leaders then blanch as the mission directs them to welcome an ill-prepared "visiting expert" from the United States who jets in for a week to lecture them on advocacy skills, racking up expenses that would pay for a year's rent for office space and a whole set of office equipment besides.

The exponential salary differentials between expatriate and local professionals are standard in the aid world, but nonetheless a source of widespread, though quiet, bitterness.

CORRECTIVE STEPS

At its worst, the external project method results in assistance activities that are poorly rooted in the recipient society, based on superficial knowledge of the local context, locked into inflexible molds, too short-lived to have much effect, and unreasonably expensive. Many democracy assistance efforts of the 1980s and 1990s have been marred by flaws reflecting these underlying shortcomings: training courses badly matched to local needs; American consultants parachuting in for short stays with little understanding of the country they are supposed to assist; equipment transfers misused or gathering dust; poorly designed study tours that end up as tourism and shopping expeditions; unread diagnostic reports written by visiting experts; mediocre, unprepared field representatives who command little respect from their local counterparts; and so forth.

The "Discovery" of Localism

With experience, aid providers and the intermediary organizations carrying out democracy programs have become increasingly aware of the deficiencies of their basic method. Some have begun to ask themselves tougher questions about how they operate and to modify their methods in response. The thrust of these modifications is to increase participation in democracy programs by people and organizations of the recipient countries, or, more briefly, increased localism. ("Localism" is used here with a somewhat different meaning than in the discussion of "going local" in civil society assistance; there it referred to moving from work in capital cities of recipient countries to outlying areas, while here it refers to a shift in emphasis from aid groups from outside the recipient countries to organizations from the recipient countries themselves.)

To a limited extent, aid providers have begun to make such changes at the assessment and design stages. Starting in the mid-1990s, for example, USAID began experimenting with participatory processes in which selected people and organizations in a recipient country help decide how USAID's democracy assistance programs should be focused. One of the first applications of this method was in South Africa, where USAID conducted a participatory assessment to help shape its post-apartheid democracy programming.

Giving people in the recipient country a direct say in the development of democracy programs for their country (as opposed merely to interviewing people in the recipient country to gain their perspectives on the political situation) hardly seems like a radical idea. But among aid providers, it is. Though valuable, it is by no means simple in practice. Selecting which people and groups in the recipient society are to be consulted becomes critical. In South Africa, for example, representatives of civil society dominated the process. Not surprisingly, their main recommendation was that the United States should concentrate its aid on civil society development—creating unhappiness in U.S. groups hoping for other areas of emphasis, such as political party aid. The "local" status of local experts is no guarantee of wisdom or neutrality. Moreover, people from the recipient country may know their political context intimately and manage to be objective but still not be good at judging where democracy aid might be most useful.

Increasing localism is making most progress with project implementation. The key here is replacing the notion that Americans involved in the assistance are *themselves* responsible for producing changes in target countries with the idea that the aid's role is to help people of the recipient countries bring about change. This is a monumentally obvious idea, yet it was absent from much of the democracy assistance of the late 1980s and early 1990s. All too often in those years, U.S. groups sent off their staff, trainers, and experts, thinking that they would be the agents of change themselves—that they would mobilize citizens in other countries around the issue of parliamentary transparency, bring about coalitions of opposition parties, persuade parliaments to adopt new committee systems, and so forth.

The shift now is toward treating people and organizations in the recipient countries like genuine partners rather than hired hands. This has many dimensions: investing significant time and effort in finding and developing local partners; designing budgets that emphasize in-country investments rather than U.S.-based expenditures; ceding real authority to people in the recipient country for decisions on project implementation; operating with transparency in the recipient country; and shunning the temptation to take credit for successes.

The shift also means breaking the habit of relying on American consultants, trainers, and experts. Aid providers are beginning to look harder for experts in the recipient countries themselves and to invest in training that can develop such experts. Training programs increasingly include the "training of trainers" rather than simply bringing in trainers from the outside for the duration of the undertaking. When it is necessary to import experts, standards for them are rising. The assumption once pervasive in many democracy projects that almost any American, merely by virtue of being a citizen of a democratic country, could be useful in a democratizing country has begun to disappear. And visiting experts are staying longer as the realization grows among aid providers that fly-in, fly-out consultants are useful only in limited circumstances.

Some American democracy groups are also making more use of third-country trainers and experts, sending Polish experts to Ukraine, Chileans to Bolivia, South Africans to Malawi, and so on around the world. The knowledge and skills they bring are often much more relevant than that of American experts, with less taint of the ugly outsider. The cultural dynamics of some regions, of course, makes such matches difficult. Guatemalans may be much happier to deal with an American trainer than a Costa Rican or an Argentine; Romanians may prefer an American to a Hungarian. Using third-country experts can help build regional cooperation by creating person-to-person links between neighboring countries that have been traditionally cut off from each other. A further advantage is banal yet significant—the use of third-country experts is often much less expensive than the use of American experts, because of lower travel costs and professional fees.

Old Lessons Learned Anew

The external project method is by no means being abandoned. Rather, it is being opened up to greater input from recipient countries. The goal is a productive marriage of external and internal efforts in which outside expert help and experience join with internal ideas, commitment, and initiative. It is interesting to note that increased localism, though still only gaining ground in democracy assistance, is an old story in development aid, dating back to the 1970s and before. What democracy promoters present now as penetrating insights about the need for participatory design, genuine local partners, and the use of local know-how has been received wisdom in development circles for decades (though many development projects have failed to follow it).

That such thinking is only now spreading in U.S. democracy assistance reflects the separation of the U.S. democracy community from the established world of foreign aid and development. Most democracy promoters came to their work from U.S. political campaigns, labor unions, congressional staff positions, law firms, or lobbying groups, not from development work. These democracy activists have brought many skills and attributes to the task—above all energy, self-confidence, and idealism. They often started off, however, with no experience in trying to stimulate or facilitate change in other societies, and sometimes with little international experience of any kind. Their initial lack of experience and their can-do outlook often led them to start with a view of democracy assistance as a matter of them going abroad to show others what to do. Accordingly, the learning curve on methods of implementation has been steep. Nevertheless, some democracy groups and democracy providers, having gained considerable practical experience over the past ten years, have become more adept at fostering local participation in their work. Progress, however, is still uneven. Visiting projects in the field, one encounters vast differences in operational sophistication, sometimes in projects that are almost side-by-side in the same country, such as the two in Romania described at the beginning of this chapter. In addition, new organizations continue to enter the field and seem determined to start from scratch, working their way mistake by mistake along the same learning curve.

Moreover, when confronted with the argument that they have a nondevelopmental approach and could learn something about implementation from the providers of development aid, many democracy promoters bristle. They see democracy promotion as dissimilar in basic ways from traditional development—more fast moving, risk oriented, and opportunity driven. Often they harbor considerable contempt for conventional development aid, seeing it as too slow moving, buried in studies and formal methodologies, and generally stuck in the past. They resist the idea that they have anything to learn from the other domain and, if anything, pride themselves on going their own way.

Even when democracy promoters accept the lessons of localism, putting them into practice can be difficult. The rhetoric of participation is easy to embrace—indeed, "participation" is probably the most overused term in foreign assistance. Yet genuinely participatory methods of project design and implementation can give rise to delays, inconsistency, and local infighting. Incorporating participation also means giving up a certain amount of control, something no aid provider does easily, whatever its stated principles. A recent analysis of participatory methods in sustainable development work highlights some of the problems:

> We should ask why, given that the need for participation has been recognized for at least the past thirty years, so little has been done to implement it up to this time. One needs only to visit programs in the field to see that staff and consultants in most development agencies are more likely to have been selected for their technical specialty . . . than for managerial, institutional development, or process and people skills. For the most part they have little understanding of their role and responsibilities in promoting ownership and commitment, and they are given little if any training, preparation, or support in performing this role. Many of the staff and consultants who are effective perform the role intuitively. . . . It is safe to surmise that most donor agencies are not structured to support participative activities in the field. . . . To implement the objective of a redefined role in promoting sustainable development, donor agencies need a better understanding of what is required at the level of interaction between donor and recipient to promote active participation by the recipient in the development process.[3]

More generally, the bureaucracies of the agencies and organizations that dispense U.S. government aid, as well as the instincts and outlook of democracy promoters, are not easy things to change. Localism looks good in theory but runs up in practice against habits that pull in the opposite direction. Genuine local ownership of aid projects is still the exception rather than the rule. Merely augmenting local participation does not ensure ownership; visiting any aid organization in Washington or in the field and listening to aid representatives talk about "our projects," "our activities," and "our results" makes one aware of how much ownership remains with the aid providers. The projects are still designed and implemented to fit the needs, habits, and demands of the funding agencies as much as to fit the local realities. The relatively short duration of most projects has not changed much. Three years is considered a long commitment, and USAID in particular pushes many projects to show results in less than six months, even when dealing with enormously complex, entrenched problems such as women's lack of political power or a government's sketchy adherence to the rule of law. The lack of flexibility also hurts projects and, at least with USAID-funded projects, may be getting worse. In the mid-1990s, USAID began shifting to a "performance management system" as part of an effort to inject corporate-style rigor into the aid bureaucracy and to show a skeptical Congress that foreign aid can deliver tangible results. Under this system, USAID projects—which USAID officials are no longer allowed to term "projects" but instead must call "results packages"—must list in advance well-defined objectives and establish highly specific, preferably quantitative, indicators of progress. Although the system is intended to foster innovation, the burdensome, often arcane process of devising objectives and indicators and getting them approved by the appropriate offices at USAID creates operational straitjackets. This system is analyzed in greater detail in the discussion of evaluative methods in the next chapter. The point here is that projects become locked into meeting predefined objectives and indicators, making it more difficult for people working on the ground to modify projects as they learn or as circumstances change. It is ironic that USAID is moving backward on flexibility at the same time that it is making progress on other issues of implementation, such as ownership, local knowledge, and cost.

Direct Grants

The external project method is the dominant method in U.S. democracy assistance, but not the only one. Aid providers sometimes use direct grants to organizations in transitional countries. This usually entails either a grants competition, with organizations in a potential recipient country submitting proposals to an aid provider, or an aid provider sending representatives into the field to meet organizations and choose recipients, or both methods combined. Once it receives funds for its project, the organization in the recipient country is responsible for implementing it. No American intermediary group is involved in the implementation. Different U.S. aid providers use this method to varying degrees for democracy programming. The Eurasia Foundation gives away a sizeable share of its funds in this way. The NED reserves close to half its grant funds for what it calls its discretionary funding (as opposed to its grants to the four core grantees), much of which goes directly to organizations in target countries. The Asia Foundation gives some direct grants to organizations in the countries in which it works. USAID has some small direct grant programs, but they constitute a minor part of its democracy work.

Direct grants are typically employed in civil society projects—to support advocacy NGOs, election monitoring groups, independent newspapers, journals, or radio stations, or labor unions. They are infrequently used with institutions of the state. USAID and other U.S. funding organizations do enter into direct agreements with justice ministries, legislatures, or other state institutions in transitional countries, but usually an American intermediary group oversees implementation of the project.

The direct grant method has several advantages. It gets the aid money directly into the recipient society. Eliminating the U.S. intermediary lowers project costs, sometimes dramatically. Providers can make small, sometimes targeted grants, increasing the flexibility and focus of the aid effort. Direct grants give the responsibility for action to people of the societies that the aid is intended to help transform. This increases the possibility that the aid programs will be carried out by people who know well the local terrain. It also helps invest the local people with ownership of the project.

The direct grant method inevitably involves difficulties and limitations of its own. Choosing among the myriad small, often new organizations that apply for such grants calls for an in-depth understanding of the recipient societies that aid providers often do not have. Aid providers almost inevitably fund the more Westernized groups—those whose leaders speak good English, know the aid lingo, and have mastered the art of grant proposals. Direct grants also require a certain tolerance of risk, since it is trickier to monitor numerous small local grants than a major contract with or grant to a U.S. intermediary.

For USAID, giving grants directly to small local organizations taxes its complicated methods for monitoring projects and heightens its fear of the misuse of funds. The strain that local grants programs can place on USAID's bureaucracy and procedures was highlighted by the problematic experiences of the agency's Democracy Network Program in Romania. Created in the mid-1990s, the program was supposed to provide more flexible, locally oriented aid to civil society in Eastern Europe, of which grants to NGOs were to be a major feature. In Romania, the grant-making body was a "Democracy Commission" consisting of representatives of the USAID mission, the USIA office, and the political section of the U.S. embassy in Bucharest, and chaired by the U.S. ambassador. Predictably, bureaucratic and political disagreements between the USAID representatives and the other members of the commission led to long delays and few grants. Moreover, not many Romanian NGOs were capable of writing proposals sophisticated enough to meet the commission's requirements. The training component (run by a U.S. intermediary organization, World Learning) ended up trying to train Romanian NGOs to write proposals acceptable to the commission—hardly the original purpose of the advocacy training program. Only thirteen grants were ever awarded. Frustrated officials at USAID terminated the grants program ahead of schedule, leaving Romanian NGOs mystified by the U.S. government's inability to give away a considerable pot of money designated for them.

Direct grants also raise the problem of dependence. Such grants constitute a source of funding in transitional societies that is not part of those societies and often not very long-lived. The grants spawn many groups that have little prospect of surviving if required to live from domestic sources alone. In addition, although direct local grants lend themselves to "seeding the field" for long-term change and supporting modest initiatives intended to produce new ideas for thought and action, they are less suited to systematic efforts to reshape large-scale institutions.

As practiced by U.S. aid providers furnishing democracy assistance, the local grants method maintains a certain externalness.

Either U.S.-based or in-country U.S. staff are often responsible for the funding decisions, as well as for the close-up monitoring and evaluation of the grants. A completely local grants method requires a further major step—the creation of local foundations that are given control over the aid funds. U.S. and European aid providers have begun to support the establishment of community foundations in some recipient countries, usually in relation to community-based development efforts. By far the most significant example of the local foundation method is the Soros foundations network, established by the financier and philanthropist George Soros.[4] This network consists of approximately thirty national foundations, primarily in Eastern Europe and the former Soviet Union. Each is run by a board of directors, managers, and staff made up in most cases of people from the host country. Within the ambit of Soros's broad goal of promoting "open societies," these people decide what program areas to pursue and what to spend their funds on. Regional offices of the network in New York and Budapest contribute technical knowledge and oversee some network-wide programs. A board of directors for the entire network approves foundation strategies and major programs. Nonetheless, the national foundations maintain a fair amount of autonomy.

The unusually deep-reaching localism of the Soros approach has some substantial benefits. Most important, it creates a notably high degree of ownership within the recipient countries. Despite Soros's personal visibility, and in some societies, his notoriety, the Soros national foundations are often perceived in their host countries as being organizations *of* those countries. The high degree of responsibility given to the local boards of directors, management, and staff builds a much deeper relationship between the foundations and the societies in which they operate than that found in conventional foreign aid projects. It also provides crucial management and operational training for the people involved. The responsibility accorded the staff makes the foundations attractive employers for talented people, which in turn often leads to good programming. The foundations bring much deeper knowledge about the local scene to their work than do the field offices of most aid organizations, with their transient expatriate staff and subordinate local employees.

The Soros method is risky. Placing local boards and staff in control of the money can lead to problems. In some cases, national foundations have given funds only to a closed circle of friends or political favorites. In other cases, most visibly in Russia, outright theft of program funds occurred. The misuse of funds, either intentional or unintentional, is of course not unknown in conventionally structured aid projects. When U.S. aid providers are told about the Soros method they typically insist that U.S. legislative requirements would not allow them to assign responsibility for grant-making to entities in recipient countries. Yet for the most part they have not tried to create such arrangements. In one innovative exception, the USAID mission in the Dominican Republic developed a project for strengthening civil society in which a board made up of Dominicans living in the country made decisions about grants to local organizations. The project proved highly successful, building both ownership among Dominicans and a reputation for good grant-making practices.[5]

THE INSTITUTIONS OF DEMOCRACY ASSISTANCE

I have focused in this chapter on the issues of implementation that confront any aid provider engaging in democracy assistance. Yet, inevitably, methods of implementation are linked to the institutional cultures and structures of the organizations that provide the assistance. I do not attempt here to examine deeply the internal workings of the main organizations that sponsor U.S. democracy aid. Nonetheless, several basic issues relating to the institutional sources of U.S. democracy aid are worth outlining while on the general question of implementation.

Too Many Cooks?

One institutional issue that arises periodically in Washington is duplication. At least five U.S. government agencies and three quasi-governmental organizations sponsor democracy aid and dozens of American intermediary groups carry out projects. Every few years, a congressman or congressional staffer will suddenly notice this situation and go on a brief crusade to investigate whether there is unnecessary duplication in U.S. democracy promotion. Typically, these episodes produce a flurry of meetings and reports in which executive branch officials explain to Congress how the whole agglomeration of agencies and organizations fits together, and the issue dies down for a time.

The multiplicity of actors in this field is not a major problem. The government and quasi-governmental organizations have developed different specialties and for the most part have divided up the pie in such a way that they are not duplicating each other's efforts. They should talk with each other more to increase their synergy and learn more from each other. The Pentagon's work on promoting democratic values in foreign militaries is far too isolated, for example, from civic education and civil-military programs that USAID and USIA sponsor. Similarly, the Justice Department's foreign rule-of-law work is too separate from that sponsored by USAID, due to institutional rivalries among all the U.S. actors involved in rule-of-law aid that dates from the 1980s. The challenges are more those of inadequate communication and synergy than of excessive duplication.

Moreover, the involvement of multiple institutions has some advantages. Different actors try different approaches, which helps the field of democracy aid evolve. Although the institutional rivalries can become unproductively intense or petty, a sense of competition among the different groups helps avoid the complacency that is inevitable when one institution has a monopoly on a field. Although people in recipient countries do at times find the diversity of U.S. actors involved in democracy aid bewildering, it sends important messages about pluralism. Having a single powerful institution that promoted democracy would send the wrong message about democratic pluralism to societies struggling to move away from centralized, authoritarian traditions.

A Troubled Institution

A second set of institutional issues concerns USAID, by far the largest source of U.S. democracy aid. As discussed in chapter 2, when the U.S. government began to get into the business of democracy aid in the 1980s, USAID was extremely wary about entering the political domain. In the 1990s, USAID took democracy promotion much more seriously. Yet democracy aid has put down shallower roots in USAID than would appear from the agency's official statements about strategic priorities. Among many career USAID officers, especially specialists in Asia, the Middle East, and Africa, the view persists that democracy promotion is at best a sideline to a core goal of socioeconomic development. Furthermore, some of these people figure that democracy promotion is a Washington fad that will fade once a new administration arrives or some other new idea comes along. Only ten years after USAID got into the democracy field, for example, did it create the first seminars training USAID officers to do democracy work. The establishment of the Center for Democracy and Governance at USAID in 1993 was an important step toward rooting democracy work within the agency. The center has received only modest budgets, however, and has had to struggle to gain influence in the agency.

The nagging question with USAID is not only commitment to democracy assistance; it is also competence. It is impossible to carry out field research on USAID's activities without being struck by the number of people, in both the U.S. intermediary groups and the recipient societies, who think ill of the organization. One hears a consistent litany of criticisms: USAID is highly bureaucratic, inflexible, micro-managing, slow, and inefficient. Horror stories abound about the elaborate and seemingly absurd hoops people have to go through to satisfy the agency's bureaucratic requirements. "Reinventing government" initiatives meant to streamline and modernize USAID in the mid-1990s seem only to have intensified the bureaucratization. The criticisms go beyond administration, to indict the highly uneven quality of personnel, missions that are "bubble colonies" out of touch with the societies in which they operate, and the habitual reliance on a limited circle of outside consulting groups, many of which are peopled by retired USAID employees.

Although USAID is a troubled organization, the contacts I have had with other countries' aid agencies have not persuaded me that they are any better. Many are afflicted with serious administrative problems of their own. Some, especially among the northern European aid agencies, are less bureaucratic when it comes to giving their money away, but they often fall short in obtaining accountability from their recipients. In addition, many other Western aid agencies seem well behind USAID in terms of attempting to think through democracy promotion, to collect lessons from experience, and to engage in institutional learning on the subject.

The Ambassadors' View

Although USAID is the largest U.S. government actor in democracy assistance, its activities in the field are overseen by the State Department—more particularly, by the U.S. ambassador in each country in which USAID works. The State-USAID relationship in this domain (which is supposed to be growing tighter as USAID is formally put under the direction of the State Department) is sometimes problematic, because State Department officers in general, and U.S. ambassadors in particular, tend to view democracy aid very differently from USAID democracy officers.

At the risk of overgeneralizing, it is hard for many ambassadors and other senior diplomats to give up old proconsul habits—to resist the view that promoting democracy in a country means favoring friends and trying to nudge or push the political process to ensure that those friends come to power and stay there. When they pay attention to democracy aid, U.S. ambassadors tend toward a narrow dual focus. First, they concentrate on elections and push hard for electoral aid packages, more than for any other kind of democracy aid. They want high-profile American observer teams there for the elections and resist arguments by the main American organizations that carry out election observing that it is better not to send observers to elections that are clearly not going to be legitimate. When observer missions arrive, the ambassadors often try to influence their statements, assuming that the observers' reports should bend to fit Washington's diplomatic interests, especially in moderating criticism of friendly governments.

Second, ambassadors and other State Department officials at U.S. embassies enthuse over study tours in which officials of the recipient country's government go to the United States for several weeks to see democracy in action. To some extent they like study tours so much because handing out visits to the United States is a way for them to build goodwill among their counterparts in the host country and to reward foreign government officials for cooperation. Yet the reasons for their enthusiasm about study tours go deeper. They tend to view democratization as a matter of getting senior officials to behave democratically. If they can just get the key political leaders, the inner circle of executive branch powerholders and the top parliamentarians to accept democratic norms, their thinking goes, the government will become more democratic. And the diplomats display a touching faith that if they can just get the necessary foreign officials to the United States for a few weeks to see democracy in action, those officials will have transformative experiences and come back armed with good ideas, even a whole new outlook on politics.

This "democracy by light bulb" theory was vividly put to me by a U.S. ambassador in Romania who asserted that he wanted to see every member of the Romanian political elite go to the United States on a democracy study tour. If they can just see democracy in practice, he insisted, they will realize what they need to do.

Not only are the ambassadors and other State Department officials drawn to the short-term methods of elections and study tours, but they often have a corresponding disdain of what they view as USAID's slow, long-term approach to democracy building. They have a horror of the agency's studies, assessments, planning documents, and the like. They want action, not statements like "It will take a generation of gradual political change." They are often particularly contemptuous of USAID's interest in civil society work, viewing the local NGO community as a fringe element and an irritant to the host government.

These differences in outlook do not necessarily deter USAID missions from carrying out their programs. They are merely another complicating factor in the design and implementation of democracy projects, another layer of bureaucracy on top of an already cluttered system. If the State Department wants to exert more control over democracy assistance, as some department officials insist, it will have to take it upon itself to learn more about the subject and stop acting on the poorly formed instincts of some diplomats. Recent efforts to bolster the role of the Bureau of Democracy, Human Rights, and Labor in this vein are a start but the more traditional parts of the State Department bureaucracy will have to expand their thinking as well.

The Private Alternative

Highlighting the shortcomings of USAID and the complications of its relationship with the State Department leads naturally to the question of whether the private alternative for democracy aid—giving responsibility to quasi-governmental but privately run organizations such as the NED, the Asia Foundation, and the Eurasia Foundation—avoids these institutional problems. These organizations are indeed less bureaucratic and slow than USAID. They are that way, however, mainly because they are so much smaller—their budgets together are less than 1 percent of the foreign aid budget that USAID oversees. Increasing their budgets substantially would bring on many of the problems that afflict USAID, especially those concerning monitoring and evaluation. The NED, for example, could not be expanded much without fundamental changes in its methods of operation and self-governance, particularly its special relationship with its four core grantees.

Similarly, if these private organizations commanded hundreds of millions of dollars of public funds to support democracy, they would call down upon themselves the sort of intensive congressional oversight that has done much to suffocate USAID's institutional culture. (NED, in fact, already attracts bouts of congressional scrutiny, which would escalate if its budgets ran to the hundreds of millions rather than tens of millions of dollars.) Moreover, these private organizations currently enjoy a certain leeway to carry out government-funded democracy promotion at some distance from U.S. foreign policy. That leeway would shrink rapidly if such organizations came to control the bulk of public funds devoted to democracy aid. The State Department in particular would begin to evince the same need to bring them under its wing that it has recently asserted with USAID. Moreover, though these private groups have some advantages of flexibility and speed over USAID, they are not without their own problems, particularly the tendency to give aid to ingrown circles of recipients and to develop ingrown leadership structures.

There is no easy private alternative to the basic institutional challenges of spending large amounts of taxpayers' money on U.S. democracy aid. The institutional shortcomings of democracy aid that USAID and other U.S. government agencies sponsor are to some extent reflections of the chronic bureaucratic problems of large federal agencies. At the same time, however, they grow out of tendencies and tensions that arise when an organization is responsible for such expenditures: the compulsion to create invasive mechanisms of oversight to ensure the money is not misspent; the tendency to engage in burdensome planning to ensure one knows what one is doing; the constant push-pull between giving authority to field offices and maintaining central mechanisms of control; the need to create detailed mechanisms of evaluation to figure out whether the aid is working and to lay a base for persuading others that the enterprise is worthwhile; and so forth down the bureaucratic line. Renewed efforts at USAID and other U.S. agencies to improve the internal mechanisms for designing and delivering democracy aid are necessary. Yet only when the American public, Congress, the policy community, and the media come to accept the value of such work will some of the pressure that creates these counterproductive institutional tendencies and tensions recede and permit more flexible, innovative mechanisms for large-scale democracy aid.

10
Giving Out Grades: Evaluation

Good implementation of democracy assistance is hard. Good evaluation is even harder, although it is necessary if programs are to be improved and resources are to be well deployed. The problem of developing a system that produces honest, insightful, and helpful evaluations is by no means unique to democracy aid. Foreign aid of all kinds has suffered from inadequate evaluations for decades. More broadly, as U.S. aid officials struggle to find some objective means of assessing the value of democracy programs, they should remember that the effects of most kinds of government assistance programs, domestic or international, are subject to fundamental debate. To take just one example, the question of how much domestic antipoverty programs have actually reduced poverty over the past thirty years in the United States continues to stir ferocious argument despite copious, well-funded research by batteries of social scientists. Given the lack of consensus on such a thoroughly researched issue, one cannot expect to achieve definitive conclusions about the effectiveness of U.S. democracy assistance abroad.

In this chapter, I start by identifying the key challenges of this important task and consider whether democracy aid is uniquely difficult to evaluate. After briefly reviewing the traditional evaluation methods I devote considerable critical attention to USAID's current effort to apply a corporate-style, quantitatively oriented "managing for results" system to democracy assistance. I close by sketching some principles for an alternative method.

THE DIFFICULTIES OF EVALUATION

Among the manifold difficulties of evaluating democracy assistance, two challenges stand out: establishing *criteria for success* and establishing the *causal links* between assistance programs and changes in the recipient societies.

In Search of Criteria of Success

In attempting to arrive at criteria for success for different kinds of democracy projects, aid providers look for objective indicators that are specific, straightforward, and relatively easy to measure. For programs to strengthen parliaments, for example, aid providers seek a definition of a good parliament, so that the program can be assessed in terms of achievement of a defined ideal. The problem of establishing such criteria—whether for parliamentary programs, media projects, local government work, or any area of democracy aid—lies mainly in trying to make objective what is inherently subjective.

Even within the confines of a single political system, agreeing on precise criteria for successful political institutions and processes is not easy. To continue the example of legislatures, a random group of American political analysts would probably agree that a good legislature has certain attributes, such as efficiency, representativeness, and relative freedom from corruption. Yet attaching specific meanings to these general terms is less simple. What, for instance, is an ideal degree of legislative efficiency? Some people might think that bills should speed through the legislature in a few days or weeks. Others would be more concerned about giving interest groups the opportunity for full consultations. Even an attribute as apparently uncontroversial as freedom from corruption does not always get everyone's agreement in practice. Some people, including many prominent politicians, regard the U.S. system of financing campaigns as perfectly acceptable. Others see it as a form of institutionalized corruption.

The same difficulty of establishing objective criteria of success holds for every institution or sector that democracy assistance programs touch. Is it possible to define for all countries the best kinds of labor unions, the right type and quantity of advocacy NGOs, or the most useful sort of local government? Even when it is possible to agree on the essential attributes of such organizations as they function in established democracies, it is not necessarily possible to reach a consensus on their role in particular transitional situations. A group of diverse political scientists might agree that independent labor unions tend to have certain characteristics, but it would be much harder for them to see eye-to-eye on what kinds or number of unions would further democratization most in a particular transitional country. It is difficult enough for Americans of different political stripes to reach even minimal agreement on such issues. It is impossible to get people from a range of political cultures to settle on detailed criteria of success for democracy assistance efforts.

The elusiveness of the value of objective criteria of success increases when one realizes that the value of democracy programs is often not their specific effects on institutions but the way they reshape the attitudes or ideas of individuals. An aid effort may provide moral support to embattled activists, build trust among different political subcultures, or enhance a spirit of possibility and cooperation among politically engaged youth. Establishing objective indicators for moral support, trust, or an enhanced spirit of possibility is an extremely difficult task.

The Causal Conundrum

The second major challenge in evaluating democracy assistance—determining whether particular political changes in a recipient country are the result of particular democracy assistance efforts—is formidable. Suppose, for example, U.S. aid providers sponsor a program to train journalists in a transitional country to be more challenging and assertive in their coverage of politics. During the life of the program or soon afterward, newspapers in the country become more diverse in their political opinions and more willing to criticize the government. These shifts might be the result of the training program, but they might have come about because of a variety of other changes—in the ownership of some of the papers, in editors' rising anger at the government, or in the political climate due to the declining health of the president. Or, for example, if an opposition party increases its showing in one national election, how do we know whether it is because of a U.S. training program for that party, a shift in the party leadership, some party chiefs figuring out better strategy on their own, a bad economy, a corruption scandal that hurt the ruling party, or some other factor?

In any society, the political environment is a swirl of events, institutions, personalities, processes, attitudes, and trends. It is rarely possible to know with any precision how external influences affect internal factors to produce political outcomes. And in the particular area of democracy promotion, U.S. democracy aid programs are usually only one element in a thicket of direct and indirect external political influences that may range from European religious groups' large-scale civic education campaigns to the introduction of foreign television shows through new cable networks.

The Question of Uniqueness

Evaluating most kinds of democracy aid is a much less straightforward task than is evaluating at least some types of social and economic programs. Simple, objective indicators of success are easier to find for programs to increase crop yields or vaccination rates than for programs to strengthen civil society or the rule of law. Similarly, assessing the causal relationship between aid programs focused on crop yields or vaccination rates and changes in those figures is almost certain to be less complex than with programs aimed at civil society or the rule of law. The fact that democracy aid is harder to evaluate than some types of social and economic aid provokes different— and usually not constructive—reactions among aid providers and democracy promoters. Some aid officials have little sympathy for the idea that democracy aid may be more subjective than other types of aid and simply try to force democracy programs through the same evaluative mechanisms used for agricultural or public health programs. As described later in this chapter, the results are usually disastrous. On the other hand, some democracy promoters take advantage of the inherent subjectivity of political change to argue that their work cannot be evaluated in any systematic way and should essentially be taken on faith.

Although democracy aid is harder to evaluate than some kinds of social and economic aid, the differences should not be overdrawn. Certain social and economic programs may have precise, objective goals, but many do not. Donor-funded land reform programs, for example, are often highly controversial, both in the target societies and in the donor agencies themselves. Criteria for the best pattern of land ownership in a country are likely to be as subjective as criteria for the best form of national legislature or the best form of labor union. What one analyst writes about the problem of subjectivity in evaluating socioeconomic aid efforts sounds exactly like what some people lament as the problem of subjectivity in evaluating democracy assistance:

> Little is known about the objective successes and failures of [aid] projects and little agreement can be reached in this respect with regard to specific projects. What some call successes, others will call failures, both opinions based on subjective and intuitive interpretations of actual and imagined events.[1]

Similarly, although for certain social and economic programs causal links between aid and sectoral changes can be ascertained relatively easily, in many areas, such as micro-enterprise development, education, and poverty alleviation, isolating discrete causal factors of change is not simple. An extensive study of project monitoring and evaluation in the agricultural domain, for example, warns of the problem of causality:

> If the measurement of change is difficult, rigorously attributing the causality of the change is almost impossible under real-life conditions, in which experimental methods and replications cannot be achieved. The experimental method developed by the natural sciences cannot usually be reproduced in evaluation studies of agricultural project participants.[2]

In short, although the challenges of evaluation are especially sharp for most democracy assistance, they are more differences of degree than of kind compared with those for other areas of foreign aid.

The Low Standard

The democracy aid community has not risen to the challenge of evaluating its own work. Many democracy groups evaluate their efforts informally and haphazardly, with many projects not evaluated at all. To some extent this is due to the belief common among democracy promoters that their work is of unquestionable value and needs no assessing. Then, too, starting with the slew of democratic openings in the late 1980s and early 1990s, democracy groups got in the mode of hurrying from one country to the next, launching programs on a crash basis. Painstaking retrospective analysis appeared an unaffordable luxury.

Among U.S. assistance providers involved in democracy work, USAID carries out by far the most project evaluations. As with most of its projects, whether in child nutrition or forest preservation, USAID does retrospective evaluations of many of its democracy assistance projects (although fewer have been carried out since the advent in the mid-1990s of the managing for results system described below). Typically in these evaluations, a small team goes to the country in question a few months after a project has ended, interviews people involved in the project, and writes a report for USAID. Although many such evaluations have been carried out, they have not advanced much methodologically over the years. They are better than not carrying out evaluations at all—which has been the habit of some other U.S. government agencies involved in the field—but, like most evaluations of development work, they have many limitations.[3]

To start with, these evaluations have not come close to solving the twin problems of finding useful criteria for success and establishing causal links between project activities and political changes. To avoid the difficulties of settling on criteria for success, they often focus on outputs rather than effects—what activities the project sponsored, how many people were trained, what equipment was donated, what conferences were held, and so forth. To the extent the evaluations examine effects, they do so in mechanical ways that leave unquestioned the aid providers' underlying assumptions about their approach and that convey little idea of the significance of the project's outputs or effects. An evaluation of a project intended to teach a legislature's staff to do better research, for example, may simply state that staff members reported learning much from the training courses. Yet the evaluation may not ask to what ends the new research skills are being used and whether they have had any substantial effects on the legislature's output. In general, evaluations focus narrowly on project performance. They do not look at how other actors in the recipient society saw the aid project, whether people in the country understood why the aid was being given, what political sensitivities the aid raised, and other questions relating to context and "fit." Furthermore, since evaluations are almost always carried out within a few months of the project's completion, findings are limited to the short term. Democracy aid providers have accumulated almost no systematic knowledge about the long-term effects of their efforts.

The information-gathering methods of the evaluations are usually as limited as the analytic scope. The evaluators talk primarily to people who were responsible for implementing the project and to project participants—that is to say, people who had a stake in the project. In many cases, the USAID officer in the recipient country who was responsible for the project sets up the evaluators' visit, chooses the people they will interview, and prepares those people for the interviews. Evaluators rarely attempt to broaden the circle of those they talk to beyond aid recipients, to people who are not direct beneficiaries of the project but are knowledgeable about the institutions or sectors targeted by the project. Moreover, evaluators make clear the official nature of their inquiry. The people interviewed thus have the strong impression that any unfavorable comments they make about the project may endanger the possibility of continued aid. This creates a powerful incentive for positive comments.

The people who carry out the evaluations are often from U.S. development consulting groups that depend on USAID contracts. They are already socialized into existing aid approaches and are not prone to question assumptions about the way aid is designed or implemented. Nor are they inclined to be too critical, because that can jeopardize relations with aid officers and hurt their group's chances of being selected to perform other evaluations or other assistance projects. In at least some cases, the evaluators are chosen by the project directors themselves; naturally project directors tend to choose people they believe will be sympathetic to the project, often with an open wink about "precooking" a friendly review. Evaluators rarely have in-depth experience in the country in which they are doing evaluations. Thus they are examining changes to the complex political fabric of societies about which they usually know little beyond what they have gleaned from project documents and one regimented visit to the country in question.

THE FALSE DREAM OF SCIENCE

By the mid-1990s U.S. aid providers were feeling pressure to get more serious about evaluating democracy assistance efforts. Before, they could argue that democracy aid was too new to justify concerted evaluation. But once hundreds or even thousands of projects and several billion dollars of aid funds had come and gone, maintaining that the field was too young to assess was no longer credible. Furthermore, the honeymoon for both democratization and democracy assistance was clearly over. When democracy was spreading rapidly in the late 1980s and early 1990s, democracy assistance shone with reflected glory. When democracy stalled in many transitional countries in the mid-1990s, however, democracy programs began to come under harsher scrutiny.

Substantial cuts in the U.S. foreign affairs budget across the first half of the 1990s also imposed greater pressure on democracy promoters to justify their expenditures. This translated into a push to come up with dramatic, easily digestible success stories for skeptical congressmen and a drive to develop evaluation methods that would prove conclusively that democracy aid, and all other kinds of aid, were making a real difference. The budget cuts also impelled aid providers to choose between programs; therefore, they sought evaluative information that would give them a solid basis for such choices.

Democracy promoters' response to these pressures has been a significant increase in discussion of evaluations and some increase in the actual carrying out of evaluations. At the National Endowment for Democracy, for example, a general lack of interest in evaluations, particularly among NED's four core grantees, has gradually given way to more attention to the subject and more frequent use of outside evaluators. The most significant institutional response has come from USAID, which has felt the greatest pressure to justify its budgets and which had additional impetus to develop new methods of evaluation because of its embrace in the mid-1990s of the Clinton administration's "reinventing government" initiative. "Reinvention" means adopting a corporate-style managing for results system with precise definitions of strategic objectives, intended results, and indicators of success. For USAID, this has meant creating an elaborate bureaucratic methodology to define its objectives in every aid-receiving country and to monitor progress toward them using quantitative indicators.[4] Although the monitoring component of the system is designed to keep track of the progress of projects, it has ended up operating as an evaluation mechanism—the results of the year-by-year monitoring exercises are used to make decisions about whether to continue projects and as general measures of success. Because of the importance of the new system for USAID and because it represents the U.S. democracy promotion community's largest effort to find a method of assessing the impact and value of democracy assistance, managing for results merits in-depth examination.

The Apparatus

The implications of USAID's adoption of the managing for results system for the design, implementation, and monitoring of its projects are vast. The goal is nothing less than a transformation of USAID's operations. Assessing the effects and value of this reorganization as a whole is beyond the scope of this study. The focus here is on the monitoring component. To understand that component, however, the fundamental elements of the apparatus must be understood. The apparatus is intricate to the point of byzantine and wrapped in the lingo of modern corporate management methods (for example, recipients of aid are now called "customers"), increasing its impenetrability. Basically, each USAID mission is required to periodically write a "results framework" to define what it seeks to accomplish. The framework has three levels: at the top are several "strategic objectives," each of which connects downward to several "intermediate results," each of which in turn is undergirded by several "performance indicators" that are to be used to measure fulfillment of the intermediate results.

Most missions are allowed to have just two or three strategic objectives. A mission may, for example, have one for economic growth, one for public health, and one for democracy. Because a mission has at most only one strategic objective for democracy, that objective is typically cast in very broad terms. In Zambia, for example, the USAID mission's strategic objective for democracy is "more sustainable multiparty democracy built."[5] In Guatemala, it is "more inclusive and responsive democracy." Missions vary the adjectives strung in front of "democracy," but the basic objective is "more democracy" or just "democracy."

The intermediate results underlying each strategic objective tend to correspond to particular sectors or institutions on the standard democracy assistance checklist, again with varying adjectives applied. In Guatemala in the mid-1990s, for example, the intermediate results of the democracy program included "more productive and transparent national legislature," "strengthened local governments more responsive to citizen interests," and "increased protection of human rights through a strengthened criminal justice system." Each intermediate result may be divided into three or four "subintermediate results," which are, essentially, more specific versions of intermediate results. In Zambia, for example, the intermediate result of "improved public debate" was broken down into subintermediate results that included "enhanced media information," "increased citizen awareness," and "better parliamentary process."

For each intermediate result and subintermediate result, the USAID mission must establish performance indicators. These are supposed to be specific, concrete, and measurable. There is a strong preference for quantitative indicators. To assess whether a "better parliamentary process" is occurring in Zambia, for example, the USAID mission will measure the "percentage of groups who report improved interactions with MPs" and the "percentage increase in MPs' use of legislative resource facilities." To assess whether "increasing effectiveness of civil society organization advocacy" is occurring, the mission will measure the "percentage increase in effective advocacy campaigns conducted by NGOs" and the "percentage increase in government interaction with NGOs." In the previous democracy program in Zambia, in the mid-1990s, the intermediate result indicator of "media are more professional and independent" was measured by the "private-sector share of newspapers" and the "private-sector share of working journalists."

For each indicator, the aid mission must determine a unit of measurement, a method of data collection, and the frequency of data collection. USAID and the American groups it funds have expended considerable effort in developing data collection methods, including surveys, focus groups, case studies, field observations, and gathering data from government sources. Targets are established for each indicator, based on figures calculated in a baseline survey. The annual targets for each indicator tend to be linear projections from the starting point, usually with little basis in the actual project planning. In the Zambia project, for example, the target for total percentage of voters registered was simply set at 50 percent for 1996, 60 percent for 1997, and 70 percent for 1998. Performance on the indicators is measured and reported each year by USAID missions to USAID headquarters in Washington in a country-by-country review process.

USAID devoted an enormous amount of time and energy to setting up the monitoring component of the managing for results system. Creating results frameworks for every project in every mission entailed huge quantities of new bureaucratic activity. Functionaries spent countless hours coming up with a compendium of sample indicators, the weighty "Indicator Handbook."[6] The many intermediary organizations that compete for USAID funds had to be brought on board as well. In the democracy promotion community, the specialized democracy organizations such as NDI, IRI, and IFES, as well as the development consulting groups that have entered the arena, also had to learn to use the system, a task few relished.

The Inadequacy of Numbers

As applied to the democracy realm, the managing for results system does have some good points. It forces people who are planning and implementing assistance projects to think carefully about and articulate clearly what they are trying to do. A great deal of vague thinking and loose language has accompanied democracy building. Phrases such as "strengthening civil society" and "making government more responsive" have been casually invoked to describe any number of things a democracy group feels like doing. The managing for results system obliges practitioners to flesh out such concepts. The system also shifts the attention from outputs to effects, getting past the often sterile exercise of counting the number of people trained, books delivered, and seminars held.

On the whole, however, the effort to assess the impact of democracy programs by using highly reductionistic indicators is a deeply flawed undertaking that is consuming vast resources, producing little useful insight or knowledge, and introducing serious distortions into the designing and implementing of such aid. The core problem is that democratization in any country cannot be broken down neatly and precisely into a set of quantitative bits. Attempting to use such informational bits as criteria of success without grounding them in sophisticated, deep-reaching analyses of the political context produces superficial and dangerously misleading pictures. One vivid example underlines this point. In 1997 a coup in Cambodia derailed the shaky democratic transition that USAID and other donors had been supporting with large amounts of political and economic assistance since the early 1990s. The USAID "Results Review and Resource Request" for Cambodia that year nonetheless reported that for its democracy projects, "progress against most SO [strategic objective] indicators exceeded expectations."[7] The report described the success of USAID-funded NGOs in "helping restore democratic momentum" and a general "growing demand for governmental accountability." The contrast between this upbeat progress report and a country reeling from a major setback in democratization was almost surreal.

The problems with the quantitative indicators become apparent if one looks closely. Consider, for example, some of the indicators commonly used to measure the success of programs for strengthening legislatures. One such indicator is the percentage of bills approved for which public hearings are held, reflecting the view of many U.S. aid providers that congressional hearings are a good marker of democracy, and the more the better. If the number of such hearings increases from, say, three to five a year in a country where a program for strengthening the legislature is under way, this will be reported as a favorable result, a "66.6 percent increase in parliamentary openness." The number of hearings may be up, however, for all sorts of reasons, possibly having little to do with the aid project or with increased openness and accountability. The speaker of the parliament may have presidential ambitions and have decided to lead a series of public hearings, no matter how unnecessary or politically biased, to raise his or her visibility. Or the increase may stem from an attempt by the ruling party to prosecute some members of the executive branch on trumped-up corruption charges, using public hearings. Mere numerical data about hearings, which is what will be generated by the assistance monitoring, conveys far too little information to be useful as a measure of legislative strengthening or democratization.

Another frequently used indicator for legislative programs is the percentage of total bills approved that were initiated by the legislature as opposed to the executive branch, the assumption being that more parliamentary initiative is a good thing in most transitional societies because it reflects less executive dominance. If an increase in the percentage of bills initiated by the legislature, say from 10 percent to 20 percent, occurs in a country where USAID is sponsoring a legislative aid program, that fact will be reported as an encouraging 100 percent increase in a key indicator of parliamentary development. Yet once again, the reasons for the apparently positive change may not have much to do with democratization. It may be that members of the executive branch spent much of the year mired in a corruption scandal and therefore did little work on their legislative agenda, sending many fewer bills to the legislature than the year before—thereby raising the percentage of bills initiated by the legislature even though that body was not any more active than in the previous year. Or the increase may be due to the formation of a coalition of extremist parties, which pushed a number of bills through the legislature—bills inimical to political tolerance and openness. In short, the figure for the percentage of bills initiated by the legislature, by itself, tells far too little to be useful as an indicator of success or failure and may reflect any number of trends, many of which are not linked to democratization.

Most of the indicators employed for democracy programs are similarly flawed. In a few areas of democracy building, naked numbers may be reliable guides to progress. Tracking the percentage of eligible voters registered, for example, is a useful way to gauge the success of a voter registration program (although other factors, such as the integrity of the registration process, are also relevant). In most cases, the numbers tell very little, and what they do tell is unclear. Reducing large elements of democracy, such as a well-functioning local government or an active civil society, down to two or three extremely narrow quantitative indicators does irremediable violence to those concepts. The propagation in USAID of a system based on such indicators for measuring the progress of democracy assistance represents the false dream of science that frequently mesmerizes Americans engaged in sociopolitical work, the belief that all those messy particularities of people and politics can be reduced to charts and statistics.

Under the managing for results system, USAID missions are allowed to present some qualitative analysis along with the numerical information drawn from the indicators. Yet, whatever the intention of those overseeing the system, the numbers end up dominating the discussions both within missions and at USAID headquarters. The strong perception of officers in the field is, in the words of one experienced USAID official in Nepal, "Washington only cares about the numbers." The qualitative analysis that missions provide about the progress of democracy aid projects ends up being supplementary at best, with little time and energy usually invested in it by either those producing it or those reviewing it.

A Distorting Process

The indicator system not only fails as a method for assessing the effects of democracy aid programs, it introduces distortions into the aid itself. Inevitably, when faced with strict, narrow criteria for success, aid officers begin to design projects that will produce quantifiable results rather than ones that are actually needed. As the indicators become established and are taken to constitute the set of accepted outcomes of democracy projects, the universe of program design shrinks to match the indicators. The evaluation tail begins to wag the program dog. In Nepal, for example, a USAID official commented to me with some regret that an apparently useful program to build consensus on policy reform among government officials had to be sacrificed because it suffered in comparison with the literacy program. The numbers on the literacy program were great, she said—tens of thousands of people reached. The numbers on policy reform—a handful of laws affected—were much less impressive. That comparing the number of individuals reached by a literacy program with the number of laws modified by a policy reform program is an obviously illogical comparison did not stop the inexorable push toward numerical analysis. In Zambia, a USAID representative remarked to me that one of the reasons the mission there planned to emphasize judicial and legislative work rather than civil society programming was that he was sure they could produce "good numbers" with the former but not the latter.

   The obsession with quantifiable indicators also works against attempts by democracy promoters to grapple with core political processes rather than merely trying to reproduce institutional forms. In the area of legislative strengthening, for example, more elaborate institutional forms often accomplish little. What the recipient country needs is attention to issues of process, such as building patterns of give-and-take and cooperation across bitterly partisan lines or encouraging legislators to tackle mundane but practical issues rather than spending all their time in public posturing on conflict-laden, symbolic topics. These sorts of process-oriented goals fit poorly into the numerical frameworks and charts that USAID now demands. The quantifiable indicators and the system that accompanies them thus unhelpfully reinforce a focus on institutional checklists and preset institutional endpoints.

The negative effects of the system also extend to the phase of implementation. In theory, once the objectives of a project are agreed on, the group that is implementing the project may use whatever methods it wishes to achieve the objectives and modify its methods as it sees fit. In practice, powerful rigidities are built into the system. Establishing indicators for a project and getting all the necessary parts of the bureaucracy to sign off on them is so time-consuming and demanding that once indicators are set they are difficult to change. It is hard to take advantage of new opportunities or to respond to the constantly shifting realities of transitional situations when one knows that one's project will be judged on whether a certain number of public hearings were held, a certain percentage of bills were initiated by the legislature, a certain percentage of bills incorporated input from the research staff, and so forth. A representative of a U.S. election aid group working on a USAID-funded project to strengthen civil society in the former Soviet Union told me about having to fill out a 104-week project activity form in advance, specifying the precise timing, topic, and participants for each training seminar—this in a country less than five years old, in which every element of political life was up for grabs and evolving day by day. The representative, who was also a poet, told me, "Thank goodness I have a literary imagination, otherwise I could not fill out such a form." The controlling assumption of the system—that democratization follows a predictable sequence of quantifiable, planned segments of sociopolitical change—represents the social engineering tendencies of foreign aid at their worst.

The indicator system strives futilely for great precision in assessing the effects of aid programs. Yet at the same time, it almost completely fails to establish causal links between the changes noted and the assistance programs. If an aid program is operating in a particular sector and one of the indicators shows a positive change, the aid provider simply ascribes that change to the program. Stated even more baldly, if something good happens in the domain in which an aid project is working, the aid provider automatically takes credit for it whether or not there is any plausible causal link. Some proponents argue that because the indicators are narrowly defined, the causal links to the aid programs are essentially built into the system. Yet even with the most tightly delimited indicators, many factors may explain a change. If, for example, an increase in voter registration occurs in a country in which an aid program to promote voter registration is being carried out, attributing that change to the program may seem logical. But the change may be due to the entry of an interesting new candidate into the electoral campaign, or to a political furor over a highly visible issue. With almost every indicator, multiple causal factors are possible. The lack of serious attention to the issue of causality and the credit-grabbing approach adopted by aid providers further reduce the credibility of the indicator system.

In addition, the system impedes successful partnership with local actors. If local advocacy NGOs participate in U.S. advocacy training seminars and then begin to represent interests to the government more effectively, U.S. aid providers say, "We have got civil society working." If the judiciary starts to process cases more quickly after some judges install U.S.-designed case management systems, U.S. aid providers happily report, "We are strengthening the rule of law." Such statements sour the recipients. The "we did that" mindset encouraged by the system works against the important idea that democracy aid is best conceived as something that can *facilitate* positive changes in the political life of other countries, through genuine partnership with local agents of change.

Often U.S. aid representatives are even hesitant to show the results frameworks they have developed for their aid projects to their counterparts in the recipient country. Aid providers will confidently insist that they have developed their plans for the legislature, judiciary, or other target institution in close collaboration with their local counterparts. Actually showing the speaker of the parliament a detailed USAID document that sets out for the next three years how many hearings or committee meetings the legislature should hold, the number of bills it should initiate, the number of meetings it should have with NGOs, and so forth, is a little hard to do. The speaker, and other political actors, are likely to find a foreign-designed master plan for the functioning of one of their key political institutions disquieting, to say the least.

The indicator system is extremely unpopular among USAID officers, at least those working on democracy building. Few think it has improved the programs; most consider it tremendously time-consuming and expensive. As career professionals, they go through the motions and implement it. In private they are skeptical, even derisive, about the system and assume it will fizzle out in a few years and be replaced with some new pet project of the next set of political appointees. Officials of the specialized democracy organizations that receive USAID funding react with disdain and resistance. They resent having to squeeze their organizations' methods through the gears of the indicator system. At the development consulting firms that implement USAID programs, the attitude is more accepting. After all, they have made a business out of mastering the arcane bureaucratic requirements of the foreign aid machinery. In fact, the more cumbersome and elaborate the requirements, the less competition the consulting firms have from other organizations in bidding for aid contracts.

Awareness is gradually growing among USAID managers of the many shortcomings of the indicator system as applied to democracy aid. Some of the democracy groups that have been forced to use the system have made their harsh opinions very directly known to USAID. The agency has attempted to respond by reassuring USAID missions that indicator performance will not be a controlling factor in decisions about allocation of new funds to missions. But the system is hard to change. It is an elaborate contraption with its own self-referential logic that must basically be accepted or rejected as a whole. Moreover, USAID cannot make an exception from the system for its democracy work. The system is being applied to all USAID's programs, from public health to population control. Democracy aid cannot opt out.

THE START OF AN ALTERNATIVE

The difficulties of evaluating democracy assistance are indeed considerable. And the responses to these difficulties by the democracy assistance community have not been weak. Democracy promoters have tended either to underdo evaluations, carrying them out haphazardly, using superficial methods, or to overdo them, elaborating overly complex, rigid methods, such as the USAID quantitative indicator system. There is a pressing need to find a workable middle ground.

Aid providers must start by accepting that definitive evaluations—objective assessments that establish with certainty the democratic value of particular aid programs—are not possible. Subjectivity in evaluations is inevitable. Interpretation is essential. Nuance is necessary. The false dream of science must be abandoned. It must be replaced with a realistic philosophy about both what kinds of knowledge evaluations can produce and the fact that promoting democracy is more an art than a science.

Next, aid organizations must clarify the purposes of their evaluations. Several different purposes are often intertwined, leading to problems. In addition to the basic audit function of making sure aid funds were spent in legitimate ways, evaluations have at least three different purposes: 1) to provide material that can be used to convince others that the aid programs are a worthwhile investment of funds; 2) to provide information necessary for managing democracy assistance projects, about what effects the programs are having, what their weak spots are, how they can be improved, and other middle-level issues relating to design and implementation; and 3) to engage in deep learning about democracy aid, to question assumptions, find new approaches, and understand how the assistance is perceived and valued within the recipient societies.

If the first of these functions—essentially the public relations function—is necessary, the procedures and products developed to fulfill it should be kept as separate as possible from the other functions of the evaluation. The public relations imperative inevitably distorts and corrupts other evaluative functions if it is mixed with them. Some USAID officials, for example, blame the shortcomings of the indicator system on USAID's desire to prove conclusively to skeptical members of Congress that foreign aid is useful. In fact, some congressional staffers say in private that they are not especially interested in or impressed by quasi-scientific, number-laden reports on the progress of democracy aid projects. If public relations is the purpose of an evaluation effort, it is best simply to emphasize stirring anecdotes, vivid testimonials, and good photographs.

In evaluations intended for the middle level, the bread-and-butter evaluations necessary for good management, the approach should be to improve on several key features of the standard evaluation described above, in which a team of evaluators is sent out at the end of a project to interview a number of people involved. One set of improvements should focus on who the evaluators are. A greater effort should be made to use people who neither work full-time for the aid organization sponsoring the evaluation nor depend on that organization for a significant proportion of their work. Aid providers fall into the trap of thinking that an outsider cannot possibly understand their work. They are wary of hard questioning from anyone not already on board the general enterprise of democracy assistance. Yet good evaluations require USAID in particular to find ways to break out of the closed circle of consultants who shuttle between USAID projects and evaluations. In addition, aid providers should more frequently employ evaluators from the recipient countries themselves. In many countries, highly qualified experts are available who know the local political scene much better and cost much less than fly-in U.S. consultants. Using in-country evaluators is not always simple—conflicting interests and local loyalties sometimes get in the way—but it can bring many benefits and is underutilized by the democracy promotion community.

A second, more extensive set of improvements should change what the evaluators do. Instead of attempting to determine whether a project produced certain preset indicators of success, the evaluators should seek to examine all effects the project had—intended, unintended, direct, indirect, material, psychological, and so on. An inquiry of this sort involves a different approach to field research by the evaluators. They should not start with or limit themselves to targeted questions, such as, "Did the training help the parliamentary research staff provide more useful advice to legislators on the main economic reform bills currently pending?" Instead, they should step back and ask the people being interviewed more open-ended questions such as, "What was the training like?" or "Describe how the training affected you." That will also help avoid the tendency of evaluators to ask questions that make plain to those being interviewed what answers the evaluators want to hear, such as, "Did the technical consultations help make the case management system easier for you to understand and more efficient to use?"

In addition, evaluators should interview a wider range of people in the recipient country. They should talk not just with those who took part in or directly benefited from the aid project in question, but with others who have not been part of the (often ingrown) circle of aid recipients yet are knowledgeable about a target institution or sector. To do so requires evaluators to cast a broader net for contacts. Aid organizations must give evaluators the leeway—as well as the time and resources—to set up their own meetings rather than relying on the aid officers in a country to set them up.

Once evaluators have examined the effects of the project in a broad manner, they should analyze them in terms of their relation to the project's goals. The goals should have been specified early on in qualitative terms yet with a reasonable degree of detail. If, for example, the project was intended to strengthen a legislature, the planning process should have required the aid providers to describe the kinds of strengthening they hoped to help bring about—greater cooperation between the contending political blocs, fuller consideration of views from interest groups, more serious deliberation by the review committees, and the like. Not all the effects of a project will necessarily relate directly to a project goal. Evaluation should assess the significance for democratization of any unintended effects encountered by asking whether they further any of the basic attributes of democratic societies, such as political openness, representativeness, accountability, or participation.

Evaluation should not simply assume that any positive changes in the targeted institutions or sectors were the result of the aid programs. Causality can rarely be ascertained with great certainty, but evaluators should at least attempt some inquiry into it. For an aid program directed at the media, for example, evaluators should try to gain an understanding of how the sector has been changing and what set of factors has been producing the changes. When they turn to the effects of the specific program under evaluation, they can put those effects into a broader causal context.

Aid providers must set aside energy, resources, and attention for less frequent but vitally important deep-learning exercises. The purpose of such efforts should be to take a ground-up look at a particular area of democracy aid—to question the assumptions that underlie work in that area to date, to penetrate the thinking of the people on the receiving end and to learn how they perceive and value the assistance, to explore the long-term and less direct effects of aid in that area, and other such issues. Deep-learning efforts require different methodologies than the more regular middle-level evaluations. They require more time and more freedom for the evaluators (who in such efforts are better considered researchers). The questions to be explored will be more open-ended and may evolve as the fieldwork advances. More extensive empirical research may be involved, including more in-depth surveys and the use of control groups. A comparative focus across several regions is often valuable.

Few of the U.S. organizations engaged in democracy aid have carried out many deep-learning exercises, although the field, still in a formative stage, could benefit greatly from such undertakings. Starting in the early 1990s, USAID did sponsor a few longer-term studies of specific areas of democracy assistance that took on some of the characteristics of deep-learning exercises. One of these studies took a comparative, in-depth look at rule-of-law aid, usefully questioning basic assumptions and suggesting new approaches.[8] A study of legislative assistance was less helpful because it became infected with a public relations purpose that led to both a reluctance to probe underlying assumptions and a marketing language that was clearly intended for Congress.

Finally, democracy promoters should look at two alternative evaluation methods that have been developed and used occasionally in other areas of development work. One is participatory evaluation, in which people from the recipient country who are directly involved in an aid project take responsibility for evaluating the project, as it goes along as well as once it is completed.[9] They identify their own indicators of success, and develop their own research methods and methods of results reporting. Participatory evaluations are a natural outgrowth of more localistic project design and implementation. They entail their own difficulties and shortcomings but have important benefits as well—above all, engaging the recipients directly in the task of assessing the value of an aid intervention.

The other method is participant-observer studies, in which a researcher "lives" with a project for an extended period, perhaps six to twelve months, for the purpose of observing its operation and effects and getting to know both the project and its context extremely well.[10] This is a quiet, slow, and expensive method that requires unusually talented evaluators, but it can produce important insights that other kinds of evaluations will miss. It is especially useful for examining areas of assistance that are not going well but do not reveal their problems easily.

Three central points about evaluation merit repeating in conclusion. Foremost, aid providers and those who stand outside the aid community looking in must accept the limitations of evaluation. Assessing democracy aid, like democratization itself, cannot be turned into a science. And in most cases, pseudoscientific efforts are worse than none at all. There is no easy solution to the challenges of determining the effects and value of particular aid projects. There is no substitute for in-depth, qualitative analysis that deals head-on with the complexities and subtleties of a recipient country's political situation. Second, aid providers must be sure to clarify their own purposes when they set out to evaluate. Confusing public relations with evaluation is a common failing. Finally, real detachment between those evaluating and those evaluated is essential. It takes surprisingly hard bureaucratic labor to establish a method that ensures evaluations that are the product of a constructive, balanced detachment. The temptations to do evaluations the easy way are ever-present, and the quality of aid suffers as a result.

11
Understanding Effects

When people outside the democracy assistance community take an interest in democracy aid—whether they are government policy makers, journalists, scholars, activists from other areas of international affairs, or members of the public—they usually arrive quickly at a basic question, "Does it work?" This question has bubbled up to the surface in policy circles again and again over the past two decades, finding little resolution and being posed each time as though for the first time. Despite thousands of democracy projects carried out in dozens of countries, billions of dollars spent, and endless reports by aid providers, there is surprisingly little conventional wisdom on the utility of democracy aid. Instead, one encounters passionate assertions from democracy promoters that such assistance is critical to the future of democracy worldwide and questioning, even derisive comments from skeptics who say that democracy cannot be exported.

Discussions or arguments about the effectiveness of democracy assistance gravitate almost inevitably to a high level of generality. When people outside the immediate community of democracy promoters ask whether such aid works, they are usually referring to macro-level effects. They do not want to know whether the U.S. aid programs in a country have successfully trained the staff of the parliament in policy analysis, endowed the electoral commission with new technical capabilities, or improved the civic awareness of some citizens. They want to know whether the democracy aid has produced democracy. It is obviously unfair to expect any one assistance project to determine the political direction of a country. Yet for the whole package of democracy aid in any one country, the question is often unavoidable.

This chapter addresses the question of effects. I first present one answer to the question of "Does it work?" and then explore how the effects of democracy aid should be understood, beyond the stock question of whether or not democracy is produced. In the second half of the chapter, I return to the four case studies, reviewing the effects that U.S. democracy programs have had in each of the countries.

MODEST RESULTS

To understand the nature and weight of the effects of democracy aid, it is useful to consider three categories of cases: countries that are moving forward in democratic transitions; countries in which attempted democratic transitions are stagnating or moving backward; and countries that have not yet experienced a significant democratic opening or breakthrough.

Speeding Up a Moving Train

For countries in the first category, democracy aid can help reinforce, broaden, and deepen democratization. To cite just some examples, electoral aid may contribute to the institutionalization of elections, both with regard to the government's competence in administering them and the public's understanding of and participation in them. Political party programs may give parties tools with which to campaign effectively and to build membership. If government officials are seriously interested in reforming major state institutions, external aid can furnish knowledge and ideas about judicial, legislative, and other institutional reforms. If the government is committed to decentralization, outside support can focus and bolster its efforts. Democracy programs can boost the formation of national and local-level advocacy NGOs, potentially increasing interaction between government and citizens and producing beneficial changes in some laws and policies bearing on various public interest issues. Aid to media groups can accelerate the growth and capabilities of independent media.

There is no guarantee that specific democracy programs will have these kinds of effects, even where the political dynamic of a country is positive. As discussed in the three middle chapters on the different types of democracy aid, there are many ways in which aid can fall short, bounce off, or even have negative effects, despite a favorable climate. A government may fail to institutionalize learning about election administration. Political parties may participate in externally sponsored training programs but continue their old habits of patronage and personalism. Even very large amounts of institutional aid may be absorbed by stagnant state institutions, to minimal effect. NGOs may multiply but accomplish little beyond providing comfortable jobs for a small, Westernized elite, and so forth.

Nevertheless, when a country is moving forward in a democratic transition, foreign democracy promoters can normally find ways to help. But in such situations democracy aid is rarely a major reason for democratization's advance. Larger underlying factors are usually responsible for the political evolution; democracy aid helps the country move somewhat more quickly in the direction it is already going.

There is no clearly identifiable set of factors that guarantees a successful future for a country that experiences a political opening and sets out to consolidate democracy. The more successful cases of democratic transition in recent years, primarily in Central Europe, East Asia, and South America, nonetheless share some or all of a set of five characteristics: major political forces that are not monolithic and have significant numbers of prodemocratic adherents; few powerful antidemocratic forces or a loss of legitimacy by existing antidemocratic forces that prevents them from blocking the democratic process; some historical experience with political pluralism; a peaceful regional setting in which democracy is spreading; and economic dynamism, or at least stability, and better than subsistence conditions for the majority of citizens.

These factors are deeply rooted, slowly evolving conditions that democracy aid does not affect in decisive, or even significant ways. Various mixes of democracy-related workshops, training courses, equipment donations, study tours, expert consultancies, and small grants may certainly reach many of the main political elites. They do not, however, fundamentally reshape the balances of power, interests, historical legacies, and political traditions of the major political forces in recipient countries. They do not neutralize dug-in antidemocratic forces. They do not alter the political habits, mind-sets, and desires of entire populations. They do not create benign regional settings. They do not alter the basic economic level or direction of countries. That democracy aid does not determine the presence or absence of the major factors contributing to democratization should not be seen as a grievous failure or fault. It is a fundamental fact about democracy aid that should be understood and accepted by all involved.

Slowing the Backward Slide

In countries where attempted democratic transitions are stagnating or slipping backward, democracy aid has few chances of reversing the trend. A series of sobering cases in recent years underscores this fact. Russia has absorbed large amounts of U.S. and European political aid, yet democracy there remains on extremely thin ice. Albania received the full range of U.S. and European democracy efforts in the first half of the 1990s before slipping into political turmoil in 1996. Cambodia saw numerous Western-funded efforts to foster elections, political parties, the rule of law, media, and civil society before the 1997 coup shattered the fragile democratic transition. Haiti became a major recipient of U.S. and other Western democracy aid after the U.S. military intervention in 1994, but political life there remains chaotic. With the democratic retrenchment that began in many parts of the world in the mid-1990s, this list could easily be expanded.

In such circumstances, aid for elections and political parties runs into walls. If an entrenched leader is determined to subvert an election, external aid can usually do little but ensure that reliable information about the electoral shortcomings is collected and disseminated. If a dominant political party is monopolizing state assets and marginalizing opposition forces, aid programs for political parties or civil society will seldom be able to do much about it. If leaders have scant interest in reforming the major state institutions or decentralizing power, aid for parliaments, judiciaries, and local government is unlikely to achieve noteworthy results. Aid to advocacy NGOs in stagnant or backsliding transitions can at least help them withstand the political pressure and serve as a haven for democratic activists. Such organizations seldom accumulate sufficient power on their own, however, to unlock a stalled or failing transition. Similarly, aid to media can help a few independent sources of information survive but rarely outweighs the power of state-controlled television and radio or keeps the government from shutting them down if it so chooses.

In short, democracy aid can keep the flame alive, as democracy promoters like to say, in transitions that are going badly, but not much more. In transitions gone wrong, just as in good transitions, democracy aid does not have a major influence on the factors that are at the root of the situation. Democracy aid cannot break up or change deeply entrenched concentrations of power or the antidemocratic outlook of the ruling forces. It cannot fundamentally alter a political culture that is steeped in hierarchical traditions, torn by ethnic divisions, or rife with populist longings. It cannot raise millions of people out of harsh poverty, provide them with a basic education, and persuade them that democracy will better their lot.

Extra Straws on the Camel's Back

In countries that are under nondemocratic rule and have not experienced a democratic opening, the effects of democracy aid are similarly minor in most cases. Dictatorships fall in different ways for different reasons. In Latin America, Africa, Eastern Europe, and the former Soviet Union from the late 1970s through the early 1990s, several underlying factors often contributed to democratic breakthroughs: sustained or acute economic decline; a pattern of inept, corrupt, and haphazard governance over many years; persistent groups of opposition activists who eventually transformed their campaigns into broad-based popular movements; a trend toward democratization in the region; and significant international pressure applied on human rights issues. Some cases in East Asia, such as South Korea and Taiwan, presented a very different pattern, in which movement from dictatorship to democracy was stimulated by economic growth rather than decline, although democratic activism by students, unions, and opposition political parties was also critical.

Democracy aid in nondemocratic contexts can contribute to a few of these factors. It can support democracy activists, but it is not a substitute for democracy groups' own courage, energy, skills, and legitimacy. Outside aid may help make possible the dissemination to the public of political information and ideas not controlled by the government. That is often a useful part of building popular support for political change, but it is not a simple route to a democratic revolution. Support for human rights groups can help draw domestic and international attention to a repressive government's human rights abuses.

These various forms of democracy aid in nondemocratic contexts can be valuable but they are secondary to internal factors and larger international ones as well. Even in Eastern Europe, where democracy promoters make their greatest claims of success in helping end dictatorships, U.S. and other Western democracy aid was not a central factor. Larger developments inside and outside the region—the decline and eventual collapse of Soviet power, the overwhelming failure of socialist economies, the powerful example of Western prosperity and freedom, and the heroic work of opposition activists in the countries—combined over decades to help bring down the communist regimes. Western aid supported many of the activists but cannot take primary credit for their accomplishments, which in the end were only one part of the broader political story.

Modest Expectations

The conclusion is the same, whether for countries moving ahead or moving backward in attempted democratic transitions or for countries that are not yet transitional: democracy aid generally does not have major effects on the political direction of recipient countries. The effects of democracy programs are usually modestly positive, sometimes negligible, and occasionally negative. In countries where democratization is advancing, democracy aid can, if properly designed and implemented, help broaden and deepen democratic reforms in both the governmental and nongovernmental sectors. In countries where an attempted democratic transition has stalled or regressed, democracy programs can help actors keep some independent political and civic activity going and, over the long term, help build civic awareness and civic organizations at the local level. In countries that have not yet experienced a democratic opening, democracy programs may help democracy activists survive and gradually expand their work and may increase the flow of political information not controlled by the government. These broad conclusions parallel findings on the effects of economic development aid. A recent major study by the World Bank reports that economic aid has some positive effects in countries that are following sound economic policies but makes little contribution in countries that follow unsound economic policies.[1]

This picture of limited effects does not mean that democracy aid does not work or is futile. It does mean that people both outside and inside the democracy promotion community must adjust their expectations so that when they ask "Does it work?" they do not mean "Does it produce democracy?" Instead, they should mean "Does it contribute to democratization and if so, in what ways?" It is certainly legitimate for skeptics to question whether taxpayer dollars should go to programs to promote democracy, but they must start from reasonable expectations. That expenditures totaling less than one-twenty-fourth of 1 percent of the U.S. federal budget fail to ensure democracy in nearly 100 countries around the world is not surprising.[2]

Numerous project evaluations and reports have argued over the past ten years that democracy programs must be accompanied by modest expectations about their ability to produce political change. Yet at least in the foreign affairs community in the United States, people continue to talk of democracy aid as though it is—or should be—a major determinant of political outcomes in other countries. When democracy stagnates in Russia, U.S. democracy aid is seen as having failed, as if a few tens of millions of dollars' worth of training and technical assistance should have transformed that vast country's political culture. When democracy triumphed in Chile in the latter 1980s, U.S. democracy promoters took credit in Washington, as though the struggle of Chilean opposition forces, the long tradition of democracy in Chile, and the powerful regional context of democratization were less significant than the scattering of small aid programs implemented late in the transition process.[3]

It is worth considering why expectations in the U.S. foreign affairs community about democracy aid are often unrealistically high. To some extent, such expectations are puzzling. Few Americans would suppose that in the United States, or even in a single state of the United States, a set of small government aid programs totaling a few million dollars a year (the approximate amount of U.S. democracy aid in most transitional countries) could have a decisive impact on major aspects of political life such as low voter turnout, poor civic education, and declining civic participation.

One reason for the high expectations is that Americans often assume that since transitional countries are going through change, they are particularly susceptible to outside influences. The idea is that while basic aspects of American political life (such as low voter turnout) are deeply engrained, in a transitional country the basic rules and practices of political life are up for grabs. In reality, however, the change in most transitional countries is much more superficial than it first appears. In many instances the underlying structures of power, as well as the sociopolitical cleavages and habits of the polity, are not much in flux.

Moreover, many Americans operate under the assumption, usually unstated, that the United States, being as powerful and wealthy a country as it is, can exert a strong influence on poor, relatively weak countries if it decides to do so. They actually imagine it is easier for U.S. actors to remedy shortcomings in *other* countries than in their own because American size and power create more leverage over other societies than their own.

Democracy promoters themselves inflate expectations through the language they use to describe their projects. They often—understandably—employ grandiose verbiage to persuade members of Congress, executive branch policy makers, and others to provide the funds they seek. Stakes are raised, and figurative or real promises are made: "You are concerned about whether Indonesia will make a successful democratic transition? Give us funds for special new programs there and we will meet the challenge." Democracy promoters also tend to live inside the world of their programs, and consequently see them as more central to the recipient countries than they really are. Inevitably they and their organizations transmit this perspective back to the policy community in Washington.

Adding up to More

The general conclusion about the limited effects of most democracy assistance is leavened by the phenomenon of cumulative effects. When democracy assistance to a particular country is extensive enough and successful enough to contribute to positive change in several sectors simultaneously, these contributions may begin to build on each other, multiplying the effects. Romania may be such a case, if one considers not just the U.S. aid efforts but the many democracy-related initiatives of other Western actors. Romania has been the recipient of a remarkably wide array of efforts sponsored by numerous Western governments, including those of the United States, Great Britain, Germany, Canada, Holland, France, Switzerland, Sweden, Belgium, and Italy; private Western foundations such as the Soros foundations, the German Marshall Fund of the United States, and the Charles Stewart Mott Foundation; and multilateral organizations, including the European Union, the Council of Europe, the United Nations Development Programme, and the Organization for Security and Cooperation in Europe. One cannot say that the work of any one of these actors has been essential or highly important. Yet it is impossible to move through Romanian society without noting that in almost every area where positive change seems to be occurring, external aid is present. That is not to say aid sparked all those points of change, but it is clearly supporting them. And the percentage of Romanians active in political and civil affairs who have received some direct exposure to or training relating to Western democratic ways is extremely high. Romania's democratic progress since 1989 is primarily the work of Romanians. Yet Western aid, taken together, has been a substantial partner.

Significant cumulation of positive effects of democracy programs does not often occur because several conditions must exist simultaneously. The country must be not too large (so that the aid is not spread too thin), the aid must be extensive and varied, and the political system must be populated with enough reform-oriented actors to take advantage of the aid. Eastern Europe and Latin America are the regions in which those conditions have been most common in recent years. In Eastern Europe, Romania and Bulgaria may be cases in which Western democratic aid has had real weight. Latin America may also have at least a few—possibly El Salvador and Bolivia—although the more successful democratic transitions, such as those in Chile and Uruguay, have not seen major outside democracy aid. Moreover, some of the countries that have received sizable amounts, including Nicaragua, Honduras, and Peru, have demonstrated how such aid can be stymied or even negated by local difficulties.

The Subjective Realm

In taking stock of democracy aid, it is important not to count only the specific institutional changes or activities that programs seek to accomplish: whether a legislature formed new committees; whether political parties established new internal rules of organization, whether certain NGOs carried out a particular advocacy campaign;

whether lawmakers modified the criminal procedure code to incorporate new language on rights; and so forth. Much of the value of democracy aid inheres in the less concrete, often more psychological or educational effects that it has on individuals who take part in or are otherwise reached by the programs. People may gain new ideas, skills, attitudes, or beliefs from the programs and apply them to future endeavors in many different domains. An aid provider may look at a legislative project and ask whether it succeeded in its stated goal of making the staff research division a useful resource for legislators. The most consequential effects of the program, however, may be quite different—skills gained by the research staff that they took with them to other jobs at policy institutes, media organizations, or political parties; a new attitude among some of the parliamentary staff that they should have a greater say in the functioning of the legislature; or the experience of some legislators working productively across party lines to solve an internal problem of their institution.

The same disjunction between the defined, external goals and the much more subjective, internalized effects occurs with every type of democracy program. It is one more factor that undermines aid providers' efforts to develop narrow, quantitative measures for assessing their programs. Democracy providers close to the ground are acutely aware of this disjunction, but they have difficulty conveying the idea back up the institutional food chain to those who provide the funds.

Although it is critical to recognize that the effects of democracy aid often go beyond specific institutional modifications, democracy promoters may be too facile in their use of that fact. Pointing to indeterminate psychological effects can be a tempting fallback when confronted with apparent failure. "Our project did not produce any visible change in the legislature, but we are sure we spread some valuable new ideas around," the argument may go. And that the effects of democracy aid may not appear until years later when ideas and skills are put to use in new settings similarly offers an easy out for problematic projects. "No effects are identifiable now," the aid provider may argue, "but we have planted vital seeds that will blossom in the future." Democracy promoters cannot assume or claim that valuable psychological, attitudinal, and educational change is occurring with every project. Badly designed or badly run projects may be devoid of such effects or may even result in negative ones—teaching recipients that attempts at change are futile, communicating poor organizational principles, or fostering corruption and dependency. If they wish to take credit for more indirect, subjective effects of their programs, democracy promoters must show that they understand from the outset what sort of broader goals they have and how their efforts will accomplish them.

The Power of Example

Though its impact is usually modest, democracy aid is one of the most important means at policy makers' disposal for advancing democratic transitions in other countries. A less direct influence, but one of equal or greater importance in some regions, is the power of example—the example of democracy as the most successful political system, the one most closely associated with prosperous, just, and peaceful societies. In Central Europe, for example, most political elites and ordinary people accept democracy as the normal, legitimate political system, even if they are unhappy with the performance of the democratic governments their countries have. That acceptance, which arguably results mainly from the examples from Western Europe and the United States, has had a powerful, even defining effect on the evolution of politics in that region in the 1990s, although it does not guarantee that democracy will succeed everywhere in the region.

A similar argument can be made for Latin America, where democracy in the past two decades has made substantial headway toward becoming the accepted norm. The United States has a mixed record in this century with the promotion of democracy in the region, but America's own relatively successful political system has been an important influence. Again, the widespread acceptance of democracy as the most legitimate political alternative is no guarantee that the many obstacles to effective, stable democracy in Latin America can be overcome. Nevertheless, it has been a critical factor helping to hold together many fragile Latin American transitions in the face of significant problems.

The influence of example is less strong in other regions. It is present to some degree in parts of the former Soviet Union, Asia, and Africa and to a limited extent in some Middle Eastern societies.

It is diluted in those regions by a less close connection with the West, frequent resentment of the West for other reasons, different and strongly embedded local value systems, and other factors. A more detailed survey would reveal tremendous variation, with some countries, such as Taiwan and South Korea, reflecting a high degree of awareness of and receptivity to the democratic example and others, such as Sudan and Afghanistan, evidencing little at all. Moreover, the example of Western democracy is not seamlessly positive. People around the world often see in American society, or in Western democratic societies in general, shortcomings that make them doubt the model.

The power of the democratic example is a much broader form of influence than democracy assistance, but there is a relationship between the two. Democracy aid reinforces the idea that democracy is a model to be emulated. By going out and promoting democracy through assistance programs that require commitment, time, and money, established democracies are showing people in other societies that they believe in democracy and think it suitable and valuable for others. Although people in recipient societies may sometimes interpret democracy promoters' intentions as being sinister or manipulative—and occasionally they are correct in doing so—on balance democracy aid contributes to the broader power of example.

CONSIDERING THE CASES

The four case studies discussed throughout this book represent a small but diverse sample of attempted democratic transitions. Two of the countries, Guatemala and Romania, managed to stay on a democratizing path during the 1990s (albeit with much wobbling) despite divergent but equally unpromising political histories—a harsh legacy of repressive military rule in Guatemala and a long, horrendous period of totalitarianism in Romania. One of the countries, Nepal, passed rapidly from democratic opening to political stagnation. And one country, Zambia, has slipped backward from democratic promise in the early 1990s toward strongman rule. A look at the main causes of the varying fortunes of these four political transitions, and a review of the effects of the U.S. democracy aid programs in each country, provide specific examples of the broad conclusions set out in this chapter about the impact of democracy aid.

Guatemala

Guatemala's democratic transition has been slow, excruciating, and littered with casualties. Nonetheless, the country made real progress in the 1990s. An impromptu coalition of major societal actors formed to defeat a self-coup by President Serrano in 1993. The civil war was brought to an end in the mid-1990s and comprehensive peace accords were signed, with negotiated provisions for far-reaching social and political reforms. Human rights abuses declined significantly. Political debate and activity became much more free and open. Civic groups of many kinds expanded their activities around the country. Although improved, the picture is still far from ideal. Some segments of the business elite and the security forces remain outside the new political bargain, and remain potential threats to democracy. Indigenous people, who make up more than half the population, are still largely citizens in name only. Political parties have not developed strong institutional structures and are unstable. Powerholders' toleration of opposition is often only skin deep. Economic power remains extremely concentrated, limiting real political pluralism.

Several major factors have kept Guatemala on a democratizing path despite the many obstacles. Most important, a significant proportion of the business community continues to hold the view (arrived at in the 1980s) that an at least formally democratic system is in its social and economic interest. The resolution of the civil war has stuck. Democracy's wide acceptance in Central America, and in Latin America in general, has helped push the Guatemalan elite to keep up with their neighbors. Since the end of the cold war, Washington has provided diplomatic support for democracy in Guatemala (despite friendly ties between members of the U.S. intelligence community and regressive elements in the Guatemalan security forces).

What role, then, has U.S. democracy aid played? The main area of emphasis of the aid—bolstering the reform of some of Guatemala's state institutions—has not had much effect. Aid for judicial reform is finally starting, after almost fifteen years, to gain some traction. The first attempts, in the late 1980s, ran up against a political establishment uninterested in the task. In the early 1990s, U.S. aid efforts helped bring about the enactment of a new criminal procedure code, though implementation of the code has been grudgingly slow. In the latter 1990s, more sophisticated efforts have established some worthwhile pilot projects to improve criminal justice structures and have at least engaged prosecutors in some training and organizational reform. Although the U.S. aid in this area has begun to yield small benefits, the troubled state of the judiciary has not substantially improved and the rule-of-law climate in the country is considered one of the weakest links in the transition.

The United States organized training courses for the Guatemalan police from the mid-1980s on, with the aim of reducing human rights violations by police officers and bolstering their investigative capabilities. There was little improvement until the mid-1990s, when human rights abuses by all security forces suddenly dropped. The change was due to the new political leadership, which pressed leaders of the security forces to stop engaging in repression. The decisiveness of this shift highlighted the weakness of the rationale of the previous ten years of U.S.-sponsored police training efforts—that police were committing human rights abuses because they did not know enough about human rights. As the government continued with police reform in the second half of the 1990s, training sponsored by the United States, Spain, and other countries did help the police acquire new skills.

Similarly, U.S. aid efforts for the national legislature, also dating from the 1980s, started to gain a footing only in the late 1990s. Earlier programs were lost on legislatures that had extremely weak commitment to reform and rapid turnover. The current U.S. program is part of a large-scale package of aid from several donors. Although this package has increased the professionalism of the staff and helped legislators focus on some procedural shortcomings, it does not change the facts that the body is heavily dominated by one party (and thus tends toward the rubber stamp) and is still of limited political importance.

U.S. aid to the Guatemalan government's human rights ombudsman, which started with the creation of the office in the 1980s, is an example of a small program that has had an important effect. The amounts of aid to the ombudsman's office have been quite limited—measured in the hundreds of thousands of dollars. The actual workings of the office have been uneven, with periods of serious drift. Nevertheless, the aid was symbolically important and contributed to changing attitudes among Guatemalan elites in the late 1980s and early 1990s about the legitimacy of human rights as a topic of political attention. That the U.S. government, under Republican administrations, made an early, visible commitment to support the office was widely noted in Guatemalan political circles.

On the nongovernmental side, there is little sign that the initial U.S. civic education program of the early 1990s had more than minor effects. A handful of Guatemalan civic groups were given money to teach Guatemalans about the value of democracy, but these efforts were shallow and were lost amid the political tension and conflict of those years. The powerful rejection by Guatemalans of the attempted self-coup by President Serrano in 1993 was a signal that citizens were rallying around the ideal of democracy. That evolution appears to have been driven by conditions that greatly outweighed the small-scale civic education efforts financed by the United States and other donors—fatigue with the civil war, the appearance of a new generation of leaders, and the changing views of important segments of the business class, among others. A U.S. program to support civil society, developed in the late 1990s, though promising, is too new at this writing to have had much effect.

Finally, the U.S. aid for the 1985, 1990, and 1995 national elections was of minor utility in helping meet some of the technical challenges faced by the electoral tribunal and conveying to Guatemalans that the United States was interested in free and fair elections. Comparing Guatemala with El Salvador makes clear the often limited effect of such technical aid to electoral commissions. The United States provided substantial technical aid to the Salvadoran electoral tribunal from the mid-1980s on, yet the tribunal performed abysmally election after election. It was racked by political divisions, and no amount of aid seemed to alleviate its lack of professionalism. In Guatemala, by contrast, the electoral tribunal has been much more professional, and has done a credible job during the same period despite a tense political climate and relatively little U.S. or other external aid.

In sum, Washington's various democracy-related programs in Guatemala since the mid-1980s have at best made minor contributions in half a dozen sectors. None of the programs has been catalytic or transformative, and many have encountered significant resistance in target institutions. The symbolic value of having the United States explicitly sponsor democracy efforts has been notable in some areas, although U.S. policy toward Guatemala has only recently clearly moved away from Washington's long, shameful record of antidemocratic machinations. The main factors that have kept Guatemala on its shaky but positive political path since the 1980s were neither shaped nor even much affected by external democracy aid. In the late 1990s, U.S. democracy projects in the governmental and nongovernmental sectors began to gain some momentum due both to learning by aid providers and the peacetime atmosphere. That is encouraging, although it is also sobering that democracy aid to Guatemala is beginning to show promise only after more than fifteen years of effort.

Nepal

In its first ten years of attempted democratic transition, Nepal, like many other countries, has achieved the forms of democracy but not the substance. Many elections have been held and power has alternated repeatedly among shifting coalitions of the three main political parties. The country enjoys a considerable degree of political freedom; political and civil rights are generally respected. Yet the formal democratic system remains badly disconnected from the society. The numerous elections, though largely free and fair, have failed to forge strong links between the government and citizens. Instead, power trades back and forth within a small circle of elite groups, all of which are far more concerned about their own interests than those of the country as a whole. The state has also failed to make progress in basic competency. Ineptitude, corruption, inefficiency, and profligacy afflict one government after another, while the crushing poverty and economic underperformance continue.

Several factors have helped keep Nepal's democratic experiment from sinking. The division of power among three different political parties has ensured that no one group is able to capture the state. The most powerful external influence on Nepal, socially, culturally, and politically, is a democratic state, India. And the once-dominant royal family seems to have accepted its shrunken political role. At the same time, equally weighty features of Nepalese society work against a deepening of democracy: the dominance of a few elite castes and the relative sociopolitical marginalization of most others; an entrenched, ineffectual civil service that saps the state's paltry resources and steadfastly defends its perquisites; the patronage-oriented organization and outlook of the main political parties; and the debilitating lack of basic infrastructure—especially roads and electricity—that leaves many Nepalese profoundly isolated.

The first wave of U.S. democracy assistance in Nepal, in the first half of the 1990s, emphasized the reform of major state institutions, above all the judiciary and the parliament. These efforts had little effect. The training courses and technical assistance for judges, legislators, and their staffs made almost no impression on institutions enmeshed in patronage politics, corruption, and inefficiency. A small program to strengthen local government started useful activities in several provinces, but was never expanded and ended almost as soon as it hit stride. The central government has taken only minor steps toward real decentralization of authority. Media aid helped furnish training for many Nepalese journalists but has had no noticeable effects on the stunted profile of Nepal's television and radio or on the well-established newspapers that dominant the print media.

The U.S. and other Western aid programs to promote civil society development since the early 1990s have fueled an NGO boom in Kathmandu. The scores of new advocacy NGOs have at least increased debate over various issues, such as women's rights and the environment. The advocacy NGO sector is beset with problems, however, including self-interested, opportunistic behavior, an over-concentration of groups in the capital, politicization, and weak ties to ordinary Nepalese. U.S. and other Western aid providers are reacting to the problems in the capital by concentrating new civil society programs on NGO development in the smaller towns and villages, but large-scale effects are probably decades away.

USAID's shift in its democracy aid from state institutions to an emphasis on empowering women in the villages and towns reflects the donors' "go local" trend in Nepal. It is still too early to assess the long-term results of that effort. The program has exposed tens of thousands of women to new ideas and taught them a range of skills useful in their everyday life. All attempts to help along the development of civil society run up against Nepal's extreme poverty and profound web of cultural traditions and divisions—two powerful constraints on change. The efforts to develop civil society can only begin to help generate broader change, but at least the programs with women are working with notably receptive recipients, the women themselves, most of whom have a strong interest in genuine change.

In general it is difficult to be optimistic about the possibility of outside democracy aid having major effects on Nepal's political life. Since the 1950s vast quantities of aid from many countries, including Britain, the United States, China, India, Japan, and the Soviet Union, flowed into the country, to depressingly little effect.[4] Despite its unusually high levels of aid (reflecting the fact that many countries competed in the cold war for influence in Nepal), Nepal remains one of the ten poorest countries in the world, with staggeringly bad socioeconomic indicators on almost every dimension. Why political aid should succeed where so much other aid has failed is not obvious.

Zambia

The widespread hopes of the early days of Zambia's democratic transition have met with disappointment. Zambia has not slipped back into outright dictatorship, but President Chiluba and his inner circle have shown increasing signs of authoritarian tendencies. They tolerate only limited amounts of political opposition, respect human rights erratically, and have obsessively persecuted their one serious rival, former president Kenneth Kaunda. The Chiluba government has pursued market reform policies, ensuring the support of the World Bank, the United States, and other Western donors despite its political shortcomings. And a certain limited amount of political space has been maintained, allowing a limited range of civic groups and opposition parties to operate. The political trend, however, is negative. What democratic reforms did occur took place in the first half of the 1990s; since then, backsliding has predominated.

At least three major factors impede democratization in Zambia. The antidemocratic political values of Chiluba and most of the ruling elite are a central problem. Also, the administrative and psychological legacy of a generation of single-party rule has exacerbated the tendency of the current ruling party to slip into a dominant-party or even single-party mode. More generally, the lack of any significant tradition of democracy, combined with widespread poverty and low educational levels in the country, mean that the population is a weak force for democracy.

The ambitious set of U.S. democracy aid projects launched in Zambia during the optimistic period after the 1991 transition generally failed to find fertile ground and were often stymied by the government's maneuvering. After successfully contributing to the 1991 national elections, for example, U.S. aid for the 1996 elections was unable to prevent Chiluba from excluding his main rival and damaging the process in other ways. The U.S.-funded election observers did at least document the shortcomings of those elections but their presence did not dissuade Chiluba from his actions. Similarly, the U.S. aid for the planned constitutional revision was useless once Chiluba decided to manipulate the process for his own purposes.

Another project involving state institutions, to improve the functioning of the cabinet office (a policy-coordinating office in the government), got somewhat further. It resulted in a manual of procedures for the office, better planning memos by certain cabinet members for proposed executive actions, and some improvement of the office's internal managerial methods. These small-scale technocratic improvements were mostly lost, however, in a problematic government. They did not lessen the widespread official corruption, the dominance of a small circle of the shady presidential advisers over decision making, and other deep-seated deficiencies of the government. Moreover, during the short life of the project (it was terminated after less than two years as part of a reduction of U.S. aid to punish Chiluba for his antidemocratic acts in the 1996 elections), the cabinet office was headed by an official known for his animus toward the World Bank and the IMF and for his generally anti-West views. Strengthening the cabinet office's role in decision-making meant strengthening this official's hand, which did not necessarily promote the sort of political and economic reforms the United States favored. Some people in the Zambian government wondered why the United States was helping an official who seemed to oppose U.S. interests. This situation reflects a feature of democracy aid that deserves more attention: aid designed to support a generic idea (such as that a strong cabinet office is good, or a strong parliamentary committee system is good) sometimes ends up supporting a particular person or clique whose broader goals are inconsistent with those of the aid providers.

The U.S. political party aid of the mid-1990s does not appear to have had any significant effect on the major Zambian political parties. The training seminars may have helped individual party activists better understand the role parties play in established democracies. This limited project could not, however, do anything to change

Zambian parties' unhealthy power configuration—a dominant party led by politicians with doubtful democratic intentions, and several weak opposition parties hobbled by various combinations of weak or out-of-date leadership, a lack of resources, and government persecution.

Although the Chiluba government permitted a small amount of independent civic activity, the U.S. and other Western democracy projects that tried to take advantage of that space were unable to accomplish much because of the deeper political constraints. U.S. aid for civic education did make possible more education activities by various Zambian NGOs and the creation of a large civic education organization, FODEP. But in a climate of decreasing pluralism and increasing human rights violations, the efforts to educate Zambians about democratic values had little noticeable impact. More specifically, many of the U.S.-sponsored efforts in this domain focused on voter education, trying to motivate people to vote in the 1996 elections. When Chiluba manipulated those elections and the main opposition parties boycotted, the voter education programs were undercut.

Finally, the U.S. media assistance provided training for scores of Zambian journalists, increasing the knowledge and skills of many of the participants. The independence, quality, and diversity of the Zambian media did not materially improve, however, because of continued government control over most of the media, the bleak economic conditions for independent media, and some bad management in what few independent publications existed.

Zambia is a cautionary lesson in the difficulties of aiding democracy in backward-sliding countries and the need for aid providers to search for alternatives to a template approach based on the assumption of a positive transition. None of the democracy aid projects carried out in the 1990s had more than marginal effects. Even though Zambia is a highly aid-dependent country (donors underwrite approximately half the national budget) and might therefore be expected to be vulnerable to donor pressure, the government was able to block U.S. and other Western efforts to keep democratization on track.

Romania

Throughout the 1990s, outside observers tended to portray Romania's political situation as a murky, grim, and only partial transition away from totalitarianism. Romania's external image suffers greatly both from stereotyped ideas that many people hold about the country—from spooky vampires to bleak orphanages—and comparison with some of its more rapidly reforming neighbors in Eastern Europe such as Hungary and Poland. In fact, Romania made substantial democratic progress in its first decade after communism, especially considering its unusually dismal starting point. Most of the major political forces now basically accept the democratic rules of the game. Regular elections have been held and political power has alternated among the dominant parties. Political and civil rights are by and large respected. Television, radio, and the print media span the political spectrum and continue to expand and mature. Many new civic groups are active both at the national and local levels and are gradually rooting themselves in the society.

At the same time, Romania's democratic transition has significant weaknesses. Most important, the country's poor economic performance (aggravated by persistently half-hearted, inchoate reform policies) has led many Romanians to associate democracy with economic hardship. The poor performance of government institutions—their corruption, inefficiency, and overly bureaucratic habits—adds to the disillusionment. Romania's political elites have failed to deal openly and effectively with the crimes of the communist era and to put that period fully in the past. As a result, national political debates often end up gravitating toward symbolic issues linked to the past rather than sticking to the practical choices the country must make for the future.

Several factors have helped keep the democratic transition basically on course despite all its difficulties. First, the discrediting of communism in Romania in 1989 was overwhelming, creating a powerful impulse, at least among urban Romanians, for deep-reaching political, economic, and social change. That impulse was slow to be realized, with significant elements of the old system clinging to power during the 1990s, but it has nonetheless been a fundamental force since the fall of Ceauşescu. Also, the demise of communism and the rise of democracy in much of the region have helped impel Romania's transition. Moreover, Romania's conception of itself as a Western and, more specifically, European society, and the powerful positive example of successful democracies in Western Europe and North America, meant that when communism fell, many Romanians instinctively believed their political destiny was democratic. Finally, Romania came to its transition with a highly educated citizenry, a passable standard of living for most people, and some democratic traditions (or at least widely accepted popular myths about a period of democracy in Romania between the world wars).

U.S. and other Western democracy aid was much less important in Romania's democratic transition than those basic underlying factors. Nevertheless, the democracy aid had positive effects in a number of sectors. U.S. democracy promoters devoted considerable effort to elections and political parties. They sought both to ensure technically credible elections and to improve the fortunes of the main parties opposed to President Iliescu and his party. Technical aid to the Romanian electoral commission for the 1992 and 1996 elections did help improve the administration of the elections and may have reduced the possibility of a last-minute, desperate attempt by hard-line elements in the government to rig or otherwise undermine the 1996 election. The U.S.-sponsored international election observer missions at the 1990 and 1992 elections gathered much accurate information about the elections that would have been unavailable otherwise. That information carried more weight outside the country than inside it; Romanians of different political camps continued to believe whatever they wanted about the validity of the elections. The U.S.-sponsored domestic observers in the 1992 and 1996 elections helped foster the idea among some Romanians that they themselves could do something about the integrity of their own elections.

With electoral outcomes, the picture is complicated. After more than six years of trying, the opposition finally defeated President Iliescu in the 1996 elections. The extent to which U.S. aid to the opposition was responsible for that victory is a matter of debate. The aid was useful to the opposition both practically and as moral support. It is unlikely, however, that it was a major factor. To start with, the U.S. aid was only one of a number of Western sources of support to the Romanian opposition—the British Conservative Party was an active ally, as was more than one German *Stiftung*, and other West European parties. Moreover, after the most intensive period of U.S. party assistance, leading up to the 1992 elections, some people who had been directly involved with the program came away frustrated, complaining that the Romanian opposition parties did not take their advice, were hopelessly stubborn, and had failed to change their personalistic, disorganized ways. There was much less U.S. aid in 1993–1996, so one has to assume that the aid did not have a decisive effect on the 1996 campaign. Those elections were not so much won by the opposition parties with skillful campaigning or attractive candidates as lost by the ruling party. The serious corruption in its ranks, the economic downturn of that year, and voters' fatigue with a president and party that had been in power since the fall of Ceauşescu combined to undermine the ruling party's position. It should also be noted that one part of the opposition that was largely excluded from U.S. and other Western aid (because of its former ties to the ruling party)—the Democratic Party led by Petre Roman—increased its share of the vote in 1996 by a percentage similar to that of the opposition parties that received U.S. aid.

In the reform of major state institutions, U.S. aid had minimal impact during Iliescu's tenure, and even after the opposition came to power. A string of U.S. (and European) legislative aid programs has exposed many Romanian parliamentarians to information about the operation of legislatures in Western democracies, trained and equipped many of the professional staff members, and helped establish a much better library and information system. These achievements have not, however, made much dent in the profound inefficiency, mediocrity, and corruption of the parliament. The victory of the opposition coalition in the 1996 elections raised hopes among aid providers that parliamentary reform would finally begin to take off. Washington accordingly renewed aid for the parliament. Yet since then, the parliament has become mired in the same sorts of infighting, deadlock, and corruption as before, leaving the recent parliamentary aid programs with little to show for their efforts.

Similarly, U.S. and European aid for judicial reform has as yet only brought minor changes at best. In the first half of the 1990s, the programs were small, the problems immense, and the government's commitment to judicial reform feeble. The U.S. efforts to strengthen the official judicial training school were lost on an organization that the government supported half-heartedly. Frequent seminars on law reform were only occasionally associated with successful law reform initiatives. After the new government took office in 1996, the prospect for judicial reform arose and external aid on rule-of-law issues increased, including work with the judiciary, police, and prisons. Reforms have slowly started to take shape in those areas, although the process will clearly be a long one and aid programs continue to meet resistance in the middle and lower reaches of various institutions.

Local government proved only marginally more amenable to external assistance than the central institutions. An initial round of local government assistance in the mid-1990s, designed to strengthen mayors' offices, had little effect. Mayors had few real powers and the central government was not much interested in decentralization. The government elected in 1996 has taken some steps to devolve financial and substantive authority. A new set of U.S. initiatives facilitated that movement with advice on the drafting of laws pertaining to decentralization, by training some local administrators to take on their new functions, and by encouraging new measures in some cities to make mayors' offices more accessible and useful to citizens.

Assistance to civil society has met with considerably greater receptivity. Together with European aid and private Western aid, U.S. aid for Romanian NGOs has helped foster the idea and the growing reality of an independent sector in Romania. NGOs have some concrete accomplishments, for example, achieving stronger legislation on human rights and prompting the adoption of greater governmental transparency. The growth of NGOs has also gotten many Romanians more involved in public affairs, broadened civic participation, and accustomed some Romanian officials to the idea of taking the interests of citizens into account in decision making. The growing NGO sector has been an arena for thought and action outside the reach of the government, something that was particularly important in the first half of the 1990s as Romanian political culture struggled painfully away from the totalitarian legacy of the Ceauşescu years.

Although external aid helped fuel NGO growth, the sector would have expanded greatly in the 1990s even without Western aid, given the new political climate. It should also be noted that the NGO sector took on an elitist character early on and has been slow to reach out of the major cities. Most of the Western-funded NGOs still find little of their financial support within the country, and the future of the sector remains uncertain, particularly given the gradual reduction in the late 1990s of Western aid for Romanian advocacy NGOs.

After some misstarts, U.S. efforts to promote independent media in Romania have met with some success. An early effort to help set up a private television station failed badly. A large dose of aid in the early 1990s to the largest pro-opposition newspaper helped that paper thrive, although the paper did not always exhibit a high degree of professionalism or political tolerance. Aid kept alive for some time a number of cultural journals for the elite, but it is not clear whether they had much influence outside their limited circles of readers. Extensive media training programs in the second half of the 1990s proved more useful. They helped ready new journalists for the expanding world of private media—private radio, independent newspapers, and private television—teaching them how to run media businesses as well as basic tradecraft. The growth of the independent media sector was an important bulwark helping keep Romanian politics pluralistic during the long rule by Iliescu. The U.S. and European aid to that sector was beneficial, though not determinative.

Together, the many components of U.S. democracy aid to Romania have made worthwhile contributions to Romania's democratic transition. The aid has built tellingly on the opportunities for growth and change in Romania's emergent civil society. Above and beyond specific outcomes for institutions and projects, the aid has exposed many Romanians to new ideas and given many talented people the chance to start making up for Romania's years of near-complete isolation from the world. It has also constituted a form of moral support to a society with a deep yearning for integration into the community of established Western democracies. At the same time, the aid is at most a supplement to the broader forces outlined above that have put and kept Romania on a democratic track. Moreover, the aid has faced significant limitations along the way. It could not bolster the weak reform impulse of the Iliescu government. Even allied with Washington's policy of favoring the opposition in the early years after Ceauşescu, the aid did not produce an opposition victory in 1992. And since the coming to power in 1996 of President Constantinescu and the former opposition coalition, democracy aid has not managed to do much to alleviate the infighting, incompetence, and inefficiency that have hampered the political and economic reforms that many people inside and outside Romania hoped the government would achieve.

PART FOUR

Conclusion

12
The Learning Curve

Since the mid-1980s democracy assistance has become a significant element of American foreign aid and foreign policy. By the end of the 1990s the U.S. government was spending more than $700 million a year on democracy aid in approximately 100 countries, with five U.S. government agencies, three major quasi-governmental organizations, and dozens of government-funded American NGOs actively involved. Although the current wave of democracy programs has forerunners, particularly in the political development, or "modernization," programs of the 1960s, it is the most extensive, systematic effort the United States has ever undertaken to foster democracy around the world. The expansion of U.S. efforts—and the rising tide of such aid from many other established democracies and international institutions—is a response to two major political developments of the past two decades: first, the acceleration of a global trend toward democracy in the 1980s and early 1990s, which pushed democracy to the top of the international policy agenda and challenged democratic countries to respond to the many political openings with help and advice; and second, the end of the cold war, which lowered barriers to international political cooperation and allowed U.S. foreign policy to shift away from its anticommunist focus to a greater interest in democracy for democracy's sake. The parallel trend toward market economics in many countries also contributed. Given their belief that democracy and market economics go hand in hand, U.S. policy makers also gained an economic rationale for promoting democracy. The revolution in information and communication technologies has further spurred the growth of democracy aid by speeding the flow of ideas and knowledge across borders.

There are many reasons for skepticism about U.S. democracy assistance (or Western democracy aid generally). Despite the increasingly lofty democracy rhetoric of successive administrations, the United States is still inconsistent in its commitment to democracy abroad, maintaining friendly relations with various nondemocratic regimes for the sake of economic and security interests. The sums that Washington devotes to democracy programs are relatively small, even compared with the rest of the not especially generous foreign aid budget. Democracy building can be a cover for partisan political intervention. Moreover, American democracy has shortcomings of its own, causing some people to question the United States' credibility as a promoter of political solutions in other countries.

Nevertheless, U.S. democracy aid merits serious attention. The United States is indeed inconsistent in its support for democracy abroad, but in many countries it is carrying out programs genuinely intended to foster democratization. The amounts of aid are not large compared with many other kinds of U.S. spending on international affairs, but they do finance thousands of projects that directly or indirectly affect millions of people. The use of such aid for partisan political purposes has generally declined since the early 1990s. And democracy as practiced in the United States certainly has many flaws, but many Americans have valuable experiences and insights on democracy to share.

MOVEMENT ALONG THE CURVE

Flush with the excitement of democracy's advances in the late 1980s and early 1990s, American democracy promoters initially brought to their work a surfeit of expectations, hopes, and illusions. Typically they started out with only a shallow understanding of what they were doing, having little relevant experience, knowledge of democratization (as opposed to democracy), and, many times, exposure to foreign political settings at all. They launched many embarrassingly simplistic or misguided efforts and met few of their goals. Over the years, however, they have acquired experience and are now progressing along a learning curve. Democracy programs are starting to have fewer obvious flaws and to reflect a pattern of constructive evolution. This pattern is uneven, partial, and often excruciatingly slow, but it is real. Yet aid for democracy abroad remains an understudied field, with the result that learning by practitioners is too often inadequately shared within the community of democracy promoters and understanding of the field is still weak within the foreign policy community and the public more generally.

Improving on Instinct

In designing democracy projects in Latin America, Asia, Africa, Eastern Europe, the former Soviet Union, and the Middle East, American aid providers have employed a core strategy based on three interrelated instincts: first, using American democracy as a model or template, whether consciously or subconsciously; second, viewing democratization as a process of "institutional modeling" in which the democratizing country attempts to reproduce the forms of institutions of established democracies; and third, assuming that democratization consists of a natural, orderly sequence of stages, from political opening, through transitional elections to democratic consolidation.

As these instincts have collided with the variegated realities of political transitions in countries around the world, they have begun to evolve. Some American democracy promoters, at least, are relying less on an American model. They are bringing in information and ideas from other established democracies or from successful new democracies. Or, less often, they are trying to help other societies develop democratic forms particular to the country's own history and culture. For many American democracy promoters, giving up the American model is difficult. Often they are unaware how American their ideas are, taking as the norm such distinctive features of American democracy as a high degree of separation of powers and a powerful NGO sector. Even if they are aware of it, they sometimes believe that American political ways are the best and should be universally emulated, little considering how they might work in other contexts.

Some democracy promoters are also acknowledging the need to move beyond formalistic attempts at "institutional modeling," such as trying to remake a dysfunctional legislature by training legislators to adopt specific institutional forms and procedures. The challenge is to coax along processes of institutional change that take account of the underlying interests and power relations in which institutions are embedded. More broadly, democratic change must be understood not as the reproduction of institutional endpoints but as the achievement of a set of political processes including the active representation of interests, the balancing of major political forces, the acceptance of democratic rules of the game, and the expansion of political participation. Deepening their conception of democratization is one of the most critical imperatives for democracy promoters, yet one in which progress has lagged. It requires much greater knowledge of the local political environment than most external actors have. It forces democracy promoters to address head-on overtly political issues—such as which political faction controls a particular institution, what benefits it gains from that control, and what might induce it to share its power—rather than hiding behind the screen of technocratic fixes. And it means thinking much harder about the socioeconomic forces that affect political life, from concentrations of economic power to interethnic tensions, and figuring out how democracy aid can be broadened to address them as well.

At the same time, democracy promoters are facing the fact that democratic transitions often do not follow an orderly sequence. Although many of the democratic transitions that blossomed in the late 1980s and early 1990s seemed rather similar at first, they have diverged into myriad political patterns. Democracy promoters are identifying various political trajectories that follow political openings and transitional elections: institutional stagnation, backsliding to semiauthoritarianism, electoral breakdown, postconflict recovery, and others. They are beginning to design democracy aid portfolios to fit the specific dynamics and obstacles of these various contexts rather than working on the assumption of a natural sequence.

The evolution of strategy marks a critical shift. Democracy aid got going in earnest when democracy was spreading dramatically. The core U.S. strategy reflected the perception of the time that almost any country could become democratic relatively quickly and painlessly if the political elite decided on it. Ten years down the road, the third wave of democracy has slowed, or even stopped. Many transitional countries are either stuck in a gray zone of weak, partial democratization or have drifted into semiauthoritarian rule. Democracy promoters are struggling to adapt. Their evolution in thinking about strategy points to the conclusion that the notion of a single best strategy for aiding democracy is an unhelpful illusion. No magic strategy is out there waiting to be found, neither for all countries nor even for one country. All three lines of development concerning strategy are moving the field toward greater variety, subtlety, and adaptability. Formulating good strategy is not a matter of finding silver bullets but instead of accepting a heterogeneous approach to models of democracy, connecting institutional change to underlying sociopolitical realities, and letting go of the belief in a single natural sequence of democratization.

Evolution at the Core

The menu of democracy aid programs is essentially the same today as fifteen years ago, with programs aimed at a by-now familiar set of targets relating to elections, state institutions, and civil society. The emphasis has shifted among the three main categories. Electoral aid has declined compared with the other two now that the phase of breakthrough elections is largely over. Aid to civil society figures much more prominently than before, because of growing enthusiasm for the idea and a certain disillusionment with aid to state institutions. Nevertheless, the tripartite democracy template still dominates; most of the changes being made reflect the evolution of approaches within each of the specific areas.

In the field of elections, the changes are sharp. Election observing has become much more sophisticated—at least those observation missions carried out by the experienced groups. What were once weekend jaunts by poorly prepared observers are now often systematic efforts over the course of months, covering the electoral process from start to finish. Similarly, aid to improve the administration of elections has become a well-developed subfield of its own. Aid providers have helped strengthen the administration of many transitional elections, and in some cases enabled election administrators to pull off elections in extraordinarily adverse circumstances.

Still, many bad elections continue to be held in transitional countries, even when administrative support is provided and observers are present. If a leader or government wants to distort or subvert an electoral process, which many still do, external electoral aid rarely stops them. The art of manipulating elections has developed just as rapidly as the art of aiding elections. Moreover, in precarious transitions, even if reasonably good elections are held, breakdowns often occur down the road when political bargains come unhinged. Over and over in the 1990s, democracy promoters excited about electoral aid have run up against the inexorable fact that elections do not equal democracy—that they are, at best, only an early step, one that often leaves underlying political problems largely untouched.

The American groups that furnish aid to foreign political parties are outgrowing their early tendency to send American consultants with little foreign experience to lecture foreigners on how to run campaigns the American way. They now usually pay more attention to the organizational development of parties and use experts who know something about non-American settings. They have also moved away from partisan approaches, except in Eastern Europe and the former Soviet Union. Despite all this, in most transitional countries, political parties remain among the feeblest links in the democratization chain. They rarely perform the basic functions that parties play in established democracies; rather they usually are either personalistic vehicles for political entrepreneurs or patronage systems for political machines. Years of political party aid from the United States and Western Europe have not changed that situation much.

Programs to support the reform of judiciaries, legislatures, and other state institutions—organized around the idea of strengthening the nonexecutive branches of top-heavy governments—constitute the largest of the three main categories of democracy aid. They have also been the most problematic, with many programs bouncing off their targets or having weak effects relative to their size. Learning has been slow in this domain—democracy promoters have had a hard time giving up their fixed models and their mechanistic notions about how to foster change in large institutions. They have made little effort to draw on the large pool of knowledge about institutional change from other parts of the development field, such as the troubled but instructive history of efforts to promote civil service reform in developing countries. Certain lessons are nevertheless making themselves felt.

Aid providers are coming to appreciate that will to reform must exist in state institutions if change is to occur. They are learning how to assess when such will is present, and when it is absent, so that they can either try to generate it or stay away. They are also starting to accept that resistance to reform in at least some levels of any given state institution is more the rule than the exception and must be dealt with. That insight is part of the emerging view of institutional change as something that is more complex than the reproduction of institutional forms and must zero in on connections between institutions and their societal contexts. This view is leading democracy promoters to use more bottom-up methods for promoting institutional change, linking civil society programs to the institutional realm.

Despite tentative progress, the enormity of the challenge is daunting. In most transitional countries, the advent of political pluralism has done little to stimulate institutional reform. Many state institutions in democratizing countries remain repositories of corruption, inefficiency, and fecklessness. Citizens' disdain for the public sector is correspondingly high. The shortcomings of judiciaries, legislatures, police, local governments, and other institutions usually dwarf the aid programs that address them. Resistance to reform is persistent and widespread. Citizen-led efforts to create pressure for institutional change are gradually multiplying but are usually very weak. The realization that institutional reform requires deeper changes, down among the interest structures and power relationships, is a necessary insight yet also one that underscores how slow and difficult such change will be.

Democracy promoters' growing emphasis on civil society is itself part of the learning curve; they are seeking to go beyond elections and state institutions, to turn democratic forms into democratic substance. Much of the first wave of civil society aid has gone to supporting NGOs devoted to public interest advocacy on a limited range of sociopolitical issues roughly conforming to the American liberal agenda. Those programs have helped fuel an NGO boom in many transitional countries and have contributed to the remarkable spread worldwide of interest in the concept of civil society.

With experience, democracy promoters are taking a harder look at the NGO world. They are pushing themselves and their recipients on the issue of representativity—asking what social base the NGOs they support really have and what relationship those groups develop with the citizens on whose behalf they claim to act. They are also taking more seriously the problem of sustainability—the fact that many of the new NGOs in transitional countries would be unable to survive without outside support, and the need either to develop local sources of support or to modify the structures of NGOs to fit the local financial realities. At the same time, democracy promoters are expanding the range of NGO advocacy they are willing to underwrite, incorporating social and economic issues and other topics not directly related to political life. They are broadening their reach in other ways as well, moving from a near-exclusive focus on large, nationally oriented NGOs based in capital cities to more work with smaller groups in towns and rural areas.

The other areas of civil society work carried out under the democracy rubric are also evolving. In civic education programs, another favorite of democracy promoters, formalistic teaching methods and abstract content are giving way to hands-on, innovative approaches more relevant to the people being taught. In media assistance, the training of journalists is still the mainstay, although in many countries the media's static ownership structures, formal or informal mechanisms of government control, and commercial pressures prevent the media from evolving as democracy promoters hope. Where the media sector is genuinely in transition, media aid specialists have developed programs, such as business training for new media actors, that help the larger transformation along.

As they log experience with civil society work, democracy promoters are starting to go beyond easy assumptions about the heroic nature of NGOs. They are also discovering that although civil society is a highly accessible place of entry for democracy aid, often much more so than reform-resistant state institutions, it is also vast. It is clearly possible to create many points of light, but producing broad changes in civic attitudes and practices or in state-citizen relations is another story. In general, civil society programs reach only a thin slice of the civil society of most transitional countries. Although democracy promoters like to talk about civil society as a simple whole ("we have brought civil society on board"), they are usually only nibbling at the edges of a realm they barely understand.

Revised Groundwork

Democracy aid often falls short in its methods of implementation. Democracy promoters have failed in many cases to seek a sophisticated understanding of the societies in which they work, resting on the misguided idea that their knowledge of democracy alone is a sufficient guide to foster democracy wherever they go. They have carried out many cookie-cutter projects only superficially adapted to local circumstances. They have sent many U.S. consultants and experts on fly-in, fly-out missions to impart political wisdom in societies they know hardly at all. Too often they have taken upon themselves the role of agents of political change in transitional societies, treating local partners as mere assistants. Countless projects have withered for lack of real ownership in the recipient countries.

Implementation is gradually improving, with increased localism the main theme of change. This theme has many facets: investing more time and energy in learning about the social and political contexts in which projects will be carried out; avoiding the use of expatriate consultants on brief stints, keeping field representatives in recipient countries for several years at a stretch; giving local partners the primary role in implementation; making greater use of experts and consultants from the recipient country; and in general, shaping projects to fit the local realities rather than attempting the reverse.

These are lessons that developmentalists in other domains have considered received wisdom for decades. Incorporating them into the democracy realm has been hard work, however, and has been only partially accomplished. Democracy promoters, inclined to hubris, are slow to give up the belief that democracy can be promoted in a one-size-fits-all manner. They resist the idea that they have anything to learn from traditional development aid, clinging to the self-aggrandizing notion that democracy assistance is a world apart. They also shy away from more localism out of fear of losing control over the aid they are providing. Greater localism also means more money going into the recipient societies rather than to the American intermediaries that usually absorb most aid dollars—anathema to many of the intermediaries, who use their Washington connections to ensure their continued share of the pie. Additionally, the bureaucracies of U.S. aid providers, especially U.S. government agencies, lack the flexibility and tolerance of risk necessary for more localism. More broadly, increasing localism in democracy aid requires changing the mindset of providers away from the view that democracy building is something "we" do to "them," toward the idea that it is something people in other countries do, sometimes with our help.

Of the many facets of democracy aid, evaluation has advanced least. Democracy programs present a challenge for evaluators because of the difficulty of agreeing on precise criteria of success in the political domain and of establishing clear causal links between specific projects and larger political trends. In most cases, during the 1990s democracy promoters either did not evaluate their programs at all or commissioned superficial evaluations by investigators lacking real independence. Only in the past several years, with the end of the post-1989 honeymoon for democratization and growing pressure to justify budgets, have aid providers begun to take the subject of evaluations more seriously.

The leading new method of evaluation, however, has been USAID's "managing for results" system—a set of mechanisms for "performance monitoring" that functions in the bureaucracy as an evaluation system. This system, USAID's interpretation of the Clinton administration's "reinventing government" initiative, has consumed enormous energy in the aid bureaucracy and in the democracy groups operating with USAID funds but has not proved useful or effective. The quantifiable indicators around which the system is built provide scant helpful information and overshadow what little qualitative analysis is performed. The absence of serious analysis connecting political trends to aid projects renders meaningless most of what information the system does churn out. The quantitative focus obliges democracy promoters to concentrate on form over substance (for instance, the number of hearings a parliament holds rather than how it structures and makes use of hearings), militating against any positive evolution of strategy. The laborious, inflexible nature of the system leads to projects that are designed to fit the system—to produce "good numbers"—rather than to fit the needs of democratizing countries.

If evaluation of democracy programs is to improve, aid providers must give up the false dream of science, the notion that the effects of democracy aid can be measured with calculators. They must accept that in-depth qualitative analysis is the only way to gain an understanding of political events and effects, and that many of the most important results of democracy programs are psychological, moral, subjective, indirect, and time-delayed. They should focus on creating mechanisms to genuinely engage independent people in evaluations as well as to explore a wider range of approaches to evaluation, including participatory evaluation. It is also important that they enforce a greater separation between evaluations pursued for different purposes—for example, auditing reviews versus long-term qualitative assessments—and not mix public relations objectives with evaluation goals.

In spite of the weakness of most evaluations, certain basic conclusions about the effects of democracy aid are now apparent. In countries where a democratic transition is moving ahead, aid can play a minor but useful role in broadening and deepening the transition. In countries where a transition has stagnated or begun to slide backward, democracy programs are rarely able to put the transition back on track, although they may support pockets of reform or help keep open some political space. In nondemocratic countries in which no visible democratic ferment is occurring, democracy programs usually can do little beyond keeping a few political candles burning. Where authoritarian regimes are actively opening up, aid can bolster the forces pressing for change, although it is not a substitute for energy and commitment from those forces. In such situations it may also facilitate different aspects of political liberalization, if external actors are willing to work quietly and patiently around the edges.

On the whole, democracy programs are at best a secondary influence because they do not have a decisive effect on the underlying conditions of the society that largely determine a country's political trajectory—the character and alignment of the main political forces; the degree of concentration of economic power; the levels of education, wealth, and social mobility; the political traditions, expectations, and values of the citizenry; and the presence or absence of powerful antidemocratic elements.

Looking at the three main categories of democracy assistance, differences in effects are visible but not dramatic. Electoral aid has relatively consistent but circumscribed effects. Programs to reform state institutions often fall short of expectations, producing significant positive effects usually only in transitional countries that are moving ahead with democratization. Programs to aid civil society help many individuals and small organizations strengthen their civic participation but rarely have society-wide reverberations. The effects of all the types of programs are often diffuse and indirect, much more so than the rationalistic approaches of democracy promoters might imply. The programs are directed at institutions and organizations but affect individuals, their greatest impact often being the transmission of ideas that will change people's behavior in other settings at other times.

DOING BETTER

I do not attempt in this concluding chapter to boil down the analysis presented in the book to four or five sweeping recommendations. One of my central purposes in delineating the learning curve for democracy aid is to encourage democracy promoters to push ahead along it as much as they can, in all its many specific dimensions: going beyond the simplistic use of U.S. models; moving from the reproduction of institutional forms to the nurturing of core political processes and values, such as representation, accountability, tolerance, and openness; coming to terms with the multiplicity of political trajectories that follow democratic openings; understanding the limits of electoralism; confronting the inadequate will to reform that hampers the reform of most state institutions; giving up the simple equation of advocacy NGOs with civil society; embracing more hands-on innovative methods of civic education; not counting on the training of journalists as a solution to media reform; taking seriously the need to synthesize top-down and bottom-up approaches rather than merely pursuing them side by side; finding a workable middle ground on evaluations between over-elaborate, mock-scientific schemes and cursory, in-house reviews; and so forth across all the areas of concern.

Obstacles to Progress

The fact that learning is taking place among democracy promoters does not mean it is occurring naturally or easily. In fact, it is a constant struggle. To start with, democracy promoters have brought to their work many unhelpful assumptions about politics and political change. Some are hubristic, such as the idea that democracy should basically be the same all over—that is, it should conform to their ideas about it, shaped by American practices. Others have less familiar but equally problematic roots that reflect an almost preternaturally benevolent view of politics. Some examples: The notion that it is a lack of knowledge that makes political actors behave undemocratically (one imagines a crooked politician slapping his forehead, "If I had only known the courts are supposed to be independent, I wouldn't have called that judge to scare him off my case!"); the fantasy that entrenched powerholders will cede power without a struggle for the sake of abstract principles; the assumption that institutional reform occurs naturally after a nondemocratic regime falls; the belief that violence and conflict are aberrations in processes of political transformations; and the idea that a country's history is largely about the past rather than being a defining element of the present.

Democracy programs too often rest on what is either a dreamy, or, seen in another light, a hollow view of politics. Democracy promoters frequently seem surprised by the most banal realities of politics—that power is only rarely given away cost-free, that principles trump interests only occasionally, that zero-sum instincts are as common as cooperative attitudes, that political violence erupts easily when power shifts are occurring, and that historical legacies, whether helpful or harmful to democratization, are extraordinarily persistent.

Also slowing progress along the learning curve is a whole set of institutional liabilities that afflict aid organizations not just in the democracy realm but in all fields in which they work. Aid bureaucracies may say they favor innovation, but at heart they crave regularity and conformity. The imperative of getting millions of aid dollars out the door on a regular basis with a high degree of fiscal accountability produces inexorable pressure to create molds and formulas that stifle innovation. Furthermore, aid providers, or at least U.S. aid providers tiptoeing on a path through weak public and congressional support, need rapid results. They may recognize that democratic change in most transitional countries is best measured in decades, but they want something to show right away for every dollar spent. On top of all this, aid providers, though they trumpet their common enterprise, instinctively compete with one another. They fret over who has the lead in a sector or country, who has access, who gets credit. They often work alongside one another, but only rarely in a genuinely cooperative fashion.

Progress along the learning curve is then not simply a matter of concentration on technical lessons and the accumulation of experience. Democracy promoters have to challenge their own ideas about politics and come to terms with how much—or how little—they really know about political change in other societies. Institutions engaged in democracy promotion must challenge their own methods of operation, asking hard questions about what imperatives actually shape their programming and how they can improve their practices.

Areas for Extra Attention

All components of the learning curve are important, but not equally so. One deserves special attention: developing good methods of implementation. The most common and debilitating weakness of democracy programs is the manner in which they are carried out—above all, the failure to fit activities to the local environment and to give people and organizations of the recipient country a primary role. Democracy promoters should certainly continue to grapple with the bigger questions, such as how to conceptualize and bring about rule-of-law development or strengthening of civil society and how to develop country strategies. Yet the knowledge of what constitutes good methods of implementation is already at hand and can make a major difference in any project, large or small. Moreover, methods of implementation sensitive to the local setting stimulate good strategy and design. They clarify what is really needed and possible to advance democracy in a particular setting and undercut democracy promoters' tendency to build castles in the air.

Three broader issues also merit greater attention. First, democracy promoters should push to build a relationship between aid for democracy and the larger, more established world of aid for social and economic development. Most democracy promoters believe that economic development and democratization reinforce each other. They have not, however, made many efforts to connect their work to the other parts of the development assistance picture. In part that is because they have been struggling to establish democracy aid as a legitimate field and so have emphasized its distinctiveness from other kinds of aid. Moreover, democracy promoters have worked from a conception of democratization focused on political institutions and processes, which downplays socioeconomic forces and trends that affect democratization. In parallel fashion, even though many traditional developmentalists came around in the 1990s to the idea that democracy can be a positive factor in development, they have shown little interest in democracy assistance, whether out of skepticism about the possibility of shaping political development through aid or concern about "infecting" their social and economic programs with overtly political content.

Efforts to explore links between political aid and socioeconomic aid began to appear in the latter 1990s but are only preliminary. Aid providers assigned the task of finding such ties quickly conclude that citizens' participation is the natural bridge between the two domains. They assert that greater participation in a public health project or a project for the development of small businesses constitutes democratic content, and that participatory development is really a form of democracy building. Although participation—however defined—is certainly valuable, this approach dissolves too easily into a jumble of unobjectionable but not very acute declarations about how participation should flourish in all areas of social, economic, and political life. Much work lies ahead just in identifying the critical connections between economic and political phenomena. Aid providers must begin assessing the effects that economic and social programs have on democratization—the political ramifications of a privatization program that deconcentrates economic power, for example, or of an agricultural program that creates new, larger interest networks across different regions. And they must begin to analyze the impact of political reform on socioeconomic development—the economic implications of opening up a legislature to greater input from citizens or increasing the media's ability to scrutinize government policy making. This is a potentially rich area of inquiry, holding out the tantalizing but formidable challenge of creating a synthesis of political and socioeconomic development work.

Second, democracy promoters should give greater attention to the role of women in democratization. U.S. democracy aid does include a growing number of undertakings directly relating to women but there remains a tendency among numerous democracy promoters to view the subject as a narrow specialty rather than as a potentially powerful approach that can usefully synthesize many aspects of the democracy agenda. A focus on the political status and role of women obliges aid providers to go beyond the forms of democracy to grapple with the substance—how different sectors of a society are participating in political life and whether political systems are representing their interests. It also ties together the all too often separate components of the standard democracy aid template. It may entail simultaneously addressing issues relating to elections and political parties (such as encouraging and preparing women candidates), state institutions (increasing the presence of women in positions of state power and the extent to which state institutions are responsive to women's concerns), and civil society (heightening the degree of civic organization and participation among women). It also stimulates democracy promoters to bridge the gap between democracy concerns and socioeconomic issues by highlighting the effect of people's social and economic situation on their political role and vice versa.

Democracy programs targeting women's issues are by no means without their complications and limitations. As in all areas of democracy aid, training efforts directed at women are often unable to overcome underlying power structures and constraints. Programs to help increase the number of women in political office may meet their numerical goals but run up against the fact that merely having more women in office does not change much. Though women's NGOs are often the most rapidly growing form of NGO in transitional countries, they still face the same problem as other donor-supported NGOs of elitism and disconnection from their intended base. Nonetheless, in carrying out field research on democracy programs, it is impossible not to be struck by the unusually intense interest and enthusiasm that democracy programs relating to women often generate. It is a domain with notably strong potential for further development.

Third, democracy promoters must help recipient countries better understand and use democracy aid. Democracy programs have expanded rapidly over the past ten years and descended on most recipient countries with little warning or explanation. Governments in transitional societies accept such aid in the hope of benefiting from it or out of reluctance to displease powerful donors by rejecting it. Officials rarely know much about the aid, however, or have a strategy for using it; they just take it as it comes. The citizens of recipient countries usually know even less. They may have heard that other countries are dispensing aid and claiming a prodemocratic role in their society, but they are unlikely to have easy access to information about the aid, or any influence over what is done. Typically, a small group of privileged people and groups in the recipient country manage to insinuate themselves into the donors' circle and to absorb some of the aid. For most citizens of transitional countries, however, democracy aid from abroad, like most of the political life in their societies, is a matter of obscure, powerful forces operating well beyond their reach.

Democracy promoters have a responsibility, still largely unmet, to help governments and citizens of transitional countries understand democracy aid and become more than passive recipients. Locally oriented methods of design, implementation, and evaluation are a step in the right direction. Yet they have an effect only project by project. Democracy promoters must mount efforts that tackle the subject as a whole, such as organizing meetings for government officials in recipient countries at which all potential democracy donors explain the sorts of aid they offer, their thinking about strategy, and their experience with such programs elsewhere. Transparency and publicity are essential if citizens are to understand, participate in, and truly benefit from such aid. Donors need to make information about their democracy programs much more widely known and available in recipient countries, in the local language, fully explaining what programs are being carried out for what purposes and with whom.

Broadening the Curve

The learning curve does not—or at least should not—apply only to democracy promoters. The goal of promoting democracy abroad is not the arcane preoccupation of a small circle of specialists. It is a broad-ranging element of American foreign policy. As such, the entire American foreign policy community—policy makers, analysts, and advocates, as well as interested journalists, scholars, and businesspersons—should attempt to achieve at least a basic understanding of the most widely used democracy promotion tool, that is, democracy aid. To do so means moving beyond overstated positions based on wishful thinking, reflexive skepticism, the single glowing anecdote, or the single glaring disaster. The policy community must do a simple but difficult thing. It must accept democracy aid for what it is—a useful element of American foreign aid and foreign policy that is gradually gaining coherence, one that is rarely of decisive importance but usually more than a decorative add-on. An acceptance of this kind does not mean democracy programs should be immune from scrutiny and criticism. Rather it means not reverting constantly to the question of whether democracy aid is legitimate, but, instead focusing on how it can be improved. Just as democracy promoters have begun to establish a foundation of knowledge and to move to the next level of issues, so too the policy community should evolve in its debates about and understanding of the subject.

Attaining a broad, stable consensus on this central point would help the field develop. It would alleviate the chronic defensiveness within the aid bureaucracy, which hobbles democracy programs with extreme aversion to risk, a mania for short-term results, and over-elaborate evaluation systems that are supposed to prove scientifically that democracy work is valuable. It might also help democracy aid obtain a more stable funding base. The rising dollar amounts of U.S. democracy aid over the 1990s give the impression that such activities proceed on a solid financial footing. In fact the situation is surprisingly shaky.

Even after major reductions in the foreign aid budget in the past decade, Congress continues to whittle away at aid, and to impose more and more restrictive earmarks on the aid budget that sharply reduce the pool of unrestricted money from which funds for democracy programs are drawn. In 1999, for example, the Democracy and Governance Center at USAID was threatened with closure for lack of funds. Around the same time, the Senate considered a measure to terminate funding for the National Endowment for Democracy. Several years before, the Asia Foundation lost two-thirds of its annual congressional appropriation. The constant uncertainty about congressional support eats up aid providers' energies in battles for survival, undercuts the ability to think and act in the long term, and makes it harder to attract high-quality people to the work. Congress's inconsistent and often inadequate support for democracy aid is just one part of a much larger problem in American foreign policy—the stubborn refusal of Congress, particularly the Republican majority, to commit the necessary resources to the core international affairs budget for aid, diplomacy, and international institutions.

Beyond the government, other parts of the policy community can and should contribute to the learning curve. The media, especially newspapers reporting on foreign political developments, should take up the subject of democracy aid more frequently and seriously. A narrow but important starting point is improving coverage of election observers. Journalists should press observers harder on their political interests in a given electoral situation but also avoid insisting on simplistic thumbs-up or thumbs-down judgments on elections. More generally, the media should go beyond haphazard treatments of democracy aid—which seem to alternate disorientingly between merciless attacks and shallow puff pieces—to examine in real depth what is being done with the many millions of taxpayers dollars.

Similarly, most scholars have neglected the subject. Many fail to appreciate how large and varied democracy aid activities have become or remain stuck in outdated assumptions about the motives and methods of democracy promoters. There remains a great need to connect serious academic thinking on democratization with the practice of democracy promotion. Many components of the subject remain woefully underexamined, such as why rule of law does or does not develop in different transitional societies and what might ameliorate the profound infirmities of political parties throughout the developing world.

Finally, the American foreign policy community as a whole must get over the tendency to see democracy aid, and democracy promotion in general, as the special province of the United States. What has been especially striking about the current boom in aid for democracy is the wide range of governments, international institutions, and private organizations that have entered the field. Virtually every established democracy in the developed world is now engaged at least to some extent in attempting to foster democracy in other countries. A thicket of different interests, many far from idealistic, lies behind these efforts. But a common outlook appears to be at work—many people in democratic societies believe their kind of political system would be beneficial for people in nondemocratic or partially democratic countries and would like to help them achieve it.

Although America has the oldest living written constitution and an unusually strong tradition of liberty, many other democracies have just as much political wisdom of their own to offer to others. The United States is the strongest military and economic power, but American efforts to affect political development in other countries are usually neither dominant nor definitive. The U.S. share of development aid worldwide, for example, has shrunk since the 1960s from more than 60 percent to less than 20 percent today. One man, George Soros, has contributed more democracy-related aid to many countries in Eastern Europe and the former Soviet Union than has the U.S. government or any other government.

Paradoxically, the tendency of many Americans to talk about democracy promotion as their country's special mission works against the mission. It fuels the suspicion, still common in the developing world, that democracy promotion is just political manipulation by the superpower. It alienates like-minded countries and discourages U.S. partnership on democracy efforts with other donors.

It reinforces some Americans' feeling that their country is alone in taking on global responsibilities and is being asked to commit too many resources to international affairs. In reality, the special American mission to spread democracy is now an even stronger calling because it is no longer only America's mission, if it ever really was.

Looking Ahead

The democratic gains in the world during the past two decades have been substantial. Yet the challenges ahead for persons committed to aiding democracy abroad remain monumental. Since the demise of Soviet-backed communism, democracy has no broad-reaching ideological rival. Nevertheless, democratic transitions can and do fail through their own weaknesses and shortcomings. And dictatorships can and do survive through their own heavy hands. Looking around the world, it is sobering to note the range of countries where democracy is fading, failing, or still nonexistent.

In most of the former Soviet republics democracy has not taken root. Russia and Ukraine have at least achieved the limited state of electoral democracy but they are profoundly troubled societies where democracy's prospects are still uncertain. In sub-Saharan Africa fewer than ten of the more than forty countries that experienced political openings at the start of the 1990s have managed to achieve even plausibly democratic systems. Civil wars, coups d'état, strongman leaders, and failing states are still common on the continent. Dictatorships dominate the Middle East, with only a few Arab countries experimenting with political liberalization and all still well short of real pluralism.

Even in the regions where democracy has made substantial progress there is no room for complacency. In Latin America, the Andean region is in political trouble. Venezuela has a populist president of doubtful democratic intentions. Peru's semiauthoritarian regime maintains a firm hold on power. Colombia's pluralistic system is being torn apart by a seemingly endless civil war. Ecuador is experiencing serious civic unrest. In Asia the democratic gains in parts of East and Southeast Asia are countered by a number of negatives: the Chinese leadership continues to oppose real political reform; Vietnam, Burma, Laos, Malaysia, Singapore, and North Korea show few signs of democratizing; and Pakistan's political life is corrupt, violent, and in decay. Indonesia is an important positive case but it has not yet brought its political opening around the corner onto a clear path of democratization. In Eastern Europe the gains in much of the region are offset by the political problems of the Balkans. Dictators still hold sway in Croatia and Serbia; Albania is only just crawling back from political chaos; and Bosnia's political and ethnic divisions are only hardening.

The analysis of democracy aid presented in this book highlights a central cautionary lesson for policy makers and other who will attempt to promote democracy in these many daunting situations in the years ahead: no dramatic results should be expected from democracy promotion efforts. Democracy aid, as well as the complementary tools of diplomatic and economic carrots and sticks, can do little to change the fundamental social, economic, and political structures and conditions that shape political life in other countries. The limitations of democracy promotion efforts are usually clear in contexts where political violence is epidemic, a dictator is firmly entrenched, or socioeconomic conditions are abysmal. Yet the limitations are still there in best-case situations where a peaceful, stable country is attempting democratization and is open to influence from the outside. Even military intervention—a tool useful only in a narrow range of circumstances—is no guarantee of democratic results. Interventions only sometimes get rid of the dictators they are directed against. Even when a full-scale invasion is mounted to ensure that the strongman is ousted, the underlying political pathologies are difficult to heal, as Haiti's and Panama's problematic politics demonstrate.

Accepting that most democracy promotion efforts do not bring about rapid or decisive change does not imply that the United States should downgrade or abandon its commitment to advancing democracy abroad. It means that democracy promotion must be approached as a long-term, uncertain venture. Policy makers must be prepared to stick to the goal for decades, to weather reversals, and to find ways to question and criticize their own methods as they go along without throwing the enterprise into disarray. The challenge, in short, is to build a cautious, realistic understanding of capabilities into the commitment. Basing a call for a democracy-oriented foreign policy on an assumption of vast American influence over other countries' political fortunes only sets up the policy edifice for a fall. Americans are so used to debating foreign policy from positions of realism and idealism, in which America's interests and capabilities are either systematically understated or overstated, that it is hard to avoid discussing democracy promotion in those terms. A position based on idealistic aspirations tempered by deeply realist considerations makes both sides uncomfortable. For democracy promotion, however, it is the only real choice.

Notes

Much of the analysis in the book is based on factual information drawn from hundreds of interviews and informal conversations with representatives of U.S. and other Western government agencies, quasi-governmental organizations, and nongovernmental organizations involved in democracy assistance, as well as with persons in many aid-receiving countries who have participated in or observed democracy programs. I give more details about the information-gathering for the four case studies in the notes to chapter 5. For the most part I do not cite specific interviews or conversations, both because many persons with whom I talked prefer anonymity, and because many of the analytic points and conclusions are drawn from an amalgam of examples and cases that cannot be attributed to any single source or small number of sources.

I have also made extensive use of many studies, reports, memos, project papers, internal evaluations, and other documents produced by aid providers or aid-implementing organizations, only some of which have been published or otherwise publicly released. I cite written sources when possible, attempting to give enough information about the document to make it possible for other researchers to locate it. In particular, with USAID documents, many of which can be found only in the files in USAID missions abroad, I try to cite USAID document numbers when they are available; these numbers help in tracking down the documents through the USAID documentation center.

Chapter 2
The Rise Of Democracy Assistance

[1] See Tony Smith, *America's Mission* (Princeton: Princeton University Press, 1994), pp. 1–176.
[2] See Robert Packenham, *Liberal America and the Third World* (Princeton: Princeton University Press, 1973), chs. 1–4.

3 The literature on modernization theory is enormous. Classic texts include Gabriel Almond and J.S. Coleman, eds., *The Politics of Developing Areas* (Princeton: Princeton University Press, 1960); Gabriel Almond and G. B. Powell, *Comparative Politics: A Developmental Approach* (Boston: Little Brown, 1965); and David E. Apter, *The Politics of Modernization* (Chicago: University of Chicago Press, 1965). For an early review of the rise and decline of modernization theory see Donald Cruise O'Brien, "Modernization, Order, and the Erosion of a Democratic Ideal: American Political Science, 1960–1970," *Journal of Development Studies*, vol. 8 (July 1972), pp. 351–78.

4 U.S. development assistance rose from $2.7 billion in 1960 to $3.6 billion by 1963. On U.S. aid levels in this period and the Kennedy administration's approach to aid generally, see W.W. Rostow, *Eisenhower, Kennedy and Foreign Aid* (Austin, Tex.: University of Texas Press, 1985), chs. 3 and 4.

5 U.S. emphasis in the 1960s on public administration or what other analysts call "development administration" is analyzed in Mark Turner and David Hulme, *Governance, Administration and Development* (West Hartford, Conn.: Kumarian Press, 1997), ch. 1.

6 On the Alliance for Progress, see Jerome Levinson and Juan de Onis, *The Alliance That Lost its Way* (Chicago: Quadrangle Books, 1970); Tony Smith, *America's Mission*, ch. 8; Ronald Scheman, ed., *The Alliance for Progress: A Retrospective* (New York: Praeger, 1988); and Packenham, *Liberal America and the Third World*, ch. 2.

7 Donald Fraser, "New Directions in Foreign Aid," *Congressional Record*, 89th Congress, 2nd session, vol. 112, no. 45 (March 15, 1966).

8 Foreign Assistance Act of 1966, Part I, Section 281(a). On Title IX generally, see Elizabeth Fletcher Crook, "Political Development as a Program Objective of U.S. Foreign Assistance: Title IX of the 1966 Foreign Assistance Act," Tufts University Ph.D. thesis, 1970 (unpublished); Packenham, *Liberal America and the Third World*; and Brian E. Butler, "Title IX of the Foreign Assistance Act," *Law and Society Review*, vol. 3, no. 1 (August 1968), pp. 115–51.

9 Princeton Lyman, chief of the Title IX division from 1968 to 1972, explained USAID's understanding of Title IX as follows: "In specific program terms, we aim to place the greatest stress in USAID's carrying out Title IX on the economic and social development

process and our instruments for this purpose. This approach corresponds to USAID's basic rationale and to its technical structure. We wish, in other words, to emphasize means by which economic development strategy and instruments can be used to maximize the opportunities for increased participation." Princeton Lyman, "Introduction to Title IX," *Foreign Service Journal*, vol. 47, no. 3 (March 1970), pp. 10, 41.

10 See Joan Coe, "Political Development and U.S. Development Assistance," prepared for the USAID Bureau of Program and Policy Coordination, USAID, May 1970, pp. 74–82.

11 The State University of New York, the University of Iowa, and the University of Hawaii all received USAID grants in the first half of the 1970s to carry out studies on legislative development and to provide technical assistance on legislative development in developing countries. These institutions generated a large amount of literature on the subject in this period. See, for example, Abdo I. Baaklini and James J. Heaphey, *Legislative Institution Building in Brazil, Costa Rica, and Lebanon* (Beverly Hills: Sage Publications, 1976) and "Legislative Development: A New Direction in Technical Assistance," *Comment*, vol. 2, no. 2 (State University of New York, February 1975).

12 See James Gardner, *Legal Imperialism: American Lawyers and Foreign Aid in Latin America* (Madison: University of Wisconsin Press, 1980); David M. Trubek and Marc Galanter, "Scholars in Self-Estrangement: Some Reflections on the Crisis in Law and Development Studies in the United States," *Wisconsin Law Review*, vol. 1974 (1974), pp. 1062–102; and John Henry Merryman, "Comparative Law and Social Change: On the Origins, Style, Decline & Revival of the Law and Development Movement," *American Journal of Comparative Law*, vol. 25, no. 3 (1977), pp. 457–91.

13 See, for example, John Schott, "U.S. Foreign Assistance Policy and Civic Education: Constraints and Opportunities," USAID Document no. PN ABI 477 (Washington, D.C.: USAID, May 1970); and C. Arnold Anderson, "Conceptual Framework for Civic Education in Developing Societies," USAID Document no. PN ABI 474 (Washington, D.C.: USAID, May 1970).

14 Accounts of the AFL-CIO's activities in Latin America in the 1960s can be found in Hobart Spalding, "The Two Latin American Foreign Policies of the U.S. Labor Movement: The AFL-CIO Top

Brass vs. Rank-and-File," *Science and Society*, vol. 56, no. 4 (Winter 1992–93), pp. 426–30; Paul G. Buchanan, "The Impact of U.S. Labor," in Abraham F. Lowenthal, ed., *Exporting Democracy: The United States and Latin America, Themes and Issues* (Baltimore: Johns Hopkins University Press, 1991), ch. 6; Cliff Welch, "Labor Internationalism: U.S. Involvement in Brazilian Unions, 1945–1965," *Latin American Research Review*, vol. 30, no. 2 (1995), pp. 61–89; and Robert Packenham, *Liberal America and the Third World*, pp. 77–80.

[15] On USAID's municipal development work in Latin America, for example, see Creative Associates International, *A Retrospective of A.I.D.'s Experience in Strengthening Democratic Institutions in Latin America, 1961–1981* (Washington, D.C.: USAID, September 1987).

[16] See John Ranelagh, *The Agency: The Rise and Decline of the CIA* (New York: Simon and Schuster, 1986), pp. 115, 131; Thomas Powers, *The Man Who Kept the Secrets: Richard Helms and the CIA* (New York: Alfred A. Knopf, 1979), p. 78.

[17] See Creative Associates International, *A Retrospective of A.I.D.'s Experience in Strengthening Democratic Institutions in Latin America, 1961–1981*, p. V-10.

[18] The late-1960s disillusionment with foreign aid is expressed in Samuel P. Huntington, "Foreign Aid for What and for Whom," *Foreign Policy*, no. 1 (Winter 1970/1971), pp. 161–89. As an example of the sort of official rethinking of foreign aid that went on at the end of the 1960s, see "U.S. Foreign Assistance in the 1970s: A New Approach," Report to the President from the Task Force on International Development (Washington, D.C.: U.S. Government Printing Office, March 4, 1970). See also Vernon W. Ruttan, *United States Development Assistance Policy: The Domestic Politics of Foreign Economic Aid* (Baltimore: Johns Hopkins University Press, 1996), p. 94.

[19] Robert M. Gates, *From the Shadows: The Ultimate Insider's Story of Five Presidents and How They Won the Cold War* (New York: Simon and Schuster, 1996), p. 96.

[20] A summary of the Project Democracy proposal submitted to Congress in 1983 is contained in "Authorizing Appropriations for Fiscal Years 1984–1985 for the Department of State, the U.S. Information Agency, the Board for International Broadcasting, the Inter-American Foundation, the Asia Foundation, to Establish the National Endowment for Democracy," Hearings and Markup

before the Committee on Foreign Affairs and its Subcommittee on International Operations, House of Representatives, 98th Congress, 1st session on H.R. 2915 (Washington, D.C.: U.S. Government Printing Office, 1984), appendix 6. See also, Thomas Carothers, *In the Name of Democracy: U.S. Policy toward Latin America in the Reagan Years* (Berkeley: University of California Press, 1991), ch. 6.

21 On the planning for and establishment of the NED see Thomas Carothers, *In the Name of Democracy*, ch. 6; Christopher Madison, "Selling Democracy," *National Journal*, June 28, 1986, pp. 1603–08; Howard Wiarda, *The Democratic Revolution in Latin America: History, Politics and U.S. Policy* (New York: Holmes and Meier, 1990), ch. 6; and U.S. General Accounting Office, *Events Leading to the Establishment of the National Endowment for Democracy; Report to Senator Malcolm Wallop* (Washington, D.C.: U.S. General Accounting Office, July 6, 1984).

22 "Promoting Democracy and Peace," Address by President Reagan to the British Parliament, London, June 8, 1982, *American Foreign Policy: Current Documents* (Washington, D.C.: U.S. Department of State, 1983), p. 18.

23 See the hearings on Project Democracy cited above. See also Joel M. Woldman, "The National Endowment for Democracy," Congressional Research Service Issue Brief, April 2, 1987.

24 Several years after Project Democracy went down to defeat in Congress, the name "Project Democracy" reappeared. Oliver North used it for the secret contra resupply operation and during the Iran-contra investigations in 1987 this fact emerged, prompting speculation about links between the illicit Iran-contra activities and the original Project Democracy initiative. The only such link was in the public diplomacy realm—the secret resupply operation appears to have had some ties to the anti-Sandinista public diplomacy operation, which had grown out of the effort to expand U.S. public diplomacy activities abroad but was not directly tied to the original Project Democracy proposal or to the National Endowment for Democracy. See Robert Parry and Peter Kornbluh, "Iran-contra's Untold Story," *Foreign Policy*, no. 72 (Fall 1988), pp. 3–30.

25 In 1984, for example, $11 million of the NED's $17 million in program grants went to the AFL-CIO's Free Trade Union Institute. See National Endowment for Democracy, *Annual Report 1984* (Washington, D.C.: National Endowment for Democracy, 1985).

26 Ibid., p. 21.

27 Ibid., p. 35.

28 See Thomas Carothers, *In the Name of Democracy*, pp. 206–10.

29 On CIA funding for Napoleón Duarte, see William M. LeoGrande, *Our Own Backyard: The United States in Central America, 1977–1992* (Chapel Hill: University of North Carolina Press, 1998), p. 249.

30 Carothers, *In the Name of Democracy*, pp. 210–15. Also on the administration of justice program see Jose Alvarez, "Promoting the 'Rule of Law' in Latin America: Problems and Prospects," *George Washington Journal of International Law and Economy*, vol. 25 (1991) pp. 287–332; Washington Office on Latin America, *Elusive Justice: The U.S. Administration of Justice Program in Latin America* (Washington, D.C.: Washington Office on Latin America, May 1990).

31 On the evolution of Reagan's policy see Tamar Jacoby, "The Reagan Turnaround on Human Rights," *Foreign Affairs*, vol. 64 (Summer 1986), pp. 1066–86.

32 Don Oberdorfer, *The Two Koreas* (Reading, Mass.: Addison-Wesley, 1997), pp. 168–71.

33 CIA backing for Solidarity is mentioned in Robert Gates, *From the Shadows*, pp. 450–51.

34 The figure for Eastern Europe is drawn from the U.S. Department of State, *SEED Act Implementation Report*, Department of State Publication no. 10616 (Washington, D.C.: Department of State, March 1999), appendix, p. 8. The figure for the former Soviet Union is an estimate drawn from information in U.S. Department of State, *U.S. Government Assistance to and Cooperative Activities with the New Independent States of the Former Soviet Union: FY 1998 Annual Report* (Washington, D.C.: Department of State, Office of the Coordinator of U.S. Assistance to the NIS, January 1999), appendix, pp. 5–6. It includes expenditures by the Defense Department's International Military Education and Training Program and Cooperative Threat Reduction Program, the Eurasia Foundation, and the Department of Justice.

35 See USAID's annual *Congressional Presentation* for the years 1994–1999.

36 World Bank, *Sub-Saharan Africa: From Crisis to Sustainable Growth* (Washington, D.C.: World Bank, 1989), p. 37.

37 Adrian Leftwich, "On the Primacy of Politics in Development," in Adrian Leftwich, ed., *Democracy and Development* (Cambridge, UK: Polity Press, 1996), p. 18.

[38] The figures in this table were obtained from the following sources or computed using the following methods: *USAID:* Figures provided by USAID Democracy and Governance Information Unit. *USIA:* There is no established method of determining the dollar amounts that USIA spends on democracy-related activities. These figures are the estimated fiscal year 1998 disbursements for those education and cultural exchange programs and international information programs that, according to the U.S. Department of State's *Fiscal Year 1999 Congressional Presentation for Foreign Operations,* increase adherence to democratic principles. *State Department:* Figures provided by the State Department, Bureau of Democracy, Human Rights and Labor Affairs. *Defense Department:* These figures represent fiscal year 1998 expenditures by the Expanded International Military Education and Training Program (E-IMET); figures provided by the Department of Defense, Program Management Division. The figure for the Newly Independent States includes IMET democracy funds and approximately $5.3 million spent on democracy promotion by the Cooperative Threat Reduction Program (CTR). CTR figures were provided by the Department of Defense, Office of Russia, Ukraine, and Eurasia, and Office of the Deputy Assistant Secretary for Strategy and Threat Reduction. *Justice Department:* Figures include fiscal year 1998 estimated disbursement for the International Criminal Investigative Assistance Program (ICITAP) and the Overseas Prosecutorial Development, Assistance and Training Program (OPDAT). ICITAP is administered by the Justice Department, but receives most of its funding from the State Department. OPDAT receives funds from both the State Department and USAID. The State Department figures in this chart do not include the funds for these programs. OPDAT figures do not include USAID-funded programs. Figures provided by the Justice Department, Criminal Division, ICITAP/OPDAT. *NED:* Figures based on program grants in the NED's *1998 Annual Report. The Asia Foundation:* According to the State Department's *Congressional Presentation for Foreign Operations, FY 2000,* the 1998 appropriation to the Asia Foundation was $8 million. The Asia Foundation spends about 75 percent of the total appropriation, or $6 million, on two areas with substantial connection to democracy building: governance and law programs and women's political participation programs. USAID-funded Asia

Foundation programs are included in the USAID line rather than in the Asia Foundation line of the table. Figures provided by The Asia Foundation. *The Eurasia Foundation:* These figures represent the grants in three areas of the Eurasia Foundation's work that are clearly democracy related: public administration, NGO development, and rule-of-law. In fiscal year 1998, 18.3 percent of the Eurasia Foundation's total grants of approximately $19.8 million went to NGO development, 6.9 percent to public administration, and 10.5 percent to rule-of-law programs. Figures provided by the Eurasia Foundation.

[39] See Edward D. Mansfield and Jack Snyder, "Democratization and War," *Foreign Affairs*, vol. 74, no. 3 (May/June 1995), pp. 79–97.

Chapter 3
Interlude For Skeptics

[1] Kishore Mahbubani, "The Dangers of Decadence: What the Rest Can Teach the West," *Foreign Affairs*, vol. 72, no. 4 (September/October 1993), p. 14. On the tension between problems with democracy at home and the confidence of democracy promoters abroad, see also Thomas Carothers, "Promoting Democracy in a Post-Modern World," *Dissent* (Spring 1996), pp. 35–40.

Chapter 4
Introducing Four Cases

[1] On Guatemala's recent political history see David Holiday, "Guatemala's Long Road to Peace," *Current History* (February 1997), pp. 68–74; Rachel M. McCleary, "Guatemala: Expectations for Peace," *Current History* (February 1996), pp. 88–92; International Institute for Democracy and Electoral Assistance, *Democracy in Guatemala: The Mission for an Entire People* (Stockholm: International Institute for Electoral Assistance and Democracy, 1998); Jennifer G. Schirmer, *The Guatemalan Military Project: A Violence Called Democracy* (Philadelphia: University of Pennsylvania Press, 1998); Kay B. Warren, *Indigenous Movements and Their Critics: Pan-Maya Activism in Guatemala* (Princeton: Princeton University Press, 1998); Georges A. Fauriol and Eva Loser, *Guatemala's Political Puzzle* (New Brunswick, N.J.: Transaction Books, 1988); Robert Trudeau, "The Guatemalan Election of 1985: Prospects for Democracy," in John A. Booth and Mitchell A. Seligson, eds., *Elections*

and Democracy in Central America (Chapel Hill: University of North Carolina, 1989), pp. 93–125; Piero Gleijeses, "Perspectives of a Regime Transformation in Guatemala," in Wolf Grabendorff, Heinrich-W. Krumwiede, and Jörg Todt, eds., *Political Change in Central America: Internal and External Dimensions* (Boulder, Colo.: Westview, 1984), pp. 127–38; Richard Millet, "Guatemala's Painful Progress," *Current History* (December 1986), pp. 413–16, 430–31; Peter Calvert, *A Nation in Turmoil* (Boulder, Colo.: Westview, 1985); Susanne Jonas, *The Battle for Guatemala: Rebels, Death Squads, and U.S. Power* (Boulder, Colo.: Westview, 1991).

2 Accounts of Nepalese politics include T. Louise Brown, *The Challenge to Democracy in Nepal: A Political History* (London: Routledge, 1996); Michael Hutt, *Nepal in the Nineties: Versions of the Past, Visions of the Future* (Delhi: Oxford University Press, 1994); Leo Rose, "Nepal and Bhutan in 1998," *Asian Survey*, vol. 39, no. 2 (February 1999), pp. 155–62; Y. N. Khanal, "Nepal in 1997: Political Stability Eludes," *Asian Survey*, vol. 38, no. 2 (February 1998), pp. 148–54; Krishna Hachheth, "Nepal in 1996: Experimenting with a Coalition Government," *Asian Survey*, vol. 37, no. 2 (February 1997), pp. 149–54; Dhruba Kumar, ed., *State, Leadership and Politics in Nepal* (Kathmandu, Nepal: Tribhuvan University, 1995); R.K. Shah, *Nepali Politics: Retrospect and Prospect* (Delhi: Oxford University Press, 1975); Anant Raj Poudyal, "The Communist-Rule Experiment," *Asian Survey*, vol. 36 (February 1996), pp. 209–15; Lok Raj Baral, "The Return of Party Politics in Nepal," *Journal of Democracy*, vol. 5, no. 1 (January 1994), pp. 121–33; Krishna B. Bhattachan, "Business as Usual," *Asian Survey*, vol. 34, no. 2 (February 1994), pp. 175–80; Anant Raj Poudyal, "The Hung Parliament!" *Asian Survey*, vol. 35, no. 2 (February 1995), pp. 161–65; Lok Raj Baral, "Politics Without Power," *Asian Survey*, vol. 28, no. 2 (February 1988).

3 For analyses of Zambian political developments see Michael Bratton, "Democracy Starts Over," *Journal of Democracy*, vol. 3, no. 2 (April 1992), pp. 81–94; Kenneth Good, "Zambia: Back Into the Future," *Third World Quarterly*, vol. 10, no. 1 (January 1988), pp. 37–53; Carolyn Baylies and Morris Szeftel, "The 1996 Zambian Elections: Still Awaiting Democratic Consolidation," *Review of African Political Economy*, vol. 24, no. 71 (1997), pp. 113–28; Julius Omozuanvbo Ihonvbere, *Economic Crisis, Civil Society, and Democratization: The Case of Zambia* (Trenton, N.J.: Africa World Press,

1996); Eric Bjornlund, Michael Bratton, and Clark Gibson, "Observing Multiparty Elections in Africa: Lessons from Zambia," *African Affairs*, no. 91 (July 1992), pp. 405–31; Keith Panter-Brick, "Prospects for Democracy in Zambia," *Government and Opposition*, vol. 29, no. 2 (Spring 1994), pp. 231–47; Human Rights Watch, *Zambia: No Model for Democracy* (New York: Human Rights Watch, May 1998); Richard Joseph, "Zambia: A Model for Democratic Change," *Current History*, vol. 91 (May 1992), pp. 199–201; Jeffrey J. Hawkins, Jr., "Understanding the Failure of IMF Reform: The Zambian Case," *World Development*, vol. 19, no. 7 (1991), pp. 839–49; Peter Burnell, "The Politics of Poverty and the Poverty of Politics in Zambia's Third Republic," *Third World Quarterly*, vol. 16, no. 4 (1995), pp. 675–90; Zambia Independent Monitoring Team, *Presidential and Parliamentary Elections in Zambia 18 November 1996* (Lusaka, Zambia: Zambia Independent Monitoring Team, 1997); Michael Bratton, "Economic Crisis and Political Realignment in Zambia," in Jennifer A. Widner, ed., *Economic Change and Political Liberalization in Sub-Saharan Africa* (Baltimore: Johns Hopkins University Press, 1994), pp. 101–28.

4 On Romanian politics see Vlad Georgescu, *The Romanians: A History* (Colombus, Ohio: Ohio State University Press, 1991); Vlad Georgescu, ed., *Romania: 40 Years* (Washington, D.C.: Center for Strategic and International Studies, 1985); Ion Mihai Pacepa, *Red Horizons* (Washington, D.C.: Regnery Gateway, 1987); Daniel N. Nelson, *Romania After Tyranny* (Boulder, Colo.: Westview, 1992); International Institute for Democracy and Electoral Assistance, *Democracy in Romania* (Stockholm: International Institute for Democracy and Electoral Assistance, 1997); Dennis Deletant, *Communist Terror in Romania: Gheorghiu-Dej and the Police State, 1948–1965* (New York: St. Martin's Press, 1999); Martyn Rady, *Romania in Turmoil: A Contemporary History* (London: IB Tauris, 1992); Bruce Haddock and Ovidiu Caraiani, "Nationalism and Civil Society in Romania," *Political Studies*, vol. 47, no. 2 (June 1999), pp. 258–74; Liliana Popescu, "A Change of Power in Romania: The Results and Significance of the November 1996 Elections," *Government and Opposition*, vol. 32, no. 2 (Spring 1997), pp. 172–86; Nestor Ratesh, "Romania: Slamming on the Brakes," *Current History* (November 1993), pp. 390–95; Thomas Carothers, "Romania: Projecting the Positive," *Current History* (March 1996), pp. 118–23;

Matei Calinescu and Vladimir Tismaneanu, "The 1989 Revolution and Romania's Future," *Problems of Communism* (January–April 1991), pp. 42–59; Vladimir Tismaneanu, "The Quasi-Revolution and Its Discontents: Emerging Political Pluralism in Post-Ceauşescu Romania," *East European Politics and Societies*, vol. 7, no. 2 (Spring 1993), pp. 309–48; Katherine Verdery and Gail Kligman, "Romania after Ceauşescu: Post-Communist Communism?" in Ivo Banac, ed., *Eastern Europe in Revolution* (Ithaca, N.Y.: Cornell University Press, 1991), pp. 117–47; Kathleen Hunt, "Letter from Bucharest," *New Yorker*, July 23, 1990, pp. 74–82.

Chapter 5
The Question Of Strategy

[1] Robert Dahl, *Polyarchy: Participation and Opposition* (New Haven: Yale University Press, 1971), pp. 2–3. A thorough review of definitional issues about democracy is set forth in Larry Diamond, *Developing Democracy: Toward Consolidation* (Baltimore: Johns Hopkins University Press, 1999), pp. 7–19.

[2] See, for example, Guillermo O'Donnell, Philippe C. Schmitter, and Laurence Whitehead, *Transitions from Authoritarian Rule: Prospects for Democracy* (Baltimore: Johns Hopkins University Press, 1986) and Larry Diamond, Juan J. Linz, and Seymour Martin Lipset, *Democracy in Developing Countries, Volume 4: Latin America* (Boulder, Colo.: Lynne Rienner, 1989).

[3] Guillermo O'Donnell and Philippe C. Schmitter, *Transitions from Authoritarian Rule: Tentative Conclusions about Uncertain Democracies* (Baltimore: Johns Hopkins University Press, 1986), pp. 37–47.

[4] Kevin F.F. Quigley, "Political Scientists and Assisting Democracy: Too Tenuous Links," *PS, Political Science & Politics*, vol. 30, no. 3 (September 1997), pp. 564–67.

[5] O'Donnell and Schmitter, *Transitions from Authoritarian Rule*.

[6] Adam Przeworski, *Democracy and the Market: Political and Economic Reforms in Eastern Europe and Latin America* (Cambridge, UK: Cambridge University Press, 1991).

[7] On the idea of African forms of democracy, for example, see Claude Ake, *Democracy and Development in Africa* (Washington, D.C.: Brookings Institution Press, 1996), pp. 132–34.

8 William I. Robinson, *Promoting Polyarchy: Globalization, U.S. Intervention and Hegemony* (Cambridge, UK: Cambridge University Press, 1996), p. 355.

9 Ibid.

10 The first major review within USAID of judicial reform programs highlighted the problem of lack of attention to will to reform on the part of the judiciaries being aided. See Harry Blair and Gary Hansen, *Weighing in on the Scales of Justice: Strategic Approaches for Donor-Supported Rule of Law Programs*, USAID Program and Operations Assessment Report no. 7 (Washington, D.C.: USAID, 1994).

11 I am indebted to Marina Ottaway of the Carnegie Endowment for the phrase.

12 See Krishna Kumar, ed., *Postconflict Elections, Democratization and International Assistance* (Boulder, Colo.: Lynne Rienner, 1998); Jennifer McCoy, Larry Garber and Robert Pastor, "Pollwatching and Peacemaking," *Journal of Democracy*, vol. 2, no. 4 (Fall 1991), pp. 102–14.

13 See, for example, International Institute for Democracy and Electoral Assistance, *Democracy and Deep-Rooted Conflict: Options for Negotiators* (Stockholm: International Institute for Democracy and Electoral Assistance, 1998); Timothy Sisk and Andrew Reynolds, eds., *Elections and Conflict Management in Africa* (Washington, D.C.: U.S. Institute of Peace Press, 1998).

14 Catharin Dalpino, *Opening Windows* (Washington, D.C.: Brookings Institution Press, 1999).

15 Information on U.S. democracy assistance is based on interviews in Washington and Guatemala City in 1997 and 1998 with representatives of USAID, the State Department, DPK Consulting, Creative Associates, ICITAP, and many Guatemalan officials and NGO representatives, as well as on many project reports and other aid documents, including Checchi and Company Consulting, *Final Report: Strategy for Guatemalan Democratic Initiatives*, USAID Document no. PD-AAZ-123 (Washington, D.C.: USAID, March 29, 1989); USAID Guatemala, *Action Plan FY1994–FY1995*, USAID Document no. PD-ABF-373 (Guatemala City: USAID Guatemala, January 1993); Richard Nuccio and David Fleischer, "Report on the Center for Democracy," USAID Document no. PD-ABF-457 (Washington, D.C.: USAID, March 28, 1990); USAID Guatemala,

Project Paper: Democratic Institutions, Amendment Number 1, USAID Document no. PD-ABJ-240 (Guatemala City: USAID Guatemala, September 1992); USAID Guatemala, *Peace in Guatemala: Inclusion, Local Empowerment, and Poverty Reduction: Strategic Plan FY 1997–2001* (Guatemala City: USAID Guatemala, undated); USAID Guatemala, *Program Description: Office of Democratic Initiatives* (Guatemala City: USAID Guatemala, December 1997); USAID Guatemala, *CDSS Update FY 1990–FY 1994* (Guatemala City: USAID Guatemala, December 1988); Partners of the Americas, *Democratic Initiatives Project in Central America: Final Report,* USAID Document no. PD-ABJ-744 (Washington, D.C.: USAID, July 1994).

[16] National Endowment for Democracy, *1986 Annual Report* (Washington, D.C.: National Endowment for Democracy, 1987), p. 38.

[17] USAID Guatemala, *Country Development Strategy Statement Update FY 1990–FY 1994* (Guatemala City: USAID Guatemala, 1988), pp. 65–70.

[18] Information about democracy programs in Nepal is drawn from interviews in Washington, D.C., and Kathmandu in 1996 and 1997 with representatives of USAID, the State Department, USIA, the Asia Foundation, the Asian-American Free Labor Institute, the National Democratic Institute, Institutional Reform and the Informal Sector (University of Maryland), Metametrics Consulting, and many Nepalese politicians, civil servants, NGO leaders, journalists, scholars, and others, and from many aid documents including, USAID Nepal, *Country Program Strategic Plan, FY 1995–2003* (Kathmandu, Nepal: USAID Nepal, May 8, 1995); Stephen Golub and Peter Sellar, *A Reassessment of the Nepal Democracy Strategy* (Washington, D.C.: USAID, July 1994); USAID, *Project Grant Agreement between His Majesty's Government of Nepal and the United States of America for the Democratic Institutions Strengthening Project,* USAID Document no. PD-ABI-286 (Washington, D.C.: USAID, September 24, 1992); Harry Blair et al., *The Nepal Democracy Strategy,* USAID Document no. PN-ABJ-119 (Washington, D.C.: USAID, June 1991); USAID Nepal, *Results Review & Resource Request: Nepal* (Kathmandu, Nepal: USAID Nepal, March 1996); Development Associates, *Asia Democracy Program Evaluation Report,* USAID Document no. PD-ABG-648 (Washington, D.C.: USAID, April 21, 1993).

[19] I have gathered information about U.S. democracy programs in Zambia from interviews in Washington and Lusaka in 1997 and

1998 with representatives of USAID, the State Department, the National Democratic Institute, ABT Associates, Southern University, PACT, and many Zambian politicians, NGO representatives, journalists, scholars, lawyers, and businessmen, as well as from many aid documents including USAID, *Democratic Governance Project Paper*, USAID Document no. PD-ABE-719 (Washington, D.C.: USAID, April 1993); National Democratic Institute for International Affairs, *The October 31, 1991 National Elections in Zambia* (Washington, D.C.: National Democratic Institute, 1992); National Democratic Institute for International Affairs, *USAID/Zambia Final Report: Zambia Strengthening Political Parties* (Washington, D.C.: National Democratic Institute, 1996); USAID Zambia, *Country Strategic Plan 1998–2002* (Lusaka, Zambia: USAID Zambia, December 1997); USAID Zambia, *Fiscal Year 1999 Results Review & Resource Request* (Lusaka, Zambia: USAID Zambia, March 10, 1997); USAID Zambia, *Zambia Democratic Governance Project: Mid-Term Review* (Lusaka, Zambia: USAID Zambia, July 18, 1995); USAID Zambia, *Zambia Democratic Governance Project: Final Evaluation* (Lusaka, Zambia: USAID Zambia, March 14, 1997); USAID Zambia, *A Review of the Components of the Zambia Democratic Governance Project managed by Southern University* (Lusaka, Zambia: USAID Zambia, 1997); Associates in Rural Development, *Democracy and Governance in Zambia: An Assessment and Proposed Strategy* (Washington, D.C.: USAID, June 1992); USAID Zambia, *Democracy and Governance in Zambia: An Assessment and Proposed Strategy* (Lusaka, Zambia: USAID Zambia, June 15, 1992); USAID Zambia, *Democracy Governance Project Paper* (Lusaka, Zambia: USAID Zambia, September 1992).

[20] I gathered information on U.S. democracy aid to Romania from interviews in Bucharest, Iaşi, Craiova, and Washington, D.C. from 1994 through 1998 with representatives of USAID, the State Department, USIA, the NED, the National Democratic Institute, the International Republican Institute, the American Bar Association's Central and East European Law Initiative, the Free Trade Union Institute, the International Foundation for Election Systems, the Institute for Democracy in Eastern Europe, World Learning, International Media Fund, International City/County Management Association, and many Romanian politicians, government officials, lawyers, businessmen, NGO representatives, journalists,

scholars, trade union officials, and others. I also drew information from numerous project reports, quarterly statements, annual reports, project papers by the U.S. organizations funding or implementing projects in Romania.

Chapter 6
Basic Steps: Elections and Political Parties

[1] For an early account of the rise of U.S. electoral assistance in the 1980s by someone who participated from within USAID, see Marilyn Anne Zak, "Assisting Elections in the Third World," *Washington Quarterly*, vol. 10, no. 4 (Autumn 1987). See also Thomas Carothers, *In the Name of Democracy*, pp. 208–10.

[2] Data on international election observing at the 1996 Nicaraguan elections were provided by the International Institute for Democracy and Electoral Assistance (Stockholm). On international election observing generally, see Yves Beigbeder, *International Monitoring of Plebiscites, Referenda and National Elections: Self-Determination and Transition to Democracy* (Dordrecht, The Netherlands: Martinus Nijhoff, 1994); David Padilla and Elizabeth Houppert, "International Election Observing: Enhancing the Principle of Free and Fair Elections," *Emory International Law Review*, vol. 7 (Spring 1993), pp. 73–132; and Guy S. Goodwin-Gill, *Free and Fair Elections: International Law and Practice* (Geneva: Inter-Parliamentary Union, 1994).

[3] David Hirschmann, *Managing Democratic Electoral Assistance* (Washington, D.C.: USAID, 1995). See also the many technical guides to election assistance produced by the International Foundation for Election Systems (Washington, D.C.).

[4] There is an enormous political science literature on elements of electoral system design. A comprehensive, practice-oriented analysis of the question of design is contained in International Institute for Democracy and Electoral Assistance, *The International IDEA Handbook of Electoral System Design* (Stockholm: International Institute for Democracy and Electoral Assistance, 1997).

[5] To get an idea of the scope and sophistication of election observation efforts, see any of the many election reports produced by the International Republican Institute, the National Democratic Institute, or the Carter Center.

[6] See for example the report by NDI and the Philippine National Citizens Movement for Free Elections on domestic election monitoring groups in Asia, *Making Every Vote Count: Domestic Election Monitoring in Asia* (Washington, D.C.: National Democratic Institute, 1996). More generally on domestic monitoring, see National Democratic Institute for International Affairs, *How Domestic Organizations Monitor Elections: An A to Z Guide* (Washington, D.C.: National Democratic Institute, 1995), and Neil Nevitte and Santiago A. Canton, "The Role of Domestic Observers," *Journal of Democracy*, vol. 8, no. 3 (July 1997), pp. 47–61.

[7] Robert Pastor, who has worked closely with Jimmy Carter in many of these mediation efforts, describes this type of intervention in Robert Pastor, "Mediating Elections," *Journal of Democracy*, vol. 9, no. 1 (January 1998), pp. 154–63.

[8] Thomas Carothers, *In the Name of Democracy*, pp. 208–10.

[9] Probably the most widely cited elaboration of this critical line was Edward S. Herman and Frank Brodhead, *Demonstration Elections* (Boston: South End Press, 1984). See also John A. Booth and Mitchell A. Seligson, eds., *Elections and Democracy in Central America* (Chapel Hill: University of North Carolina Press, 1989).

[10] Thomas Carothers, "The Observers Observed," *Journal of Democracy*, vol. 8, no. 3 (July 1997), pp. 17–31.

[11] The 1998 Armenian elections provoked considerable differences and controversies among the various international organizations observing the elections. On these controversies, see Commission on Security and Cooperation in Europe, *Report on Armenia's Presidential Election, March 16 and 30, 1998* (Washington, D.C.: Commission on Security and Cooperation in Europe, June 1998).

[12] International Republican Institute and National Democratic Institute for International Affairs, *Restoring Democracy in Cambodia: The Difficult Road Ahead* (Washington, D.C.: International Republican Institute and National Democratic Institute, August 29, 1997); International Crisis Group, *Cambodia's Elections Turn Sour* (Brussels: International Crisis Group, September 10, 1998); Tina Rosenberg, "Hun Sen Stages an Election," *New York Times* (August 30, 1998), sec. 6, p. 26.

[13] Ted Bardacke, "Cambodia Polls Fair, Says Observer Group," *Financial Times*, July 28, 1998.

[14] The U.S. government statement is in the State Department Briefing of June 27, 1995. The Republican Institute statement was released in "Haiti Election Alert," June 27, 1995.

[15] Jørgen Elklit and Palle Svensson, "What Makes Elections Free and Fair?" *Journal of Democracy*, vol. 8, no. 3 (July 1997), p. 43.

[16] Krishna Kumar, ed., *Postconflict Elections, Democratization and International Assistance* (Boulder, Colo.: Lynne Rienner, 1998); Terrence Lyons, *Voting for Peace: Postconflict Elections in Liberia* (Washington, D.C.: Brookings Institution Press, 1999).

[17] See Marina Ottaway, "Angola's Failed Elections," in Kumar, ed., *Postconflict Elections, Democratization and International Assistance*, pp. 133–52.

[18] International Institute for Democracy and Electoral Assistance, *Democracy and Deep-Rooted Conflict: Options for Negotiators* (Stockholm: International Institute for Democracy and Electoral Assistance, 1998); Timothy D. Sisk, *Power Sharing and International Mediation in Ethnic Conflicts* (Washington, D.C.: U.S. Institute of Peace Press, 1997).

[19] Marina Ottaway and Theresa Chung, "Debating Democracy Assistance: Toward a New Paradigm," *Journal of Democracy*, vol. 10, no. 4 (October 1999).

[20] Fareed Zakaria, "The Rise of Illiberal Democracy," *Foreign Affairs*, vol. 76, no. 6 (November/December 1997), pp. 22–43.

[21] Robert Kaplan, "Was Democracy Just a Moment?" *Atlantic Monthly* (December 1997).

[22] There is almost no secondary literature on political party assistance. In this section I have drawn on many interviews and informal conversations with current and former representatives of the two U.S. political party institutes, as well as with many people in recipient countries in Africa, Latin America, Eastern Europe, Asia, and the former Soviet Union who have participated in or observed their programs. I have also consulted the annual reports, newsletters, and other written products of the two party institutes. An early, useful article is Joshua Muravchik, "U.S. Political Parties Abroad," *Washington Quarterly* (Summer 1989), pp. 91–100. See also USAID Center for Democracy and Governance, *USAID Political Party Development Assistance* (Washington, D.C.: USAID, April 1999).

[23] There is little available in English on the work of the German party foundations or other West European party programs. An

excellent examination of the German party foundations' work in Eastern Europe is set out in Ann L. Phillips, "Exporting Democracy: German Political Foundations in Central-East Europe," *Democratization*, vol. 6, no. 2 (Summer 1999), pp. 70–98. See also Michael Pinto-Duschinsky, "Foreign Political Aid: The German Political Foundations and Their US Counterparts," *International Affairs*, vol. 67, no. 1 (January 1991), pp. 33–63.

24 On IRI's work in Romania, see Thomas Carothers, *In the Name of Democracy*, pp. 35–44.

25 USAID Center for Democracy and Governance, *Technical Annex C: Democracy* (Washington, D.C.: USAID, 1995), p. 12.

26 Letter from Rep. Frank R. Wolf (R-Va.) to Secretary of State Warren Christopher, October 8, 1996.

27 See letter from Kenneth D. Wollack to Louis Zanardi in appendix XIV of U.S. General Accounting Office, *Promoting Democracy: Progress Report on U.S. Democratic Development Assistance to Russia* (Washington, D.C.: U.S. General Accounting Office, February 1996).

28 David M. Farrell, "Political Consultancy Overseas: The Internationalization of Campaign Consultancy," *PS, Political Science & Politics* (June 1998), pp. 171–76.

Chapter 7
From the Top Down: State Institutions

1 Herman Schwartz, "Shaping the New Eastern Europe," *Legal Times*, February 10, 1992, p. 19. The actual opportunities for considered processes of constitutional design, whether or not external advisers have a role, are fewer than might be expected, due to the fact that many transitions occur rapidly and push countries into hasty periods of constitutional change. See Donald Horowitz, *Constitutional Design: An Oxymoron?* (Norton, Mass.: American Society for Political and Legal Philosophy, 1998). An insightful account of one American adviser's involvement in constitution rewriting in the Czech and Slovak Republics in the early 1990s is given in Eric Stein, *Post-communist Constitution-making: Confessions of a Comparatist (Part I)* (San Domenico, Italy: European University Institute, 1992).

2 Jon Elster, "Constitution-Making in Eastern Europe: Rebuilding the Boat in the Open Sea," *Public Administration*, vol. 71 (Spring/

Summer 1993), p. 193. See also, Robert Sharlet, "Legal Transplants and Political Mutations: The Reception of Constitutional Law in Russia and the New Independent States," *East European Constitutional Review,* vol. 7, no. 4 (Fall 1998), pp. 59–68.

3 USAID Zambia, *Fiscal Year 1999 Results Review & Resource Request* (Lusaka, Zambia: USAID Zambia, March 10, 1997), p. 28.

4 On the rule of law generally, see Ian Shapiro, ed., *The Rule of Law* (New York: New York University Press, 1994); Franz Neumann, *The Rule of Law: Political Theory and the Legal System in Modern Society* (Dover, N.H.: Berg, 1986); Allan C. Hutchinson and Patrick Monahan, *The Rule of Law: Ideal or Ideology* (Toronto: Carsell, 1987); Barry Weingast, "The Political Foundations of Democracy and the Rule of Law," *American Political Science Review,* vol. 91, no. 2 (1997), pp. 245–63.

5 An excellent overview of the economic rationales for judicial reform is presented in Richard E. Messick, "Judicial Reform and Economic Development: A Survey of the Issues," *World Bank Research Observer,* vol. 14, no. 1 (February 1999), pp. 117–36.

6 Thomas Carothers, "The Rule of Law Revival," *Foreign Affairs,* vol. 77, no. 2 (March/April 1998), pp. 95–106.

7 On police aid generally, see the seven manuals in the series on *Themes and Debates in Public Security Reform* produced by the Washington Office on Latin America (Washington, D.C., 1998/1999). On ICITAP, see Charles T. Call, "Institutional Learning Within ICITAP," in Robert B. Oakley, Michael J. Dziedzic, and Eliot M. Goldberg, eds., *Policing the New World Disorder* (Washington, D.C.: National Defense University Press, 1998) pp. 315–63.

8 See for example, Public Interest Law Initiative, *Symposium on Public Interest Law in Eastern Europe and Russia: Symposium Report* (New York: Columbia Law School, 1997).

9 For an example of public interest law advocacy in one country, the Philippines, see Stephen Golub, "The Growth of a Public Interest Law Movement: Origins, Operations, Impact and Lessons for Legal System Development," in G. Sidney Silliman and Lela Garner Noble, eds., *Organizing for Democracy: NGOs, Civil Society and the Philippine State* (Honolulu: University of Hawaii Press, 1998), pp. 254–79.

10 The most comprehensive review of lessons about rule-of-law aid is contained in four manuals written by Linn Hammergren, issued

in August 1998 by the USAID Center for Democracy and Governance: *Institutional Strengthening and Justice Reform*, USAID Document no. PN-ACD-020; *Judicial Training and Justice Reform*, USAID Document no. PN-ACD-021; *Code Reform and Law Revision*, USAID Document no. PN-ACD-022; *Political Will, Constituency Building, and Public Support in Rule of Law Programs*, USAID Document no. PN-ACD-023. See also Harry Blair and Gary Hansen, *Weighing in on the Scales of Justice: Strategic Approaches for Donor-Supported Rule of Law Programs*, USAID Program and Operations Assessment Report no. 7 (Washington, D.C.: USAID, 1994); National Center for State Courts, *Lessons Learned: Proceedings of the Second Judicial Reform Roundtable* (Williamsburg, Va.: National Center for State Courts, 1996); U.S. General Accounting Office, *Promoting Judicial Reform to Strengthen Democracies* (Washington, D.C.: U.S. General Accounting Office, September 1993); World Bank, *World Bank and Legal Technical Assistance: Initial Lessons* (Washington, D.C.: World Bank, January 1995); USAID, *A.I.D.'s Experience With Democratic Initiatives: A Review of Regional Programs in Legal Institution Building* (Washington, D.C.: USAID, February 1990).

[11] Edgardo Buscaglia, "Obstacles to Judicial Reform in Latin America," in Edmundo Jarquín and Fernando Carillo, eds., *Justice Delayed: Judicial Reform in Latin America* (Washington, D.C.: Inter-American Development Bank, 1998), p. 20. There is no comprehensive review of the U.S. experience with promoting judicial reform in Latin America. I have based my assessment on dozens of interviews and conversations since the late 1980s with U.S. officials and Latin American judges, lawyers, and other participants in the programs. See also Washington Office on Latin America, *Elusive Justice: The U.S. Administration of Justice Program in Latin America* (Washington, D.C.: Washington Office on Latin America, 1990); Margaret Popkin, *Justice Delayed: The Slow Pace of Judicial Reform in El Salvador* (Washington, D.C.: Washington Office on Latin America, December 1994); José Alvarez, "Promoting the 'Rule of Law' in Latin America: Problems and Prospects," *George Washington Journal of International Law and Economy*, vol. 25 (1991), pp. 281–332; Thomas Carothers, *In the Name of Democracy*, pp. 210–15; Hugo E. Frühling, "Judicial Reform and Democratization in Latin America" (unpublished paper, 1995); Luis Pásara, "La Justicia en Guatemala," *Diálogo* (Guatemala), vol. 2, no. 3 (March 1998).

[12] Linn Hammergren, "Donor Assisted Judicial Reforms: An Overview of USAID Experience and Some Emerging Lessons" (unpublished paper, 1999), p. 7.

[13] Ronald M. Childress, "The Children's Crusade: Reflections on American Assistance to the Russian Federation, 1993–1996," (paper presented to the 1998 Annual Meeting of the American Association for the Advancement of Slavic Studies); Woodrow Wilson School of Public and International Affairs, *Project Report on the Role of Foreign Aid for Legal Reform Programs in the Russian Federation* (Princeton: Princeton University, January 1999); Robert Sharlet, "Legal Transplants and Political Mutations: The Reception of Constitutional Law in Russia and the New Independent States." On the weaknesses of Western rule-of-law aid efforts generally, see András Sajó, "Universal Rights, Missionaries, Converts, and 'Local Savages'," *East European Constitutional Review*, vol. 6, no. 1 (Winter 1997), pp. 44–49.

[14] USAID Guatemala, *Stocktaking of 1986–1991 Administration of Justice Program* (Guatemala City: USAID Guatemala, October 1991); Checchi and Company Consulting, Inc., *Final Report: Evaluation of the Harvard Law School Program, Guatemala*, USAID Document no. PD-ABA-849 (Washington, D.C.: USAID, 1989).

[15] Thomas Carothers, *Assessing Democracy Assistance: The Case of Romania*, pp. 51–57.

[16] Author interviews with Nepalese participants and observers of U.S. judicial aid programs, and with former Asia Foundation Nepal office staff members, December 1996.

[17] See Linn Hammergren, *The Politics of Justice and Justice Reform in Latin America: The Peruvian Case in Comparative Perspective* (Boulder, Colo.: Westview, 1998), pp. 270–76.

[18] USAID has produced many reports and evaluations of its legislative aid programs. Some of the most useful include, Hal Lippman and Jan Emmert, *Assisting Legislatures in Developing Countries: A Framework for Program Planning and Implementation*, USAID Document no. PN-ACA-902 (Washington, D.C.: USAID, October 1997); Ryan S. McCannell, *Legislative Strengthening: A Synthesis of USAID Experience* (Washington, D.C.: USAID, May 1995) and a series of five country studies of legislative aid, in Poland, the Philippines, El Salvador, Bolivia, and Nepal, issued by the USAID Center for Development Information and Evaluation in 1995 and 1996. There is little recent secondary literature on the subject.

[19] Congressional Research Service, *Parliamentary Assistance Programs: Final Report* (Washington, D.C.: Library of Congress, May 18, 1998), p. i.

[20] Hal Lippman and Joel Jutkowitz, *Legislative Strengthening in El Salvador*, USAID Document no. PN-ABS-549 (Washington, D.C.: USAID, 1996).

[21] Michael Calavan, Jan Emmert, et al., *Strengthening the Legislature and Democracy in the Philippines*, USAID Document no. PN-ABS-535 (Washington, D.C.: USAID, 1995).

[22] USAID Guatemala, *Guatemala Project Paper: Democratic Institutions, Amendment Number 1* (Guatemala City: USAID Guatemala, September, 1992), p. 5.

[23] Richard Nuccio and David Fleischer, *Report on The Center for Democracy* (Washington, D.C.: USAID, March 28, 1990), p. ii.

[24] On USAID approaches to decentralization see Ronald W. Johnson, *Decentralization Strategy Design: Complementary Perspectives on a Common Theme*, USAID Document no. PN-ABW-981 (Washington, D.C.: USAID, August 1995); Center for Democracy and Governance, *Handbook on Programming for Democratic Decentralization* (Washington, D.C.: USAID, forthcoming); Harry Blair, *Spreading Power to the Periphery: An Assessment of Local Governance* (Washington, D.C.: USAID, September 1998).

[25] Commonwealth Secretariat, *Decentralization for Development: A Select Annotated Bibliography* (London: Commonwealth Secretariat, 1983).

[26] On the evolution of decentralization programs across the past three decades, see John M. Cohen and Stephen B. Peterson, *Methodological Issues in the Analysis of Decentralization*, Development Discussion Paper no. 555 (Cambridge, Mass.: Harvard Institute for International Development, October 1996).

[27] Harry Blair, *Assessing Democratic Decentralization: A CDIE Concept Paper* (Washington, D.C.: USAID, November 6, 1995), p. 39. U.S. decentralization assistance has itself not been very decentralized. Just four countries, Egypt, the Philippines, El Salvador, and Indonesia, accounted for almost two-thirds of total U.S. decentralization aid from the late 1980s to the mid-1990s.

[28] G.S. Cheema and D.A. Rondinelli, eds., *Decentralization and Development: Policy Implementation in Developing Countries* (Beverly Hills: Sage Publications, 1983); G. Hyden, *No Shortcuts to Progress: African*

Development Management in Perspective (London: Heinemann, 1983); P. Mawhood, ed., *Local Government in the Third World: the Experience of Tropical Africa* (Chichester, UK: Wiley, 1983); Harry Blair, "Participation, Public Policy, Political Economy and Development in Rural Bangladesh, 1958–85," *World Development*, vol. 13, no. 12 (December 1985), pp. 1231–47; and Kirsten Westergaard and Muhammad Mustafa Alam, "Local Government in Bangladesh: Past Experiences and Yet Another Try," *World Development*, vol. 23, no. 4 (April 1995), pp. 679–90.

29 Eliza Willis, Christopher de C.B. Garman, and Stephan Haggard, "The Politics of Decentralization in Latin America," *Latin American Research Review*, vol. 34, no. 1 (1999), pp. 7–56.

30 James Manor, *The Political Economy of Democratic Decentralization* (Washington, D.C.: World Bank, 1999).

31 Harry Blair, "Supporting Democratic Local Governance: Lessons from International Donor Experience—Initial Concepts and Some Preliminary Findings" (unpublished paper, August 1996), pp. 13–14.

32 George C.S. Benson, *Political Corruption in America* (Lexington, Mass.: Lexington Books, 1978), p. 137.

33 On the Philippine program see Gary Hawes, *Local Development Assistance Program: Impact Evaluation* (Washington, D.C.: USAID, March 1995).

34 Johanna Mendelson Forman and Claude Welch, *Civil-Military Relations: USAID's Role* (Washington, D.C.: USAID Center for Democracy and Governance, July 1998), p. 16. See also The American University Democracy Projects, *Civil-Military Relations in Latin America: Lessons Learned*, USAID Document no. PN-ABX-344 (Washington, D.C.: USAID, 1995).

35 Joseph S. Nye, Jr., "Epilogue: The Liberal Tradition," in Larry Diamond and Marc F. Plattner, eds., *Civil-Military Relations and Democracy* (Baltimore: Johns Hopkins University Press, 1996), p. 153.

36 Ibid.

37 Barbara Geddes, *Politician's Dilemma: Building State Capacity in Latin America* (Berkeley: University of California Press, 1994), p. 41.

38 Ibid., p. 27.

39 James G. March and Johan P. Olsen, *Rediscovering Institutions: The Organizational Basis of Politics* (New York: Free Press, 1989), pp. 56–57.

[40] Linn Hammergren highlights the distinction between these two different reasons for lack of will to reform in state institutions in *Institutional Strengthening and Justice Reform* (Washington, D.C.: USAID, August 1998), p. 84.

[41] Moisés Naím, *Latin America's Journey to the Market* (San Francisco: Institute For Contemporary Studies, 1995).

Chapter 8
From the Bottom Up: Civil Society

[1] Gordon White, "Civil Society, Democratization and Development (I): Clearing the Analytical Ground," *Democratization*, vol. 1, no. 3 (Autumn 1994), p. 379. The literature on civil society is huge. Some recent books include Ernest Gellner, *Conditions of Liberty: Civil Society and its Rivals* (New York: Allen Lane, 1994); John Hall, ed., *Civil Society: Theory, History, Comparison* (Cambridge, UK: Polity Press, 1995); Adam B. Seligman, *The Idea of Civil Society* (New York: Maxwell Macmillian International, 1992); John Keane, *Civil Society: Old Images, New Visions* (Stanford: Stanford University Press, 1998); John W. Harbeson, Donald Rothchild, and Naomi Chazan, eds., *Civil Society and the State in Africa* (Boulder, Colo.: Lynne Rienner, 1994). David Rieff asks some usefully pointed questions about the concept of civil society in "Civil Society and the Future of the Nation-State," *The Nation*, February 22, 1999, pp. 11–16.

[2] Gordon White, "Civil Society, Democratization and Development (I): Clearing the Analytical Ground," p. 379.

[3] In a typical statement about how democracy promoters at USAID have viewed civil society, Harry Blair introduces a USAID-sponsored study of civil society assistance with the following specification: "Here civil society is taken to mean those organisations existing in the space between the state and the family that both enjoy autonomy from the state *and seek to have a significant influence on public policy*" (italics added). Harry Blair, "Civil Society and Building Democracy: Lessons from International Donor Experience," in Amanda Bernard, Henny Helmrich, and Percy B. Lehning, eds., *Civil Society and International Development* (Paris: North-South Centre of the Council of Europe and Development Centre of the OECD, 1998), p. 66. See also Gary Hansen, *Constituencies*

for Reform: Strategic Approaches for Donor-Supported Civic Advocacy Programs, USAID Program and Operations Assessment Report no. 12 (Washington, D.C.: USAID, February 1996).

[4] Robert Putnam, *Making Democracy Work: Civic Traditions in Modern Italy* (Princeton: Princeton University Press, 1993), p. 167.

[5] Ibid.

[6] A few examples of the enormous body of writings on NGOs and development include David Hulme and Michael Edwards, *NGOs, States and Donors: Too Close for Comfort?* (New York: St. Martin's Press, 1997); John Clark, *Democratizing Development: The Role of Voluntary Organizations* (West Hartford, Conn.: Kumarian, 1990); David Korten, *Getting to the 21st Century: Voluntary Action and the Global Agenda* (West Hartford, Conn.: Kumarian, 1990); and Roger Riddell and Mark Robinson, *NGOs and Rural Poverty Alleviation* (Oxford: Oxford University Press, 1996).

[7] Little systematic research has been carried out on corruption among NGOs in developing or transitional countries. I base this conclusion on many conversations with aid officials and NGO activists in the case study countries and other countries in which I have worked.

[8] USAID, *Zambia Democratic Governance Project: Final Evaluation* (Washington, D.C.: USAID, March 14, 1997), p. 11.

[9] Ibid.

[10] On the issue of sustainability and resource mobilization for NGOs, see Ann Hudock, "Sustaining NGOs in Resource-Dependent Environments," *Journal of International Development*, vol. 7, no. 4 (1995), pp. 653–67; J. Bennett and S. Gibbs, *NGO Funding Strategies: An Introduction for Southern and Eastern NGOs* (Oxford: INTRAC, 1996); and S. Vetter, "Resource Mobilization: The Business of Grassroots Development," *Grassroots Development*, vol. 19, no. 2 (1995), pp. 2–11.

[11] The survey, sponsored by the Washington Post and Harvard University, found a widespread, profound lack of knowledge among Americans about the American political system. *Washington Post*, January 26 and 29, 1999, p. A1.

[12] Christopher Sabatini, Gwendolyn Bevis, and Steven Finkel, *The Impact of Civic Education Programs on Political Participation and Democratic Attitudes* (Washington, D.C.: Management Systems International, January 27, 1998).

[13] Michael Bratton and Philip Alderfer, "The Effects of Civic Education on Political Culture: Evidence from Zambia," *World Development*, vol. 27, no. 5 (1999), pp. 822.

[14] Management Systems International, *An Evaluation of the Program of Education for Participation* (Washington, D.C.: Management Systems International, August 1989), p. v.

[15] America's Development Foundation, *Final Report of the Civic Education Project* (Alexandria, Va.: America's Development Foundation, undated), pp. 8, 12. For an evaluation of some of the NED's civic education work in Guatemala and elsewhere in Latin America, see Sally Yudelman and Lucy Conger, *The Paving Stones: An Evaluation of Latin American Civic Education Programs* (Washington, D.C.: National Endowment for Democracy, March 1997).

[16] Interview with USAID/Guatemala officer, March 1997.

[17] See USAID Center for Democracy and Governance, *The Role of Media in Democracy: A Strategic Approach* (Washington, D.C.: USAID, June 1999).

[18] USAID Center for Democracy and Governance, "Media Law Reform in New Democracies," *Democracy Dialogue* (Washington, D.C.: USAID, July 1998).

[19] Some lessons from the experience of aiding media in Romania are set out in Peter Gross, *Mass Media in Revolution and National Development: The Romanian Laboratory* (Iowa City: Iowa University Press, 1996), ch. 6.

[20] A discussion of the relationship between media assistance and the economic and political conditions affecting media development is contained in Noreene Janus and Rick Rockwell, *The Latin American Journalism Project: Lessons Learned* (Washington, D.C.: USAID, November 1998).

[21] See chapter 2, note 14.

[22] Checchi and Company Consulting, *Evaluation of the 1986–90 A.I.D. Cooperative Grant no. 519-0321-A6219-00 The American Institute for Free Labor Development (AIFLD)*, USAID Document no. PD-ABB-187 (Washington, D.C.: USAID, September 29, 1989), p. 1.

[23] Peter Accolla, *Evaluation: AIFLD Cooperative Agreement 524-0316-A-00-5065-00* (Washington, D.C.: USAID, March 25, 1996), p. 4. The evaluation noted that "more than 80 percent of the funds allocated to CPT [Nicaraguan Permanent Workers Congress]-affiliated organizations had been utilized primarily to subsidize

operations costs of trade union organizations" but that despite this large aid influx, "the CPT was no longer a cohesive group of unions and was about to disperse."

24 John H. Sullivan, Jerome T. Barrett, and Kate D. Iskander, *Joint Management Review and Evaluation Report: U.S. Assistance to the Egyptian Labor Movement*, USAID Document no. PD-ABF-571 (Washington, D.C.: USAID, November 1992), p. 11.

Chapter 9
Making It Work: The Challenges of Implementation

1 Janine Wedel, *Collision and Collusion: The Strange Case of Western Aid to Eastern Europe, 1989–1998* (New York: St. Martin's Press, 1998); Matt Bivens, "Aboard the Gravy Train," *Harper's* (August 1997); David Samuels, "At Play in the Fields of Oppression," *Harper's* (May 1995); Ronald M. Childress, "The Children's Crusade: Reflections on American Assistance to the Russian Federation, 1993–1996," (paper presented to the 1998 Annual Meeting of the American Association for the Advancement of Slavic Studies).

2 USAID Zambia, *Zambia Democratic Governance Project: Final Evaluation* (Lusaka, Zambia: USAID Zambia, March 14, 1997), p. 28.

3 Albert R. Wight, "Participation, Ownership, and Sustainable Development," in Merilee S. Grindle, ed., *Getting Good Government: Capacity Building in the Public Sector of Developing Countries* (Cambridge, Mass.: Harvard Institute for International Development Press, 1997), pp. 369–412.

4 On the work of the Soros foundations see Open Society Institute, *Building Open Societies: Soros Foundations Network 1998 Report* (New York: Open Society Institute, 1999); Kevin Quigley, *For Democracy's Sake: Foundations and Democracy Assistance in Central Europe* (Washington, D.C.: Woodrow Wilson Center Press, 1997); Thomas Carothers, "Aiding Post-Communist Societies: A Better Way?" *Problems of Post-Communism*, vol. 43, no. 5 (September/October 1996), pp. 15–24.

5 Marcia Bernbaum and Guillermo Marquez, *Final Evaluation of USAID/DR Strengthening Civil Society Activity* (Santo Domingo, Dominican Republic: USAID Dominican Republic, December 1, 1996).

Chapter 10
Giving Out Grades: Evaluation

[1] Roger C. Riddell, *Foreign Aid Reconsidered* (Baltimore: Johns Hopkins University Press, 1987), p. 197.

[2] Dennis J. Casley and Krishna Kumar, *Project Monitoring and Evaluation in Agriculture* (Baltimore: Johns Hopkins University Press, 1987), p. 119.

[3] A number of works that examine the problem of evaluation in development assistance highlight a fairly consistent set of problems with the evaluations typically performed by development agencies. See for example, Claus C. Rebien, *Evaluating Development Assistance in Theory and Practice* (Brookfield, Vt.: Ashgate Publishing, 1996); B.E. Cracknell, ed., *The Evaluation of Aid Projects and Programmes* (London: Overseas Development Administration, 1984), pp. 21–44; Joseph Valadez and Michael Bamberger, *Monitoring and Evaluating Social Programs in Developing Countries* (Washington, D.C.: World Bank, 1994), pp. 111–58; Robert Cassen and Associates, *Does Aid Work?* (Oxford: Clarendon Press, 1994), pp. 86–95.

[4] Some USAID officials also assert that the agency's emphasis on quantitative indicators of success is mandated by the Government Performance and Results Act of 1993 (Public Law 103–62) which requires every government agency to establish performance goals and to express such goals in "an objective, quantifiable, and measurable form." In fact the GPRA only requires performance goals at the broad program level, not for every individual project or activity. In addition, the act has waiver provisions that allow agencies to petition for alternative approaches for expressing performance goals or to forego stating performance goals if such goals prove impractical. Enough flexibility exists in the GPRA that USAID does not have to carry out its performance management system in as strictly a quantitative fashion as it is currently configured. USAID management has been eager to make the agency a showcase of the Clinton administration's reinventing government initiative, however, and thus has not pressed for a more flexible interpretation of the GPRA, in order not to give any impression of softness in its approach to reinvention.

[5] The various labels cited in the text for strategic objectives, intermediate results, subintermediate results, and indicators are drawn

from USAID documents produced by the relevant USAID missions from 1996 to 1998. Many of these documents are unlabeled and undated and are not part of any larger citable document. Some of the Zambia quotes are drawn from USAID Zambia, *Promises to Keep: From Reforms to Benefits for Zambians, Country Strategic Plan 1998–2002* (Lusaka, Zambia: USAID Zambia, December 1997), annex 1.

[6] USAID Center for Democracy and Governance, *Handbook of Democracy and Governance Program Indicators* (Washington, D.C.: USAID, August 1998).

[7] USAID Cambodia, *Results Review and Resource Request* (Phnom Penh, Cambodia: USAID Cambodia, February 1, 1998), p. 4.

[8] Harry Blair and Gary Hansen, *Weighing in on the Scales of Justice* (Washington, D.C.: USAID, 1994).

[9] Rebien, *Evaluating Development Assistance in Theory and Practice*, ch. 5.

[10] Lawrence F. Salmen, *Listen to the People: Participant-Observer Evaluation of Development Projects* (Oxford: Oxford University Press, 1987).

Chapter 11
Understanding Effects

[1] World Bank, *Assessing Aid: What Works, What Doesn't, and Why* (Oxford: Oxford University Press, 1998).

[2] The 1998 federal budget is approximately $1.7 trillion. Democracy expenditures are about $700 million for the year, as discussed in chapter 2.

[3] In an example of bold credit-taking for democracy assistance, the political commentator Charles Krauthammer wrote in 1991, "NED funds helped 200,000 poor voters get the small photographs required to vote in the 1988 Chilean referendum. That referendum ended the Pinochet dictatorship. The program cost $25,000." Charles Krauthammer, "Shortchanging Democracy: Why Kill the Most Cost-Effective Program in Government?" *Washington Post*, June 21, 1991.

[4] Nagendra Singh, *Foreign Aid, Economic Growth and Politics in Nepal* (New Delhi, India: Anmol Publications, 1996), ch. 9.

Bibliography

This is a list of selected works on democracy assistance and democracy promotion. It does not cover democratization generally; it concentrates on the much more limited body of writing that analyzes efforts by external actors to assist or promote democracy. It is primarily made up of secondary sources; it does not include the many annual reports, project papers, and other documents produced by aid agencies and democracy promotion organizations, with the exception of some overview studies by USAID.

General

Afkhami, Mahnaz. "Promoting Women's Rights in the Muslim World," *Journal of Democracy*, vol. 8, no. 1 (January 1997): 157–66.

Allison, Graham T., Jr., and Robert P. Beschel, Jr. "Can the United States Promote Democracy?" *Political Science Quarterly*, vol. 107, no. 1 (Spring 1992): 81–98.

Bivens, Matt. "Aboard the Gravy Train," *Harper's* (August 1997).

Brinkley, Douglas. "Democratic Enlargement: The Clinton Doctrine," *Foreign Policy*, no. 106 (Spring 1997): 111–27.

Burnell, Peter. "Good Government and Democratization: A Sideways Look at Aid and Conditionality," *Democratization*, vol. 1, no. 3 (Autumn 1994): 485–503.

Carothers, Thomas. "Democracy Assistance: The Question of Strategy," *Democratization*, vol. 4, no. 3 (Autumn 1997): 109–32.

──────. "Aiding Post-Communist Societies: A Better Way?" *Problems of Post-Communism* (September/October 1996): 15–24.

──────. *Assessing Democracy Assistance: The Case of Romania*. Washington, D.C.: Carnegie Endowment for International Peace, 1996.

──────. "Promoting Democracy in a Post-Modern World," *Dissent* (Spring 1996): 35–40.

———. "Democracy Promotion Under Clinton," *The Washington Quarterly*, vol. 18, no. 4 (Autumn 1995): 13–28.

———. "Recent U.S. Experience with Democracy Promotion," *IDS Bulletin*, vol. 26, no. 2 (April 1995): 62–69.

———. "Democracy and Human Rights: Policy Allies or Rivals?" *The Washington Quarterly*, vol. 17, no. 3 (Summer 1994): 109–120.

———. "The NED at Ten," *Foreign Policy*, no. 95 (Summer 1994): 123–38.

———. *In the Name of Democracy: U.S. Policy Toward Latin America in the Reagan Years*. Berkeley: University of California Press, 1991.

Cohen, John M. "Foreign Advisors and Capacity Building: The Case of Kenya," *Public Administration and Development*, vol. 12 (1992): 493–510.

Crawford, Gordon. "Foreign Aid and Political Conditionality: Issues of Effectiveness and Consistency," *Democratization*, vol. 4, no. 3 (Autumn 1997): 69–108.

Creative Associates International. *A Retrospective of A.I.D.'s Experience in Strengthening Democratic Institutions in Latin America, 1961–1981*. Washington, D.C.: USAID, September 1987.

Crook, Elizabeth Fletcher. "Political Development as a Program Objective of U.S. Foreign Assistance: Title IX of the 1966 Foreign Assistance Act," Tufts University Ph.D. thesis, 1970 (unpublished).

Dalpino, Catharin E. *Anchoring Third Wave Democracies: Prospects and Problems for U.S. Policy*. Washington, D.C.: The Institute for the Study of Diplomacy, Georgetown University, 1998.

———. *Opening Windows*. Washington, D.C.: Brookings Institution Press, 1999.

Dalpino, Catharin E., and Mike Jendrzejczyk. "Has the Clinton Administration Done a Good Job of Promoting Democracy in Asia?" *The CQ Researcher*, vol. 8, no. 27 (July 24, 1998).

Dawisha, Karen, ed. *The International Dimension of Post-Communist Transitions in Russia and the New States of Eurasia*. Armonk, N.Y.: M.E. Sharpe, 1997.

Diamond, Larry. *Developing Democracy: Toward Consolidation.* Baltimore: Johns Hopkins University Press, 1999.

———. *Promoting Democracy in the 1990s: Actors and Instruments, Issues and Imperatives.* Washington, D.C.: Carnegie Commission on Preventing Deadly Conflict, 1995.

———. "Promoting Democracy," *Foreign Policy,* no. 87 (Summer 1992): 25–46.

———. "Promoting Democracy in Africa: U.S. and International Policies in Transition," in John W. Harbeson and Donald Rothchild, eds., *Africa in World Politics: Post-Cold War Challenges.* Boulder, Colo.: Westview Press, 1995.

Farer, Tom J., ed. *Beyond Sovereignty: Collectively Defending Democracy in the Americas.* Baltimore: Johns Hopkins University Press, 1996.

Flickner, Charles. "The Russian Aid Mess," *The National Interest* (Winter 1994/1995): 13–18.

Geddes, Barbara. *Politician's Dilemma: Building State Capacity in Latin America.* Berkeley: University of California Press, 1994.

Gershman, Carl. "The United States and the World Democratic Revolution," *The Washington Quarterly,* vol. 12, no. 1 (Winter 1989): 127–40.

Gordon, David F. "On Promoting Democracy in Africa," in Marina Ottaway, ed., *Democracy in Africa: The Hard Road Ahead.* Boulder, Colo.: Lynne Rienner, 1997: 153–63 .

Green, Jerrold D. "USAID's Democratic Pluralism Initiative: Pragmatism or Altruism?" *Ethics and International Affairs,* vol. 5 (1991): 215–31.

Grindle, Merilee S., ed. *Getting Good Government: Capacity Building in the Public Sector of Developing Countries.* Cambridge, Mass.: Harvard Institute for International Development, 1997.

Halperin, Morton H., and Kristen Lomasney. "Guaranteeing Democracy: A Review of the Record," *Journal of Democracy,* vol. 9, no. 2 (1998): 134–47.

Hendrickson, David C. "The Democratist Crusade: Intervention, Economic Sanctions, and Engagement," *World Policy Journal,* vol. 11 (Winter 1994/1995) 18–30.

Henry, Clement M. "Promoting Democracy: USAID, at Sea or off to Cyberspace?" *Middle East Policy,* vol. 5, no. 1 (1997): 178–90.

Hook, Steven W. " 'Building Democracy' through Foreign Aid: The Limitations of United States Political Conditionalities, 1992–96," *Democratization,* vol. 5, no. 3 (Autumn 1998): 156–180.

International Institute for Democracy and Electoral Assistance. *Democracy and Deep-Rooted Conflict: Options for Negotiators.* Stockholm: International Institute for Democracy and Electoral Assistance, 1998.

Joyner, Christopher C. "The United Nations and Democracy," *Global Governance,* vol. 5 (1999): 333–57.

Kagan, Robert. "Democracy and Double Standards," *Commentary,* vol. 104, no. 2 (August 1997): 19–26.

Kegley, Charles W., Jr., and Margaret Hermann. "A Glass Half Full? U.S. Intervention and the Promotion of Democracy," *Futures Research Quarterly,* vol. 13, no. 1 (Spring 1997): 65–84.

Kibble, David G. "Monarchs, Mosques, and Military Hardware: A Pragmatic Approach to the Promotion of Human Rights and Democracy in the Middle East," *Comparative Strategy,* vol.17, no. 4 (October 1998): 381–91.

Lancaster, Carol. "Governance and Development: The Views from Washington," *IDS Bulletin,* vol. 24, no. 1 (1993) 9–15.

Leftwich, Adrian, ed. *Democracy and Development: Theory and Practice.* Cambridge, U.K.: Polity Press, 1996.

———. "Governance, Democracy and Development in the Third World," *Third World Quarterly,* vol. 14, no. 3 (1993) 605–24.

Lowenthal, Abraham F., ed. *Exporting Democracy: The United States and Latin America.* Baltimore: Johns Hopkins University Press, 1991.

Meernik, James. "United States Military Intervention and the Promotion of Democracy," *Journal of Peace Research,* vol. 33, no. 4 (November 1996): 391–420.

Moore, Mick, and Mark Robinson. "Can Foreign Aid Be Used to Promote Good Government in Developing Countries?" *Ethics and International Affairs,* vol. 8 (1994): 141–58.

Moss, Todd J. "U.S. Policy and Democratisation in Africa: The Limits of Liberal Universalism," *The Journal of Modern African Studies,* vol. 33, no. 2 (1995): 189–209.

Muravchik, Joshua. *Exporting Democracy: Fulfilling America's Destiny.* Washington, D.C.: American Enterprise Institute Press, 1991.

Newberg, Paula, and Thomas Carothers. "Aiding—and Defining—Democracy," *World Policy Journal,* vol. 13, no. 1 (Spring 1996): 97–108.

O'Brien, David, and Luciano Catenacci. "Towards a Framework for Local Democracy in a War-Torn Society: The Lessons of Selected Foreign Assistance Programmes in El Salvador," *Democratization,* vol. 3, no. 4 (Winter 1996): 435–58.

Olsen, Gorm Rye. "Europe and the Promotion of Democracy in Post-Cold War Africa: How Serious is Europe and for What Reason?" *African Affairs,* vol. 97, no. 388 (July 1998): 343–67.

Ottaway, Marina, and Theresa Chung. "Debating Democracy Assistance: Toward a New Paradigm," *Journal of Democracy,* vol. 10, no. 4 (October 1999).

Packenham, Robert A. *Liberal America and the Third World: Political Development Ideas in Foreign Aid and Social Science.* Princeton: Princeton University Press, 1973.

Payne, Julian H. "Economic Assistance to Support Democratization in Developing Countries: A Canadian Perspective," *Development,* vol. 3 (1992): 12–16.

Phillips, Ann L. "Exporting Democracy: German Political Foundations in Central-East Europe," *Democratization,* vol. 6, no. 2 (Summer 1999): 70–98.

Pinto-Duschinsky, Michael. "The Rise of 'Political Aid'," in Larry Diamond, Marc Plattner, Yun-han Chu, Hung-mao Tien, eds., *Consolidating the Third Wave Democracies.* Baltimore: Johns Hopkins University Press, 1997: 295–324.

Pridham, Geoffrey, Eric Herring, and George Sanford, eds. *Building Democracy? The International Dimension of Democratisation in Eastern Europe.* New York: Leicester University Press, 1997.

Quigley, Kevin F.F. "Political Scientists and Assisting Democracy: Too Tenuous Links," *PS, Political Science & Politics*, vol. 30, no. 3 (September 1997): 564–67.

———. *For Democracy's Sake: Foundations and Democracy Assistance in Central Europe*. Washington, D.C.: Woodrow Wilson Center Press, 1997.

Quinn, Frederick. *Democracy at Dawn: Notes from Poland and Points East*. College Station, Tex.: Texas A&M University Press, 1998.

Riccardi, Andrea. "Promoting Democracy, Peace, and Solidarity," *Journal of Democracy*, vol. 9, no. 4 (Fall 1998): 157–67.

Robinson, William I. *Promoting Polyarchy: Globalization, US Intervention, and Hegemony*. Cambridge, U.K.: Cambridge University Press, 1996.

Samuels, David. "At Play in the Fields of Oppression," *Harper's* (May 1995).

Sisk, Timothy, and Andrew Reynolds, eds. *Elections and Conflict Management in Africa*. Washington, D.C.: U.S. Institute of Peace Press, 1998.

Smith, Tony. *America's Mission: The United States and the Worldwide Struggle for Democracy in the Twentieth Century*. Princeton: Princeton University Press, 1994.

Stevens, Mike, and Shiro Gnanaselvam. "The World Bank and Governance," *IDS Bulletin*, vol. 26, no. 2 (April 1995): 97–105.

Travis, Rick. "U.S. Security Assistance Policy and Democracy: A Look at the 1980s," *The Journal of Developing Areas*, vol. 29, no. 4 (1995): 541–62.

Turner, Mark, and David Hulme. *Governance, Administration and Development*. West Hartford, Conn.: Kumarian Press, 1997.

Vásquez, Ian. "Washington's Dubious Crusade for Hemispheric Democracy," *Policy Analysis*, no. 201, CATO Institute (January 12, 1994).

Vitalis, Robert. "The Democratization Industry and the Limits of the New Interventionism," *Middle East Report*, vol. 24 no. 187 (March 1994).

Wedel, Janine R. *Collision and Collusion: The Strange Case of Western Aid to Eastern Europe, 1989–1998*. New York: St. Martin's Press, 1998.

———. "U.S. Aid to Central and Eastern Europe: Results and Recommendations," *Problems of Post-Communism* (May/June 1995): 45–50.

Whitehead, Laurence, ed. *The International Dimensions of Democratization: Europe and the Americas*. Oxford: Oxford University Press, 1996.

———. "Concerning International Support for Democracy in the South," in Robin Luckham and Gordon White, eds. *Democratization in the South: The Jagged Wave*. Manchester, U.K.: Manchester University Press, 1996: 246–50.

Wiarda, Howard J. *Cracks in the Consensus: Debating the Democracy Agenda in U.S. Foreign Policy*. The Washington Papers, vol. 172. Westport, Conn.: Praeger Publishers, 1997.

———. *The Democratic Revolution in Latin America: History, Politics and U.S. Policy*. New York: Holmes and Meier, 1990.

Williams, David. "Governance and the Discipline of Development," *The European Journal of Development Research*, vol. 8, no. 2 (December 1996).

Zakaria, Fareed. "The Rise of Illiberal Democracy," *Foreign Affairs*, vol. 76, no. 6 (November/December 1997): 22–43.

Civil-Military Assistance

Cope, John A. *International Military Education and Training: An Assessment*, McNair Paper, no. 44. Washington, D.C.: Institute for National Strategic Studies, October 1995.

Danopoulos, Constantine P., and Daniel Zirker, eds. *The Military and Society in the Former Eastern Bloc*. Boulder, Colo.: Westview Press, 1999.

Forman, Johanna Mendelson, and Claude Welch. *Civil-Military Relations: USAID's Role*. Washington, D.C.: USAID Center for Democracy and Governance, July 1998.

Huntington, Samuel, P. "Reforming Civil-Military Relations," *Journal of Democracy*, vol. 6 (1995): 9–17.

Mares, David R. *Civil-Military Relations: Building Democracy and Regional Security in Latin America, Southern Asia, and Central Europe.* Boulder, Colo.: Westview Press, 1998.

Rhame, Thomas G. "Security Assistance Programs: Promoting Democracy in the Post-Cold War Era," *Army*, vol. 46, no. 6 (June 1996): 25–31.

Ulrich, Marybeth Peterson. "U.S. Assistance and Military Democratization in the Czech Republic," *Problems of Post-Communism*, vol. 45, no. 2 (March/April 1998): 22–32.

Civil Society Assistance

Bebbington, Anthony, and Roger Riddell. "The Direct Funding of Southern NGOs by Donors: New Agendas and Old Problems," *Journal of International Development*, vol. 7, no. 6 (1995): 879–93.

Blair, Harry. "Civil Society and Building Democracy: Lessons from International Donor Experience," in Amanda Bernard, Henny Helmrich, and Percy B. Lehning, eds., *Civil Society and International Development.* Paris: North-South Centre of the Council of Europe and Development Centre of the Organization for Economic Cooperation and Development, 1998.

―――. "Donors, Democratisation and Civil Society: Relating Theory to Practice," in David Hulme and Michael Edwards, eds. *NGOs, States and Donors: Too Close for Comfort?* New York: St. Martin's Press, 1997: 23–42.

Bratton, Michael, and Philip Alderfer. "The Effects of Civic Education on Political Culture: Evidence from Zambia," *World Development*, vol. 27, no. 5 (1999): 807–24.

Diamond, Larry. "Rethinking Civil Society: Toward Democratic Consolidation," *Journal of Democracy*, vol. 5, no. 3 (July 1994): 4–17.

Foley, Michael W. "Laying the Groundwork: The Struggle for Civil Society in El Salvador," *Journal of Interamerican Studies and World Affairs*, vol. 38, no. 1 (1996): 67–104.

Fowler, Alan. "Non-governmental Organizations as Agents of Democratization: An African Perspective," *Journal of International Development*, vol. 5, no. 3 (1993): 325–39.

Hadenius, Axel, and Fredrik Uggla. "Making Civil Society Work, Promoting Democratic Development: What Can States and Donors Do?" *World Development*, vol. 24, no. 10 (1996): 1621–39.

Hansen, Gary. *Constituencies for Reform: Strategic Approaches for Donor-Supported Civic Advocacy Programs*. USAID Program and Operations Assessment Report no. 12. Washington, D.C.: USAID, February 1996.

Hearn, Julie. "Foreign Aid, Democratisation and Civil Society in Africa: A Study of South Africa, Ghana and Uganda," Discussion Paper no. 368. Brighton, U.K.: Institute of Development Studies, University of Sussex, March 1999.

Hudock, Ann. "Sustaining NGOs in Resource-Dependent Environments," *Journal of International Development*, vol. 7, no. 4 (1995): 653–67.

Hulme, David, and Michael Edwards, eds. *NGOs, States and Donors: Too Close for Comfort?* New York: St. Martin's Press, 1997.

———. *Beyond the Magic Bullet*. West Hartford, Conn.: Kumarian Press, 1996.

Hyden, Goran. "The Challenges of Analysing and Building Civil Society," *Africa Insight*, vol. 26, no. 2 (1996): 92–106.

Kenzenkovic, Kevin, and Nedzida Salihovic-Galijasevic. "Association Building in Bosnia and Herzegovina," *Public Management*, vol. 81, no. 4 (April 1999): 21–23.

Macdonald, Laura. "A Mixed Blessing: The NGO Boom in Latin America," *NACLA Report on the Americas*, vol. 28, no. 5 (March 1995): 30–35.

———. *Supporting Civil Society: The Political Role of Non-governmental Organizations in Central America*. New York: St. Martin's Press, 1997.

Ndegwa, Stephen N. *The Two Faces of Civil Society: NGOs and Politics in Africa*. West Hartford, Conn.: Kumarian Press, 1996.

Pearce, Jenny. "Civil Society, the Market and Democracy in Latin America," *Democratization*, vol 4, no. 2 (Summer 1997): 57–83.

Quigley, Kevin F.F. "Towards Consolidating Democracy: The Paradoxical Role of Democracy Groups in Thailand," *Democratization*, vol. 3, no. 3 (Autumn 1996): 264–86.

Reilly, Charles A., ed. *New Paths to Democratic Development in Latin America: The Rise of NGO-Municipal Collaboration.* Boulder, Colo.: Lynne Rienner, 1995.

Rieff, David. "Civil Society and the Future of the Nation-State," *The Nation* (February 22, 1999): 11–16.

Robinson, Mark. "Strengthening Civil Society in Africa: The Role of Foreign Political Aid," *IDS Bulletin*, vol. 26, no. 2 (April 1995): 70–80.

Sabatini, Christopher, Gwendolyn Bevis, and Steven Finkel. *The Impact of Civic Education Programs on Political Participation and Democratic Attitudes.* Washington, D.C.: Management Systems International, January 27, 1998.

Siegel, Daniel, and Jenny Yancey. *The Rebirth of Civil Society: The Development of the Nonprofit Sector in East Central Europe and the Role of Western Assistance.* New York: Rockefeller Brothers Fund, 1992.

Van Rooy, Alison, ed. *Civil Society and the Aid Industry.* London: Earthscan Publications, 1998.

White, Gordon. "Civil Society, Democratization and Development (I): Clearing the Analytical Ground," *Democratization*, vol. 1, no. 3 (Autumn 1994): 56–84.

Elections Assistance

Anglin, Douglas G. "International Monitoring of the Transition to Democracy in South Africa, 1992–1994," *African Affairs*, vol. 94, no. 377 (1995): 519–43.

Beigbeder, Yves. *International Monitoring of Plebiscites, Referenda and National Elections: Self-Determination and Transition to Democracy.* Dordrecht, The Netherlands: Martinus Nijhoff, 1994.

Bjornlund, Eric, Michael Bratton, and Clark Gibson. "Observing Multiparty Elections in Africa: Lessons from Zambia," *African Affairs*, no. 91, no. 384 (July 1992): 405–31.

Carothers, Thomas. "The Observers Observed," *Journal of Democracy*, vol. 8, no. 3, (July 1997): 17–31.

Carroll, David J., and Robert A. Pastor. "Moderating Ethnic Tensions by Electoral Mediation: The Case of Guyana," *Security Dialogue*, vol. 24, no. 2 (1993): 163–73.

Elklit, Jørgen, ed. *Electoral Systems for Emerging Democracies: Experiences and Suggestions*. Copenhagen: Danish Ministry of Foreign Affairs, 1997.

Elklit, Jørgen, and Palle Svensson. "What Makes Elections Free and Fair?" *Journal of Democracy*, vol. 8, no. 3 (July 1997): 32–46.

Evered, Timothy C. *United Nations Electoral Assistance and the Evolving Right to Democratic Governance*. Livingston, N.J.: Center for U.N. Reform Education, 1996.

Garber, Larry, and Glenn Cowan. "The Virtues of Parallel Vote Tabulations," *Journal of Democracy*, vol. 4, no. 2 (April 1994): 95–107.

Goodwin-Gill, Guy S. *Free and Fair Elections: International Law and Practice*. Geneva: Inter-Parliamentary Union, 1994.

Herman, Edward S., and Frank Brodhead. *Demonstration Elections*. Boston: South End Press, 1984.

Hirschmann, David. *Managing Democratic Electoral Assistance*. Washington, D.C.: USAID, 1995.

International Institute for Democracy and Electoral Assistance. *The International IDEA Handbook of Electoral System Design*. Stockholm: International Institute for Democracy and Electoral Assistance, 1997.

Koenig-Archibugi, Mathias. "International Electoral Assistance," *Peace Review*, vol. 9, no. 3 (September 1997): 357–64.

Kumar, Krishna, ed. *Postconflict Elections, Democratization, and International Assistance*. Boulder, Colo.: Lynne Rienner, 1998.

Lyons, Terrence. *Voting for Peace: Postconflict Elections in Liberia*. Washington, D.C.: Brookings Institution Press, 1999.

McCoy, Jennifer, Larry Garber, and Robert Pastor. "Pollwatching and Peacemaking," *Journal of Democracy*, vol. 2, no. 4 (Fall 1991): 102–14.

National Democratic Institute for International Affairs. *How Domestic Organizations Monitor Elections: An A to Z Guide*. Washington, D.C.: National Democratic Institute, 1995.

Nevitte, Neil, and Santiago A. Canton. "The Role of Domestic Observers," *Journal of Democracy*, vol. 8, no. 3 (July 1997): 47–61.

Padilla, David, and Elizabeth Houppert. "International Election Observing: Enhancing the Principle of Free and Fair Elections," *Emory International Law Review*, vol. 7, no. 1 (Spring 1993): 73–132.

Pastor, Robert. "Mediating Elections," *Journal of Democracy*, vol. 9, no. 1 (January 1998): 154–63.

Reilly, Ben, and Andrew Reynolds. *Electoral Systems and Conflict in Divided Societies*, Papers on International Conflict Resolution, no. 2. Washington, D.C.: National Academy Press, 1999.

Zak, Marilyn Anne. "Assisting Elections in the Third World," *The Washington Quarterly* (Autumn 1987): 175–93.

Evaluation

Berlage, Lodewijk, and Olav Stokke, eds. *Evaluating Development Assistance: Approaches and Methods*. London: Frank Cass Publisher, 1992.

Brown, Deryck R. "Evaluating Institutional Sustainability in Development Programmes: Beyond Dollars and Cents," *Journal of International Development*, vol. 10, no.1 (1998): 55–69.

Cassen, Robert, and Associates. *Does Aid Work?* Oxford: Clarendon Press, 1994.

Cracknell, B.E. "Evaluating Development Assistance: A Review of the Literature," *Public Administration and Development*, vol. 8 (1988): 75–83.

Dhungana, Josefina O. "A Participatory Way of Evaluating a Participatory Communication Project," *Media Asia*, vol. 23, no. 1 (1996): 42–46.

Golub, Stephen. "Assessing and Enhancing the Impact of Democratic Development Projects: A Practitioner's Perspective," *Studies in Comparative International Development*, vol. 28, no. 1 (Spring 1993): 54–70.

Lefevre, Pierre, and Concepcion Garcia. "Experiences, Perceptions and Expectations of Local Project Actors on Monitoring and Evaluation: A Case Study in the Philippines," *Journal of International Development*, vol. 9, no. 1 (1997): 1–20.

Picciotto, Robert, and Eduardo Wiesner. *Evaluation and Development: The Institutional Dimension.* New Brunswick, N.J.: Transaction Publishers, 1998.

Reckers, Ute. "Participatory Project Evaluation: Allowing Local People to Have Their Say," *Nomadic Peoples,* vol. 39 (1996): 163–70.

Rebien, Claus C. *Evaluating Development Assistance in Theory and in Practice.* Aldershot, U.K.: Avebury, 1996.

Salmen, Lawrence F. *Listen to the People: Participant-Observer Evaluation of Development Projects.* Oxford: Oxford University Press, 1987.

Taschereau, Suzanne. *Evaluating the Impact of Training and Institutional Development Programs: A Collaborative Approach.* Washington, D.C.: World Bank, 1998.

World Bank. *Assessing Aid: What Works, What Doesn't, and Why.* Oxford: Oxford University Press, 1998.

Labor Union Assistance

Buchanan, Paul G. "The Impact of U.S. Labor," in Abraham F. Lowenthal, ed. *Exporting Democracy: The United States and Latin America, Themes and Issues.* Baltimore: Johns Hopkins University Press, 1991: 155–87.

Cook, Linda J. *Labor and Liberalization: Trade Unions in the New Russia.* New York: Twentieth Century Fund Press, 1997.

Spalding, Hobart A. "The Two Latin American Foreign Policies of the U.S. Labor Movement: The AFL-CIO Top Brass vs. Rank-and-File," *Science & Society,* vol. 56, no. 4 (Winter 1992/1993): 421–439.

Welch, Cliff. "Labor Internationalism: U.S. Involvement in Brazilian Unions, 1945–1965," *Latin American Research Review,* vol. 30, no. 2 (1995): 61–89.

Legislative Assistance

Baaklini, Abdo I., and James J. Heaphey. *Legislative Institution Building in Brazil, Costa Rica, and Lebanon.* Beverly Hills: Sage Publications, 1976.

———. "Legislative Development: A New Direction in Technical Assistance," *Comment*, vol. 2, no. 2, State University of New York (February 1975).

Lippman, Hal, and Jan Emmert. *Assisting Legislatures in Developing Countries: A Framework for Program Planning and Implementation*, USAID Document no. PN-ACA-902. Washington, D.C.: USAID, October 1997.

McCannell, Ryan S. *Legislative Strengthening: A Synthesis of USAID Experience*. Washington, D.C.: USAID, May 1995.

Local Government Assistance

Beaumont, Enid. "Democracy and Public Administration Reform Linked," *Public Manager*, vol. 28, no. 1 (Spring 1999): 47–50.

Blair, Harry. *Assessing Democratic Decentralization: A CDIE Concept Paper*. Washington, D.C.: USAID, November 6, 1995.

Buss, Terry F., and Roger Vaughan. "Training and Technical Assistance for Local Government in Hungary: A Critique and Suggestions for Reform," *East European Quarterly*, vol. 29, no. 3 (September 1995): 384–407.

Campbell, Tim E. J. *Innovations and Risk Taking: The Engine of Reform and Local Government in Latin America and the Caribbean*. Washington D.C.: World Bank, 1997.

Cohen, John, and Stephen B. Peterson. *Administrative Decentralization: Strategies for Developing Countries*. West Hartford, Conn.: Kumarian Press, 1997.

Crook, Richard Charles, and James Manor. *Democracy and Decentralization in South Asia and West Africa: Participation, Accountability, and Performance*. Cambridge, U.K.: Cambridge University Press, 1998.

Johnson, Ronald W. *Decentralization Strategy Design: Complementary Perspectives on a Common Theme*, USAID Document no. PN-ABW-981. Washington, D.C.: USAID, August 1995.

Manor, James. *The Political Economy of Democratic Decentralization*. Washington, D.C.: World Bank, 1999.

USAID Center for Democracy and Governance. *Handbook on Programming for Democratic Decentralization*. Washington, D.C.: USAID, forthcoming.

Media Assistance

Githongo, John. "Civil Society, Democratization and the Media in Kenya," *Development*, vol. 40, no. 4 (1997): 41–45.

Gross, Peter. *Mass Media in Revolution and National Development: The Romanian Laboratory*. Ames, Iowa: Iowa State University Press, 1996.

Janus, Noreene, and Rick Rockwell. *The Latin American Journalism Project: Lessons Learned*. Washington, D.C.: USAID, November 1998.

Myers, Mary. "The Promotion of Democracy at the Grass-roots: The Example of Radio in Mali," *Democratization*, vol. 5, no. 2 (Summer 1998): 200–16.

O'Neil, Patrick H., ed. *Communicating Democracy: The Media and Political Transitions*. Boulder, Colo.: Lynne Rienner, 1998.

————. *Post-Communism and the Media in Eastern Europe*. Portland, Oreg.: Frank Cass, 1997.

USAID Center for Democracy and Governance. *The Role of Media in Democracy: A Strategic Approach*. Washington, D.C.: USAID, June 1999.

Political Party Assistance

Burnell, Peter, and Alan Ware, eds. *Funding Democratization*. Manchester, U.K.: Manchester University Press, 1998.

Muravchik, Joshua. "U.S. Political Parties Abroad," *Washington Quarterly*, vol. 12, no. 3 (Summer 1989): 91–100.

Pinto-Duschinsky, Michael. "Foreign Political Aid: The German Political Foundations and Their U.S. Counterparts," *International Affairs*, vol. 67, no. 1 (1991): 33–63.

USAID Center for Democracy and Governance. *USAID Political Party Development Assistance*. Washington, D.C.: USAID, April 1999.

Rule of Law Assistance

Alvarez, José. "Promoting the 'Rule of Law' in Latin America: Problems and Prospects," *George Washington Journal of International Law and Economy*, vol. 25 (1991): 287–332.

Blair, Harry, and Gary Hansen. *Weighing in on the Scales of Justice: Strategic Approaches for Donor-Supported Rule of Law Programs*, USAID Program and Operations Assessment Report no. 7. Washington, D.C.: USAID, 1994.

Carothers, Thomas. "The Rule of Law Revival," *Foreign Affairs* (March/April 1998): 95–106.

Chua, Amy L. "Markets, Democracy, and Ethnicity: Toward a New Paradigm for Law and Development," *Yale Law Journal*, vol. 108, no. 1 (October 1998): 1–107.

Elster, Jon. "Constitution-Making in Eastern Europe: Rebuilding the Boat in the Open Sea," *Public Administration*, vol. 71 (Spring/Summer 1993): 169–217 .

Faundez, Julio, ed. *Good Government and Law: Legal and Institutional Reform in Developing Countries*. New York: St. Martin's Press, 1997.

Gardner, James. *Legal Imperialism: American Lawyers and Foreign Aid in Latin America*. Madison: University of Wisconsin Press, 1980.

Golub, Stephen. "The Growth of a Public Interest Law Movement: Origins, Operations, Impact and Lessons for Legal System Development," in G. Sidney Silliman and Lela Garner Noble, eds., *Organizing for Democracy: NGOs, Civil Society and the Philippine State*. Honolulu: University of Hawaii Press, 1998: 254–79.

Hammergren, Linn A. *The Politics of Justice and Justice Reform in Latin America: The Peruvian Case in Comparative Perspective*. Boulder, Colo.: Westview Press, 1998.

———. *Institutional Strengthening and Justice Reform*, USAID Document no. PN-ACD-020. Washington, D.C.: USAID Center for Democracy and Governance, 1998.

———. *Judicial Training and Justice Reform*, USAID Document no. PN-ACD-021. Washington, D.C.: USAID Center for Democracy and Governance, 1998.

————. *Code Reform and Law Revision*, USAID Document no. PN-ACD-022. Washington, D.C.: USAID Center for Democracy and Governance, 1998.

————. *Political Will, Constituency Building, and Public Support in Rule of Law Programs*, USAID Document no. PN-ACE-023. Washington, D.C.: USAID Center for Democracy and Governance, 1998.

Hoeland, Armin. "The Evolution of Law in Eastern and Central Europe: Are We Witnessing a Renaissance of 'Law and Development'?" in Gessner Bolkmar, Armin Hoeland, and Csaba Varga, eds., *European Legal Cultures*. Dartmouth, N.H.: Aldershot, 1996.

Huggins, Martha. *Political Policing: The United States and Latin America*. Durham, N.C.: Duke University Press, 1998.

Jarquín, Edmundo, and Fernando Carrillo, eds. *Justice Delayed: Judicial Reform in Latin America*. Washington, D.C.: Inter-American Development Bank, 1998.

Merryman, John Henry. "Comparative Law and Social Change: On the Origins, Style, Decline and Revival of the Law and Development Movement," *American Journal of Comparative Law*, vol. 25, no. 3 (1977): 457–91.

Neild, Rachel. *Themes and Debates in Public Security Reform: A Manual for Civil Society*. Washington, D.C.: Washington Office on Latin America, 1998.

Oakley, Robert B., Michael J. Dziedzic, and Eliot M. Goldberg, eds. *Policing the New World Disorder: Peace Operations and Public Security*. Washington, D.C.: National Defense University Press, 1998.

Ratliff, William, and Edgardo Buscaglia. "Judicial Reform: The Neglected Priority in Latin America," *Annals of the American Academy of Political and Social Science*, vol. 550 (March 1997): 59–71.

Sachs, Jeffrey, and Katharina Pistor, eds. *The Rule of Law and Economic Reform in Russia*. Boulder, Colo.: Westview Press, 1997.

Sajó, András. "Universal Rights, Missionaries, Converts, and 'Local Savages'," *East European Constitutional Review*, vol. 6, no. 1 (Winter 1997): 44–49.

Sevastik, Per, ed. *Legal Assistance to Developing Countries*. Dordrecht, The Netherlands: Kluwer Law, 1997.

Sharlet, Robert. "Legal Transplants and Political Mutations: The Reception of Constitutional Law in Russia and the New Independent States," *East European Constitutional Review*, vol. 7, no. 4 (Fall 1998): 59–68.

Skolnik, Sam. "Charges of Fraud, Waste Prompt Probe of Justice Department Training Programs," *Legal Times* (September 21, 1998): 2.

———. "Ex-DOJ Official Claims Bid to Keep CIA Out of Police Training Program Cost Her a Job," *Legal Times* (March 1, 1999): 1.

———. "DOJ Curbs Foreign Programs' Spy Contacts," *Legal Times* (March 22, 1999): 12.

Stein, Eric. *Post-Communist Constitution-Making: Confessions of a Comparatist (Part I).* San Domenico, Italy: European University Institute, 1992.

Trubek, David M., and Marc Galanter. "Scholars in Self-Estrangement: Some Reflections on the Crisis in Law and Development Studies in the United States," *Wisconsin Law Review*, vol. 1974 (1974): 1062–102.

U.S. General Accounting Office. *Promoting Judicial Reform to Strengthen Democracies.* Washington, D.C.: U.S. General Accounting Office, September 1993.

Washington Office on Latin America. *Elusive Justice: The U.S. Administration of Justice Program in Latin America.* Washington, D.C.: Washington Office on Latin America, May 1990.

World Bank. *World Bank and Legal Technical Assistance: Initial Lessons.* Washington, D.C.: World Bank, January 1995.

Index

Accountability, 46
ActionAid, 228
Afghanistan, 314
African-American Institute, 42
Agree, George, 307
Albania, 44, 69, 92, 148, 154, 199, 351
Alfonsín, Raúl, 33
Algeria, 110
Alliance for Progress, 22
American Bar Association (ABA), 7, 258
American Center for International Labor Solidarity, 7, 32, 245
American Federation of Labor-Congress of Industrial Organizations (AFL-CIO), 24–25, 30–32, 37; in Guatemala, 115; in Romania, 119; and implementing aid, 258; and union aid, 244–47
American Institute for Free Labor Development (AIFLD), 244–45
Angola, 111, 124, 134, 137, 239
Aquino, Corazon, 37
Arbenz Guzmán, Jacobo, 66
ARD, 7
Argentina, 33, 139, 152, 207, 267
Aristide, Jean-Bertrand, 43, 144
Armenia, 5, 92, 109, 130
Asia Foundation, 7, 43, 52, 54, 177, 348; and implementing aid, 271, 278; and media aid, 236; and Nepal, 72, 173; and NGO aid, 213
Australia, 104
Austria, 142
Azerbaijan, 5, 60, 109, 130

Baker, James, 74
Baltic nations (Estonia, Latvia, Lithuania), 41, 240

Bangladesh, 43, 187
Belarus, 92
Belgium, 142, 150, 310
Birendra (King), 67, 71
Blair, Harry, 194
Bolivia, 4, 43, 141, 267
Bosnia, 41, 134, 137, 166, 239, 351
Botswana, 99
Brazil, 24, 33, 36, 139, 207, 244
Brock, William, 30
Budgets, aid: democracy assistance, 6, 39, 41, 48–53, 54, 59, 61, 120–121, 264–65, 278–79, 331, 332, 348; foreign aid, 61, 116, 278–79, 288, 348, 349
Bulgaria, 4, 41, 144, 148, 311
Burma, 44, 57, 95, 350
Burundi, 42, 239
Buscaglia, Edgardo, 170–71
Bush, George H.W., 3, 5, 41–42, 56–57, 74, 89, 208; and Romania, 74
Business, 105–06, 224; in Guatemala, 74, 75, 315; in Zambia, 118

Cambodia, 43, 92, 306; and aid strategy, 109–10, 124; and aid to institutions of state, 172, 176; and elections aid, 127, 135, 137, 141, 154; and evaluation, 291–92
Cameroon, 92
Canada, 12, 104
CAPEL (Inter-American Center for Electoral Promotion), 35–36
Carnegie Endowment for International Peace, 13
Carter Center, 7, 73, 126
Carter, Jimmy, 4, 28–29, 33, 128; and Guatemala, 66
Castro, Fidel, 21

About the Author

Thomas Carothers is vice president for global policy and co-director of the Democracy and Rule of Law Project at the Carnegie Endowment for International Peace. An international lawyer and political scientist, he has worked on democracy programs for over ten years with a number of American and international organizations and carried out extensive field research on democracy aid in Eastern Europe, the former Soviet Union, Latin America, Africa, and Asia. He is the author of two previous books on democracy promotion, *Assessing Democracy Assistance: The Case of Romania* (Carnegie Endowment, 1996) and *In the Name of Democracy: U.S. Policy toward Latin America in the Reagan Years* (University of California, 1991). He has also published many articles on international affairs in major journals and newspapers.

Prior to joining the Carnegie Endowment, Mr. Carothers was an attorney at Arnold & Porter in Washington, D.C. and served in the Office of the Legal Adviser of the U.S. Department of State. He has also been an International Affairs Fellow of the Council on Foreign Relations and a Guest Scholar at the Woodrow Wilson International Center for Scholars. He is a graduate of Harvard Law School, the London School of Economics, and Harvard College.

About the Carnegie Endowment

The Carnegie Endowment for International Peace is a private, non-profit organization dedicated to advancing cooperation between nations and promoting active international engagement by the United States. Founded in 1910, its work is nonpartisan and dedicated to achieving practical results. Through research, publishing, convening and, on occasion, creating new institutions and international networks, Endowment associates shape fresh policy approaches. Their interests span geographic regions and the relations among governments, business, international organizations, and civil society, focusing on the economic, political, and technological forces driving global change. Through its Carnegie Moscow Center, the Endowment helps develop a tradition of public policy analysis in the states of the former Soviet Union and improve relations between Russia and the United States. The Endowment publishes *Foreign Policy,* one of the world's leading journals of international politics and economics, which reaches readers in more than 120 countries and several languages.

Carnegie Endowment
for International Peace
1779 Massachusetts Ave., N.W.
Washington, D.C. 20036
Tel: 202-483-7600
Fax: 202-483-1840
E-mail: carnegie@ceip.org
Web: www.ceip.org

Carnegie Moscow Center
Ul. Tverskaya 16/2
7th Floor
Moscow 103009
Tel: 7-095-935-8904
Fax: 7-095-935-8906
E-mail: info@carnegie.ru
Web: www.carnegie.ru